BETWEEN WORLDS

BETWEEN WORLDS

John A. Broadus

THE SOUTHERN BAPTIST SEMINARY
AND THE PROSPECTS OF THE NEW SOUTH

ERIC C. SMITH

LOUISIANA STATE UNIVERSITY PRESS ❧ BATON ROUGE

Published by Louisiana State University Press
lsupress.org

Copyright © 2026 by Louisiana State University Press
All rights reserved. Except in the case of brief quotations used in articles or reviews,
no part of this publication may be reproduced or transmitted in any format or by
any means without written permission of Louisiana State University Press.

DESIGNER: Kaelin Chappell Broaddus
TYPEFACES: Garamond Premier Pro, text; Bourbon, Cabazon,
Isherwood WF, Scotch Modern, display.

Cover and frontispiece photographs courtesy Archives and Special Collections,
James P. Boyce Centennial Library, Southern Baptist Theological Seminary.

Cataloging-in-Publication Data are available from the Library of Congress.
ISBN 978-0-8071-8522-3 (cloth: alk. paper) —
ISBN 978-0-8071-8630-5 (pdf) — ISBN 978-0-8071-8629-9 (epub)

For Coleman, Crockett, and Clarabelle

thy children like olive plants round about thy table.
Behold, that thus shall the man be blessed that feareth the Lord.

—PSALM 128:3–4

·→>>❖·❀·<<←·

And for Keith Harper

Most men will proclaim every one his own goodness:
but a faithful man who can find?

—PROVERBS 20:6

And a certain Jew named Apollos, born at Alexandria, an eloquent man, and mighty in the scriptures, came to Ephesus. This man was instructed in the way of the Lord; and being fervent in spirit, he spake and taught diligently the things of the Lord, knowing only the baptism of John.

—ACTS 18:24–25

CONTENTS

Photographs follow page 98.

ACKNOWLEDGMENTS

Solomon once wrote, "Better is the end of a thing than the beginning thereof" (Eccl 7:8). Perhaps the very best thing about reaching the end of this project is looking back on all the people who have kindly helped me along the way. I am so grateful for you all.

Of the many fine people who assisted me in tracking down sources, Adam Winters, archivist at the James P. Boyce Centennial Library at Southern Seminary, deserves first mention. Adam answered questions and provided materials even as the library underwent extensive renovations. I also appreciate Jake Stone, Casey McCall, and Garrett Walden, who all connected me with various Broadus resources. Thanks also to Matthew Shrader, author of a terrific study on Alvah Hovey, who kindly shared copies of the Broadus-Hovey correspondence. About halfway through this project, I joined the faculty at Broadus's Southern Baptist Theological Seminary, where my administrators, faculty colleagues, and students have all blessed me with their interest and conversation about the book. Thank you!

I was thrilled when Rand Dotson, editor in chief at LSU Press, was willing to give my manuscript a chance. Thank you, Rand, for the opportunity, and thanks to all at LSU Press who have labored to bring this book to publication. I am also indebted to a number of gifted scholars who read all or portions of the manuscript. These include James Patterson, Beth Schweiger, Scot Danforth, and Bill Leonard, along with another anonymous reviewer. Each of these readers strengthened the finished product tremendously by their keen and generous insights. My friends Jeremy Isbell and Ray Van Neste, who also read early versions of this book, sharpened my thinking with their questions and encouraged me with their enthusiasm. Thank you!

Occasionally I have the privilege of leading Southern Seminary students out to Cave Hill Cemetery in Louisville, where Broadus and many former faculty members await the resurrection. As we wander among the headstones, we discuss the history of the seminary and reflect on the wisdom of Ecclesiastes 12. When students invariably cite our Cave Hill pilgrimage as their favorite part of the class, I tell them it is just one of many ways that I am trying to follow in the footsteps of my longtime hero, Timothy George, who did the same for earlier generations of seminarians. Thank you, Dr. George, for your example and personal encouragement.

In the course of writing this book, no individual has invested more in me than Keith Harper. His interest, availability, and expert guidance have been extraordinary. This book is immeasurably better, and it was a whole lot more fun to write, because of Keith. Our friendship is the very best gift that I take from this experience. Thank you!

As always, I am so grateful for Candace. Unlike Lottie Broadus, she would *never* let her husband galavant all over the world without her—and I would never want to. Walking with Broadus has only deepened my love for her, and for our children. I understand something of Broadus's ambition to do something significant with my life. But as I watch Coleman, Crockett, and Clarabelle grow up like olive shoots around our table, I am reminded where true significance is found. With my work put away, we gather around their mother's latest wonderful meal to sing the Doxology, read books aloud, identify birds out the back window, and lay all sorts of family plans. In a brief flash of clarity, I realize that I am up to my neck in what the Bible calls "the blessing of the Lord." I receive these, and all his good gifts, with a heart of humble thanks.

❦ BETWEEN WORLDS ❦

INTRODUCTION

I N THE SPRING OF 1867, John Albert Broadus received an invitation to preach the commencement services at Washington College in Lexington, Virginia. As a nationally renowned preacher, Broadus received dozens of similar invitations each year, but this one bore special significance. It came from the college's new president, Robert E. Lee. Broadus had spent the late summer months of 1863 living in the camps with Lee's Army of Northern Virginia, ministering to Confederate troops in the devastating months after Gettysburg. He had preached to as many as five thousand soldiers on occasion, and he helped lead a massive revival, later memorialized in the popular volume *Christ in the Camp.* Four years later, on the other side of Confederate defeat, General Lee wanted to hear Broadus preach hope again.

Though honored by the invitation, Broadus regretfully informed Lee that he could not afford the travel expenses. "Almost all those who had been wealthy before the war were now really poor," he explained elsewhere, "numerous families, formerly prosperous, or at least comfortable, had not a dollar of money for many months after the close of the war." Broadus had certainly fallen far from his own antebellum comfort, sometimes going eighteen months without collecting a salary in the grim, postwar years. His family bought groceries on credit, and survived on the garden produce supplied by the backcountry Baptists to whom he preached. But Lee persisted, through their mutual friend J. William Jones: "Tell him we are as poor as church mice, but would most gladly pay four times the amount in order to have one of his gospel sermons and have the pleasure of his society."[1] Broadus bought a ticket to Lexington.

He almost did not make it. Standing on the platform of the Gordonsville depot, he watched the approaching train he intended to board and realized that it was not stopping. But he judged the train to be moving slowly enough, and decided to jump aboard as it passed—to his instant regret. "I seized the iron rods with my two hands, was immediately dragged from my feet, and found myself between the platform and the moving car, holding by my hands, and dragged over the crossties, sadly near the terrible wheels," he recounted to his wife. Only by enormous effort did he pull himself to safety onto the train. An unknown passenger scolded him for his "great folly" as Broadus rubbed a bruised ankle. "If my life is spared long, it is greatly to be feared that I shall do a variety of foolish things, but I feel at present a strong confidence that I shall never again try to get on a train in motion," he wrote sheepishly.[2]

Broadus had a marvelous time in Lexington. He was "treated with great respect and kindness" wherever he went, both he and his company reminding one another of pleasanter days in the Old Dominion. He preached to a packed house in a local Presbyterian church, took tea with the professors, and caught up with old classmates from the University of Virginia. He called on General and Mrs. Lee at home, and paid his respects at the tomb of Stonewall Jackson. After the visit, he and Lee would exchange friendly letters until the former general's death in 1871.[3]

Broadus's warm reception among Confederate royalty is not surprising, given his impeccable southern pedigree. Born in Culpeper County, Virginia, in 1827, he was raised by a respected state politician, from whom he learned the ways of southern honor that indelibly shaped his view of the world. White mastery was central to this worldview. Like his father, Broadus would own slaves, and even after emancipation he never shed the class commitments or racist assumptions he first absorbed on Edge Hill Plantation. After experiencing a call to preach, he attended the University of Virginia, focusing on classical languages and graduating valedictorian with a master's degree in 1850. He maintained close ties with the university, a citadel of southern gentility, and occasionally served as its professor and chaplain. As pastor of the Charlottesville Baptist Church, he zealously served the sectional goals of the Southern Baptist Convention, founded in 1845. Though he initially opposed secession, Broadus supported the Confederacy, defending its righteousness, praying for its victory, ministering to its troops, and grieving its demise. After the South's catastrophic defeat, he remained "proudly and nobly jealous for his own native South," and gave his best energies to preserving its cultural institutions, especially the Southern Baptist Theological Seminary. His

1865 covenant with his colleagues, "Suppose we all quietly agree that the seminary may die, but we'll die first," has been valorized in the denomination as a symbol of postwar southern resilience. "Dr. Broadus was a Southerner in every sense of loyalty to the local and social environment and tradition in which he was born and in which he lived his whole life," observed one admirer.[4]

This book explores the life, ministry, and southern identity of John A. Broadus, one of the most consequential religious figures of late nineteenth-century America. Over the last two-thirds of the nineteenth century, he participated in his home region's tumultuous transition from the Old South to the New, and helped shape the religious culture that emerged on the other side. At first glance, the Confederate camp evangelist seems a straightforward representative of Lost Cause religion. After all, just two years after his death, the Sons of Confederate Veterans formed a "John A. Broadus Camp" in his honor. By 1905, the Broadus camp boasted several hundred members, who toasted their namesake at their Confederate reunions from Louisville's plantation-style Galt House Hotel. But as Steve Longenecker has argued, the Lost Cause, like all popular movements, was "a house with many rooms," and one in which Broadus occupied a unique corner.[5]

Broadus was a realist who accepted Confederate defeat and urged white southerners to adapt to their new social conditions. He preached peace on both sides of the Mason-Dixon Line after the war. "We have one country—North, South, East, West—we are one," he told a Boston audience. "God bless the *United States!* Let us love one another." He became a beloved, peace-making American patriot, praised as both "a Southerner in every sense" and "a truly national man." Broadus spent months each year preaching to northern Baptists and evangelicals. He delivered addresses at America's most esteemed institutions, received honors from Yale, Princeton, and Harvard—the latter awarded him an honorary degree at its 250th anniversary—and turned down the presidencies of Vassar College, Brown University, and the University of Chicago. Back home, he advocated for many aspects of a modern New South. He cautioned against bitter sectionalism, cultivated wealthy northern benefactors—his close friend John D. Rockefeller called him "the wisest man living"—and encouraged the development of southern industry and urban centers. Broadus's brand of Lost Cause-ism promoted the South's restoration to American life and reconciliation with white northerners. Many of the latter, weary of war and Reconstruction, eagerly received his message, even if Black Americans lost in the bargain.[6]

Yet while Broadus wished, with his friend Isaac Taylor Tichenor, to "lay the foundations of a new society," he also intended to "preserve the distinctive principles which have made southern society what it is." He refused to countenance the formal reunification of northern and southern Baptists, for one thing. And, though he came to repudiate slavery, he ever maintained that an elite class of educated white men should provide leadership for the South, and emphasized their paternalistic duties to Blacks and poor whites alike. He condemned lynching and endorsed universal education while confidently advancing scientific racism. Broadus rejected seminary applicants who possessed "a drop of negro blood," and thereby helped to lay the groundwork for Jim Crow social policies. In these ways and more, he reflected what Dewey Grantham once termed the South's struggle to reconcile "progress and tradition." Broadus's life helps us better understand the complicated southern religious story.[7]

→»»✿❦✿«««←

North and South comprise only one set of the polarities that Broadus bridged in nineteenth-century America. He stood prominently among E. Brooks Holifield's "gentleman theologians" in the antebellum South, embodying "the religious sentiments of the common folk, distinguished by fervor and commitment," while simultaneously projecting the image of "a gentleman, exalted and elevated through character, erudition, and professional status." Broadus's dual persona of cultural elite and man of the people flavored all that he did, not least his preaching. Listeners praised his sermons in large part for their power to connect with every class of listener. Adopting a simple, conversational style that aimed to explain the Bible clearly and "access the doors of men's hearts," he rarely failed to win his audience. "'The common people heard him gladly,' and the most thoughtful and cultured never failed to be greatly edified," recalled one witness. In 1889, Broadus delivered the prestigious Lyman Beecher Preaching Lectures at Yale Divinity School, cementing his reputation as a premier American pulpiteer. The Broadus preaching style revolutionized the southern pulpit in the late nineteenth century, thanks in no small part to his celebrated textbook *A Treatise on the Preparation and Delivery of Sermons* (1870), which remains the most popular preaching manual in American history.[8]

He expanded his multi-generational influence by founding the Southern

Baptist Theological Seminary in 1859. Baptists did not require an educated ministry, and they had flourished in antebellum America by flooding the frontier with ardent revival preachers. Yet as Southern Baptists embarked on their "pilgrimage toward respectability," Broadus joined other denominational leaders in a quest to elevate the quality and status of their ministry. Indeed, William Whitsitt called "the promotion of higher theological cultivation among our Baptist people" Broadus's "supreme object of exertion." Broadus designed an innovative curriculum that would equip the least cultivated preachers with professional knowledge and ministry skills, while also offering specialized academic training for future scholar-leaders of the denomination. Seminary leadership required political sensitivity to the Convention's various subgroups, including the urban and rural, Southeast and Southwest, elite and folk cultures, centrists and localists, Calvinists, Arminians, Landmarkers, and more. He quipped that Baptists "had as much culture as Presbyterians and as much ignorance as Methodists," but he could speak to them all.[9]

Broadus also mediated between traditional evangelical orthodoxy and modern scholarship. In the latter decades of his career, new ideas related to science, historicism, and higher biblical criticism reshaped America's theological landscape. In 1879, seminary trustees dismissed his protege and German-trained colleague Crawford Toy for undermining a classic evangelical view of biblical inspiration. The Toy episode proved traumatic for Broadus in every way, bringing him under denominational scrutiny and prompting him to reevaluate his approach to raising up a learned ministry. In his remaining years, he offered a generation of evangelicals grappling with biblical authority a model of scholarly conservatism—updated, learned, yet reverential toward the Bible. The nation's top scholars respected Broadus's work in Greek and New Testament (including his 1886 *Commentary on the Gospel of Matthew*), even as his commitment to the Bible's verbal plenary inspiration grew out of step with the American academy.

In his personal life, Broadus also found himself caught between powerful, conflicting forces. Reared among prominent Virginians, he developed by his teenage years an unquenchable desire to "rise and be eminent" in the world. In the same period, his earnest evangelical conversion and call to Baptist ministry provided counterbalancing demands for humility and the surrender of his own will to God's. He spent his life struggling to harness these potent, competing claims. He set ambitious professional goals and worked a relentless schedule as a professor, pastor, denominational leader, author, and circuit speaker. By his early twenties, he had attained to a modest religious celebrity that would only increase to the end of his life. At the same time, his drive for success created an oppressively busy lifestyle, separated him for long periods from his wife and children, and overburdened his fragile body, which could never quite meet the stern demands he placed upon it. If bridging disparate cultures serves as the major theme of Broadus's public life, then managing the interlocking tensions of ambition, humility, fame, family, health, and public duty supplies the dominant motif of his private life.

--->>>•⊱•⊰•<<<---

An 1869 profile of Broadus in the *Richmond Dispatch* suggests something of his appeal to his contemporaries. The account describes him as "A young looking man of some forty years, with dark hair, keen eyes, and shoulders bent by study. When the countenance is lighted up by the animation of speaking, there is a wonderful play of emotion in his face; but ordinarily he looks calm and imperturbable." Though he had "no superior in intellect and scholarly cultivation in the Baptist denomination in the South," other charms softened his persona. "He has a peculiarly winning smile, attracts by the gentleness and suavity of his manner, and talks like one who has the subject of discussion under perfect acquaintance and control," the reporter observed. "His conversation is alike attractive to the *savant* and to the student, to the wise and well-informed, and to those not enjoying those advantages."[10]

As this admiring piece suggests, Broadus arose as an attractive and formative religious leader in nineteenth-century America by moving skillfully among many worlds. He was an urbane gentleman with a commoner's touch, a sophisticated scholar with a revivalist's instinct, an unrepentant Confederate with a national appeal, and a man of the Old South with a modern vision for the New. At many points in Broadus's life, John R. Sampey's "interpreter" metaphor seems to best capture him: "He could interpret Southern people to Northern audiences, and Northern people to Southern audiences," skillfully crossing various cultural boundaries to communicate his message. At other times, the harrowing incident at the Gordonsville train depot provides a more apt image: two hands gripping a moving train, two feet flailing over the passing rails, one desperate man scrambling to safety as he is pulled into a future beyond his control.[11]

Given his stature in the history of American Christianity, it is surprising that Broadus has never been the subject of a full critical biography. In 1901, his son-in-law A. T. Robertson published his hagiographical *Life and Letters of John Albert Broadus.* The adoring Robertson makes no claims of objective analysis, but his impressive assemblage of primary source materials still makes his book the starting point for any researcher. Since then, work on Broadus has largely been limited to denominational pieces and seminary dissertations. In 2008, a cohort of Southern Baptist scholars published *John Broadus: A Living Legacy,* a collection of appreciative essays in conjunction with the Southern Baptist Theological Seminary's 150th anniversary. I have benefitted immensely from these previous studies, as well as from the extensive John Broadus Papers housed at the James P. Boyce Centennial Library Special Collections and Archives at Southern Seminary in Louisville, Kentucky. Many fine historical works of southern religion have also informed my understanding of Broadus's broader milieu. With help from these and many other earlier researchers, I hope to provide a personal portrait of Broadus that situates him in the larger story of nineteenth-century American life.[12]

The task of interpreting Broadus has grown more daunting over the past decade. Southern Baptists venerated him throughout the twentieth century; his piety, preaching, scholarship, and gentility seemed to represent the best of the denomination's founding era. Since the 1870s, the president of the Southern Baptist Convention has opened business at the annual meeting with a ceremonial whack of the "Broadus gavel." In 1933, the Southern Baptist publishing house took the name of "Broadman Press" (today B&H Publishing Group) to honor Broadus and his co-laborer Basil Manly Jr. Public streets bear witness to Broadus's enduring influence, including Broadus Street in Fort Worth, Texas, where the founders of Southwestern Baptist Theological Seminary viewed him as a guiding light. His influence pervades the Southern Baptist Theological Seminary in Louisville, Kentucky, one of the world's largest evangelical seminaries today. Images and quotations of the founder grace the institution's decorous hallways, and his memory is regularly invoked in classrooms, chapel messages, and conversations. In 1999, the seminary christened the colonial-stye Broadus Memorial Chapel, featuring at its center an exquisite, elevated pulpit, reflecting Broadus's status as "the father of modern expository preaching." As late as 2008, celebrating Broadus's "living legacy" with a major denominational publication seemed uncontroversial.[13]

This is no longer the case. A series of highly publicized, racially charged crimes in the late 2010s (including a fatal incident in Broadus's own Charlottesville, Virginia, centered on a statue of Robert E. Lee) renewed a heated national discussion about memorializing slaveholders and the Confederacy. In response, the Southern Baptist Theological Seminary released a detailed report in 2018 of the history of slavery and racism at the institution. The report revealed Broadus and the founders as having been "deeply involved in slavery and complicit in the defense of slavery." Broadus made headlines in the summer of 2020 when the *Washington Post* reported SBC President J. D. Greear's decision to retire the venerable Broadus gavel before the upcoming annual meeting. Cries went up to purge Broadus from every aspect of denominational life, even as loyal partisans protested the "canceling" of a man who had contributed so much of value. In the midst of the tumult, Southern Seminary President Albert Mohler noted that "you can't tell the story of the SBC without John Broadus." "We can't erase history," he added. "We must reckon with it."[14]

This book is my attempt to reckon with the significance of John A. Broadus, in all its historical complexity. When Broadus reflected on the Civil War in the 1890s, he urged "even those who most strongly condemn the views entertained" by Confederates like himself to "care enough for historical truth and personal justice to take . . . pains towards understanding our position."[15] The purpose of this study is neither to praise Broadus nor to bury him—doubtless frustrating readers inclined to do either. I hope instead to simply arrive at a better understanding of this major figure from the past. As he freely admitted, he did and thought "a variety of foolish things" in his lifetime, alongside his many inspiring achievements. By taking an honest, updated look at his life, perhaps we can learn from both.

One

DETERMINED TO BE SOMETHING

T HE BOY STOOD nervously with his father on the platform as the crowd gathered. It was 1839, and Edmund Broadus, Whig candidate from Culpeper County, Virginia, was in the middle of a reelection campaign for the state legislature. This race had been particularly tight, and Broadus had delivered so many speeches that he had finally shouted himself hoarse. As the people now meandered toward him, he had no voice left.

But Edmund's youngest son, John Albert Broadus, knew the speech as well as he did—John had read a copy aloud to his father over and over at home, until it was memorized. The twelve-year-old seemed in some ways a natural speaker. As a small boy he had amazed neighbors with his perfect mimicry of the Baptist preacher's most recent sermons, and he often entertained the Broadus house guests by standing on the kitchen table and reading from the pages of the *Religious Herald,* Virginia's state Baptist newspaper. He had been reared, in fact, in a family of professional talkers—politicians, school teachers, and preachers. So today, after Edmund beckoned him over, John cleared his throat and delivered the speech. We don't know much else about that day, except that it was probably John A. Broadus's first public address. And we know that Edmund Broadus won that election.[1]

John A. Broadus was born into an age of orators. In antebellum America, the individuals of greatest consequence were usually those who could speak with power and eloquence on the public stage. The Old South, which invested such significance in the impressive public appearance, gave particular honor to the rhetorical arts. One historian, noting the antebellum South's preoccupation with stirring speakers and debating societies, referred to the region's "cult of oratory." Southern orators typically rose to prominence in the arenas of politics, law, or the military. But as Robert Elder has pointed out, the evangelical pulpit increasingly became a pathway to recognition in southern society in the nineteenth century. By "wielding words" that accessed the deep mysteries of the human heart, antebellum preachers could gain entrance to "one of the most hallowed spheres of honor" in southern culture.[2]

John Broadus would come to understand all of this as well as any of his contemporaries. "But printing can never take the place of the living word," he once observed. "When a man who is apt in teaching, whose soul is on fire with the truth which he trusts has saved him and hopes will save others, speaks to his fellow-men, face to face, eye to eye, and electric sympathies flash to and fro between him and his hearers, till they lift each other up, higher and higher, into the intensest thought, and the most impassioned emotion—higher and yet higher,—till they are borne as on chariots of fire above the world,—there is a power to move men, to influence character, life, destiny, such as no printed page can ever possess."[3] He received his first taste of the electric power of the spoken word among the Broadduses of Virginia.

→》》✣☙《←

Broadus traced his family's origins to Wales, where they had spelled their name Broadhurst (the suffix "hurst" refers to a wooded hill or knoll). The family had migrated to the Old Dominion early in the eighteenth century, and grew numerous in the Virginia Piedmont. There was some disagreement among the Virginia Broadduses about the proper Americanization of their family name. Most preferred "Broaddus," with some prominent family members known to bristle at the exclusion of the second "d." It was John's progressive father, Edmund, along with his brothers, William and Andrew, who first simplified the spelling to "Broadus," after their father's death. (William and Andrew would revert back to the traditional spelling, under pressure from the family's two-d advocates.) However it was spelled, the Broaddus name was well-known in Virginia by the time of John's birth in 1827. Broadduses were not unusually wealthy; they were farmers, schoolteachers, country lawyers, railroad workers, and preachers. They were, however, men of southern honor, members of Virginia's middling gentry class, known for their sociability, learning, and especially for their piety. To a man, Broadduses were Baptists.

Since the mid-eighteenth century, the Baptist movement had been a powerful religious force in Virginia. The rowdy Separate Baptists had first invaded the genteel and orderly world of Anglican Virginia in the 1750s and 1760s. Appealing to Virginia's lower classes with their plain preaching, emotional worship, sensory rituals, and contempt for the pretentious tobacco aristocracy, Separate Baptists exploded numerically in the decades before the Revolution. Their proliferation provoked a violent backlash of persecution from the ruling class of Anglican planters. Nineteenth-century Virginia Baptists like the Broadduses recalled this period of their history with pride, regaling one another with tales of courageous forbears enduring whippings, surviving drownings, and suffering imprisonments and other indignities for the Baptist gospel—particularly in John Broadus's own Culpeper County. During the Revolution, these despised Baptists shrewdly bartered their desperately needed military service with colonial leaders for full religious liberty under the new state constitution, aided by statesmen like Thomas Jefferson and James Madison.[4]

John Broadus's Episcopalian grandmother, Susannah Ferguson Broaddus, had been converted and baptized by one of those early Virginia Baptists, John Leland. The rugged pietist Leland represents well the religious radicalism of eighteenth-century Virginia Baptists. He was a farmer-preacher who refused to accept a ministerial salary, taking pride in his sunburnt neck and calloused hands. He was a persevering itinerant, riding—and, if his horse went lame, walking—the Virginia countryside to preach the gospel. Self-taught and scornful of college-educated ministers, Leland led emotional revivals and testified of ecstatic visions and dreams. When Leland preached, he wept and roared, cracked jokes, spun tales, and mocked Virginia's refined clergy with sarcasm and coarse language. Leland's popular preaching gained a tremendous following among Virginia plain folk, and he even collaborated with James Madison over religious freedom issues. Yet Leland always remained an outsider in elite southern society.[5]

By John A. Broadus's day, Baptist marginalization was a chapter in the heroic past. After tremendous numeric growth through the revivals of the Second Great Awakening, Virginia Baptists now constituted a cultural majority. Moreover, unlike Leland and his eighteenth-century compatriots, Virginia Baptist preachers had come to occupy an increasingly respectable station in broader southern society. John needed to look no further than his own family to demonstrate Baptist growth and respectability. He could count more than a dozen Baptist preachers in his family in the nineteenth century. "No other family has given to our ministry so many able men," commented one contemporary. These preaching Broadduses cut a very different figure in Virginia society than had John Leland.[6]

Born a generation after Leland, in 1770, John Broadus's distant uncle Andrew Broaddus was perhaps the most celebrated Baptist preacher of antebellum Virginia. He was also a gentleman. Neatly dressed, graceful in motion, and fastidious in his manners, Broaddus was the picture of "cultivated taste" in the pulpit. "His style was always chaste, sometime rising to the beautiful," remembered Richmond College President Robert Ryland, "his gesticulation was appropriate, easy and impressive, never violent, over-wrought or pompous." Broaddus's voice "had nothing of the whine—nothing of the affected solemnity of tone about it. It was musical, flexible and capacious. His whole carriage in the pulpit was mild and graceful." Yet for all his refinement, Andrew Broaddus remained a revivalist, especially skilled in "the pathetic." He knew well "how to touch the delicate chords of passion in the human heart, but he did not abuse his skill by constant exercise." Many considered him "the most perfect orator" they had ever heard; even Henry Clay praised Andrew Broaddus as "the past master of eloquence."[7]

Andrew Broaddus was just as impressive outside the pulpit. He published an array of works with the American Baptist Publication Society—hymnals, church histories, children's catechisms, and polemical pieces against the infidel Thomas Paine's *Age of Reason* and Alexander Campbell's Disciples of Christ movement. For his elevation of Baptist culture, Columbian College conferred on Broaddus the Doctor of Divinity degree in 1843. The finest city churches in Baptist America—in Richmond, Norfolk, New York City, and Philadelphia—courted Broaddus as their pastor. Yet he chose to spend his life preaching to the Virginia Baptists of Caroline, King and Queen, and King William counties. In return, they fairly worshipped him. Andrew Broaddus represented well the interplay of evangelical piety and southern honor culture that would characterize the antebellum period; when John heard him preach at the great Baptist meetings, he thrilled to claim the distinguished pulpiteer as his kin.[8]

John Broadus also observed the upward mobility of Virginia's Baptist ministry in his father's two preaching brothers, "Kentucky Andrew" (so-called for his Kentucky ministry, and to distinguish him from the older, more famous Andrew Broaddus) and William F. Broaddus. John was especially close to his gregarious Uncle William. Affable, opinionated, and slightly eccentric (the sight of a cat made him physically ill), the portly William Broaddus would figure prominently in John's life until William's death in 1876. William wrote to his nephew frequently, badgering him with job opportunities and advising him in all matters, partnering with him in revivals and denominational work, and would one day help him raise money for the fledgling Southern Baptist Theological Seminary. But before all that, William F. Broaddus provided John with another model of cultured Baptist ministry.[9]

Like Andrew Broaddus, William combined revival preaching with social respectability. He was an educator, keeping a school most of his life. He also zealously endorsed the growth of a central Baptist denomination, an important step in Baptist sophistication in the early nineteenth century. As Beth Schweiger has shown, a denomination afforded Baptist ministers influence beyond the local congregation, through the benevolent work of Sunday schools, temperance societies, and foreign missions. Many rural Virginia Baptists opposed denominational activity as a dangerous innovation that usurped local church authority, lacked biblical precedent, and corrupted the simple Baptist piety of their forefathers. Among these backward-looking Baptists was old John Leland, now relocated to Massachusetts, but still vocal into the 1830s. Yet, as compelling as their case may have been, the "antimissionary" or "Primitive" Baptists found their message undermined at every turn by the aggressive efforts of William F. Broaddus. Some said that he, more than anyone else, "broke the power of the anti missionary spirit in Northern Virginia among the Baptists."[10]

In another important step of Baptist professionalization, William Broaddus also campaigned for a salaried ministry. When a Kentucky church told him they could not promise a definite salary, but would "try to do their best for him," William retorted that he would show up to preach on the same terms: "if I have nothing else to do, and if it suits me, I suppose you may look for me, but I could not promise definitely. Since you can not promise me any definite salary," he reasoned, "I thought it was only fair that I should not promise you any definite service." This was a long way from Leland, who had gloried in never drawing a salary. Rural Baptists criticized William for his worldly airs—"My salary was too high, my sermons too pointed, my language too lofty, my hair too long, my visits too seldom, my reproofs too severe, my discipline too rigid, my wife's cap too fine, my daughter's dress too costly, my sons too high minded, my horse too fat & a thousand other things had been conjured up to show that I was not the man for Lexington," he chuckled. William Broaddus knew that he could find plenty of appreciative Baptist audiences in the town churches of Fredericksburg, Charlottesville, and Richmond.[11]

Historians like E. Brooks Holifield, Beth Barton Schweiger, and Robert Elder have drawn attention to the rise of genteel, professional Baptist preachers like the Broadduses as signals of modernity in the nineteenth-century South. Though these pastors never abandoned their heartfelt piety or revivalist message, they did so not as wild camp meeting leaders, but as polished orators, graceful and rational. The most versatile could still connect with ordinary folks in country meetinghouses, but they were also at ease in the distinguished pulpits of elegant, tall-steepled city churches. These new Baptist preachers were no longer wandering itinerants, but professional men who drew regular salaries, owned slaves, and mixed comfortably with lawyers, doctors, merchants, politicians, and other respectable members of southern society. They valued learning, culture, and self-improvement. They read copiously, established educational institutions, and received honorary degrees. They were denominational advocates who exercised a regional, not merely local, influence. They wrote articles in Baptist newspapers and published books with Baptist presses. They promoted innovative Baptist causes and traveled by train to Baptist state conventions. They formed a bridge between an older world of southern honor and a modern world of professionalism, institution-building, and a general preoccupation with progress. These "gentleman theologians" were the ministerial models John A. Broadus observed as a boy in the Broaddus family. By the end of the nineteenth century, this model of southern Baptist sophistication would reach its apex in John himself.

→>>✣✦✣<<←

The decisive influence of John Broadus's childhood was not a preacher, but a politician. Known as "Major" Edmund Broadus for his activity in the Culpeper County militia, John's industrious father farmed, operated a sawmill, and taught school in the poor region of Culpeper County known as "The Pines." But Edmund was best known as a statesman, in an era when politics was an object of fanatical interest to every red-blooded Virginia white man. Beginning in 1826, Edmund served twenty years in the state legislature as a proud member of the Whig Party. The Whigs had formed in opposition to the popular Jacksonian

Democrats in the 1830s, and rallied around Andrew Jackson's arch-rival, Kentucky Senator Henry Clay. Edmund Broadus was an ardent Clay man, and his sons followed in his way. Ascribing to Clay's "American System," Whigs supported a strong central government that could shape the United States economically through an interventionist policy that included a national bank, protective tariffs, and government subsidies for internal improvements. They wished also to actively shape the moral culture of America by promoting causes like temperance societies and public education. To the end of his life, John Broadus retained the Whigs' forward-leaning posture and burden to "uplift" southern society. But on slavery, the premier moral issue of the day, Henry Clay's Whigs compromised to preserve the Union. Clay advocated for gradual emancipation while still owning slaves, as did Edmund Broadus. No one defended Whig policies more effectively in the Virginia Piedmont than Edmund, said to be "the only man who could handle the Democrats" in the always hotly contested Culpeper County.[12]

Like his preaching brothers, Edmund Broadus was a "clear and forcible speaker." But his chief political strengths lay in his knowledge of legislative matters, his integrity, his common sense, and his popular touch with the people. He was a southern gentleman with immense personal magnetism, praised for his courtly manners, cheerful disposition, and devout evangelical piety. Friends recalled how he stood out from the cutthroat political culture of Jacksonian Virginia with his "calm, quiet, easy, and courteous demeanor," discussing issues of state in plain talk over a clay pipe. Constituents knew him as a devoted member of the Mount Poney and New Salem Baptist churches who often housed the preacher under his own roof, as an active participant in the Baptist denomination, and as a vigorous temperance advocate. The Major became one of the most popular men in his part of Virginia, and he never lost an election. A caucus of Virginia Whigs once approached Edmund about running for governor, but he demurred on the grounds that the governor's expenses would impoverish his family. Edmund's youngest son, John Albert, adored him.[13]

Edmund Broadus married Nancy Simms in 1812, but he was so broke that they had to move in with Nancy's parents. He put back the dollar a day he made on the Simms farm until he could open a field school and teach. As they slowly built their fortune, Edmund and Nancy welcomed four children into the world. James Madison Broadus, born in 1812, was fourteen years older than John and became one of his closest friends throughout his life. After James came Martha in 1814, and, eight years later, Caroline. Both sisters would always hover over their baby brother, John Albert, and acted as his second mothers into his early adulthood.

Edmund Broadus cultivated close relationships with his children. Every evening, John rushed to his father's side as he recounted the events of his day. Edmund invited John to stay and listen to the wide-ranging adult discussions that took place at the Broadus supper table, which often included family members, political fat-chewers, or the local Baptist minister. When Edmund rode out to inspect the farm, he invariably hoisted John onto the saddle behind him. While the boy's legs were still too short to spread across the back of "Old Prince," he was clinging to his father's waist, listening to stories and explanations of how the farm worked, and to all of Edmund's little moral lessons. John accompanied his father everywhere—on visits to neighbors, to the courthouse on business, and to militia musters. This constant exposure to his father's world matured him rapidly; young cousins remembered how, at a young age, John and his father "sat and talked like two men." John frequently drew on this intimate relationship with his father in future sermons and articles. "So pleasantly father used to talk as we rode along together," John would recall in an article for Southern Baptist children:

> Dear father, he was so wise and so kind; he would tell me stories, and explain things about the plantation, and often tell me how a boy ought to do, about one thing or another. I remember that one day I pulled down a neighbor's fence, so we could ride across the field, and, in putting it up, I left the top rail lying down, because it was heavy; and father said, 'No, no, my boy, put it up; whenever you pass through a gate, or draw-bars, or a fence, always leave it at least as good as you found it.' To this day I think of that, when passing through anything of that sort, and I am sure it is a very good rule. About all sorts of things, children, whether great or small, try to do just like your father and others tell you, and you'll be glad of it when they have long been dead and you are growing old.[14]

Replacing a fence rail may have been a commonsense act of neighborly courtesy, but it also reinforced the concept, so central to southern honor, that one's identity was rooted in communal opinion. For the same reason, Edmund Broadus would train his son to publicly exercise self-restraint and genteel manners, to offer public apologies for public wrongs, and to refuse to submit to slights and insults. "When my father died, he thought he was leaving his son a scholar and a gentleman," Broadus would later declare.[15]

John was also close to his mother, Nancy. Plump and of medium height, Nancy was gentle and quiet, rarely raising her voice. Yet she held the children to high standards and managed the household with firm efficiency. With Major Broadus frequently away on political business, Nancy learned to keep the farm, mill, and household operating smoothly. As a man, John would often quote his mother's favorite aphorisms, such as "the fire would not burn were the hearth not swept," when he rose to sweep the floor. Nancy also developed the Broadus children's cultural tastes. She taught them to enjoy long winter evenings in the company of a good book, and instilled in them a love of flowers and beautiful music. Her dignified domesticity helped form a lasting image of "true southern womanhood" in John's mind.[16]

→»❖❖«←

In 1837, Edmund Broadus purchased a three-hundred-acre farm and sawmill about six miles from the Culpeper Courthouse, in the shadow of the majestic Blue Ridge Mountains. He would name it "Edge Hill." The farm included a large white house big enough for all the Broaduses and their constant stream of guests. In the serenity of Edge Hill, John raced through the orchards, fished the mill pond, drank from the clear springs, rode his horse across the rolling fields, and clambered over the Blue Ridge foothills. It was at Edge Hill that he developed a love of extended walks in the countryside and a romantic bent of mind that remained with him for life. From his desk in bustling Louisville, Kentucky, he would indulge in a sentimental paean to his childhood:

> My early home, my early home,
> Whene'er I think of thee,
> How many thronging memories
> Come sadly over me.
> I see again the old white house,
> Half hidden by the trees;
> I hear the carol of the birds,
> The humming of the bees;

I stand beside the clear old spring,
Where oft I stood of yore,
I watch them boiling, bubbling up,
Those waters, bright and pure.[17]

These reflections indicate the deep influence of Romanticism on Broadus's thinking. Nearing fifty years old by Broadus's formative period, the Romantic movement reverenced nature not merely as a rugged backdrop for the human struggle, but as a world of beauty and wonder in which thoughtful individuals could make contact with the sublime. English Romantic poets like William Wordsworth—Broadus's favorite throughout his life—encountered a sense of the holy by observing daffodils and streams, wandering fields and forests. To a new degree, these Romantics focused on feelings, intuition, and the imagination rather than mere rational thought. They also idealized childhood as a nostalgic period of innocence, freedom, simplicity, spontaneity, and creativity. It is difficult to overstate how deeply each of these Romantic themes would shape Broadus. His famous preaching textbook, for example, instructs preachers to "observe, contemplate, commune with nature" in order to "awaken and invigorate" the powers of imaginations. "A certain indefinable sympathy exists, by a law of our being, between external nature and ourselves," he instructed. "Its forms and hues have a meaning for us more subtle than language conveys, and excite in us strange longings and kindling of soul, till we idealize all we behold." Modern Romanticism would influence many of nineteenth-century America's greatest pulpiteers, including Horace Bushnell, Henry Ward Beecher, and Phillips Brooks.[18]

Commingling with Edge Hill's bucolic attractions was the ugly reality of slavery. John's earliest playmates were a pair of Black slave boys named Henry and George. As John raced and fished and made up secret languages with the boys, he silently assumed the relative darkness of their differing skin pigmentations determined different levels of intelligence. Henry and George also taught John to swear, and so he associated them with a lower standard of morality. The behavior of "Uncle Dick," the Black waggoner known to lie to get out of trouble, reinforced these assumptions. John's warmest memories were attached to "Uncle Griffin," an amiable older man who took him on his knee Sunday afternoons to tell Br'er Rabbit stories. John remembered how sad he was the day Uncle Griffin told him he was now too old for the tales; the old man understood their subversive implications for southern race relations.[19]

Edmund Broadus often displayed a genuine humanity toward his Black neighbors. Virginia law required emancipated slaves to leave the state, but on at least two occasions Edmund Broadus petitioned the General Assembly to allow specific Black men to remain in the commonwealth with their families. One Armistead Johns had shown himself to be "a very humble, respectful, industrious negro, and seems to be much attached to his wife, to her master and family and to the neighbourhood," and "that his whole conduct goes to show that he studies to make him self useful to the white people and of good character with all." Similarly, the former slave Robin, "a handy man with tools in various ways" and now nearly sixty years of age, "would prefer returning to slavery to losing the society of his wife." Edmund Broadus argued that forcing respectable Black men like Johns and Robin to leave their wives violated "the cause of humanity itself."[20]

But while the Broaduses spoke of their own slaves in family terms, they also transparently expected them to serve their comforts and conveniences. When John's sister Caroline married in 1849, Edmund offered to give her a slave girl named Maria as a wedding present. "It would be well to have some little body who could nurse the child, bring water and wood, etc.," Caroline considered, but, "we do not ask this if it involves a sacrifice on father's part." John learned early to view enslaved persons as plantation commodities that could be given as gifts or sold for cash if necessary. The presence of enslaved persons in his young world imperceptibly molded his outlook on society as an obvious and divinely ordered class hierarchy.[21]

--->>·❖·❖·<<<--

Learning no less than mastery marked the genteel southerner, and education ran in the Broadus blood. At a time when just 9 percent of Virginia's white children were enrolled in school (compared to 73 percent in Massachusetts), Edmund Broadus cultivated his children's intellectual development with marked intentionality. He filled the house at Edge Hill with books and periodicals. From the children's earliest days, he and Nancy read aloud to them, and as soon as possible had them reading on their own. John read assiduously: the novels of James

Fennimore Cooper, Jonathan Swift's *Gulliver's Travels, Robinson Crusoe,* works of Shakespeare, and the Virginia Baptist *Religious Herald.* On a typical night at the Broadus home, Edmund kept a bright fire fueled by pine knots roaring in the hearth; while he quietly reviewed his papers in the corner, John read aloud to his mother and sisters as they sewed. To the end of his life, John would see education, next to evangelical religion, as the key to southern progress.[22]

From the ages of five to seven, John walked a mile and a half to Albert Tutt's "field school." There, in a single, open room, John learned his lessons on a long, backless wooden bench, elbow-to-elbow with classmates of all ages. He quickly outpaced the older boys. When John turned ten, Edmund opened a school of his own to supplement the family income, assisted by John's brother, Madison. John was one of forty scholars in Edmund's field school, which included several adult learners. At thirteen, John walked six miles to attend a classical grammar school taught by his uncle Albert G. Simms. There he read classical literature like Virgil, Livy, and Horace, in Latin. Like most antebellum southern elites, he would always idealize the order, intelligence, and refinement of the ancient Greek and Roman cultures. He often read ahead of the rest of the class, earning himself the nickname "hustler." Though decidedly bookish, he also learned to imitate his father's winsome manners, and made friends easily. Among his closest schoolmates was the future Confederate General A. P. Hill.[23]

In 1840, Edmund Broadus had to travel frequently on political business, and John took a year off from school to oversee the farm and the sawmill. Naturally pale and thin, he spent the year hardening his muscles through constant manual labor: splitting rails, plowing fallow ground, mowing fields, binding wheat, raking hay, pulling fodder, and mending fences. His year of intensive farm work rounded out his adolescent development, throwing him alongside laboring men, Black and white, who never read a page of Horace or Virgil. These experiences ensured that, though he would devote his adult life to academic study, he could identify with working people. Aristocratic in much of his outlook, he nevertheless moved easily among common men. But his year as a farmer also convinced him that he preferred a professional lifestyle; he had no desire to spend his days laboring under the hot sun. In 1843, sixteen-year-old John announced that Uncle Simms had sent him home from school, for he had nothing left to teach him. His seemingly idyllic, Old South childhood was drawing to a close.[24]

·→》》❖·❖·《《←·

Broadus was also coming of age spiritually. At sixteen, he had not yet professed his faith in Jesus Christ, though he had come close after observing the baptism of his older sister Martha. "I thought that day I would do so, and, for some time, tried to avoid improper conduct, and to be particular about reading the Bible and prayer," he later remembered. "But I did not know my own sinfulness, did not appreciate my need for a change of heart, did not turn from the love of sin to holiness, nor cast myself, as guilty and hopeless, upon the mercy God offers in Christ our Savior," he said, "And so it all wore away."[25]

In 1843, he attended a series of "protracted meetings" held by the Mount Poney Baptist Church, which had been in the pastoral charge of John Leland nearly seventy years earlier. Protracted meetings were revival services held on consecutive days, designed to awaken members of the community to their need for conversion. Both the mechanism of the protracted meeting and the focus on individual conversion it promoted were characteristic of the modern evangelical movement. The practice existed in tension with older conceptions of southern honor, which rooted one's identity in communal opinion rather than in the subjective, inner life and encouraged young men like John to resist the public emotional displays associated with revival meetings. Under the pointed preaching of Charles A. Lewis and Barnett Grimsley, John experienced conviction of his sins. He labored under a sense of guilt for many days, uncertain if the salvation offered from the Baptist pulpit could be his. Finally, a friend drew him aside and quoted to him a promise from Jesus: "All that the Father giveth me shall come to me; and him that cometh to me I will in no wise cast out" (John 6:37). "Can't you take hold of that, John?" his friend asked. He did. Shortly after John announced his newfound faith, Reverend Cumberland George of the Mount Poney Baptist Church baptized him in Mountain Run, just outside of Culpeper.[26]

·→》》❖·❖·《《←·

By age seventeen, John Broadus was already ambitious to "be somebody." "The reflection that I have now arrived at an age when it is necessary that I commence striving to be what I wish to be, a man possessed of those solid qualities which alone can gain the esteem of the intelligent and virtuous, has often troubled me," he wrote in 1845. The yearning to achieve public honor—particularly among "the intelligent and virtuous"—would endure among the most prominent themes of John's life. On the one hand, nothing could be more natural than for a young man of the Old South to thirst for prominence; an obsession with appearance and opinions stood at the heart of honor culture. At the same time, his newfound evangelical piety compelled him to reject raw ambition as so much worldly pride and vanity. He would grapple with his drive to excel and his desire to honor God until his dying day.[27]

However he ascended in the world, he would have to leave the farm to do it. Broadus seems never to have considered remaining at Edge Hill beyond adolescence. Surrounded by public men of consequence throughout his childhood, he was determined to become one himself, gripped by what his father called "a laudable desire to be eminent." He was not yet sure how to attain those lofty goals, but it would certainly require a university education. Though his distinguished family members were all self-taught, Broadus, filled with "the dreams of young ambition," set his heart on attending Thomas Jefferson's University of Virginia, in Charlottesville.[28]

First, he would need to earn some money, and also shore up his Latin, Greek, French, and higher math through private study. He could accomplish both objectives by following the Broadus tradition of opening a country school for a year or two. It would be hard work, but sacrifices were all part of the path to self-improvement that John wished to travel. Through the help of some family connections, he secured a place in Clarke County, where he would keep school in the home of William Sowers at Rose Hill. Edmund confessed by letter that "the anxiety I feel for your welfare at this moment (one hundred miles from you) overpowers me." But Edmund, still grounding his son in the rudiments of southern honor, trusted that John could convert the experience to his benefit. "Remember that 'religion is the chief concern, that honor and honesty is the road to preferment,' and that 'modesty is a quality that highly adorns youth,'" Edmund advised. He also sent along his watch for John to use in his classroom. On the lonely ride through the Shenandoah Valley, John often felt "very sad, as drawing a lengthening chain when I was going away from home, mother, sisters." But, as he admitted later, he also indulged in "many wild dreams in that wild spot, of education, of competence, of reputation, which I never dared to hope could be realized."[29]

He quickly discovered the trials of a first-year southern school teacher. Few of his students displayed much initiative, and, since he was barely older than many of them, discipline proved an ongoing problem. One mother pulled her two daughters from the school, blaming John's inability to manage the classroom. The meager enrollment depressed him. His sister Carrie urged him to act "in such a manner as to give people no just excuse for saying anything rude or unkind about you, and then just take it for granted that they do not, and you will be much happier. See if you do not."[30] Sisters Carrie and Martha wrote faithfully during his Clarke County sojourn, keeping him abreast of local news, fussing over his wardrobe, and sending him care packages.

Dreams of greatness felt remote inside that dismal schoolhouse, but Edmund's letters encouraged John. Edmund recalled his own early struggles as a young school teacher, and urged perseverance. "All of us must rise by degrees," he counseled, "and although a laudable ambition to become eminent should be indulged, yet we ought not to expect to rise too rapidly. . . . I know you must succeed, because you have the elements, but you must plod for it *and make yourself.* This all have to do, or it is never done; but success at once would be a miracle and would destroy every claim to merit, which consists in overcoming difficulties."[31] The self-made statesman knew from experience how rugged the road to self-improvement and honor could be.

In the summer of 1844, John began keeping a diary for his sisters to read. Besides his schoolhouse mishaps, he recorded his attempts at poetry and his own course of private studies. He spent one night each week reading newspapers. He commenced studying Greek in 1845, expecting to master it by the end of 1846. He also began to make his way in Clarke County social life. Reflecting his father's influence, he joined the local militia, wrote letters to local newspapers, took an active role in the Sons of Temperance and Berryville Total Abstinence Society, and enrolled in an eighteen-week geography course that met at night. He also taught a weekly Bible class in the Berryville Sunday school. By April 16, 1845, John had arisen to the post of Sunday school superintendent, requiring him to recruit, train, and encourage other teachers.[32] The young gentleman was finding his place in antebellum society.

He was also becoming a flirt. Back in Culpeper County, pretty girls had intimidated John, but his inhibitions now rapidly fell away. "I am glad to hear that the ladies do not frighten you now," wrote his friend William Morton in August 1844. "I always told you that they would not." Increasingly, John found the fairer sex distracting him from university preparation. "Next week I shall go to the singing school again and get my head full of girls, and then good-bye, Greek," he wrote. When his friend T. W. Lewis kiddingly called him a "ladies' man," he replied, "I lament that I so well deserve the name. Ofttimes I determine and redetermine, resolve and reresolve that I will not waste so much time in fluttering around the fair, but it really seems that I *cannot* help it." In years to come, he would often vent the amorous feelings stirred by his love interests in letters and diary entries. As a good Baptist, however, he drew the line at attending dances; that, he left to the Episcopalians.[33]

Whenever John was alone again, he struggled with his life's calling. Sometimes he believed that he had the raw ability to rise and make his mark in the world. "I feel that nature has given me the ability to be something," he confided to Edmund, "and I am determined that I will strive to be something, and I am determined that I will strive to rise." His candid yearnings to "be something," to "strive," and to "rise" in the world, reflective of the aspirations of countless enterprising, middle-class Virginians in the early nineteenth century, would never leave him. Antebellum America offered numerous opportunities of upward mobility for diligent and ambitious white men—but which was his path of ascent? He often found himself "discouraged by the seemingly insurmountable difficulties that are before me. I have been troubled too, by the fact that I cannot decide what to make of myself." His students' dismal progress discouraged him from a teaching career, and Edmund steered him away from law and politics. The Major urged John to pursue medicine, and soon he was perusing anatomy books and studying skulls at night with a local physician.[34]

When his friend T. W. Lewis suggested a career in preaching, John admitted that he had considered it. "But I always come to the conclusion that preaching is not my office," he wrote. He did not think himself "qualified" for the job. "I know that my mental capabilities are, in some respects, not inconsiderable, but I was not 'cut out' for a public speaker; I have not that grace of manner and appearance, that pleasing voice, that easy flow of words, which are indispensably necessary in him who would make impressions on his fellows by public speaking."[35] Broaduses held public speaking to high standards. Still lacking direction, he determined, at his father's urging, to teach a second year in Clarke County before applying to the university.

→»»❖•❖«« ←

Like many Virginia farmers, Edmund Broadus suffered financial hardships during the depression that followed the Panic of 1837. He had sunk money into a failed Culpeper gold mine in 1835, and afterward lost much in security debts. Money would be a problem for the rest of his life. In 1849, he sold eight of his slaves to repay his debts, for a total of $3,689. "The sale of father's negroes came off yesterday, and was quite as good a one as could have been expected," John's brother, Madison, would inform him. "Father gets money from Sam Rixey, $1200 to pay his other debts here, so in some sense he may be said to be out of debt." The human cost to the displaced slaves, whose names unfortunately do not survive, did not figure into Madison's reckoning. Their sale likely separated them from family; perhaps they would also be sentenced to the brutal laboring conditions of the southwest cotton plantations. But, "at least [Edmund] will be free from annoyance. Help me to rejoice over this blessed consummation."[36] The number of slaves at Edge Hill reminds us that Broadus was raised to occupy the Old South's ruling class, one that sold human beings and divided families for ready cash and to relieve "annoyance."

In 1846, Edmund's ongoing debt led him to open correspondence with Joseph C. Cabell of the University of Virginia. The university had recently created the position of "steward," to oversee the room and board of thirty-two "state students" attending on scholarship. For a well-known state legislator like Edmund, it was humbling to apply for the post of steward, though attachment to Virginia's center of learning helped him maintain something of his reputation. The *Richmond Times-Dispatch* declared that "a more judicious selection could not have been made in all Virginia." For John, Edmund's stewardship secured his place in the student body. In the fall, he would commence the study of medicine at the University of Virginia. In afteryears, the memory of Edmund's sacrifice stirred deep emotion. "Oh! The dear memories that come up in saying this of a father who . . . broke up a pleasant home, and spent his last years in most uncongenial employment and amid pecuniary losses, solely that his son might receive the education for which he had not dared hope," he recounted in a sermon. "How that son thanks him more and more every year—how he thanks God for such a wise and noble father."[37]

—⊰⊱—

With these plans in place, John attended the annual meeting of the Potomac Baptist Association in Upperville on August 11, 1846. Associational meetings were significant events in Baptist life, drawing together ministers, denominational representatives, and engaged lay people from across the region. Associational meetings provided a forum to hear reports, plan denominational strategies, and stir enthusiasm among the churches. That enthusiasm had reached an all-time high in 1846, just one year since southern Baptists had separated from northern Baptists over slavery. Annual meetings were as much festival as business meeting, providing a major social gathering to which the Baptist faithful looked forward throughout the year.

Associational delegates could expect to hear preaching of the highest quality. This year's preacher was A. M. Poindexter, then acting as fundraising agent for the Baptist Columbian College in Washington, D.C. After hearing Poindexter, John thought "he had never before imagined what preaching might be." Poindexter himself enhanced the impressive sermon. Tall and slim with flashing, blueish-gray eyes, his "figure was graceful and pleasing, and his action was natural, varied, and often extremely commanding." Poindexter was known as an unusually clear thinker and powerful orator who, "by his logic and pathos . . . carried all before him." He was also college-educated, a published author, and a successful and well-recognized agent for various denominational causes. He had just recently received an honorary Doctor of Divinity degree from Columbian College. Like John's uncles, Poindexter embodied what E. Brooks Holifield called the "gentleman theologians" of the antebellum era.[38]

Poindexter preached on Christ's parable of the talents, from the twenty-fifth chapter of Matthew. The parable told of a master who entrusted three stewards with different amounts of money (talents) to invest and develop while he was away. Upon his return, the master inspected each steward's work, and rewarded them accordingly. Poindexter applied the parable to a call to preach. John sat riveted as Poindexter spoke eloquently of "consecrating one's mental gifts and possible attainments to the work of the ministry." John later recalled how Poindexter "seemed to clear up all difficulties pertaining to the subject; he swept away all the disguise of self-delusion, all the excuses of false humility; he held up the thought that the greatest sacrifices and toils possible to a minister's lifetime would be a hundredfold repaid if he should be the instrument of saving one soul."[39]

With his forbears, Broadus always maintained the necessity of a personal, supernatural call to preach. Earlier generations of Baptist ministers "felt themselves inwardly *called* to the ministry," he noted. Broadus judged their conception of the pastoral office to be "thoroughly correct." Indeed, Broadus chafed at speaking of the ministry as "a *profession*." "One ought not to choose the ministry at all as he might choose to be a lawyer, physician, teacher, or editor," he insisted, "but it ought to be entered upon from a sense of *duty* to God and man." At the same time, through Poindexter, he may have recognized that the pulpit could supply the long-sought opportunity to "be something." As Robert Elder notes, "after 1830, the influence wielded by prominent evangelical clergy could be viewed without much contradiction as a ripe field for the righteous ambitions of the young men of the South." John would fiddle with the calculus of how to win honor for the glory of God for the next fifty years. At the moment, he just needed to speak to his pastor, Reverend Barnett Grimsley, who he found after the closing prayer. "Brother Grimsley, the question is decided," he said through tears, "I must try to be a preacher."[40]

Two

ON THE RISE

ROADUS SAT WITH his University of Virginia classmates, listening to
them discuss the various southern cities and historic estates from which
they hailed. Finally, one turned to him and asked, "And you, Broadus, where
were you born?" Broadus replied that he "was born at the Poor House." He was
half-joking, for his father had overseen the county home for the poor back in
Culpeper, and Broadus had enjoyed a genteel upbringing among numerous slaves
on the Edge Hill estate. But he certainly felt poor now, a scholarship student
among the sons of the state's elite families.[1]

University of Virginia founder Thomas Jefferson had dreamed of a republican institution that would educate white males from across the social spectrum.
"It is safer to have the whole people respectably enlightened than a few in a high
state of science and the many in ignorance," Jefferson had declared. But Jefferson
so overspent in the construction of his university that only the wealthiest planters' sons could afford to attend for its first twenty years. Finally, in 1845, Virginia
legislators approved a state scholarship program. At least one student from each
of the thirty-two senatorial districts in Virginia would be able to attend the university for at least two years without tuition fees. These "state students" would pay
no more than $60 for room and board, and would live with Edmund Broadus,
the university-employed "steward." John Broadus was among the first Virginians
to receive a scholarship. He knew that he began his ascent from a lower rung than
did most of his peers. In later years, he would take satisfaction in repaying the
university the scholarship money he had received.[2]

Jefferson had insisted that his school bear no religious affiliation. "This institution will be based on the illimitable freedom of the human mind," he trum-
peted in 1820, "For here we are not afraid to follow truth wherever it may lead,

nor tolerate any error so long as reason is left free to combat it." Jefferson's largely secular vision unsettled many of Virginia's evangelical leaders, who suspected the old philosopher of sowing infidelity among its sons. Indeed, Jefferson predicted privately that the young men of his day would all die Unitarians, as the Enlightenment continued its triumphant march through the republic. By the time Broadus enrolled in 1846, the public still looked upon the school as "governed by influences more or less hostile to religion" and as "a centre of impiety." But after Jefferson died in 1826, a pious Board of Visitors member named General John Hartwell Cocke intervened to alter this perception. A wealthy planter and aggressive moralist, Cocke had long chafed against the university's irreligious culture, and now acted decisively to improve the student body's notorious moral laxity. He enforced school uniforms, 5 a.m. wakeup calls, and strict control over student spending. Cocke also appointed a school chaplain and replaced Jefferson's deistic professors with men of sober evangelical piety, such as the Methodist Gessner Harrison and the Presbyterian minister William H. McGuffey.[3]

Thus, Broadus entered a university pulled between the Old South's rowdy honor culture and the civilizing influences of modern evangelicalism. In the spring of 1846, students brawled with a traveling circus company after one young Virginian threw a lit cigar into the lion's cage. A few months earlier, in January of 1846, a gang of students set the great lawn ablaze. The year prior, in April of 1845, students donned masks and terrorized the campus night after night, riding horses up and down the lawn, firing pistols, launching bricks through glass windows, and battering doors to splinters. Professor Gessner Harrison repeatedly suffered assault from students, and on one occasion was threatened in his study at gunpoint. In the most notorious incident of all, a rioting student in 1840 shot and killed law professor John A. G. Davis. Yet with the growth of an evangelical presence on campus, the leavening of hardworking state students, and the more consistent application of discipline, the hell-raising culture slowly abated during Broadus's student days. His own roommate, W. A. Whitescarver, shared his Baptist piety, academic seriousness, and aspirations to the pastorate. Whitescarver married John's sister Carrie in 1849, and the two men remained lifelong friends. "He is the only man I never found anything wrong in," Broadus would say. "We talk about saints. William is one."[4] Saints remained in short supply at the University of Virginia, but Broadus's experiences there expanded his understanding of southern society.

Until 1848, Broadus and the other state students lived with Edmund Broadus in a house donated by James Monroe. Edmund still had lessons of evangelical honor to teach his son. After John "uttered some language of severe criticism" against a fellow student at the Debating Society, the insulted victim sent a written demand for an apology. John considered his classmate haughty, and so sent by a friend a half-hearted note. When Edmund learned of this, he insisted that John's station required more grace. "John, John, this will never do. You were wrong; such style of speech was wholly inconsistent with your profession and purposes in life. You must forthwith send an unconditional apology." His opponent demanded a public apology, and so John humbled himself at the next society meeting for "giving way to sinful anger and unseemly sarcasm." One witness noted that "John A. Broadus was not naturally of a very meek disposition," but the apology reinstated him in the community. "I could perceive in the countenances of all around me a manifestation of unusually heightened respect and admiration for Mr. Broadus and a corresponding disapprobation and contempt for his adversary," recalled G. W. Hansbrough. "From that hour John A. Broadus stood, as ever since he stood, on a plane infinitely higher, whilst [his opponent] sank to a much lower one." Restoring honor through a sincere apology (rather than through violence) provides a telling insight into the ways in which antebellum evangelicals could appropriate southern culture even as they transformed it.[5]

John and Edmund Broadus grew even closer in June of 1847, at the end of his first year. John received word that his mother, Nancy Broadus, was dying of heart disease. John rushed through the door of her room just in time for her death. Edmund Broadus would soon remarry, to Miss Somerville Ward. John loved his stepmother "most sincerely," and would take her into his own home after his father died.[6]

→>>✣✤✣<<←

The university's rigor jarred John, who found himself far behind in many subjects. Back in Culpeper County, friends had called him "hustler" for sailing ahead of the class; university classmates now called him "a plodder" and questioned his intellect. He devoted whole vacations to Greek, and drilled Will Whitescarver on Greek forms over long walks. The two became known for burning the lamp all night, Broadus taking over in the early morning hours after Whitescarver retired from his late-night studies. In time, Broadus's hard work showed, and he won the respect of his peers. "He demanded of himself the best he could do in all that he did," noted classmate F. H. Smith. "If genius is the ability and willingness to do hard work, he was a genius." He so impressed his professors that three of them contracted Broadus to tutor their own children. One of his pupils recalled his instruction as "all work and perfect teaching." Finding his young charges stumbling through McGuffey's Second Reader, he soon had them "with Caesar, at war with Gaul," and singing in chorus with the aid of his tuning fork. "The price of all success is *toil,* hard and unremitting," he declared to the Jefferson Society in his second year.[7]

Broadus owed much of his progress to his professors, several of whom shared his evangelical convictions. One of these was William H. McGuffey, chair of moral philosophy since 1845. McGuffey is best known for his ubiquitous primary school "readers," which remained popular in American children's education into the twentieth century. Broadus frequently praised McGuffey, who employed Socratic questioning with his students, for teaching him to think. One day McGuffey asked, "What do you think of the author's statement?" Broadus replied, "I have never thought about it." "Think about it now and give your idea," pressed McGuffey. Broadus called it a "turning point in his life." He also admired McGuffey's piety. An ordained Presbyterian minister, McGuffey held to a moderate Calvinism and was a popular preacher in Charlottesville churches of all denominations. He instituted morning prayer meetings for students, twenty minutes before 7 every day. McGuffey also took pains in his classroom to defend the Christian faith from its cultured despisers. "Nothing could have been grander than the continued attack he made on atheism and infidelity," recalled one sympathetic student.[8]

Broadus grew even closer to Gessner Harrison, professor of ancient languages. Harrison had been one of the university's first three graduates and was appointed to the faculty at the age of twenty-one as part of J. H. Cocke's moral reformation. He would remain at the university for nineteen years. A student of the latest German linguistic theories, Harrison became known for his innovative methods in philology and published several books in the field. The average university student often complained of "Old Gess's humbuggery." "The careful explanation of case-endings, tense-signs, and mood vowels seems to them a great waste of their extremely precious time," Broadus remembered. But Broadus was fascinated. Harrison was an exacting grader who once passed only twenty-six students out of 150 in his senior Latin class. Outside the classroom, Harrison was renowned for his devoted Methodist service. He conducted a weekly Sunday school for slaves and poor whites in the Ragged Mountains. Harrison's favorite motto was "Sirs, brothers, *fear God and WORK*."[9] Broadus never recovered from it.

→»·❖·❖·«←

As Broadus acclimated to his academic duties, he found time to engage in student life. He joined the Jefferson Society debate team and jousted with the next generation of Virginia lawyers and politicians. He also sang in the chapel choir and edited the short-lived "Jefferson Monument Magazine." Broadus impressed his peers as "a loyal Christian," taking a leading part in McGuffey's morning prayer meetings and accompanying Harrison to the nearby Ragged Mountains to teach Sunday school. He also enrolled in the Sons of Temperance chapter that Edmund founded at the university.[10]

And he began to preach. On June 4, 1849, Broadus delivered his first Sunday morning sermon at McGuffey's Mount Eagle Presbyterian Church, an indication of the university's broadening impact. He selected for his text Psalm 62:8, "God is a refuge for us." A little girl in the audience remembered her surprise at seeing the "slightly built, dark-hair youth, scarcely twenty years of age," rising in the pulpit in McGuffey's place. "There was something in his manner very entreating, very touching, very convincing," she wrote. The next month, Broadus preached to his home church, New Salem Baptist in Culpeper, from 1 Timothy 4:8, "For bodily exercise profiteth little: but godliness is profitable unto all things, having promise of the life that now is, and of that which is to come." His earliest efforts suggested "superior talents" for the pulpit. In September, the Charlottesville Baptist Church called him as their permanent preacher. He declined so that he could focus on his studies.[11]

By his final semester, Broadus's demanding schedule began to wear on his health. Learning to manage his physical limitations as he sought to maximize every opportunity would become a major theme of his life. He resolved to set aside his studies each afternoon in order to take daily walks in the fresh air. The arrangement became more pleasant still when he convinced Gessner Harrison's daughter, Maria, to accompany him.[12]

-->>◆·☙·《《←-

In the spring of 1850, Broadus completed his master of arts degree, the highest then available in the South. Most Virginia Baptists never attended college at all, and those who did were often satisfied with one or two years of formal study. Broadus's peers selected him as the class valedictorian, and he prepared a commencement speech on "Human Society in Its Relation to Natural Theology." Yet in the midst of these happy days, Edmund Broadus's health plummeted. On June 27, two days before graduation, Broadus was at the Major's bedside. "I shall not make my graduating speech," he told his father. "Yes," Edmund replied, "for I am dying." After upending his life to provide an education for his son, Edmund died two days before Broadus graduated as valedictorian. In his absence, Gessner Harrison declared that the university had never produced a finer student.[13]

Years later, Broadus's son-in-law, A. T. Robertson, would declare that the University of Virginia "exerted . . . an overmastering power on John A. Broadus's whole nature." The university broadened his cultural and religious outlook, throwing him among Presbyterians, Methodists, Episcopalians, and plenty of irreligious southerners. Broadus himself credited the school for instilling in him "this spirit of work, a noble rage for knowing and for teaching." More than anything, the university reinforced his father's ideal of learned Old South gentility mixed with evangelical piety that forever marked Broadus. It was there, as Steve Longenecker observes, Broadus imbibed "an environment that nurtured a distinctive Virginia brand of Southernness." He was ready for a career as a sophisticated southern linguist and pulpiteer.[14]

-->>◆·☙·《《←-

Exhausted from his hectic university course, Broadus sought a transitional job before entering the pastorate. He found it in a teaching position at the plantation home of J. H. Cocke in Fluvana County. The job did not begin until October, and the interim period allowed John time to woo Maria Harrison. He passed many hours in the Harrisons' parlor, listening to Maria play the piano. Broadus later credited her for introducing him to "the spirit-moving power that dwells in music." In future years, he would buy her pieces of sheet music in the cities he visited. Maria encouraged his own musical interests, and urged him to take up the flute. He attempted to accompany her, but his clumsy efforts spoiled her polished performances. "Indeed, I think of only one thing I am able to do well," he wrote, "and that is—*love you.*" They made plans to marry before the end of the year. "It seems to me I love you more and more, dear Maria, as that day approaches," he wrote that fall, "and I have an idea that it is even so with you. Oh, that your hopes of enjoyment in the society of the man you love may not be disappointed! Sometimes I cannot but fear, yet such times come not often—you were made to be loved, I will love you, you will be happy."[15] He was rarely afraid to reveal his feelings, by letter or in the pulpit.

Along with the blossoming of love, the summer of 1850 brought more preaching opportunities in a variety of southern evangelical churches. After a sermon before a full congregation at Gessner Harrison's Charlottesville Methodist Church, Broadus admitted to Maria that "I fear they won't continue to turn out so for me, for I spoke almost an hour, I reckon, and am afraid there seemed to be a great deal of youthful extravagance in what was said." Still, it was increasingly clear to those who heard him that, as his brother Madison wrote, "you can preach." On Monday, August 12, an ordination presbytery at New Salem Baptist Church formally set him apart for gospel ministry.[16]

But to preach as a gentleman theologian, Broadus could not just pour out his heart; he needed to study. An older peer proposed a stack of resources—in Old Testament criticism, church history, biblical encyclopedias, books of biblical geography, Greek commentaries, theological periodicals, the works of English Puritans, and various collections of Baptist sermons. Soon, Broadus was also working through the tomes of Francis Turretin, Timothy Dwight, and Andrew Fuller, all reflecting the strong appeal of Reformed, rational orthodoxy among Baptists in the Old South.[17]

In the spring of 1851, John consulted his uncle "Kentucky Andrew" Broaddus as to "how far Calvinism should be carried." Reconciling the determining activity of God and the freedom and responsibility of man was a perennial subject of debate for the South's Baptists. Anti-missionary, or Primitive, Baptists believed that the Broadduses had compromised the old doctrines of God's predestining grace with their modern denominational machinery and revivalism. The influence of the rapidly growing Methodist and Disciples of Christ movements had further weakened Calvinism's influence in the South. Yet Uncle Andrew encouraged John to avoid the path of a "controversialist." Theological jousting was a favorite sport among frontier Baptists, but the genteel Broadduses preferred to live above the fray. John should not concern himself "with isms," and simply preach the Bible as it came to him—to "know nothing among the people but Jesus Christ and him crucified," Andrew wrote. This basic biblicism ultimately led Andrew to affirm a broad Calvinism—"that God always acts in accordance with an eternal purpose." At the same time, Andrew noted that when Christ and the apostles appealed to men, they "recognized no impediment in the way of any, but called 'all men everywhere to repent.'" This, Andrew contended, was "the safe plan." Broadus took his uncle's counsel to heart. He would promote an updated, evangelical Calvinism consistent with the denominational activism of Southern Baptists, and leave the polemics to others.[18]

→›››❖‡❖‹‹‹←

At the end of September, Broadus traveled to Fluvanna County to assume his teaching duties. J. H. Cocke had constructed his Bremo Plantation home on three thousand prime acres along the James River in 1819 under the oversight of master craftsman John Neilson, who helped build Jefferson's Monticello. During the Civil War, Mary Anna Custis Lee, wife of Robert E. Lee, would stay at Bremo with the Cocke family after fleeing her own home at Arlington. "It is certainly a pretty and pleasant place," Broadus wrote to Maria. Cocke had founded Bremo Seminary to drill his own self-discipline and moral rectitude into his sons, and into those of his genteel friends. Broadus had charge of thirteen students, including Cocke's two grandsons.[19]

He had forgotten the demands of teaching. "Certain it is, I have to *work hard,*" he wrote to Maria at the end of the first week. Thirteen students of scattered ages and learning levels placed a heavy burden on a single instructor. He taught five different Latin classes. Two of the boys studied Greek, two took geometry, four he taught algebra, and one boy basic arithmetic. The thirteenth student, "little Mosely," was so much younger than the rest that he followed a different course altogether. "I find it difficult to 'arrange the lectures,'" Broadus confessed. He also led the boys in a course of "Scripture history," hoping to interest them in reading their Bibles. Classroom discipline remained a headache; more than one angry parent would write to Broadus to protest an unruly son's expulsion from Bremo. Broadus suggested that Maria could help him review the boys' lessons once they were married, though he assured her that he was not trying to make her into "a country schoolmaster's assistant." "It is bad enough to be a country schoolmaster's wife," he admitted. He had far grander visions for their life together, though he gathered that God intended this humbling season for his good. "It is good for us sometimes to be troubled, since it drives us to the Great Comforter; for it is good to feel our weakness and insufficiency, and then go to the Source of Strength."[20]

Broadus's responsibilities at Bremo included preaching regularly to Cocke's slaves. Like his friend Thomas Jefferson, Cocke had a complicated relationship with slavery. On the one hand, he denounced the institution as "the great Cause of all the Chief evils of our Land," and opposed it so forcefully that a proslavery neighbor once physically attacked him. Cocke worked actively for the colonization movement and established a farm in Alabama that ostensibly was to train slaves for freedom in the colony of Libera. He advocated for gradual emancipation, believing masters were obligated to prepare their slaves for liberty by civilizing them. At Bremo, Cocke labored to reform the morals, manners, and spirituality of his enslaved workers. He required hard work, prayer, and he forbade gambling, profanity, alcohol, and adultery. He also constructed a chapel for them in 1835. "I am glad to learn your willingness to preach to our people at our chapel," he told Broadus. "Christians in our country have an awful account to settle for their neglect of the slave population. I have long been desirous to do what I could in that way; would to God I could say my skirts were clear." On the other hand, despite his public activism, Cocke emancipated few slaves in his lifetime or in his will. He told his Alabama slaves that those who met his high behavioral standards would be freed to Liberia, but only fourteen apparently ever qualified.[21]

Cocke's paternalistic attitude toward his enslaved workers cast him as the benevolent father over a great household. Historians have demonstrated how white paternalism propped up the slaveowner's sense of superiority, enhanced his honor in the community (setting him apart from both his slaves and the brutal "white trash"), helped legitimize the slave system to his troubled conscience, and usefully reinforced slave dependence. As an evangelical, Cocke's paternalism also meant providing gospel ministry for his slaves, which is where Broadus came in. "The people listened, whether with pleasure and profit I cannot know," Broadus wrote to Maria after a sermon at the slave chapel. His uncle Andrew Broaddus had been "the most prominent Baptist advocate of slave missions in Virginia," according to Charles F. Irons, and Broadus also promoted slave ministry throughout the antebellum period. In an 1856 address to the Albemarle Baptist Association, he encouraged pastors to reach out to slaves with "a judicious blending of practical instruction with appeals to the feelings." He urged masters to read, explain, and apply Bible stories to house servants, and to make special visits to the field hands for the same purpose. Broadus's stress on feelings and stories reflected a common assumption that Black listeners could not understand doctrinal messages. Albert J. Raboteau and others have shown that slaves often listened dutifully to white preachers like Broadus, then slipped off afterward for their own services.[22]

Broadus's later reflections on antebellum slave ministry demonstrate a troubling mixture of evangelical piety and white southern racism. He clearly believed the souls of Black men and women to be worthy of his most strenuous labors, though he also never questioned their inherent inferiority. "By no means was all done that ought to have been done," he wrote in the 1890s, but, "when and where has this been the case about anything?" he asked.

But thousands and ten thousands of Christian men and women did feel the burden of these lowly souls laid upon themselves, did toil faithfully and often with great sacrifice to bring them to the Savior, and lovingly to guide their weak and ignorant steps in the paths of Christian life. Certainly there was among them, in some respects, a very low standard of Christian morality, as is usually the case with ignorant converts of any degraded race. But there are many still living who can testify, from personal observation and effort, that not a few of these negro Christians gave real and gratifying evidence of being Christians indeed. They were not black angels, as some romantic readers of romance half imagined, nor yet black demons, as some who hated them then and now would have us believe; they were and are simply black men, from among the lowest races of mankind, yet by no means beyond the reach of saving Christian truth and loving Christian culture. Some of us remember them with strange tenderness of feeling, like that of foreign missionaries for their lowly converts, and find it painful to see them grossly misrepresented, either by fanciful eulogy or foolish censure.[23]

Broadus's assessment, featuring assumptions of Black dependence, white superiority, and the benevolent intentions of masters, fits comfortably within a Lost Cause literature that helped southern whites justify the slave system in retrospect. Long after he left Bremo Plantation, Broadus maintained this posture of evangelical paternalism. He stressed the white man's duty of Black uplift, as both a Christian and a man of southern honor.

—>»❖❖«<—

On November 13, 1850, Broadus and Maria were married at the Harrison home. The union may have raised a few eyebrows among his Baptist brethren; not only was Maria Harrison a Methodist, she had never professed personal faith in Christ. Yet for aspiring gentleman pastors in the antebellum era, such marriages were not uncommon. Southern preachers on the rise often married above their social station, acquiring a fortune and a status-boost in the bargain. When one Methodist minister married a Mississippi planter's daughter around this time, a newspaper reported, "There seems to exist a powerful attraction between divines of note and females of this class."[24] No doubt many factors contributed to Broadus's choice of Maria Harrison.

On their part, the Harrisons did not hesitate to pledge Maria to the Baptist preacher. "[Maria] was married a little more than a month ago to a young Baptist minister who graduated here last June as M. A., and who is a young man of much promise," Gessner Harrison wrote to a friend. "He has no fortune, but has an uncommonly excellent education and fine abilities. I think he is well calculated to make her happy, and we have willingly committed her to the care of the same Providence which has guided us hitherto."[25] John and Maria honeymooned in Philadelphia, where the itinerary included a concert featuring Jenny Lind, the Swedish opera sensation then on tour in the States. Broadus's marriage capped a year of unparalleled transition. In 1850, he had buried his father, graduated from the University of Virginia, been ordained a Baptist minister, and now was married to a southern lady of substance. He had taken every step to "rise" and to "be something" that he had hoped.

By the spring of 1851, Broadus began receiving invitations to teach and preach. The first serious offer came from Georgetown College, a Baptist school in Kentucky's Bluegrass region. His uncle William F. Broaddus, a Board member at

Georgetown, informed John by letter of his unanimous election to the faculty as professor of ancient languages. William took it for granted that John would accept. "Our denomination is strong and wealthy in Kentucky, and the college is rapidly rising in their affections," William wrote. Other advice soon poured in. Gessner Harrison compiled an enumerated list of reasons why "a man of higher aim" like Broadus should decline. Meanwhile, Madison Broadus and William McGuffey both urged him to take the job as a launching pad to greater things. In the end, Broadus declined the Georgetown professorship; he was loathe to leave Virginia, and he was itching to preach.[26]

Other opportunities quickly followed. On a trip to Richmond in 1851, the prestigious First Baptist Church invited him to preach on a Sunday night. The auditorium was "crowded to overflowing," one observer noted. He also recalled his first impression of Broadus:

> He was so youthful in appearance, so frail, so diminutive, an old brother sitting by whispered in my ear, "He will fail." Soon with slow and graceful step he approached the desk and announced the opening hymn. In clear tones, with no tremor of voice or manner, he read the several stanzas and took his seat. The old brother whispered again, "He will not fail." And fail he did not; he fully sustained his early fame. His sermon was equal to the demands of the occasion,—no gush, no attempt at mannerism or display of learning; it was the pure gospel in simple, earnest, well-chosen diction, and impressively delivered.

Broadus so impressed one wealthy attendee, James Thomas, that Thomas told him to buy $80 worth of books for himself, and to send him the bill. It was among the first of many occasions when Broadus's preaching inspired generous sponsorship.[27]

His success in Richmond led to a deluge of invitations. Richmond's Grace Street Church extended a unanimous call to be their pastoral supply while the regular minister traveled Europe. The Baptist church in Lynchburg also made several efforts to obtain his services, as did churches in Petersburg and Scottsville. From Maryland came calls by Baptist churches in Huntingdon and Rockdale. He was also asked to open a school near Charlottesville. The flattering invitations served heady wine to a twenty-five-year-old, but he declined them all. One member at the Rockdale church observed that "the brilliant young preacher was destined to a loftier flight and could not under any circumstances have long re-mained there."[28] Spiritual concerns played an important role in Broadus's voca-tional decisions, but he also weighed his options in terms of location, salary, and platform.

Two letters from Charlottesville settled the issue. The University of Virginia was creating a new position for an assistant instructor in the ancient languages department, and wanted Broadus to work alongside his father-in-law, Gessner Harrison. He would earn $700 a year and have full use of the library. About the same time, the Charlottesville Baptist Church reissued their pastoral call. The dual invitations from Charlottesville opened the door for Broadus to pursue his passions for both preaching and the academy. He accepted both calls.[29]

Yet he also had some inkling of the dangers of dividing his energies. He wrote a letter to the church to clarify what they could expect of him. "As the arrangement proposed is somewhat peculiar it is exceedingly desirable to both the Church and myself that there be no ground left for misapprehension in any respect," he wrote. "I think it is proper for me to state as distinctly as possible what I understand to be the duties expected to be performed, they being in fact also, the extent of labor which I felt it at all practicable for me to undertake." He intended to limit his labors to preaching two messages every Sabbath and leading the weekly prayer meeting. He would be exempted entirely from the customary pastoral duties of visiting the poor and the sick; he would visit members as he could, but he made no promises.[30] Clearly, Broadus was apprehensive of assuming this "double-burden," as he would come to describe it, and anxious to meet the expectations of both the school and his congregation in his pursuit of evangelical honor. As he would learn throughout his life, serving two masters was no easy task. Still, at twenty-five, he was the pastor of a visible town church and an assis-tant instructor at the University of Virginia. He was on his way.

Three
GENTLEMAN PASTOR

IN THE FALL OF 1851, Broadus took a crucial step in his rise to evangelical eminence: he moved to the town of Charlottesville. The arrival of the Louisa Railroad Company in 1850 had transformed the once secluded agricultural hamlet into a bustling and prosperous southern center, with a population of three thousand by the Civil War. Charlottesville now formed "an important link in the connection of the metropolis with the West," explained the *Virginia Historical Register*. "The traveler may now leave Richmond soon after six in the morning, arrive at Charlottesville at one, and reach Staunton the same night." The railroad also boosted Charlottesville's economy, attracting the cotton and woolen mills of the Charlottesville Manufacturing Company in 1852. Within a decade, these mills would supply Confederate uniforms. Other signs of progress included an influx of consumer goods in stores, the construction of new buildings, and the proliferation of clubs and social organizations. Richmond resident James Thomas judged Charlottesville to be "a very delightful and a very important place, perhaps none more so, in some respects."[1]

Serving a southern town church required a particular ministerial profile. Town dwellers aspired to respectability in their dress, speech, purchasing, and leisure habits—and in their worship. Increasingly, town folk like the Charlottesville Baptists expressed preferences for a more polished and professional minister: one who would minister to their spiritual needs while also serving their self-image as people of intelligence and refinement. Broadus fit the profile neatly. All ministers should cultivate "the spirit, habits and manners of *gentlemen*," he believed. After all, "if it is not important for a preacher and pastor to be a gentleman, for whom is it important?"[2]

Kinship counted for a lot in the Old South's genteel hierarchy; Broadus was the son of a beloved state senator and a descendant of Virginia's first family of Baptist preachers. His Broaddus bloodline also welcomed him into a larger network of the South's best people. If learning was necessary for gentility, few Virginians could best Broadus. "His having been the first of our preachers to come before the public with the halo of a splendid University career on his head, was undoubtedly much in his favor at the start," remembered Baptist George B. Taylor. Observers marveled at Broadus's "extraordinary" knowledge of art, science, and literature. As Erskine Clarke notes, educated white southerners shared a "distant love affair with the classical world of Greece and Rome," seen in their Greek revival homes, bestowal of Roman names on their slaves, and frequent allusions to Horace and Tacitus. Broadus was himself so steeped in this world that he was rumored to dream and think in Greek. He relaxed by reading *The Odyssey*, gave learned discourses on "Education in Athens," and instructed University of Virginia students in the classics.[3]

Genteel southerners also prized sociability, and Broadus's manners, charm, and personal warmth drew comment wherever he went. Observers credited him with "a consideration and a courtesy, a witchery of personality which made him the center of any social gathering in which he appeared." One effusive acquaintance declared that "people listened and wanted only to listen as he talked. There was a refinement of manner and a consideration for the feelings of others which enabled him to draw out the best that was in his companions." So affable was Broadus that he could even "talk on quite smoothly" with a roomful of Yankees over southern slavery, and charm a northern woman who was reading *Uncle Tom's Cabin* in a train car. "She was very Northern, and I intensely Southern," he told Maria, "but we agreed to disagree, and got on pretty well."[4]

Utilizing Daniel Hundley's 1860 analysis, Broadus belonged to the Old South's upwardly mobile middle class. He was never fabulously wealthy, but he was socially connected, earned a respectable salary, and occupied the esteemed positions of town minister and university assistant instructor. He was also a slave owner, reporting three enslaved persons in his 1854 Albemarle County tax report. He regularly discussed the purchase of slaves with his brother. Madison Broadus urged him to purchase a sixteen-year-old girl named Margaret, for instance, at a price between $20 and $30. Considering Margaret "a pretty fair chance," Madison assured Broadus that "if she does not please you, she can be returned at any time.

She is black but comely, I mean she has a pleasant countenance, and might be made to have a genteel appearance." Though there is no indication that either Broadus brother sexually mistreated their female slaves, Madison's unsettling remarks about young Margaret's appearance indicate how slavery inherently objectified human beings. Broadus oversaw the discipline of his slaves but often delegated the unpleasant task. Maria reported that when the young slave Reuben failed to carry out her instructions, she "had to have Reuben whipped," adding that "he has done remarkably well since." Maria regularly complained of the unreliability of her servants. When Broadus wrote to longtime slave Dick Hackley, he filled his letters with the affectionate language of a benevolent patriarch. One Hirand Hansbrough, owner of Dick's daughter, Nelly, indicated that Dick and Nelly were both "very anxious" that Broadus should hire her, for the price of $36, which suggests a certain benevolence. (It does not appear that Broadus did purchase Nelly.) Broadus flavored his mastery with evangelical piety and Whiggish interest in uplift.[5]

The spirit and habits of a gentleman were open to any preacher willing to pursue them. Whether a man had been "reared in refined homes" or came from "very inferior advantages," he could, "by force of native delicacy and generosity of feeling, and by diligent use of the best social opportunities . . . become a noble gentleman," Broadus believed. Prepared by both breeding and cultivation, Broadus stepped behind the Charlottesville Baptist pulpit as one of Brooks Holifield's "genteel clerical elite." But he did not simply look the part of an impressive town minister; he "could *preach.*"[6]

-→>>∻⁂∺<<←-

Broadus's appearance in the pulpit underwhelmed at first. He was a small, slight man, rarely above 130 pounds in his lifetime. With "a broad forehead, an unusually large head," and a neatly trimmed beard, he looked more like a retiring scholar than a dynamic orator. Nor did he employ an aggressive delivery. Many Baptist preachers achieved their ends through force of volume, rate of speech, and animated gesture. Abraham Lincoln, who heard many an old-fashioned Baptist sermon as a boy, remarked, "When I hear a man preach, I like to see him act as if he were fighting bees." Broadus's delivery, by comparison, was "quiet and unostentatious." He kept his voice calm—some called it "singularly sweet"—and spoke in a natural, conversational tone, with minimal gestures. His pulpit manner was described as warm, friendly, under control; listeners felt he treated them with "exquisite respect."[7]

Despite deep learning, Broadus chose the clearest and simplest language, "a style so much like that of a mere child," as one listener put it. He modeled his sermons after his father's political stump speeches, honing what Broadus called "my clear and simple style" to engage diverse audiences of ordinary people. One hearer compared his rhetoric to Lincoln's: "conversational . . . simple and flexible and virile." The success of Broadus's natural method would transform Baptist pulpit ideals. Generations of preachers would forsake grandiloquence for Broadus's unadorned, conversational explanations of Bible texts. Some lamented that he "ruined Southern Baptist preaching."[8]

He preached without notes. Broadus believed this "free preaching" was "calculated to produce the greatest and most lasting effect upon those who hear the sermon delivered." While he lost some "precision and prettiness of expression," he made up for it in "power of thought" and the ability to "touch their hearts." Despite the unstudied appearance, Broadus "worked hard to make it look easy," as Steve Longenecker put it. He could spend "hours of distressing anxiety and laborious working" simply selecting his sermon text, and found a full day of uninterrupted labor "too little to prepare a sermon." Eventually, Broadus's efforts yielded a sermon skeleton on a half sheet of "foolscap paper" folded lengthways. He would then privately "run over the arrangement till the whole was familiar"; he rarely carried the skeletons into the pulpit. Preaching without notes allowed Broadus to focus on his listeners, not a script. He could adapt his message to the audience on the spot, always seeking access to "the door to men's hearts."[9]

He spoke with a passion, sincerity, and depth of emotion that often moved his audiences to tears, "emitting power continuously," according to one early listener. Friend George B. Taylor attributed Broadus's inspiring preaching to his personal piety. He never manufactured pulpit feelings, Taylor said, but "preserved his emotions fresh and sweet" through regular communion with God. Broadus once confided to Taylor that he "never dared to preach unless he could spend at least two sober hours in immediate preparation" of his heart. Some called him "a mystic." He could also be called a Romantic, preaching so that his listeners would not merely understand rational truths, but feel what he had felt. "There are supreme moments in which all the energies and experiences of a man are concentrated with the highest intensity upon focal points, and it is curious how things blaze," he commented after one engagement. The preaching experience sometimes left Broadus "so fiercely excited" that he had trouble falling asleep that night.[10]

A reviewer would one day sum up Broadus's mature preaching with a single word: "winningness." The skill of winning an audience could in many respects be traced to his own native abilities and charm, though he was also quick to credit the supernatural blessing of God. He also knew that the power of persuasive speech was a learned art, with principles laid down by the classical orators, whom he studied from his earliest days. "Everybody who can speak effectively knows that the power of speaking depends very largely upon the way it is heard," he wrote. "If I were asked what is the first thing in effective preaching, I should say sympathy; and what is the second thing, I should say sympathy; and what is the third thing, I should say sympathy." Broadus arose as one of the nation's most effective preachers because he could elicit this sympathy—he could win his audience—as well as any preacher of the nineteenth century.[11]

→>>✦✦✦<<←

Broadus's preaching attracted such crowds in Charlottesville that by the fall of 1852 he was raising funds to build a more spacious meetinghouse. A new building signified both the young pastor's success and another step of religious refinement for the Charlottesville Baptists. At the same time, overseeing a building campaign further complicated the job of the already busy minister. "I find a general anxiety, especially among the ladies, to have it done, and hope it will be arranged now, and finally," he wrote to Maria. "It will cost me much trouble and labor this week, and will require more wisdom than I have, to harmonize and control." Like many of his peers, Broadus found the demands of a successful town pastorate to be a mixed blessing. Managing popularity was a burden the Broadus family was only beginning to appreciate.[12]

Meanwhile, his assistant teaching position at the University of Virginia amounted to a second full-time job. His duties required him to live on campus with father-in-law Gessner Harrison, who welcomed Broadus's arrival as a relief from his own crushing workload. Enrollment in the school of ancient languages was skyrocketing, from thirty-three students in 1843 to 259 by the 1855–1856 session. For years, Harrison had borne sole responsibility for every level of Latin and Greek at the university, and many considered Harrison's professorship to be as taxing as any other two. He now gratefully rolled much of the grunt work onto his eager son-in-law. In the classroom, Broadus drilled students according to the traditional university method. He closely questioned each pupil about the day's lesson and insisted on minute accuracy. After class, he graded his interminable stack of Greek and Latin exercises in his room on the West Lawn. As an idea of the load Broadus was pulling, the university board appointed Harrison a second assistant in the fall of 1855, and by the fall of 1866 it appointed a second professor of ancient languages to handle Greek, while Harrison retained Latin.[13]

On breaks, Broadus walked and talked with students. He impressed them with his own aggressive private studies, especially in New Testament Greek. "Though I may not become an authority, yet I wish to be able for myself to form an independent judgment on all questions of New Testament interpretation," he told George Taylor. His friend recalled visiting Broadus in his study and finding him "at his table covered with lexicons and other books of reference, a shade over the lamp and one over his eyes, intense seriousness in his face, in a word the typical hard student." Taylor could not help but think his pace of work was making an old man of him; Broadus "already had the stoop of the man who sits much at the desk, and when in repose, his face seemed almost sad."[14]

Others also commented on his diminished vitality. Six months into his Charlottesville assignment, W. H. Harrison admonished him in a candid letter to take better care of himself. Everyone knew that "God had committed to you great talents with the promise of rare usefulness," Harrison wrote. But unless Broadus got more rest and exercise, "the cistern would soon be broken and the jewel which he had chosen change its casket." Harrison had already shared these concerns with him in the Bremo days; Broadus's responsibilities had since doubled. Harrison listed a string of famous, talented men who had cut their lives short through "overstudy and continual neglect and of transgression of God's physical laws." "And you, dear sir, will not be an exception," he scolded. "Your course must be short unless you change it speedily."[15] Loved ones would always fret over his health and workload, but by September 1852 Broadus knew Harrison was right. With Maria having given birth to their first child, Eliza Somerville, he had new reasons to take care of himself. He booked a trip to the spa at Rawley Springs, Virginia.

-→>>-✢-✥-<<←-

Ten miles west of Harrisonburg at the foot of the Appalachian Mountains, the resort at Rawley Springs had been a popular tourist destination since 1825. Charlene M. Boyer Lewis has shown that the Virginia springs "epitomized refinement and grace" and served as a playground for the South's planter class. Visitors from Alexandria, Baltimore, Washington, and beyond traveled to the springs for health, for pleasure, and also to signal their aristocratic stations. Though the South's fashionable set engaged in plenty of worldly shenanigans at the springs, a substantial number of affluent evangelicals also frequented the spa, like Broadus's former employer, J. H. Cocke. Broadus even preached at the spas on occasion, the *Richmond Dispatch* noting how "the gay belles and beaux of his audience were thrilled by the magic of his simple eloquence." But mostly, he came to rest. Guests praised the healthy mountain air and thought the famous spring water, which contained elevated levels of carbonic acid, had powerful medicinal value. (Maria herself enjoyed bathing in the springs.) Those who clambered up Lover's Leap took in one of the finest views in Virginia, and found the sheer beauty a powerful tonic. They also enjoyed the services of an attentive staff, both free and enslaved. Broadus expressed regret at "being thus absent from my wife and our babe," but he promised Maria that he would relax.[16]

Yet he could not forget all his troubles. His sister Carrie, Broadus's confidant and wife of his best friend, Will Whitescarver, had died just weeks earlier. Carrie's Christian faith consoled Broadus, but also reminded him that he had no such comfort about Maria. It seems curious that a Baptist preacher would marry an apparently unconverted woman, though the arrangement was not entirely uncommon among nineteenth-century evangelicals, especially the upwardly mobile. As Broadus described Carrie's joy in the presence of her Savior, he pleaded with Maria to settle her own accounts with God: "My dear Maria, be a Christian, with all your heart, now." Maria responded that his letter, while painful, had prompted her to seek salvation. Broadus, rejoicing that she was now "fairly in the right way," asked her to wait to join the church "at a time when I can be present," Maria agreed, though she would pass over her husband's Baptist church and unite with the Methodists of her father. This remarkable example of female agency within a traditional southern marriage testifies to the modernizing influence of evangelical faith in the antebellum South; it was one of many ways that southern evangelicalism "mixed the old and the new."[17]

Broadus's convalescence at Rawley Springs seemed to restore both body and soul. For five years, he had driven himself in relentless sedentary work, questing to "rise" and "be something." These efforts had yielded substantial results, but had also impaired his health. Now basking in the glory of the Blue Ridge, his spirit seemed to expand by the day, as he wrote to Maria:

> I love to see the steep hills, I love to climb them. I love to stand, as I did this morning on the summit of a precipice, and look down over the little glen between the mountains, with its dashing stream that really seems to have fretted itself into a fury, actually foaming with rage because the rocks won't get out of its way—to take off my hat and let the breeze that sweeps down the glen play on my brow, cooling its heat and blowing back the hair, and making me feel free and fresh and joyous, till I almost think I am a man, or rather till I feel myself a boy again. I dream over for a moment of some of my boyhood's dreams about a hunter's life in the woods and on the mountains. I do love this, and verily I have almost grown romantic in speaking of it.[18]

Broadus would often wax romantic about the splendor of the outdoors, especially in Virginia. He would also follow the cycle of overwork, health crisis, and retreat to the springs for the rest of his life. But by mid-September, it was time to resume his Charlottesville burdens.

—⟫❖⟫❖⟫⟪—

Broadus's time away prompted reflection on the Charlottesville Baptists. Services had been well-attended so far, but conversions were sparse. Many of his unsaved attendees seemed "careless" about their souls, and the professing Christians were "greatly lacking in fervor and zeal." He had attempted to intervene in the spring of 1852 by scheduling a day of humiliation, fasting, and prayer. The event spawned a two-week series of sunrise prayer meetings for revival, and Broadus found that "the members, especially the sisters, increased much in fervor of feeling." Most of the men remained spiritually aloof, a common complaint among southern evangelical ministers. These matters weighed heavily as Broadus returned from

Rawley Springs. "Oh, that I could see sinners among my people converted!" he wrote to Maria. "It lies like a burden on my heart, the thought that there are so many unconverted men and women who look to me for almost their only instruction, so many on the road to hell, with no voice but mine to warn them of their danger and invite them to Jesus." He traced the church's malaise to his own failings. "Alas! How cold have been my warmest feelings, how dull my most earnest appeals. The Lord in mercy forgive me, that so often, so constantly, I have neglected my duty. I know that I am not fit to be the instrument of good—the Lord take me and fashion and temper me, and then use me for his glory." The growing sophistication of antebellum town Baptists did little to dampen their commitment to revivalism, so central to the southern religious experience since the so-called Great Revival of 1800–1805.[19]

To his delight, Broadus found the Charlottesville Baptists altered on his return; they were "exceedingly attentive, and even serious." He immediately sent for Uncle William F. Broaddus to preach a series of protracted meetings. Virginia Baptist preachers often helped one another promote revival in this way—William would frequently call on Broadus to drop everything and assist him in his own meetings in the coming years. Staging a protracted meeting was just the sort of modern machination that had drawn the ire of the South's Primitive Baptists since the 1820s. But while William and John were both Calvinists, they affirmed a degree of human instrumentality in the salvation of sinners. William hurried to his nephew's aid, and from October 20–24 he preached "to large congregations, and with great power and earnestness." When William left to keep another engagement, Broadus continued to assemble the people daily for sunrise prayer meetings and evening sermons from guest preachers. He preached only once himself, focusing instead on prayer, pastoral visitation, and organization. If respectable Baptist ministers like the Broadduses had not lost their appetite for revivalism, their style differed markedly from the raucous, brush-arbor variety in the frontier South. Broadus praised Charlottesville's revival services as "very quiet and solemn," noting how "there was frequently felt a realizing *sense* of the Divine presence, which could not but impress the heart." He would always prefer a more dignified religious atmosphere, one marked by "solemn stillness," and not "the boisterous."[20]

Broadus baptized twenty-three new converts on November 10; the revival would yield forty conversions in all. "O what joy, in seeing men and women turn to the Lord, over whom my heart had often yearned in anxiety!" he exulted.

Broadus wrote up an account for the *Religious Herald*. In an evangelical practice stretching back to the First Great Awakening, he wished to testify of God's mighty work; he also wished to publish his success to *Herald* subscribers. John sensed the competing claims of piety and ambition even as he wrote his report. "And O! Deliver me from foolish vanity," he prayed. "Cleanse me of that plague spot of my soul. And help me, in gratitude and adoring love to say, 'Not unto us, O Lord, not unto us, but unto *thy name* give glory, for thy mercy, and for thy truth's sake.'" With his fellow southern town pastors, Broadus developed a "carefully calibrated view of ambition," one that reconciled the irrepressible "urge to excel in the human heart" with the holy wish to submit all to the glory of God.[21]

→»»❖⧫❖««←

The revival clarified for Broadus that he could no longer bear the double-burden of the church and university. "I live a month every day," he complained to Maria. She worried about her husband's health. "I should be glad for Mr. Broadus to go about in the country some now as he does not look very well," Maria wrote to John's sister Martha, noting that "he cannot spare time enough to do him good." Broadus resigned his position at the University of Virginia in the spring of 1853. The university lamented his departure, and would try to lure him back in 1856 as the chair of Greek and Hebrew, and later as the chair of moral philosophy.[22]

He now poured all his energies into the church. On Sunday nights, he transformed the Charlottesville meetinghouse into his classroom, presenting didactic Bible lectures, distributing printed notes, and displaying large maps. His scholarly presentations attracted more visitors from the university's student body and faculty. He also launched a new series of weeknight lectures, ranging from detailed studies of biblical figures to church history topics to practical matters, such as "family prayer" and "profanity." Each lecture cost hours of preparation, and he began corresponding with well-known northern theologians regarding resources. He asked Presbyterian Charles Hodge of Princeton Seminary to recommend the best edition of Calvin's *Works,* and wrote to northern Baptist Alvah Hovey of Newton seminary about the early church fathers. "I rejoice that any one of my brethren should be making such inquiries," Hovey replied. "We have a great work to do for ourselves in the department of ch. history."[23] Hovey became a lifelong friend.

Broadus could now make more pastoral calls, the lack of which had been some cause for complaint in the church. Town ministers often grumbled about the time lost and vacuous chatter endured in home visits, but Broadus proved skillful in directing conversations to spiritual issues. He claimed to know of more decisions for Christ derived from his home interviews than from his preaching. Broadus's winsomeness was particularly evident with the church's children and youth, who testified to his almost "clairvoyant" gift in diagnosing their soul troubles. They in turn repeated his sayings and sought his advice.[24]

Like all Baptist pastors, Broadus oversaw the discipline of wayward members. The process involved a range of church actions, from gentle remonstrance to formal expulsion from membership. Here, too, Broadus's practice suggests a growing concern for respectability. Baptist discipline had traditionally been a public affair, with the painful details of a member's offenses laid bare at regular congregational meetings. But Broadus preferred more discreet methods, handling sensitive cases within the privacy of a discipline committee. He consulted Richmond pastor J. B. Jeter about this innovation, and Jeter commended his wisdom. He assured Broadus that Baptist church independence permitted latitude in such matters, so long as he violated no direct biblical commands. Yet Broadus's discretion could not entirely eliminate the unpleasantness of discipline. One W. E. Elliott, for example, expressed his "great consternation" at learning that he was "excluded," and protested his injustice in a series of letters to Broadus.[25]

Freedom from the university also facilitated further engagement in denominational activity. Broadus began contributing regularly to the *Religious Herald* newspaper. Founded in Richmond in 1828, the *Herald* "was called into existence by the spirit of organization, which had then just taken possession of Virginia Baptists." Its contributors included leading Virginia Baptists like George B. Taylor, A. M. Poindexter, R. B. C. Howell, and Jeter, who co-purchased the paper and became its senior editor in 1865. Baptist newspapers proliferated in the antebellum South, but the *Religious Herald* arose as the flagship periodical for the denominational Baptists, and "a grand factor in promoting denominational unity." By the 1850s, it had reached twenty-five hundred subscribers. Among Broadus's frequent articles in the *Herald* was his 1854 "Essay on the Best Mode of Preparing and Delivering Sermons," which helped solidify his reputation as an authority on the subject. Publication in the *Herald* provided an important status symbol for professional Baptist ministers. For example, R. B. C. Howell fumed when the paper snubbed his speech on the early Baptists of Virginia. "How does it happen that it has never been noticed in the *Religious Herald,* except in about two lines, announcing its reception at that office? Was this design? How could it have been an oversight?" Howell fussed to Broadus. But Broadus seems to have rarely felt the sting of exclusion in these days. The *Herald* soon listed his name among those of other prominent city pastors as an associate editor.[26]

Broadus engaged in every level of denominational life. He attended meetings, served on committees, offered reports, and delivered sermons to fellow ministers. This began with the local Albemarle Baptist Association, which consisted of thirty-eight churches by 1859. Broadus pastored the largest church in the association (around eight hundred members by 1859), and was elected moderator on three different occasions. In 1855, he hosted the statewide Baptist association in Charlottesville. Broadus welcomed Virginia's leading Baptists into his new church building, preached a rousing sermon, and was elected president of the state Foreign Mission Board. Entertaining guests at the state meeting brought excitement for Maria Broadus as well. As the wife of the prominent host pastor, she spent the week accommodating a house full of Virginia Baptist dignitaries. Maria set up extra beds and made pallets on the floor, crammed the Broadus children into a room with her mother-in-law, and sent for extra food from the country. "I dreaded having so many persons to provide for, being entirely without experience in these matters," she confessed to Broadus's sister Martha. But Maria received ample help from Somerville Broadus and other friends. Though her duties were confined to the domestic sphere, the week proved as gratifying for Maria as for John. She beamed to see her husband "the object of so much admiration," and declared that she "felt more proud of him than ever before." "It must be a pleasure to you," she wrote Martha, "to know that he possesses influence, and that it is all for good and not for evil."[27]

If hosting a denominational meeting provided one signal of rising influence, traveling to meetings represented another. Trips to Richmond, Staunton, or Fredericksburg, usually by rail and in the company of pastoral colleagues, injected into pastoral life an excitement, professional camaraderie, and prestige unknown to rural ministers. The May meetings of the Southern Baptist Convention (biennial throughout the 1850s) carried Broadus to high-profile cities across the South— Baltimore in 1853, Montgomery in 1855, Louisville in 1857, and Richmond in 1859. As a messenger, or delegate, from the Charlottesville Baptist Church, Broadus took a visible role in these meetings. At Baltimore in 1853, he accepted appointment to a committee on "New Foreign Fields," and two years later he delivered a report on "the destitution of the Bible in Foreign Lands." At Richmond in 1859, he was listed in the program as a vice president of the Bible Board in Nashville, gave a committee report on the need for foreign missionaries, and was elected to preach the annual sermon in Savannah in 1861.[28] Broadus had accessed an elite circle of denominational Baptists, enjoying influence far beyond his local congregation.

Denominations, as Beth Schweiger has pointed out, "were progressive institutions in the Old South," a modern means of mobilizing local congregations for a variety of benevolent religious causes. For white Southern Baptists, the most important of these causes were home and foreign missions. The Southern Baptist Convention had formed in 1845 when northern Baptists refused to continue partnering with southern Baptist slaveholders. Promoting missions required Baptist pastors to lead their local congregations to give beyond their own local spheres, and this was no easy task. Charlottesville Baptist Church members criticized Broadus for collecting foreign missions offerings while the church remained in debt for its new building, for instance. "Do you think that after being blessed of God in building a house for our comfort and convenience we ought to neglect the lost souls out yonder for whom Christ died?" Broadus retorted. The missions sermon he preached the next day not only resulted in a generous missions offering, but the church also showed up at his house with the money to pay off the building debt. Broadus raised $540 from his church in 1853, more than his own salary as pastor. Meanwhile, to Broadus's Primitive Baptist cousins, the entire missions fundraising enterprise seemed like a modern apostasy from the simple religion of their forbears.[29]

With his fellow Baptist denominationalists, Broadus also promoted the progressive cause of women's education. Baptist female academies flourished in the antebellum South—Virginia alone claimed Valley Union Seminary, Richmond Female Institute, and Albemarle Female Institute (AFI). Broadus helped open the latter, a college-level school for women sponsored by the Albemarle Baptist Association, in 1853. He served as president of the trustee board, he designed the school's curriculum on the model of the University of Virginia, and he hosted the school in the church's basement. "Many of our girls are now receiving a fairly good education, and women are so quick in picking up and turning to account a knowledge of general literature," he later remarked, "that our young men must get a better education than has been common, or they will in many cases find themselves unpleasantly inferior to their wives." AFI would, in time, play a critical role in his personal life.[30]

Some progressive Virginia Baptists also invested their energies in regulating alcohol abuse, a cause long sacred in the Broadus family. By the mid-1850s Broadus was a popular speaker for a number of temperance organizations. "I love the cause of Temperance and to its support and defense I am resolved to contribute my mite," he declared in an early speech. "O Christian, is it not your duty, as a patriot and a philanthropist, as a lover of your country and a lover of human kind, to unite with your fellow-citizens in putting a stop to the ravages of this cruel foe, this fell destroyer of the peace and happiness of mankind?" He joined the Sons of Temperance, founded in 1844 as Virginia's most socially respectable Temperance organization. Modeled after the Masons and the Odd Fellows, the Sons of Temperance was an upscale fraternity for white, middle-class Virginians, complete with insurance benefits, elaborate regalia, initiation rites, and fraternal mottoes. Members wore a white collar, white tassels, and a red, white, and blue rosette. They memorized complex rituals and secret passwords. Broadus arose to the office of "Grand Worthy Patriarch" within the organization, and was elected in 1855 to represent Virginia at the national meeting. Like his denominational activities, participation in this fraternal order further signaled his insider status in southern society.[31]

Public speaking activities outside his congregation enhanced Broadus's regional celebrity. He received invitations from across the state—to assist friends in revival meetings at Fluvanna and Fredericksburg, to fill pulpits in Richmond and Petersburg, and to deliver paid lectures to the Young Men's Society. When the Fredericksburg Baptist Church could not contain the crowds that Broadus drew in a June 1853 visit, the meeting moved to the Presbyterian church, where he preached to "some twelve hundred people," with many forced to leave for lack of seats. His audience exhibited "not only excellent attention but much feeling— many wept," he told Maria. The next night, Broadus delivered a simple message to another overflow crowd. "I spoke of Jesus the Saviour, the all-sufficient, the loving, the only Saviour, and warned them not to reject him, not to put off, warned them to flee the wrath to come," he wrote. Again, the response was overwhelming. "Many wept; strong men, they say, and near to the door where the atmosphere is often so chill, were weeping like children."[32]

Richmond College student W. E. Hatcher stood among the starstruck. "He thrilled the people with immense magnetism," Hatcher recalled decades later. "For weeks afterwards I found myself saying things like Broadus. He threw a matchless spell over people that carried them away. Forty years ago people would worship Broadus, as the most wonderful thing you ever heard." If the response sounds exaggerated, it highlights the honor that antebellum southerners paid to gifted orators. "Your name was in the mouth of more than one friend with whom I met," William Broaddus told John after a trip abroad. "One preacher declared that 'he would give all of this world's goods'—and he has quite a large stock of wealth—'if he could preach as you preach.'"[33] If Broadus had sought a vehicle for prominence, he had found it in the southern pulpit.

Yet it was not that simple. Broadus naturally enjoyed the praise, but all the "distinction and lionizing" also troubled his evangelical conscience. Praise tempted him to pride and loaded him with greater pressure to perform. "I know that I am exciting expectations, to meet which will require more effort than I have ever made before," he wrote Maria. "Besides, I know I am grievously prone to overestimate men's opinions of me and lamentably inclined to be vain when I ought to be humble. Pray for me, Maria, that a little applause may not be permitted to turn my weak head and bewitch my silly heart in that I may remember my nothingness and my entire dependence for all true success on the Divine blessing."[34]

Preaching fame brought other challenges. Letters now arrived daily, requesting his input on a remarkable range of topics. Many correspondents he knew, but others were anonymous—like the writer struggling over which denomination to join, or the Charlottesville resident seeking spiritual assurance. "My heart is cold and hard," wrote the latter. "I beg you to write me from the *first* step to the last of *what I must do to be saved.*" Another unnamed enquirer, troubled over past sins of fornication and "uncleanness," had found hope through a Broadus sermon, and now wished the pastor to recommend comforting Bible verses. Churches that were unable to secure Broadus's pastoral services begged him for recommendations. "We want a Brother who is strictly a Disciplinarian, a Warm hearted Go ahead minister of Christ—a Brother full of the Spirit," wrote Oliver

Lillibridge from Savannah, Georgia. "One who will love all, and take sides with none, One who will cry aloud and spare not, a brother who in time of revival shall be the Instrument in the hands of God of Winning Souls to Christ, a Brother of great Christian Deportment and One who will Command great Respect And by no means what may be termed a sleepy Preacher."[35] Baptist ministry in town churches had by the 1850s already accrued definite professional standards; not just any preacher would do. Perhaps no individual in the nineteenth century helped match more Baptist pastors and churches than Broadus.

Correspondents often laid startlingly intimate matters before him. These included Doctor Stuart White, who expressed deep concern for his unmarried male patients. With no legitimate sexual outlet, White explained, they frequently suffered from involuntary nocturnal emissions, or, worse, resorted to "uncleanness." White deemed both occurrences destructive to physical and mental health; he knew young men driven to the insane asylum over the guilt of sexual impurity. These patients desperately needed "the healthy exercise of the organs of generation" once or twice a week, White believed—yet their university studies and demanding clerkships rendered marriage impractical. For the sake of health, therefore, White had urged the regular patronizing of prostitutes. "I begin to think that Mr. Jefferson was not far wrong when he built his whore-houses," he confessed. But White also feared transgressing God's Law. What should he do? Broadus's response, unfortunately, does not survive. He would never meet many of his correspondents. But after hearing him preach or reading his articles, they felt that they knew him, and could trust him to bear their burdens. He would do so for the next forty years.[36]

->>>✤✦<<<-

Broadus's influence expanded in the spring of 1855, when friends urged him to accept the chaplaincy of the University of Virginia. Worship was still noncompulsory at Jefferson's school, but faculty and students had for years supported chaplains in two-year appointments. They selected Virginia's ministers, marked by "a spirit of unity, broadmindedness and devotion," from a variety of denominations. From Richmond, J. B. Jeter pressed Broadus to accept. "It is important that the post should be well filled," Jeter wrote. "I still think that *you* are the man, if any arrangements for supplying your church can be made, best suited for the place." William Broaddus also urged him to take the position, noting that the chaplaincy would further the Baptist interest among students, and could lead to a call to a larger church for his nephew.[37]

At the encouragement of his own church, Broadus finally relented. "It has cost me (and does still) much bitterness and grief," he told Will Whitescarver. "But it seems to be needful. It will be an injury to the church, but some church had to lose its pastor," he reasoned. The chaplaincy did not pay particularly well, but he spied other advantages. "I shall gain nothing to myself, except having more time for study and careful preparation, no week services, and three months' vacation; and I greatly need time for general religious and other reading," he confessed. The church voted unanimously to retain Broadus as minister during his chaplaincy, and would employ an associate pastor for the interim. Broadus hesitated to promise that he would resume the pastorate in two years, as the church requested. Though he "confidently calculated" to return, such a written commitment seemed to "forestall Providence."[38] He would keep his options open.

The Charlottesville church called Alfred Elijah Dickinson to hold Broadus's place as associate pastor. Dickinson seemed a natural fit as Broadus's stand-in. Born in Orange County in 1830, Dickinson was three years younger than Broadus, but unlike his diminutive senior minister, he was a man "of massive form, towering like Saul." Dickinson admired Broadus, sharing his vision of an educated ministry and a modern denominational life for the Baptist South. Dickinson had graduated from Richmond College before earning a master's degree from the University of Virginia, where he had known Broadus as a teacher. Before coming to Charlottesville, he had also served the Goshen Association as a colporteur missionary, and had partnered with Broadus in several revivals. Dickinson would embrace the Charlottesville assignment with "very active and zealous labors," and lead a revival of over one hundred conversions. Broadus assisted Dickinson throughout his chaplaincy, and the two men formed an enduring friendship. Both would rise to more prominent roles in Virginia and Southern Baptist life, and collaborate often to the end of the nineteenth century. Denominational ministry forged a tight-knit brotherhood among elite Southern Baptists like Broadus and Dickinson.[39]

Broadus's hopes for a slower pace in the university chaplaincy were disappointed. "I expected, when I determined to come here, to do much study in general. Thus far, I have done hardly anything," he complained in May 1856. He preached twice each Sunday, made regular pastoral visits to faculty and students, served on a variety of university boards and committees, and was in constant demand as a speaker. "Have been run very hard to-day with a multitude of little matters, and am completely broken down," he wrote to Maria. "It's a distressing thing to be counted a smart young man, and have to be going about speechifying when one is tired beyond endurance. And then to come home Friday night, and have to preach twice on Sunday. Well, a stout heart, and old sermons, can conquer many difficulties."[40] The three-fold cord of ambition, prominence, and physical exhaustion wound about him throughout his ministry.

The university proved a challenging field for revival. Broadus took a religious survey of the student body and recorded ninety-five converted young men, including thirty-five Baptists. As he worked to expand this number, he encountered a variety of obstacles. School holidays disrupted the spiritual momentum built up over the semester. Chapel audiences did not expect "immediate results" from preaching as the church did, resulting in fewer conversions. And despite many lively Christians on campus, Broadus found that "there can be little unity of action and of feeling, not only because of denominational differences, but because their association with each other is temporary."[41]

Yet he enjoyed great popularity on campus. Students considered him "a gentleman of rare culture and attainments," and respected both his learning and piety. The hall was usually full for his voluntary chapel services, and forty students petitioned him to publish his sermon "The Apostle Paul as Preacher" in 1857. In later life, he occasionally met former students who testified to his impact as chaplain. J. E. Poindexter, later an Episcopalian rector, claimed that Broadus was the first person to ever ask him about his salvation. Another student, a religious skeptic from California, returned to campus asking for Broadus, calling him "the only man who ever affected me about religion." The formation of numerous prayer groups under his ministry prompted the organization of a YMCA. His tenure as university chaplain contributed to his lifelong bent toward interdenominational relationships, but he developed especially close attachments with Baptist university students, such as J. William Jones, Crawford Toy, and J. C. Hiden. These young Baptists revered Broadus, according to Hiden, "only 'this side of idolatry.'" Each would eventually follow him to the Southern Baptist Theological Seminary.[42]

The chaplaincy also invited more preaching appointments. In the fall of 1856, Broadus preached in most of Virginia's major cities, as well as in Philadelphia and

New York City. When New York's First Baptist Church lost its venerable pastor Spencer H. Cone, they asked Broadus to fill the pulpit. But religious celebrity exacted a cost. Maria, home with now three daughters, complained more than once of John's extended absences. "Oh, how glad I am that this week is almost over and that the time for your return is growing a little nearer," she wrote. "You talk about trials Mr. Broadus. Let me tell you that they seem like trifles compared with the great sacrifice I make of my own enjoyment every time that we have to be separated," she said. He admitted that her grievances had merit. "I was affected today by reading of a lawyer's wife," he wrote to Maria from a train car, "who complained that her husband was so busy, and when at home so tired, that he never took time to talk to her and pursue the studies together for which they both had a taste, and her life was lonely. I believe I have done wrong, even while meaning to do right." Yet fame was conflicting, even for Maria. At the same time that she mourned their frequent separations, she also basked in the glow of her husband's growing reputation. "You would have been gratified to see the favor with which a speech of Mr. Broadus was received," she wrote to his sister Martha. "I felt more proud of him than ever before, and am sure it would have done your heart good to see your brother the object of so much admiration. I am so much afraid of seeming foolishly proud of Mr. Broadus."[43]

Passing a familiar stream by rail one spring afternoon in 1856 prompted Broadus to reflect on the previous decade. He had forded this particular stream dozens of times as a nineteen-year-old, when he was scraping up money for university as a Clarke County school teacher. "Many wandering thoughts would pass across my mind as I journeyed there alone," he recalled to Maria, "many wild dreams in that wild spot, of education, of competence, of reputation, which I never dared to hope could be realized." Seeing the place again, his heart "swelled with an emotion rarely felt; the thoughts of years long passed came trooping back—the ambitious but despairing dreams of youth were remembered as if I had just waked from the dreaming; and Maria! I thought, and tried to be grateful, that Providence has done almost more for me than I dreamed."[44]

⟶⟫⟩❖❖⟨⟨⟵

Broadus returned to his Charlottesville pastorate in 1857, among the most popular evangelical preachers in the South. "[You are] just now the standard of excellence by which intellect, scholarship, and preaching talents are measured in this region," crowed Uncle Andrew Broaddus. Suitors from church and academy alike pressed him with new opportunities. The University of Virginia offered the chair of Greek in 1856 (when he declined, the chair went to the celebrated Basil Gildersleeve), and Columbian University in Washington its professorship of ancient languages. Mercer University in Georgia extended him its presidency, as did Wake Forest College in North Carolina. His denominational brethren in Virginia urged him to keep preaching. "I feel quite unwilling that you should exchange the pulpit for a professor's chair," J. B. Jeter wrote in 1856. "We have a great lack of ministers, especially educated and effective ministers."[45] Broadus's personal fame elevated the whole Baptist enterprise.

He had his pick of churches, too. From Richmond, Basil Manly Jr. dangled the Leigh Street Church pulpit. The church could only pay $1,000 per year, but Manly, as president of the Richmond Female Institute, could supplement that salary with a teaching position. Besides, Richmond offered advantages to a professional pastor like Broadus that could not be quantified—"your opportunities of extensive and permanent influence, your advantages of society, literary culture, and ministerial intercourse, etc., etc., etc. would be very great here," Manly coaxed. Other pastoral invitations stretched from the East Street Church in Washington, D.C., all the way out to Sacramento, California. More than one group of persistent correspondents from California pleaded with him to relocate to the West Coast in the wake of the Gold Rush, at the handsome salary of $3,000 a year. Wealthy Baptists from the Walnut Street and Jefferson Street churches in Louisville, Kentucky, courted him to come start a new church in their growing city, as well.[46]

As never before, his preaching gifts opened the doors of wealth, fame, and influence. But Broadus turned down every offer. Madison Broadus wondered that his younger brother would "so obstinately (may I say) persist in being poor when you could so easily have an ample living, to see you thus persist in refusing to be placed above the pains of poverty."[47] Broadus suspected that he would not remain in Charlottesville forever. But for now, the right opportunity simply had not presented itself.

four
CASTING THE DIE

I N MAY 1855, John A. Broadus traveled by rail to the Southern Baptist Convention in Montgomery, Alabama. As new passengers boarded west of Augusta, a young man "of large figure and smooth, youthful face," obviously wealthy and well-bred, stepped aboard. Two of Broadus's companions immediately sprang up to greet him. "Yonder is a man I want you to know," one remarked as he returned to Broadus. "He is a minister of ability and thorough education, and full of noble qualities. His father was a man of great wealth and he is now very generous in his gifts. He is going to be one of the most influential Southern Baptists. I want you to know him." The stranger was twenty-eight-year-old James Petigru Boyce. At the Montgomery Convention, Boyce would press a long-cherished plan to establish a theological seminary for Southern Baptists. Broadus could not yet know the leading part he would play in Boyce's scheme.[1]

America's first theological seminary had opened some fifty years earlier. New England Congregationalists, committed to an educated ministry but concerned by the religious decline of the older colleges, founded Andover Theological Seminary in Massachusetts in 1808. Andover immediately set a new standard for professional ministry education, offering a three-year curriculum, a full-time faculty, and a well-stocked library. Massachusetts Baptists quickly replicated Andover's model and opened Newton Theological Institute in 1825. By 1855, Boyce and other genteel Southern Baptists wanted a seminary of their own.[2]

Southern Baptists had already established colleges in most southern states by 1850. Many of these schools housed small theological departments for training pastors. Mercer University in Georgia, for instance, employed John Leadley Dagg, Southern Baptists' premier theologian. But these departments, scattered unevenly across the South, were small, under-resourced, and unable to provide the full ministerial education of a seminary. Dagg himself counseled young Basil Manly Jr. to study at Newton rather than with him at Mercer. But going north posed other problems. With political tensions over slavery escalating, southern evangelicals loathed to send their sons north for education. At Newton, just outside Boston, Manly complained of insult, antislavery propaganda, and suspicious doctrine. His sour experience prompted his transfer to Princeton Theological Seminary, which was friendlier to Manly's old-school Calvinism and to his slaveholding sensibilities. These very issues had factored into white southern Presbyterians founding Union Theological Seminary in Virginia in 1823, and Columbia Theological Seminary in South Carolina in 1828. After separating from their northern brethren in 1845, Southern Baptist elites were now ready to take the same step. "The South needs one Theological Seminary of high grade, equal to Andover, or Newton," declared one editorial. As Mitchell Snay has shown, antebellum religious institutions served sectional as well as denominational aims.[3]

But while certain denominational leaders agitated for a seminary throughout the antebellum period, they also encountered a "generally prevailing want of just appreciation for thorough theological education" among their brethren. The underfunded Baptist colleges resisted establishing a rival institution. Most rank-and-file Baptists viewed an educated ministry as elitist and unnecessary. Virginia's A. M. Poindexter favored a seminary, but admitted that educated Baptist ministers in the past had been "deficient in that adaptation to the wants of the masses, which constitutes one of the most valuable qualifications in a minister, and the absence of which nothing else can compensate." To a greater degree than their highbrow southern Presbyterian friends, Southern Baptist ministers had to maintain a popular touch to remain relevant.[4]

By 1857, the seminary movement found the visionary leader it needed in James P. Boyce. Born on January 11, 1827, just two weeks before Broadus, Boyce had enjoyed a privileged childhood in Charleston, South Carolina. Growing up in the home of Ker Boyce, president of the Bank of Charleston and perhaps the wealthiest man in antebellum South Carolina, Boyce developed the exquisite tastes and manners of an Old South aristocrat. He loved paintings and music, appreciated elegant book bindings and lavish flower gardens, kept up with the latest fashions in clothing and home decor, and oversaw a large staff of slaves. After his conversion in 1846, Boyce shocked his spiritually ambivalent father by announcing his intention to be a Baptist preacher rather than a financier.

He studied at Brown University under the Baptist Francis Wayland, and then at Princeton Theological Seminary, where he imbibed the academic Calvinism of professors Charles Hodge and Samuel Miller. Returning to South Carolina, Boyce accepted appointment as professor of theology at Furman University in Greenville. But he had already set his heart on recreating his own Princeton Theological Seminary for Southern Baptists.[5]

Boyce took a great stride toward that dream on July 30, 1856, in Greenville, South Carolina. In the morning, he presented to the state Baptist convention the first viable plan to raise an endowment for the seminary. South Carolina Baptists would lead the way by donating $100,000—this included Furman University's theological endowment, worth an estimated $26,000, plus an additional $74,000, which Boyce would raise from the state's churches. The school would be located in Greenville. The other southern states would jointly raise another $100,000. South Carolina Baptists accepted his proposal. But Boyce's work for the day had only begun. That evening, in his inaugural faculty address at Furman University, Boyce delivered a speech he called "Three Changes in Theological Institutions." It was his manifesto for an innovative seminary plan adapted to the needs of Southern Baptists.[6]

First, Boyce proposed the creation of a popular seminary. Diverting from the Andover model, he wished to forego the requirement of prior university training, making the school accessible to "those who actually constitute the mass of our Ministry." Boyce's mentor, New England Baptist educator Francis Wayland, had already urged Baptists to so "popularize" their seminaries. After all, Baptists believed that God called to preach whomsoever he willed, and four-fifths of Baptist ministers had no formal education. Boyce affirmed these realities. Yet he also frankly judged uneducated Baptist ministers to be "of comparatively little value to the Churches." Untrained preachers "soon find themselves exhausted of their materials, forced to repeat the same topics in the same way, and finally to aim at nothing but continuous exhortation, bearing constantly upon the same point, or as is oftentimes the case, destitute of any point at all." Boyce argued that even partial seminary training offered immense value to these rustic exhorters, allowing them to "improve themselves as to occupy positions of greater respectability and usefulness." He also hoped to elevate the general culture of country Baptist preachers by educating them in the same classrooms as university graduates, "men of polished education, of well trained minds, capable of extensive usefulness in

the cause of Christ." Boyce believed that training all of the denomination's ministry candidates—both the haves and have-nots—side-by-side would ease the social
divisions then evident among Southern Baptist clergy. "The young men should
be so mingled together as to cause each class to recognize the value of the others,
and thus truly to break down entirely any classification," he declared.[7]

But while Boyce longed to lift up the masses, he also burned to build world-
class scholars. He considered Baptist dependence on German scholarship to be
"a sore evil," and it vexed him to see his denomination relying on pedobaptist
textbooks that ridiculed their convictions. "We owe a change to ourselves, as
Christians," he declared, "bound to show an adequate reason for the differences
between us and others." So, alongside his popular classroom, Boyce proposed
a rigorous graduate studies program, modeled on the master's degrees of the
country's best universities, and resourced with a fully furnished library. Perhaps
only the top 5 percent of Baptist students would or could pursue such a course,
yet the "value to the denomination" of this elite leadership corps would more
than repay the investment.[8]

Finally, Boyce wished to ground the seminary in a conservative confession of
faith. Here, the influence of Francis Wayland gave way to that of Princeton Theological Seminary. Wayland's New England Baptist tradition tended to recoil from
written creeds as coercive, extra-biblical innovations, and many Southern Baptists
shared this aversion. The "Restoration" movement of Alexander Campbell in
recent decades had intensified popular suspicion of creeds in the Baptist South.
But Boyce traced his own Baptist lineage to the British Particular Baptists, who
celebrated the wisdom of written theological confessions. Charleston's First Baptist Church had catechized Boyce in the Westminster Calvinism of the Charleston Confession, and Samuel Miller of Princeton had reinforced Boyce's creedal
convictions. Boyce devoted many pages of his speech to convincing skeptical
Southern Baptists of the biblical, historical, and contemporary basis for theological confessions. He intended his seminary to stand as an orthodox bulwark
against popular doctrinal aberrations in the South, including the Campbellite
heresy and frontier Arminianism. Boyce proposed that the seminary adopt a new
statement of faith, one amenable to most Southern Baptists, and that it should
require strict subscription of all faculty members (though not of students). For
Boyce, one vital purpose of a seminary was to be, in Erskine Clarke's words, "the
means of nurturing and transmitting theological tradition." Boyce wanted just

such a confessional school to standardize Southern Baptist orthodoxy, preferably in the mold of Old Princeton.[9]

-→>>-✢-✚-<<←-

Broadus shared Boyce's desire to elevate Southern Baptist ministry. On the one hand, he affirmed that "every one should be encouraged to preach who feels moved to preach, and whom the churches are willing to hear." Indeed, he believed that this democratic stance comprised the "fundamental Baptist idea of the ministry" and had contributed to the Baptist ascendance over America's pedobaptist denominations. Broadus admired cultivated Presbyterian and Anglican clergy, but they had failed to reach "the masses of the people" in the early nineteenth century—masses who "sympathiz[ed] most strongly with preachers who were but little superior to themselves in general culture." Thus, he was "not ashamed of the fact that I belong to a body of Christians which has a great number of comparatively uneducated ministers. I think that in our past this has been unavoidable." But Broadus also knew that conditions had changed in the Baptist South. By the 1840s, southern Baptists ministered in towns and cities to a wealthier, better educated, and more refined middle class. This required greater professionalism in the pulpit. "Things are changing, changing fast as to education, and we must change with them," he declared, "and if our Baptist churches have not wisdom to see that the conditions which justified our past as to our ministry are changing and rapidly ceasing to justify them, then they will pay the penalty of their lack of wisdom."[10]

Yet Broadus questioned certain aspects of Boyce's seminary plan, and voiced his concerns in an April 1857 *Religious Herald* article. Boyce's required doctrinal statement for seminary faculty unsettled Broadus, for one thing. Presbyterians might all look to a single confessional document like Westminster, but Baptists had no such standard. Would Boyce now create such a confession himself, and then hold all Southern Baptist ministers—or at least those who trained them—to it? To Broadus, reared in a Virginia tradition that valued the gentlemanly discussion of ideas, Boyce's vision seemed a bit heavy handed. The seminary model itself also concerned Broadus. He favored a broad-based education for ministers, one like he had received at the University of Virginia, that acquainted a young man with the arts and humanities, and expanded his vision of the world. The typical American seminary education struck Broadus as overly narrow, tending to stamp ministers into a single, rigid mold that rendered them ineffective in real Baptist churches. Broadus thus insisted that the seminary's design "must not be left exclusively to men who have themselves been educated at existing seminaries." Boyce needed input from those with a different educational background from his own. He needed the input of someone like Broadus.[11]

Broadus soon received his opportunity. In May 1857, a special Education Convention appointed him to a "Committee on Plan of Organization" for a Southern Baptist seminary. Led by Boyce, the committee would prepare a detailed plan for the seminary over the next year and report back to the Education Convention in the spring of 1858. Boyce asked Broadus to design the seminary's curriculum, one uniquely suited for Southern Baptist ministry. "I am glad to be on the committee," Broadus wrote to Maria, "though it will be a most difficult task, everything for the success and usefulness of the institution depending on its system of instruction."[12]

In the following months, Broadus studied seminary catalogues and corresponded with educators such as Philip Schaff of Mercersburg Seminary. Yet he drew his deepest inspiration not from existing seminaries but from the great German research universities and his own University of Virginia; these would always be his gold standards of academic excellence. "To provide an institution which shall at once furnish thorough and extensive training to those who want it, and a little help to those who have desire and preparation for but little, must of course be difficult," he admitted to a friend. Yet the longer Broadus worked at it, the more he relished the challenge of designing a new kind of seminary.[13]

He ultimately settled on two innovative features. The first was an elective curriculum modeled after the University of Virginia. On this plan, the seminary could be divided into eight departments, or "schools," allowing each student to select courses "according to his taste and preparation." The second major innovation was a core curriculum based on the study of English texts, with ancient languages offered in separate courses for advanced students. At the end of an eight-month academic year, students would receive diplomas from each school in which they had received a passing grade. To earn a "general diploma" and become a "full graduate," students must complete the entire curriculum, typically a three-year process. With an elective system that included plenty of English-based classes, each student could "do that for which they have preparation, turn of mind, and time or patience, and get credit for exactly what they do." Whether students took every course or only a few, all would still profit from their studies. Broadus believed this unique curriculum design would help "counteract the tendency to formalism, to making men all on one pattern, which has so commonly characterized the theological seminaries of the country."[14] His curriculum finalized, Broadus assumed that he had fulfilled all of his duties to the Southern Baptist seminary.

→→)→❖→¾→((←

In October, Broadus also completed his chaplaincy at the University of Virginia. This meant a return to the pastorate. The Charlottesville Baptist Church had prospered in his absence, and it purchased a parsonage for the Broaduses. Maria Broadus was "delighted" by the new home. But after birthing three children in four years, Maria had grown feeble. By July 1857, she weighed only ninety-one pounds, and Broadus deemed her health "radically bad." Leaving their three daughters with his stepmother, he took Maria on a circuit of Virginia's resort springs. He left her briefly to confer with his seminary committee colleagues in Richmond, but Maria quickly sent for him to return. "I have gained all the benefit that is at all probable, and I want to leave," she wrote, signing her letter, "your affectionate, lonely, little wife." Broadus hurried back, and they remained at the springs through the end of August. But on October 21, Maria Broadus died at the age of twenty-five. When Broadus told her that she was dying, she responded, "Well, tell me about Jesus." Eliza and Annie Broadus recalled two of their uncles carrying them through the night to say goodbye to their mother; she asked the family to sing "Rock of Ages" around her bed.[15]

Too grief-stricken to preach the following Sunday, Broadus took comfort in the Calvinist doctrine of God's providence. "I know it is terrible, but it was God, even *your* God, who did it, and we know he maketh *all* things work together for good to them that love him," wrote one widowed friend. "He *gave*. He *took*. He can restore. HE doth all things well." "Experience has taught me how to sympathize with you," wrote J. B. Jeter, who had already buried two wives. "I need not point you to sources of consolation. You know them. You have directed others to them, receive instruction from your own lips—show how well you can practice the precepts you have earnestly enforced on others. Be still, and know that the Lord is God. Kiss the rod that smites you. 'It is the Lord; let him do what seemeth him good.'" His brother, Madison, offered more pragmatic counsel. "It seems to you now that the void can never be filled, but I tell you the free world will presently press in from all around and the void that cannot be filled, and the wound that cannot be healed will be forgotten," Madison wrote. "You will soon find enough in the world around you, to occupy you fully, to excite your hopes and stimulate your energies." Madison knew that his younger brother would heal best by getting back to work. Broadus did indeed throw himself into pastoring, preaching, and tweaking the seminary curriculum.[16]

-→>>❖-❖-<<←-

The first week of May in 1858, forty-four registered delegates of the Southern Baptist Education Convention met in Greenville to adopt the committee's seminary plan. They accepted Broadus's curriculum, along with the charter Boyce had written, and a new confession of faith called the Abstract of Principles, prepared by Basil Manly Jr. Finally, they elected the founding faculty. The Convention unanimously voted Broadus as professor of New Testament and homiletics (preaching).

Suddenly, a new career choice confronted him. Having long desired to "do something and to be something," was this his moment of destiny? With convention leaders "pressing it upon him," Broadus left for Charlottesville in a quandary, and reached home "still utterly undecided." His peers considered him to be the lynchpin of the seminary plan. "The real decision rests with *you,*" wrote Basil Manly Jr., who had also been elected to the faculty. "If you decline, I think Poindexter (elected as seminary fundraising agent) will," Manly conjectured. "If he and you decline, I certainly shall." Charleston pastor E. T. Winkler, another faculty nominee, would also decline if Broadus did. This would leave only Boyce, Manly wrote, "to look rather cheerlessly for new associates, men of more self-sacrifice . . . or else he too must give up the ship, a grand *finale* indeed, after all that has been said and done." Manly rested the entire enterprise on Broadus. "The question seems brought to our door, and laid at our feet. So far as you are concerned, shall this seminary live, or disgracefully die?"[17]

Broadus spent an uneasy next week consulting advisors in Charlottesville, Alexandria, Fredericksburg, and Richmond. Most stridently opposed his accepting the position. A committee from the Charlottesville Baptist Church lodged a formal, written protest. Wealthy church member William P. Farish wrote to

Broadus that he was "deeply grieved to learn you entertain the thought." Farish was a country preacher himself, and he saw little worth in a seminary. "To take valuable ministers from prominent positions to teach twenty or thirty young men to become preachers, many of whom are made worse by it, and none bene- fitted (as those who have minds are tied down to what they learn), is too great a sacrifice," he opined. In Charlottesville, Broadus occupied "the most important position known to the denomination, and the only minister of my knowing that can reach the young men coming to the University, thus sending out an influence beyond anything you can hope for at Greenville College."[18]

After ten miserable days, Broadus declined his faculty appointment. "After more anxiety and difficulty than I ever before experienced, I have at length de- cided that I cannot leave here," he wrote to Boyce, though he assured him, "If anything I can conceive could make me feel it right to leave this post, it would be the Seminary; but I dare not to go away." Manly called his decision the semi- nary's "death-blow," dooming all hope of a Southern Baptist seminary for another twenty-five years. It sounded dramatic, but, as Manly predicted, A. M. Poindexter subsequently refused his own appointment, and E. T. Winkler reversed his de- cision to leave First Baptist Charleston. It seemed to be all Broadus's fault. Sarah Rudolph Manly muttered that he had acted dishonorably. After enjoying the fanfare of being "published all over the country," he had shirked the responsibility and sacrifice the seminary required.[19]

→»❖✦«←

But other matters occupied Broadus in the summer of 1858. He had met twenty- two-year-old Charlotte Eleanor Sinclair, a student at Albemarle Female Institute. She came from a wealthy Episcopalian family, raised outside Charlottesville on the five hundred-acre Locust Grove Plantation. After the death of her father, George Sinclair, in 1851, Lottie's mother, Ruth, had taken charge of the extensive grounds and approximately twenty enslaved laborers. By July, Broadus was writ- ing Lottie long, passionate letters. At thirty-one, he was "now old enough to be thoughtful, and young enough to be devoted." He lavished her with praise and pet names, and confessed to watching her secretly, with throbs of unrequited love. "For many months, I have never heard your name even casually mentioned without a thrill, have never seen you on the street or at the church, without trembling," he declared. He composed verses for her, and kissed locks of her hair. He discussed with her the preparation of his sermons, chattered about his love of riding and life with his daughters, and suggested books for her to read. By September, he was signing his letters as "your lover" and planning a wedding. Yet Maria had been dead for less than a year. With his high profile in the school and the church, and with the Harrison family's feelings to consider, Broadus courted Lottie with extreme caution. He passed letters through the Institute's principal, John Hart, and Lottie's mother, Ruth, and he asked Lottie to burn all their correspondence.[20]

Broadus was smitten with Lottie Sinclair, but he also needed help with his three young daughters. "Great as is your loss, theirs is much greater," Madison Broadus had written upon Maria's death. "No other human being can fully fill a mother's place." Time had confirmed his judgment. Broadus's daughters remembered him as a tender and affectionate father, riding them on his foot, singing songs of Mother Goose and Robert Burns, and leading hymns at family prayers. Yet Maria had assumed total responsibility for the girls' care, allowing Broadus to maintain the active schedule of a denominational leader. After her death, he continued to travel, leaving his daughters for a week or more with young women like Julia Somers and Margarett Swann, or with his stepmother, Somerville Broadus. Letters reveal the pull that Broadus felt between home and public life. "Annie has been quite sick today," Margarett Swann wrote in December 1857, as Broadus preached a revival in Richmond. The doctor had "examined her lungs and said she had pneumonia," though "tonight he called, applied a blister, and pronounced her much better." Swann reported that Lida "is very well and sends her love and says she wants to see you mighty bad and you must come home real soon." In June 1858, Somerville Broadus informed him that the girls "talk about papa every day, say they wish you may not have to go from home again to stay so long—they send their love and say they will try and be good children." It could not have made for easy reading.[21]

The conflict between attentive fatherhood and denominational influence was emerging as another aspect of Broadus's struggle with ambition. An August letter to Lottie reveals that his early dreams of eminence had not dimmed. He confessed "to high thoughts, to noble aspirations." He still "longed to be worth something in the world." Passing through Alexandria by train, "there came over me, fresh and strong, such feelings as I thought I had conquered years ago; the ambition to gather riches and fame, that I might lay all at the feet of one I love. But no! There is a worthier ambition—to labor for the salvation of men and the glory of God. Riches are little worth compared with this highest usefulness." As with many southern evangelicals, Broadus found the line between godly stewardship of gifts and the drive for personal greatness to be exceedingly fine.[22]

Lottie Sinclair agreed to help him find it. On New Year's Day 1859, Broadus presented her with a trio of wedding presents. "Three little gifts from three little girls," he called them: a writing desk from Eliza, a traveling bag from Annie, and a thimble from baby Maria. Broadus and Lottie exchanged vows early on January 4 at Locust Grove, William Broaddus officiating. For the second time, Broadus had "married up," now to an Episcopalian lady of property (Lottie would soon receive immersion into the Baptist church). They honeymooned in New York City.[23]

→»✦✦«←

By March 1859, Broadus found that his weekly pastoral responsibilities in the large Charlottesville church were wearing him out. He agreed to reconsider his seminary appointment. Boyce, who had grown disconsolate over the whole business, was elated. "Your simple name will be a tower of strength to us," he wrote, and immediately pressed his case. Through the seminary, Broadus could shape a generation of ministers, and by them reach "every quarter of the globe and the hearts of every class of men." "What do we need now among the Baptists?" Boyce asked. "A number of educated men to aid in forming the public sentiment of the churches. In our cities and towns and villages we have conservatism, but we have not enough for the country; and behold the radicalism and the demagogism that is rife." Boyce's urgency communicates the passion of many elite Southern Baptists for raising the denomination's standards. "Ought you not to make the sacrifice," he pleaded, "are you not called by God to enter upon this work?"[24]

On April 21, Broadus yielded. "I tremble at the responsibility of the thing either way and hesitate to write words which must be irrevocable," he wrote. "But . . . if elected, I am willing to go. May God graciously direct and bless, and if I have erred in judgment, may he overrule, to the glory of his name. *Jacta est alea* [the die is cast]." In May 1859, the Convention elected Broadus to the faculty, along with Manly, and Mercer theology professor William Williams. Boyce celebrated the completion of the bright, youthful, sophisticated team. The seminary had brought together "four of us who can feel like brothers indeed toward each other."[25]

Baptist institutions across the South immediately awarded the young professors with honorary Doctor of Divinity degrees. Broadus received a D.D. from Richmond College, and another from William & Mary. He knew that it looked "slightly ridiculous," revealing his denomination's insecurity about its status in general, and the young faculty's inexperience in particular. "What a formidable array of D. D.'s it makes!" he joked. Puff pieces in the Baptist press further exaggerated the new professors' learning, dignity, and piety. Broadus, dubbed "the most distinguished Baptist minister in Virginia" by one newspaper, was "remarkably gifted as a pulpit orator," combining "uncommon intellectual powers and attainments" with a "degree of modesty and meekness that gives ample proof of the higher attainments which he has made as a Christian." "It is a phenomenon to meet a man so rarely gifted, and yet so seemingly unconscious of his superiority."[26] It felt like an overcompensation to Broadus, embarrassing him.

Nor did the public relations campaign convince the Southern Baptist public. Broadus's Uncle William had left his pastorate to serve as the seminary's agent in Virginia, predicting that he could raise $25,000 by October 1860. He instead met resistance across the state. "My work moves slowly," William wrote in June, "much opposition." To rural Baptists, the seminary was the pet project of a few ambitious city preachers. In their hands, the seminary would perpetuate denominational elitism and a stratified ministry, and reduce what little influence the rural brethren still held in Southern Baptist life. These same pietistic Baptists set little store by theological education, believing that academic work made "straight-jacket preachers." Meanwhile, urban Southern Baptists congenial to education resented competition with their state colleges, and Virginia Baptists grumbled that the seminary "took [Broadus] out of Virginia." Still others expressed concerns about the seminary's doctrine, some thinking Broadus "not quite sound on close communion," and others that Boyce was "an ultra-Calvinist." By the end of 1860, William Broaddus reported "a hard year of it. Opposition to 'Theological Schools' has met me at every step."[27] His frustrations foreshadowed a persistent popular resistance to the seminary.

Its most formidable opponent was J. R. Graves of Nashville, Tennessee. Born in Vermont in 1820, Graves had migrated to the South in the early 1840s, eventually landing in Nashville as the editor of the influential *Tennessee Baptist* newspaper. Southern Baptists, especially in the southwestern states, loved Graves's colorful, pugnacious style, and his newspaper reached a circulation of thirteen thousand by 1860. Graves contended aggressively for a narrow set of Baptist identity markers that he called "Landmarkism." Fiercely localist and sectarian in character, Landmarkers flatly denied the reality of a "universal church." The New Testament only recognized local congregations obedient to Christ's commands, they argued, which meant that Baptist churches alone were authentic; other denominations were nothing more than "religious societies." Graves strictly prohibited sharing pulpits with ministers of other denominations (known as "pulpit affiliation," a common practice among town Baptists like Broadus), as well as accepting baptisms performed by non-Baptists (known as "alien immersion," a less common practice). Landmark policies took deepest root in the frontier states of the old southwest, where Baptists battled with Methodists, Presbyterians, and Campbellites for supremacy. In this rough-and-tumble environment, the swashbuckling Graves had by 1850 become a cult hero. He also remained at constant odds with genteel eastern Baptists like the seminary founders. "Nashville will try to crush [the seminary] like everything else Atlantic," Broadus sighed in a letter to Manly.[28]

Graves opposed educating ministers at a centralized seminary rather than at state Baptist schools like Union University in Murfreesboro, Tennessee, where he was a trustee. He criticized the faculty's theology, as none held his Landmark views. He cast the seminary founders as elites who would "manufacture a sleek, dainty race of ministerial exquisites, who were to compose the literary aristocracy of our ministry." Graves's criticisms highlighted the fractured identity of white Southern Baptists, described by historian Paul Harvey as "urban versus rural, Southeast versus Southwest, settled places versus frontier." The seminary would always contend with doctrinal, cultural, and personal conflicts within its own denomination, but Broadus tried to remain philosophical. "As to pleasing everybody, I suppose it must be our lot, the balance of our lives to have various persons all the time finding fault with us," he wrote to Boyce. "There are people in abundance who don't mean to be pleased with anything we can do."[29] His words would prove prophetic; they would need as much political skill as theological acumen to succeed.

Broadus's Charlottesville neighbors sniffed at his move to Greenville; by their lights, anything south of Virginia was simply "a homogenous swamp." Some of them amused Broadus by questioning if he would be able to find clean drinking water in upcountry South Carolina. But Greenville, now a town of around three thousand, had flourished in the 1850s; the completion of the railroad in 1853 had brought a new prosperity to the city, leading to the construction of several public buildings, including a new courthouse, three churches, Baptist-led Furman University, and the Greenville Baptist Female College. The establishment of the seminary made Greenville a center for Baptist education in the South, "a sort of Athens and Jerusalem in one to the Baptists of the Palmetto State," Broadus called it.[30]

Admittedly, the setting was modest. "The requisites for an institution of learning are three *b*'s,—bricks, books, brains," Broadus once quoted. "Our brethren usually begin at the wrong end of the three *b*'s; they spend all their money for bricks, have nothing to buy books, and must take such brains as they can pick up." Boyce determined not to make that error. Whereas the Southern Presbyterians of nearby Columbia Theological Seminary met in the antebellum mansion of Ainsley Hall, across the street from Wade Hampton's stately home, Boyce settled for renting the old Greenville Baptist meetinghouse, left vacant after the church built a fine new Greek Revival structure in town. He divided the church building into two lecture rooms and a library, furnished with books from Furman University's theological library and his personal collection, which numbered in the thousands. Boyce believed he owned "almost every important exegetical work of modern date, with many others," and that Manly would add "fifteen hundred to two thousand" of his own.[31]

Twenty-six students enrolled that first term, comprised of a cross-section of white Southern Baptist manhood. W. L. Ballard was a forty-five-year-old "plain country pastor" from South Carolina, who Broadus remembered as "a deeply pious man and a deeply earnest student." Ballard would remain only one session, though he reportedly preached much better afterward. Other students hailed from prominent Baptist families, such as C. H. Ryland, son of Richmond College president Robert Ryland, who went on to be "warmly loved and very influential." J. A. Chambliss of Alabama would also fill "a number of important pastorates," including long stints in Richmond and in Charleston. The brightest star of all was the Virginian Crawford Toy, a Broadus protege and former teacher at Albemarle Female Institute. Like Broadus, Toy had earned a master's degree from the University of Virginia; he was now preparing for a missionary career in Japan. "Toy is among the foremost scholars I have ever known of his years, an uncommonly conscientious and devoted man," Broadus wrote. John and Lottie Broadus "greatly enjoy[ed] [Toy's] society," and boarded Toy and fellow UVA alum J. William Jones at their home. Virginians always tended to flock together.[32]

Yet, as Boyce had hoped, a ministerial fraternity also developed across the diverse student body. They attached affectionate nicknames to one another, such as "our theologian," "our Greek," and "our preacher." They gathered by the Greenville waterfalls for moonlit discussions and established a debating society named for English Baptist Andrew Fuller. They held "cottage prayer meetings" for spiritual awakening, passed out evangelistic tracts, and started Sunday schools in Greenville's rural environs. "This has been a place for growth in piety as well as knowledge," Broadus beamed after the first term. Between studies, extracurricular activities, and ministry endeavors, students found the seminary to be a fast-paced environment. "I never knew how to be real busy till I came here—this whole place is a veritable bee-hive," wrote one.[33]

Accepting students of all education backgrounds posed certain academic challenges. John R. Sampey thought the early admission standards quite low, with "many students" failing every course they took and the seminary producing only six "full graduates" in its first eight years. Manly considered the inaugural class overall "a valuable body of men," though he noted "2 or 3 dull chances." He wrote that his students "groan over the Hebrew," finding the language "a daghish sort of business altogether." Yet the teaching quality could also be uneven. Manly privately acknowledged that Hebrew had been his worst subject in school. "I am learning Hebrew myself, slowly, and my classes are learning it, still more slowly, of course," he wrote. More than once, he consulted the brilliant Crawford Toy about the Hebrew lesson before class.[34]

Of his new colleagues, Broadus had been least acquainted with William Williams. Student C. C. Brown believed that Williams "resembled a farmer more than a great teacher. One meeting him on the street might have thought he had come to town to sell grain or potatoes." But Williams, a Harvard Law graduate, possessed a keen, logical mind. Students marveled at the clarity of his lectures and regarded him to be an excellent preacher. Williams's fellow Georgian and future Confederate Vice President Alexander H. Stephens pronounced him "the Daniel Webster of the American pulpit." Broadus enjoyed the more glamorous preaching reputation, but students debated as to whether or not the unassuming Williams might, in fact, be his equal.[35]

Thirty-two-year-old Basil Manly Jr. was the tense, bespectacled son of Southern Baptists' most distinguished leader, University of Alabama President Basil Manly Sr. Manly had struggled to find his niche since graduating from Princeton, with pastorates in rural Alabama and Mississippi, as well as in prestigious Richmond, all failing to satisfy. Broadus considered Manly to be "the most versatile of men." He was a highly regarded preacher, had published a popular hymnbook in 1849, and could teach almost any subject on short notice. But this was also his undoing, as Manly often found himself distracted and directionless, flitting from one interest to the next. Also tending to melancholy, Manly was hard on himself and others. "I don't think Williams can stand much work," he wrote to his parents, "or is as willing to do as much as the rest." Broadus fared better in Manly's evaluation; he had "good powers of work," though Manly worried that he had "taxed them rather too severely" and would drive himself into a sickbed, thus adding to Manly's own workload.[36] Broadus and Manly nevertheless became so close that Manly would name two of his children after Broadus.

But to Broadus, Boyce was the most impressive of the faculty. Besides theology professor, Boyce served as faculty chairman, seminary treasurer, and chair of the five-member executive committee. He was involved in every major decision of the school. Boyce traveled widely to raise the endowment, and, when funds ran short, he made up the difference himself. In 1861, he would sign two bonds for $50,000, pledging to pay the sum lacking in raising the endowment on behalf of the other southern states. After the death of his father in 1854, Boyce could have passed the rest of his life as a careless heir, with a personal estate valued at $330,000 in 1860.[37] Critics reproachfully referred to the school as "Boyce's seminary," but his personal investment was unmatched.

The founding faculty were all young, sophisticated, and well educated. They were also all moderately wealthy slave owners. The 1860 Greenville District census reported that William Williams owned five slaves, Basil Manly Jr. owned seven, Boyce twenty-three, and Broadus two. (Manly and Boyce likely owned many more slaves outside of Greenville.) Together, they would mold a new generation of Baptist "gentleman theologians," instilling in their students both a theological tradition and "an ideological undergirding to a southern way of life."[38]

→>>❖⃰❖<<←

But less than two months into the opening term, Broadus's strength collapsed. He called it an attack of "indigestion," which then "settled down into confirmed and obstinate dyspepsia." He lost so much weight that he required bed rest. "I take ups and downs, and am still wholly unable to work," he wrote in February, "ten minutes of continuous close thinking will make me sick. I have been, personally, favored much, in being able to read, almost always, but only what was light, and excited no particular desire to comprehend or remember."[39]

The other faculty picked up his classes, and Boyce took him to Charleston to convalesce while he conducted business. He attended to Broadus like a mother. "He wrapped his friend in a wonderful overcoat, a miracle of softness and warmth, and when he reached Charleston carried him in his own arms from the carriage into his room at the hotel," Broadus recalled. "He seemed strong like a giant, and he was tender as a woman." Broadus marveled at Boyce's boundless energy and strength. Unlike his feebler colleagues, Boyce's health was "superb, and his powers of endurance seemed almost unlimited." He urged Broadus to take regular exercise on one of his many fine ponies; his wife and daughters rode daily with an enslaved groom in the countryside. Broadus did so, but by March was "still feeble, and very easily thrown back. It is hard to be prudent."[40]

He staggered to the seminary's first commencement on May 28, 1860. Denominational dignitaries traveled in to adorn the festivities, with Basil Manly Sr. preaching to the graduating class. Not one year later, Manly would accompany Jefferson Davis and Alexander Stephens by carriage to the Alabama State House, where he would pray down God's blessing on Davis's presidency of the newly formed Confederate States of America. Boyce's heartfelt words at the commencement reportedly moved many to tears, and Basil Manly Jr. introduced a new hymn for the occasion. It has been sung at every subsequent commencement:

Soldiers of Christ, in truth arrayed,
A world in ruins needs your aid:

A world by sin destroyed and dead;
A world for which the Savior bled.

His gospel to the lost proclaim,
Good news for all in Jesus' name;
Let light upon the darkness break
That sinners from their death may wake.

Morning and evening sow the seed,
God's grace the effort shall succeed.
Seed times of tears have oft been found
With sheaves of joy and plenty crowned.

We meet to part, but part to meet
When earthly labors are complete,
To join in yet more blest employ,
In an eternal world of joy.[41]

The ceremony held a variety of meanings for its participants, but it must have been particularly gratifying for Boyce. Four years earlier, he had pledged himself to an institution that would "take the mass now uneducated and make them capable and efficient workmen for God." For Southern Baptists, a popular religious body forged in the fires of revival, the seminary's first commencement represented a critical step in what Nathan Hatch has termed the evangelical "pilgrimage toward respectability." As Robert Elder has observed, these southern religious institutions "served the larger goal of conforming the clergy and their sermons to the emerging ideal of gentility, the language in which urban and educated southerners increasingly expressed the demands of honor in the antebellum period."[42]

As for Broadus, he was looking forward to a four-month vacation in Charlottesville. But tragedy struck in July when four-year-old Maria died of diphtheria. "Oh, my daughter!" he wrote to Boyce. "But the will of the Lord be done. I have stood by the deathbed and the grave of father and mother and sister, of wife and child; I am confident they are all safe in heaven; God help those who are left to follow them there." A week after little Maria's death, Broadus left his family for a month at the Virginia springs. "Dearest, I hope to live a good many years still, if it please Providence, and I mean to try very hard to improve during this trip," he promised Lottie. By the end of August, he reported that "I shall never again have vigorous health, that is clear, but I think it reasonable to hope that, if I can have some moderate degree of sense about exercise and eating, I may stand work tolerably well."[43] When he returned to Greenville, he found that the town had contracted secession fever.

Five
THE GREAT DISRUPTION

THE PRESIDENTIAL CANDIDACY of Abraham Lincoln in the fall of 1860 chastened Broadus's excitement about the seminary's climbing enrollment. "If Lincoln is elected, and South Carolina secedes alone, we'll be in a sweet fix," he wrote to Boyce in August 1860. The Republican candidate from Illinois advocated restricting the spread of slavery to new states, a policy that most white southerners believed endangered slavery in every state. After a decade of sectional unrest, South Carolinians had threatened secession from the Union throughout the summer of 1860. Madison Broadus began playfully addressing his letters to Broadus in "Greenville, Empire of South Carolina." More soberly, both Broadus brothers expressed concern over South Carolina's "hot haste, and hush! hush! hush! No-time-to-listen-to-you policy."[1]

Both Union-first Virginia Whigs, John and Madison Broadus considered secession a "humiliation." Their father's political party had disintegrated in the course of the tumultuous 1850s, but most of the old Virginia Whigs, including General Winfield Scott and Robert E. Lee, initially opposed secession. Even upon Lincoln's election in November 1860, Madison was willing to suspend judgment on the Illinoisan, in hopes that "a Henry Clay Whig could not well be far wrong." As Bertram Wyatt-Brown has argued, this Whiggish reluctance to promote radical change characterized many white southern clergy in 1860 and 1861. "Will it not be sad," J. B. Jeter of Richmond wrote to Broadus, "if between Northern fanaticism and Southern rashness the best government that the world has ever seen, the work of our revolutionary fathers, the admiration of the friends of freedom in all nations, and the last refuge of republican liberty, should perish?"[2]

The rest of the seminary faculty, hailing from across the South, ranged the spectrum of secession views. Boyce, the financier, opposed secession on pragmatic grounds. His father, Ker Boyce, had been a strongly pro-Union Whig in Charleston and actively opposed South Carolina's secession movements in the 1830s. Lincoln concerned Boyce and Broadus, but both believed that secession portended disaster for the South, for slavery, and for the seminary. But the Georgian, William Williams, was strongly secessionist, and Basil Manly Jr. "mildly so" (a step removed from his fire-eating father, Basil Manly Sr.). Despite their divergent political opinions, Broadus insisted that "neither that, nor anything else, has ever caused the slightest jar among us."[3]

After Lincoln's election, the South Carolina legislature called for a convention at the end of December 1860 to decide on secession. Though traditionally a stronghold of Union sentiment, Greenville quickly followed the rest of the state in secession enthusiasm. Fire-Eaters such as Furman University president and Baptist minister James C. Furman kept the town stirred with speeches, meetings, and rumors. Broadus recalled how these men "persuaded the people in general that the only way to conserve their State independence, their property, and their characteristic civilization was to quit the Union and secede to establish a Confederation of the Southern States." On November 15, the Greenville Minute Men mustered at a newly erected Liberty Pole, where they raised a flag featuring a single star above the state's Palmetto tree and the word "secession." The Furman University Riflemen saluted the flag with a volley and gave three cheers for "the New Republic." Boyce ran as a pro-Union candidate for the secession convention, and was soundly defeated.[4]

On December 20, 1860, the South Carolina secession convention unanimously adopted an ordinance dissolving all connections with the United States. The aging Charleston lawyer and Unionist James L. Petigru, for whom James Petigru Boyce had been named, muttered that South Carolina was now "too small to be a nation, and too large to be an insane asylum." Boyce himself also groaned at the course of these events. "God deliver us from the follies to which, out of it, the fire-eaters will try to carry us, and the civil discord that will thus come upon us!" he wrote to his sister after the secession convention. "As sure as we do not arrange some propositions for the North, we shall have to go through a long and bloody war."[5]

Broadus shared Boyce's disappointment over South Carolina's decision. "I was most earnestly opposed to the action of the State in seceding, and deeply regret it now," he wrote in January 1861, "I have at this hour no sympathy with secession." But like many white southerners, Broadus's primary allegiance lay with his state. Madison Broadus articulated their shared position from Virginia later that spring. "I am not a secessionist—the word angers me now—but I am a Virginian," Madison wrote. "Virginia in the Union, if men were wise enough, unselfish enough, virtuous enough to appreciate and preserve a union, is my favorite idea—but if Virginia cannot belong to the Union without servile degradation from Northern aggression and domination, then I am for Virginia and nothing else at present." John Broadus also believed that his "duty" as a citizen and a man of honor required sharing in the fate of his state, and of the new Confederacy to which it belonged, whatever the consequences. "South Carolina is going to the devil," he sighed, "and I'm going with her."[6]

--»»❖❖«« --

Broadus's reticence regarding secession reflected no sympathy with northern abolitionism. Into the 1860s, he continued to view slavery as being biblically based, morally legitimate, fundamental to the social order, and the foundation to his own self-image as a white, southern man of honor. At the time of secession, he, along with the rest of the seminary faculty, still owned multiple slaves. He considered buying several more during the war. Boyce called himself an "ultra pro-slavery man" and made it clear that it was "as a pro-slavery man that I would preserve the Union"; he predicted that secession meant war, and war meant abolition.[7]

None of the seminary faculty published extensive defenses of slavery, but they shared the views of their white Southern Baptist peers who did. "I entertain no doubt that slavery is right, morally, socially, politically, religiously right," declared Broadus's friend I. T. Tichenor. Slavery could not be a sin, because the Bible never explicitly condemned it as such. Instead, Scripture regulated the master-slave relationship with the highest ethical standards. Long after the war, Broadus continued to make this case from New Testament passages such as Paul's letter to Philemon. He admitted that slavery was not a desirable state, but he also insisted that it was lawful. He was also quick to point out how much good the sovereign

God had worked through slavery, bringing countless Africans to hear the gospel. Most Black Americans saw these pious white interpretations as hopelessly self-serving. The slaveholder's gospel, Frederick Douglass sneered, "more than chains, or whips, or thumb-screws, gives perpetuity to this horrible system."[8]

Broadus did not deny the many evils connected with slavery. He viewed the kidnapping of African men and women for profit as a grievous sin, condemned in the Bible as "man-stealing." He acknowledged also that slaves could suffer shamefully at the hands of wicked masters, as depicted luridly in *Uncle Tom's Cabin*. He lamented incidents of physical and sexual abuse, the callous dissolution of slave marriages and families, and the gross spiritual neglect of enslaved persons. But he could not believe these crimes were intrinsic to slavery itself; he insisted that they were isolated incidents, censured by respectable white community members. The historical record suggests a different story, one in which abuse was inherent to and widespread in racial chattel slavery. Yet Broadus struggled to see through his cultural conditioning—and a thick glaze of evangelical paternalism—to his complicity in a wicked system. He defended an "ideal slavery," in the abstract, in which abuse was rare, masters and slaves submitted to God's Law, and all benefitted from the relationship. Drawing from New Testament household codes, he viewed himself as the godly patriarch of a divinely ordered family, attending to his slaves' physical and spiritual needs and guiding their childlike steps.[9]

One observes some dynamics of this paternalistic relationship in a November 1860 letter Broadus received from longtime family slave Richard Hackley. Known as "Uncle Dick," Hackley wrote from Charlottesville, where he attended to Broadus's stepmother. (Broadus also hired out Hackley to work for other men for up to $60 a year.) Addressing Broadus repeatedly as "my dear master," Hackley professed to write "to show you that I think of you often." Echoing Broadus's own political views, Hackley expressed his wish that "Mr. Lincoln or no such man may ever take his seat in the presidential chair. I do most sincerely hope that the Union may be preserved." Certain "white gentlemen" had informed Hackley of South Carolina's threatened secession, but he hoped "she won't leave, as that would cause much disturbance and perhaps fighting. Why can't the Union stand like it is now?" The amiable exchange may have reinforced Broadus's confidence in the benevolence of biblically regulated slavery. Yet, while Hackley perhaps loved Broadus sincerely, he may have also calculated his remarks. Identifying himself as Broadus's "devoted servant," he indirectly requested to visit his wife.

"I have been wanting to go up and see my wife," he wrote, "but have not been able, but will do so soon, I hope. Next year I should like to live nearer her." The comment should have prompted reflection for Broadus, who bore some responsibility for separating the family. Dick Hackley had earlier requested that Broadus purchase his daughter, Nelly, so that they could be together, though it does not appear that Broadus ever did so. Hackley's disappearance from Broadus's life after emancipation suggests that their family ties were not as strong as Broadus may have believed.[10]

White southern clergy took comfort in defending slavery with the literal text of Scripture, even as northern abolitionists appeared willing to jettison orthodox views of the Bible. In this, as Mark Noll has argued, the Civil War represented a theological crisis for Americans as well as a political one; the slavery debates would forever change the way that Americans treated, and trusted, the Bible. Broadus prided himself on his strictly biblical worldview, but he had also spent a lifetime absorbing extra-biblical and racist assumptions from his white southern honor culture. In his view, Black southerners were "lowly souls" of a "degraded race," "from among the lowest races of mankind," and needed white ministers to "guide their weak and ignorant steps on the paths of Christian life." These blithe assertions owed more to Thomas Jefferson's *Notes on the State of Virginia* than to any text of the Old or the New Testament.[11]

--->>·❖·❖·<<--

The seminary rallied behind the new Confederacy. After the close of the second term in May 1861, many students enlisted as chaplains or soldiers in the Confederate Army. Broadus himself returned home briefly to Virginia, after stopping to deliver the commencement address at the University of North Carolina. But on June 16 he found himself preaching before two Virginia regiments. They were stationed at a small town in Prince William County called Manassas, near Bull Run Creek. The first major battle of the war would erupt there one month later. On July 21, Washington dignitaries and ladies traveled the thirty miles west of the capital to observe the battle as a lark, bringing picnic lunches and anticipating an easy Yankee rout of the rebels. Several chaotic hours of sloppy maneuvers and hard fighting later, the Confederate Army drove the Federals from the field, the latter retreating to Washington without orders. White southerners crowed that the war would soon be won.

The jubilant mood prevailed the next week at the South Carolina Baptist Convention in Spartanburg, where Broadus had been assigned to preach. Yet instead of grandstanding, he issued a sober warning from Psalm 44:6–8: "For I will not trust in my bow, neither shall my sword save me. But thou hast saved us from our enemies, and hast put them to shame that hated us. In God we boast all the day long, and praise thy name for ever." Broadus urged on his peers an "entire dependence on Providence, and the great importance of not taking everything for granted from a single success." He believed the South's cause to be good, but the Confederacy would only prevail if it fought a different kind of war than its northern combatants: they must lean humbly on the arm of the Lord, rather than the arm of the flesh. His message received mixed reviews. Some disappointed listeners privately expressed that Broadus "was not quite up to the requirements of the occasion." For many white Southern Baptists, Broadus wrote, lacking a "more thoughtful" and "true and scriptural doctrine of providence," any question of God's support of the Confederacy was out of bounds. "Our Southern cause was right. The right must succeed. Yes, the right had succeeded, and this must continue. Such was the feeling of many good men," he recalled. As Harry Stout has shown, for both South and North, the embrace of an ardent civil religion played a crucial role in prosecuting the long and bloody war.[12]

Steeped as they were in southern honor culture, most seminary students could not remain at their desks with a war on. Enrollment declined from thirty-one to twenty in the fall of 1861, and dwindled further over the term. "Every now and then some one of these twenty would find himself unable to continue studying, and go off to volunteer with his friends," Broadus remembered. "We studied on as best we could." Even Boyce left with the army. When local lawyer and Baptist Sunday School Superintendent C. J. Elford formed a new regiment in Greenville, he asked Boyce to serve as his chaplain. Boyce spent the fall in camp with the 16th South Carolina Infantry Regiment, then traveled with them to Charleston in December. He preached, held prayer meetings, and handed out Bibles, hymnbooks, and other Christian literature. The soldiers' spiritual apathy sobered Boyce. "You cannot know how tenderly my heart yearns over them," he wrote to Broadus. "How many, after all, must go unprepared into the presence of God. I feel like preaching all the time and would do it if I thought I could accomplish more that way. But alas for the unwillingness of men to hear the gospel."[13]

Back in Greenville, Broadus and the rest of the faculty attempted to hold the school together. By March, only eight students remained. Boyce, still in the field, advised Broadus to cancel May commencement exercises and dismiss the term early, hoping to reopen in the fall of 1862.[14] That summer, Boyce attempted to gain seminary students the same exemption from the general conscription granted to clergy. (Broadus, curiously, would claim in his memoir of Boyce that the seminary sought no such exemptions.) When this plan failed, Boyce recommended that the seminary suspend operations for the duration of the war. He endeavored to continue paying faculty salaries, but Confederate currency was already depreciating, and even that was quickly running out. He encouraged the faculty to supplement this meager income by pastoring country churches.[15]

Accordingly, Williams and Manly relocated some sixty miles south, where they both served multiple churches in the Abbeville District. Manly purchased a plantation near the town of Ninety-Six, South Carolina, bringing with him thirty slaves from Greenville and Alabama, and hiring an overseer. Williams rented a farm in Whitehall, South Carolina, near Greenwood, and hired out one of his slaves at $100 a year. Broadus remained in Greenville. He picked up Boyce's former pastoral charge, Cedar Grove Baptist Church, and preached often at other places. By 1864, Broadus was pastoring four different country churches simultaneously: Clear Spring, Cedar Grove, Williamston, and Siloam, each meeting one Sunday per month. Whether he realized it or not, the ease and comfort of his Old South world were over.[16]

-->>>�֍✿✿✿‹‹‹--

Broadus now threw the Confederacy his full support. At the 1863 Southern Baptist Convention in Augusta, Georgia, he drafted a report on "the state of our country" and a set of resolutions supporting the Confederate government. His committee affirmed the war to be both "just and necessary," and it expressed confidence in the South's "ultimate success." He did not assume a southern monopoly on God's favor. Employing the old Puritan jeremiad, he cautioned his neighbors that "our sins have deserved the terrible calamities that God has set upon us," and urged upon them "penitence, humiliation and a hearty turning to God." The Convention adopted his resolutions unanimously.[17]

Weak health prevented Broadus from enlisting as a chaplain, but he ministered regularly to Confederate troops in other ways. In February 1862, he received a request to write a religious pamphlet for soldiers, aimed at combating the vices of camp life—a major concern for southern evangelicals. Broadus penned "We Pray for You at Home," a six-page evangelistic tract playing on the soldier's longing for hearth and family. Besides entreating God for victory and personal safety, Broadus reminded the Confederate soldier that, "we pray for your soul":

> We know it must be hard for you, amid the distractions of camp life, the alternate excitement and *ennui,* the absence of home influences and the associations of the sanctuary, to fix mind and heart on things above. . . . We pray that you may be inclined and enabled to commit your soul to the divine Savior, who died to redeem us, and ever lives to intercede for us, and who with yearning love is ever saying, "Come unto me." We pray that the Holy Spirit may thoroughly change your heart, bringing you truly to hate sin, and love holiness, and may graciously strengthen you to withstand temptation, and give you more and more the mastery over yourself, and the victory over every enemy of your soul. Whether it be appointed you to fall soon in battle, or years hence to die at home, may God in mercy forbid that you should live in impenitence and die in your sins.

Printed with a hymn by Manly, "Prayer for the Loved Ones from Home," Broadus's popular tract circulated widely among the armies of northern Virginia throughout the war.[18]

In 1863, Broadus received an invitation to evangelize CSA soldiers more directly. Seminary student J. William Jones, now a chaplain in the Army of Northern Virginia, pleaded with Broadus to spend the summer as a missionary to the troops. After several cajoling letters, Jones informed Broadus that Stonewall Jackson himself had requested his services. Jackson in the spring of 1863 was the most celebrated soldier in the world, thanks to his remarkable Shenandoah Valley Campaign of 1862. He was also a devout Presbyterian. "Write to [Broadus] by all means and beg him come. Tell him that he never had a better opportunity of preaching the gospel than he would have right now in these camps," Jackson apparently told Jones. Broadus relented. He would spend July, August, and most of September ministering to the Army of Northern Virginia, while also posting articles as a war correspondent for the *Charleston News and Courier*. Jackson, according to Jones, was thrilled. "When Doctor Broadus comes you must bring him to see me," the general said. "I want him to preach at my headquarters, and I wish to help him in his work all I can." But the previously invincible Jackson died of wounds from the battle of Chancellorsville before the two could meet.[19]

Broadus crossed into Virginia the last week of June, making his way to General Robert E. Lee's camp in Winchester. He first stopped in Lynchburg to visit his brother, Madison. Watching the sun rise from Madison's front porch, Broadus realized how much he had missed his home state. "It is a pleasant morning, and my heart glows at the thought that I am in Virginia again," he wrote to Lottie. He extolled at length, as he often did, the familiar rivers, valleys, and even the "glorious green grass" of the Old Dominion. Victory seemed within Confederate grasp that morning. Lee had just staged a daring invasion of the North, hoping to break Lincoln's resolve with a decisive victory in the heart of Union territory. On July 1, the armies clashed near a little town in south-central Pennsylvania called Gettysburg. After three brutal days of fighting, Lee's men had suffered twenty-eight thousand casualties (while inflicting twenty-three thousand) and a devastating loss that altered the course of the war. Broadus reached Winchester on July 3, just as reports were trickling in. By July 7, Lee's battered army began straggling back in, with thousands of wounded soldiers desperate for medical attention.[20]

In the "confused whirl" of those first chaotic days in Staunton, Broadus found few opportunities to preach, but he resolved to "do all he can in the hospitals." "As things get quiet in the wards, I can go in and sing and pray and sometimes talk," he wrote to Lottie, "and in some way or other I may get a chance to preach some during the week, with plenty of chances for Sunday." On July 8, he passed out coffee, buttermilk, and slices of buttered bread to wounded soldiers returning from Gettysburg. When they ran out of butter, the servers scrambled eggs to spread on the bread instead. Broadus worked until "the supplies were exhausted, and everybody broken down, and still the wounded were pouring in." Intense suffering surrounded him. The basement of a local Presbyterian church had been converted into a hospital, but "the men, disliking the close room, were lying everywhere, in the enclosure before the church, and on the steps, and in the vestibule. So it is at all churches, and one never goes in or out among these poor fellows lying on their pallets or blankets, wounded or sick, without thinking of the Pool of Bethesda," he wrote.[21] The trauma of the field hospital seemed a world apart from the orderly environments of church and academy Broadus had always known.

Soon he was preaching multiple times a day. Even recycling old sermons, he struggled to keep pace with the need. "Oh, it is so hard to preach as one ought to do!" he wrote to Lottie. "I long for the opportunity, yet do not rise to meet it with whole-souled earnestness and living faith, and afterwards I feel sad and ashamed." He held services daily in local churches of all types—Lutheran, Presbyterian, Methodist, and Baptist. At other times, he assembled soldiers for services in the camps. Boyce had been discouraged by the soldiers' spiritual indifference in the war's early months, but Broadus now found a different reception. "There is no mistake about it that a large proportion of these soldiers are deeply interested in the subject of religion," Broadus told A. E. Dickinson, now serving as Virginia Baptist superintendent of colportage. "Any experienced preacher would see it, from the way they listen to preaching; and in private, not only are all respectful, but many cordially welcome religious conversation, and avow, without the slightest hesitation, their desire to be Christians," he wrote. "My heart warms toward the soldiers. . . . The Lord be thanked for the privilege of telling them about Jesus."[22]

By the middle of August, Broadus had joined the army at Orange Court House on the Rapidan River, where a massive revival had broken out. Ministers of all denominations held services day and night in every camp, drawing enormous, attentive crowds. "Many wept during the sermon, and not at allusions to home, but to their sins, and God's great mercy," he reported. Soldiers responded to preaching by streaming forward for "special prayer," seeking salvation and repentance for their backsliding. At one service, 610 soldiers reportedly came forward, with 200 professing conversion. On one Confederate Fast Day, J. William Jones estimated that five thousand soldiers gathered at sunset to hear Broadus, among them Generals Robert E. Lee, A. P. Hill (Broadus's childhood friend), Dick Ewell, and Jubal Early. Broadus preached a favorite sermon from Proverbs 3:17, "Her ways are ways of pleasantness, and all her paths are peace." "I have heard him preach from that text several times, but never with the pathos and power that he had that day," recounted Jones:

He caught the vast crowd with his first sentence, and held, and thrilled, and moved them to the close of the sermon. There were times when there was scarcely a dry eye among those gathered thousands. . . . It was touching to see the commander-in-chief and his great lieutenants and other officers, the very flower of our Confederate chivalry, mingling their tears with those of "the unknown heroes" of the rank and file—men who never quailed in battle, and trembling and not ashamed to weep under the power of the simple preaching of the glorious gospel of our Lord Jesus. At the close of the service they came by the hundreds to ask an interest in the prayers of God's people, or profess a new-found faith in the Lord Jesus Christ.[23]

Ministers were in constant demand in the Confederate camps. Jones conducted up to four baptismal services in different camps in a single day, never changing out of his wet clothes. Broadus pleaded for more Baptist preachers in the *Religious Herald*. "It is impossible to convey any just idea of the wide and effectual door that is now opened for preaching the gospel in the Army of Northern Virginia," he wrote on September 1. "The Holy Spirit seems everywhere moving among us. These widespread camps are a magnificent collection of camp-meetings. Brethren, it is the noblest opportunity for protracted meetings you ever saw. The rich, ripe harvest stands waiting. Come, brother, thrust in your sickle, and by God's blessing, you shall reap golden sheaves that shall be your rejoicing in time and eternity."[24]

Thousands professed faith in Christ in the Army of Northern Virginia in August and September of 1863. Though camp ministry entailed none of the elegance of Virginia's fine town churches, Broadus declared it to be "the most thoroughly delightful of all [my] ministerial experiences." Among Lee's desperate soldiers, Broadus encountered "none of the dull decorum and Dead-Sea formality which often embarrass the preacher's efforts in church, no thousand miles of cold air between the preacher and the nearest hearer,—nothing but live men, who came because they pleased, and listened because they liked; among whom you could stand, and lay your hand on a man's head if you chose, and look right into his eyes, and talk, man to man, about the highest things in time and eternity."[25]

Historians have drawn attention to the important role that these camp revivals played in boosting southern morale for the bloody fighting of 1864. According to James McPherson, "it may not be an exaggeration to say that the revivals of

1863–64 enabled Confederate armies to prolong the war into 1865."[26] After the war, Confederate revival narratives also became an important instrument for promoting Lost Cause mythology for Broadus's friends, especially J. William Jones. By recounting the extraordinary religious exercises of the Confederate camps, white southerners comforted themselves that God had indeed been on their side; defeat did not indicate God's disapproval of their cause, but the purification of his chosen people.[27] Regardless of how eulogizers leveraged the awakenings during and after the war, countless soldiers in both northern and southern armies found that the harrowing experiences of combat turned them to seek God with renewed fervency.

In the pages of the *Religious Herald,* A. E. Dickinson pressed Broadus to remain with the army, much to Lottie's annoyance. Broadus expressed openness to the idea "if my health were vigorous," but camp life wore on him. One night he slept "on a little wooden frame, having under me an oilcloth and a blanket to soften the plank, and another blanket for cover, with overcoat for pillow." The camp food and coffee disagreed with his delicate digestive system. Between the hot days under the sun and sleeping in the damp night air, he caught more than one cold; these settled in his throat and limited his preaching.[28]

Finally, Broadus found himself forced, "like a broken artillery horse, to go to the rear and graze." He dragged up to his mother-in-law's Locust Grove Plantation home the first week of August, feeling "very weak and prostrate." He collapsed gratefully onto a familiar bed in the cool house. "I could, perhaps, stand a soldier's life as a soldier, but with all the anxiety and nervous exhaustion attendant upon a preacher's work, which even before I went to Greenville used often to bring me into great prostration, I could not stand it," he admitted to Lottie.[29]

·—➤》❖┊❖《◄—·

As he recuperated at Locust Grove, Broadus learned how difficult the war and his absence had been on his family in Greenville. Besides caring for the girls and little Samuel (Lottie would give birth to another baby, Eleanor, the day after Christmas 1864), Lottie taught school to four students, along with some music lessons, and had begun to sell milk and vegetables. She led the girls into the countryside on foraging expeditions to further supply the table. "Our walks in the woods were frequent, with wildflowers to pick, blackberries or nuts to gather, or even acorns to feed the pig," daughter Eliza remembered. "Crab apples to make jelly, and persimmons were roadside finds, and down by the river was a kind of ivy that made a dye for the glove material that Mamma used to such great advantage, selling the gloves for a good price, as well as supplying the family." Lottie made and re-made the girls' dresses, "turning upside-down and wrong-side-out everything that could possibly be used." As Drew Gilpin Faust has explored, the war required slaveholding women like Lottie Broadus to become "mothers of invention," redefining southern womanhood in the process. Broadus praised Lottie's fortitude from Charlottesville. "You have acted nobly, my dear wife, in submitting so patiently to my absence, and I'm sure you'll bear it still. Whatever good I can do here, you deserve the credit much more than I do." From this point forward, their southern honor would be defined more by noble endurance than by patrician ease.[30]

The war had taken its toll on the family in other ways. Uncle William Broaddus was arrested in the summer of 1862 and held in a Washington, D.C., prison for a month, until a prisoner exchange could be arranged; his house in Fredericksburg had been destroyed in the battle there. While at Locust Grove, Broadus plucked a piece of evergreen from the grave of Lottie's brother Sam, who had fallen in combat. Saving a piece to wear on his lapel, Broadus sent the rest to Lottie. As he contemplated his own mortality, he poured out his heart in letters back home. "Lottie, it is possible—of course it is—that I may not see you anymore. Four weeks, four weeks and I may cease to breathe. So I'll tell you right now, here in the still night, in the room where at this hour we have often fallen asleep together, in the house where I first won your timid consent to be my bride, that I love you now more than ever before, more and more every year of the five—that I love you as much as I ever loved any other, or ever could have learned to love anyone that lives." Despite his fears, Broadus arrived home in mid-September. He resumed the pastoral charge of his distant country churches and began teaching two classes of young women, one in German and one in English literature. Unable to afford a gift at Christmas, Broadus composed a poem for Lottie instead.[31]

For now, at least, Lottie Broadus still relied on the daily services of enslaved workers. She expressed relief in 1863 to "have found at last a woman to sew for me, who suits me admirably." She was "a colored woman belonging to a Charleston lady, at Mrs. Long's," who "sews very rapidly, neatly, & is just what a servant ought to be." Other slaves, like the young woman Mary, were less cooperative.

Lottie related how Mary "was caught in quite a scrape" when found with a stolen pair of shoes. Though local law demanded "120 [lashes] & 1 month imprisonment" for Mary, friends of the Broadus family interceded, and "got her off with 40." "She did not seem to mind [the lashes] all," Lottie remarked. "Did not whimper while being whipped and came home laughing. Perfectly hardened!"[32]

Despite occasional disturbances, the Broaduses still considered their slaves, paradoxically, to be both part of their family and a flexible and lucrative financial investment. As late as November 1864, Broadus engaged in the selling of slaves. Boyce offered to hire a carpenter and a blacksmith Broadus had offered him, leaving Broadus with "nine field hands and the seamstress and . . . six children" for him to either sell or hire out. "I should say that for such a lot you ought to get all expenses and taxes paid," Boyce advised. "The *trio* ought to pay very handsomely." But time was running out on such arrangements. William Broaddus would report in 1863 that six of his own slaves had escaped to freedom in the previous year: Louisa (age 17), Lewis (age 21), Patsy (age 23), Caroline (age 16), and "Patsy's two children (ages 5 and 3)." For the Broaduses, emancipation would mean the sudden loss of household help, outside income, and the direct control over Black behavior. With other former slaveowners, they would work out new ways to exercise paternalistic oversight of their Black neighbors, and so fulfill the call of white southern honor.[33]

--->>>❖❖《《←-

Though the seminary remained suspended for the duration of the war, Broadus found a wider sphere of influence within the Southern Baptist Convention. During the war years, Broadus and Manly advanced their shared goal of establishing organized Sunday school work and producing centralized religious literature for Southern Baptists. Before the war, Southern Baptists had published religious literature, mostly Bibles, through its Bible Board in Nashville. But after Nashville fell to the Union and many of the Board's officers were arrested, the Convention voted at its 1863 meeting to close the Bible Board. Manly immediately rose to recommend the creation of a new board, this one focused on promoting "the establishment, enlargement, and higher efficiency of Sunday Schools." Part of the larger voluntarist movement birthed out of the Second Great Awakening, Sunday schools had become an important means for education, evangelism, and benevolence for Protestants in the north. Churches and individuals—the work was done by both clergy and lay people—opened Sunday schools, usually in unchurched or underserved areas, to teach the Bible, basic literacy, and meet material needs of poor children. The Sunday school movement stands as a classic example of evangelicalism's modern impulse toward progress and organization.[34]

Both Manly and Broadus had cut their ministerial teeth on Sunday school work. Manly called it "the nursery of the Church, the camp of instruction for her young soldiers," and "the great missionary to the future." He argued that Sunday school was too important for Southern Baptists to leave to disorganized, individual efforts; it demanded strong, centralized, denominational direction. The Convention granted Manly's request, though the Board met some of the same resistance that the seminary had encountered. Southern Baptists with a strong Jacksonian streak disliked the creation of another bureaucratic institution. Many questioned the timing of the venture. J. R. Graves opposed the efforts for personal reasons; he had formed his own "Southern Baptist Sunday School Union" in 1858 to advance Landmark principles. Still other Southern Baptists, otherwise favorable to the concept, expressed concern over the controlling influence that the seminary faculty would exercise over the literature. "It will not do for the Greenville professors to do all the book-making," remarked A. E. Dickinson. The seminary's fingerprints were indeed all over the new Sunday School Board: the home office was located in Greenville, with Manly serving as president and Boyce named to the Board as a trustee. All four seminary faculty would contribute regular written pieces. On October 1, 1863, the Board hired Broadus as corresponding secretary for $300 a year.[35]

Broadus oversaw the publication and distribution of Sunday school literature for all ages. Within months of its formation, the Board had published the *Confederate Sunday School Hymn Book,* Boyce's *A Brief Catechism of Bible Doctrine,* Virginia Baptist George B. Taylor's *Hints for Originating and Conducting Sunday Schools,* and *The Sunday School Primer,* which taught basic reading lessons. Broadus employed many modern promotional methods; he printed ninety thousand "Reward Tickets" to motivate young pupils to complete their lessons, for example. He also urged the Board's volunteer "missionaries" to drum up subscriptions across the South, and advertised in denominational and secular newspapers. Materials generally sold well, even in wartime.

One of the Board's most successful ventures was *Kind Words for the Sunday*

School Children, a monthly children's newspaper begun in 1866. Broadus noted that "Children are rather pleased than otherwise that theirs should be a little paper, strikingly different from the papers for grown people." He recruited seminary colleagues and leading Southern Baptist pastors to contribute articles. "Happy the man or woman who, by two or three hours of careful writing, can say something attractive and instructive to many thousands of dear children—something which may tell upon their life-long welfare, and their everlasting salvation," he wrote. Most of the authors used whimsical pen names, such as "Harry Hinter," "Cousin Will," and "Junior." For years to come, Broadus would carve out time to write children's articles as "J. A. B.," "J. Lovechild," "J. L.," "Theophilus," and "Zerubbabel." *Kind Words* endured through multiple eras of the Sunday School Board before being retired in 1929.[36]

Southern evangelicalism is commonly understood to have neglected social concern to promote a narrow conversionist message. Yet Sunday schools, in addition to spreading the gospel message, comprised an important vehicle for Southern Baptist social Christianity. In the days before public schools, Sunday schools provided moral formation and basic educational training for otherwise illiterate children, both white and Black. Broadus noted before the Southern Baptist Convention in 1866 how "a large proportion of the children of our country have now no means of learning to read but in the Sunday School." In the 1860s, Sunday schools also supplied a significant outlet for compassion ministries to children orphaned by the war.[37]

Broadus also used Sunday school to expand the spiritual leadership of Southern Baptist laypeople, especially women. Nonordained Sunday school workers, in "laboring for the benefit of a little flock," could find "their gifts and graces developed and exercised" without ever engaging in pulpit ministry, Broadus explained. Southern Baptist women had an especially vital role to play in Sunday school work. As Manly pointed out in 1863, with so many Southern Baptist men away at war, Sunday school ministry could go on because of "that never failing and invincible corps of reserves, the sisterhood." Through Sunday school work and missions support, women took on an increasingly prominent role in the male-dominated Southern Baptist Convention in the latter nineteenth century.[38]

As secretary of the Board, Broadus vigorously advocated for the creation of new Sunday schools across the South. He found that most churches could be "stirred up to a more lively interest in this great work, but that until thus stirred up, the great mass of them will continue to have no School, or one which is conducted with little zeal or benefit." Many pastors were too absorbed by the war and its effects to take Sunday school seriously. Female Sunday school workers often required special encouragement to step into leadership of a school. Teachers who did not see immediate results from their labors grew discouraged and needed reminding "that they are sowing seed for a lifetime and for eternity." "Only here and there are found persons who can 'kindle their own fire,' and keep it burning ever brightly," Broadus acknowledged. He accordingly appointed "General Missionaries" for each state, who in turn drafted local missionaries to "establish and build up Sunday Schools at all the churches they can reach." When the seminary reopened in 1866, Broadus promised Lottie to "positively and altogether" retire from the Sunday School Board. Yet, when the Board repeatedly failed to secure his successor, he continued the work without pay.[39]

The Sunday School Board struggled after the war, and Broadus considered the accomplishments of its first three years to be "sadly little." Still, its establishment represented a major step of denominational sophistication. "Tell Brother Manly to push on," Thomas E. Skinner wrote to Broadus in 1863. "I am a centralization Baptist. For 18 centuries we have frittered away our strength, usefulness, and piety for want of cooperation," he added. Skinner believed that the best way to show the importance of a strong denomination was "to present an efficiency suddenly before their eyes as to dazzle away their objections and unwittingly secure their cooperation. The Sunday school movement is calculated to bring this about." Despite a persistent minority protest from Landmarkers and other individualistic, rural Baptists, institutionally minded denominationalists like Skinner and Broadus would continue to nudge Southern Baptists toward a modern, centralized, efficiently run denomination in the late nineteenth century.[40]

Broadus's leadership of the Sunday School Board also encouraged an enduring Southern Baptist separatism in American Christianity. Though Broadus contributed to northern publications, he also contended that Southern Baptists should produce their own literature. He affirmed good work in northern organizations like the American Sunday School Union, American Baptist Publication Society, and American Tract Society, but judged many of their products unsuitable for southerners. "[T]he new books, published within the last few years, are somewhat frequently found to contain allusions to the war, made in accordance with the views and feelings of the Northern people," he noted. "However natural it may be that such allusions should be acceptable to them, it is equally natural that they should be unacceptable to us." By developing their own extensive network of publishing houses, schools, and missions boards in the late nineteenth century, Southern Baptists would promote an isolated, regional ethos that would extend at least to the end of the twentieth century. Broadus would attain tremendous popularity in the North after the Civil War, but never at the expense of his southern identity.[41]

→》》✤·✤·《《←

The final two years of the war brought grim days to Greenville. Townspeople gathered every afternoon at the railroad depot to await the delivery of newspapers from Charleston. The local Presbyterian pastor would stand on the platform to read the casualty list in a loud voice. Nearby, the pine coffins of Greenville's war dead piled high, waiting to be claimed. On April 11, 1865, Broadus doubted that peace would come in his lifetime. "I take it there will now be war in the country fully as long as you or I will live," he wrote to Manly. While holding out hope "that our children may live to see independence, and maybe our grandchildren, happiness," Broadus had now forfeited many of his own personal dreams from before the war. He had considered himself in 1863 to be "a man of bare ambition, with fondly cherished hopes of doing some good, and of gaining the good opinion of men." Yet now, "all thought of doing this or that 'after the war,' must, I fear, be abandoned." Still, there was always the possibility of divine intervention. "But 'man's extremity is God's opportunity.' As wonderful things have happened in history as that our cause should now begin to rise and prosper," he concluded. He did not know that two days earlier Lee had surrendered at Appomattox.[42]

Greenville, previously spared any fighting, would see some of the war's final action. A small brigade of Union cavalry entered the town on May 2, 1865, intent on intercepting Jefferson Davis on his southward flight from Richmond. Greenville resident Caroline Gilman heard her servants shouting "the yankees are coming!" and ran to her piazza to see the invading army looting the Main Street shops. Reaching Boyce's mansion at the edge of town, the northern soldiers commandeered his horses and "proceeded to plunder the entire house, bursting open closets and wardrobes and trunks, and flinging everything about, in the wild search for precious things." Finding Boyce himself, they held pistols to his head and "demanded to know what had become of his wife's diamonds and other jewelry." Boyce had sent these valuables away the day before. After they "stormed, and threatened to burn and kill," the soldiers left with Boyce's watch, some clothes, and whatever items they could carry off. Gilman recalled seeing one soldier wearing Boyce's fine overcoat, and "light[ing] one of [his] segars."[43]

Broadus lost nothing of value in the raid, but the cavalry did find $30,000 in cash from the Bank of Charleston that was hidden at Hamlin Beattie's store. "Ah, they were old hands," he muttered bitterly. "Walt Whitman ought to have written a so-called poem in their praise." The Greenville raid marked the end of John Broadus's Civil War. The charmed life he had led for nearly forty years had been completely upended. If the old ambitions, the "fondly cherished hopes of doing some good," still burned within him, he must learn how to attain them in a different world.[44]

This portrait was taken during Broadus's student days at the University of Virginia, where he developed "a noble rage for knowing and for teaching." He would remain intimately connected to the old southern institution for the rest of his life.

A. T. Robertson, *Life and Letters of John Albert Broadus* (Philadelphia, Pa.: American Baptist Publication Society, 1901), 134.

Determined to "rise and be something," Broadus by his early thirties had established himself as one of the South's premier evangelical preachers. In 1859, he shocked many by accepting an appointment to the founding faculty of the Southern Baptists' first theological seminary.

Archives and Special Collections, James P. Boyce Centennial Library, Southern Baptist Theological Seminary.

James Petigru Boyce convinced Broadus to join the tenuous seminary enterprise in 1859, and they labored for its survival until Boyce's death in 1888. Broadus memorialized his friend and "their life work" in his 1893 *Memoir of James Petigru Boyce*.

Archives and Special Collections,
James P. Boyce Centennial Library,
Southern Baptist Theological Seminary.

Basil Manly Jr. served with Broadus on the faculty of Southern Seminary at the institution's founding, and returned again in the 1880s, staying until his death in 1892. Broadus called Manly "the most versatile of men," and Manly named two of his children after Broadus.

Archives and Special Collections,
James P. Boyce Centennial Library,
Southern Baptist Theological Seminary.

The former meetinghouse of Greenville's First Baptist Church served as the humble home of the Southern Baptist Theological Seminary. Broadus's Charlottesville friends were horrified that he would exchange refined Virginia for the "homogenous swamp" of South Carolina.

Archives and Special Collections, James P. Boyce Centennial Library, Southern Baptist Theological Seminary.

Typically neat and scholarly in appearance, Broadus posed for this photograph on Canal Street in New Orleans. He may have done so when vacationing there on the munificence of his good friend John D. Rockefeller.

Archives and Special Collections, James P. Boyce Centennial Library, Southern Baptist Theological Seminary.

The brilliant Old Testament scholar
Crawford Howell Toy was like a
younger brother to Broadus. His
dismissal from Southern Seminary
in 1879 over the inspiration of
the Bible was the most wrenching
episode of Broadus's career.

Archives and Special Collections,
James P. Boyce Centennial Library,
Southern Baptist Theological Seminary.

Lithographs such as this one from
1881 occasionally accompanied
Broadus's numerous publications.
The 1880s were the most productive
of Broadus's literary life.

Atla Digital Library.

The seminary expanded
its footprint in downtown
Louisville at the end of
the nineteenth century,
based largely on Broadus's
fundraising success among
northern businessmen like
John D. Rockefeller. From
top to bottom are New
York Hall (1888), Memorial
Library (1890), and Norton
Hall (1893).

Archives and Special
Collections, James P. Boyce
Centennial Library, Southern
Baptist Theological Seminary.

Broadus succeeded James P. Boyce as the second president of the Southern Baptist Theological Seminary, serving from 1888 until his death in 1895. In his final lecture, just before his death, he urged his students to be "men 'Mighty in the Scriptures.'"

The wealthy Norton family paid for this handsome monument to Broadus in the seminary founders' plot in Louisville's Cave Hill Cemetery. The monument bears a curious inscription for the preacher: "On earth there is nothing great but man. In man there is nothing great but mind."

Southern Seminary dedicated Broadus Memorial Chapel, modeled after the oldest Baptist church in America, in 1999. The colonial-style worship space, accented by the elevated pulpit, memorializes the Broadus preaching tradition in Southern Baptist life. In 2020, the seminary installed a plaque outside the chapel acknowledging Broadus's participation in antebellum slavery.

Archives and Special Collections, James P. Boyce Centennial Library, Southern Baptist Theological Seminary.

Six

SURVIVAL

T HE END OF THE Civil War left Broadus, at thirty-eight, in the ruins of the southern society he had so recently ascended. After enjoying a string of apparently unbroken successes in his early life, he now entered what he would describe as "a long period of struggle and suffering, darkened by the frequently recurring fear of ultimate failure." The prospects of the seminary, closed since 1862, were particularly bleak. Its former supporters "had not a dollar of money." Boyce had suffered his own reversals and would spend the decade patching up his father's estate, paying back some $180,000 in debts. Basil Manly Jr. and William Williams wished to abandon the school for more stable employment, but at a tense faculty meeting in August 1865 Broadus galvanized his colleagues with a personal vow: "Suppose we quietly agree that the Seminary may die, but we'll die first."[1]

Broadus's pact would prove to be the defining commitment of his life, and has since lived on in denominational lore. Viewed through a broader lens, it also illumines how some southern elites grappled with the shame and despair of Confederate defeat. Their dream of a neoclassical southern republic shattered, many leading white southerners now desperately threw themselves into preserving their cultural institutions against the backdrop of Reconstruction poverty and humiliation. This "noble struggle" was essential to the Lost Cause. Broadus looked back proudly on it in 1893:

> We knew . . . that the Southern whites were upon the whole a high-toned people. They had submitted to the arbitrament of war, and would keep their word; but they had not lost all self-respect and self-reliance. They had nothing to be ashamed of in the way they had struggled against overwhelming superiority of

resources. The returned soldiers could talk without fear about the battles they had fought. There was pluck in the people. Most of all, we felt a submissive trust in Providence. Through all the dark years our people had been trying to do their duty according to their light, and multitudes only wanted to know what was their duty now.[2]

Broadus's memory of Reconstruction indicates the pivot made by many southern whites after Appomattox. Disgraced by military defeat, emancipation, and political reconstruction, they could vindicate their honor by displaying the virtues of courage, duty, determination, self-sacrifice, and religious devotion. For Broadus, this meant bending all his ambitions to the task of making the seminary, and the Southern Baptist Convention, live. Indeed, admirers testified of his relentless efforts on behalf of these institutions as though he were still fighting a war: time and again, he "sprang into the breach, seized the standard and commanded courage." "All had been lost," as Gaines Foster observed, "save honor."[3]

→›››✢✤‹‹‹←

Broadus deeply resented Reconstruction. "You brethren at the North think that you have a great deal for which to forgive the South for the four years of war," he grumbled to a Brooklyn audience in 1869. "I will not discuss that. But I tell you, brethren, we of the South have a great deal for which to forgive the North *for the four years since the war.*" He and Boyce initially held out for a return to normalcy when Boyce was elected a delegate to the 1865 South Carolina constitutional convention. Boyce and his fellow antebellum elites attempted to restore prewar social conditions to South Carolina, asserting that the state was still "a white man's government," and passing the infamous Black Codes. Throughout Reconstruction, Broadus longed to see white Democratic control reinstated, believing that "the intelligence and property of the State must control the State government."[4]

But in September 1866, Company H of the 6th Infantry Regiment marched into Greenville to enforce Federal order. The U.S. Congress would overturn the Confederate dream, beginning in March 1867, with the First and Second Reconstruction Acts. Congress nullified all former Confederate state governments (Tennessee excepted) and instituted five military districts in their stead. To re-enter the Union, the rebel states had to open voter polls to all male citizens, elect a new constitutional convention based on universal male suffrage, write new state constitutions approved by Congress, and disband all military organizations. Southern states must also ratify the Fourteenth Amendment, guaranteeing equal protection and due process rights to all citizens, including former slaves, and prohibiting many former Confederate leaders from federal and state offices. Governor James L. Orr fumed that few people in history had "been required to concede more to their conquerors than the people of the South." Delegates at a Black political meeting in Charleston saw it differently. "We ask for no special privileges or peculiar favors," they declared. "We ask only for even-handed Justice, or for the removal of such positive obstructions as past, and recent Legislators have seen fit to throw in our way, and heap upon us."[5]

The 1868 South Carolina constitutional convention, which included seventy-three Black delegates out of 124, produced a progressive new constitution modeled after Ohio's. Henry D. Green of Sumter County sneered that it was "a negro constitution, of a negro government, establishing negro equality." The new constitution gained ratification behind the state's large Black voting bloc, and the Republican Party swept the next state elections. After 1868, seventy-five of the 124 members of the House were Black, as were ten of the thirty-two senators, all Republicans. Blacks would attain greater political power in South Carolina than in any other state—in 1872, Blacks made up a full 61 percent of the state legislature. For Black freedmen, Reconstruction was an era of "intense joy" that carried "a Millennial sense of living at the dawn of a new era." Meanwhile, white South Carolinians bemoaned the state's "Africanization"; for an honor society based on white superiority, the shame could hardly have gone deeper. As Paul Harvey has observed, the phrase "Freedom's Coming" carried very different meanings across the slaveholding South.[6]

In a matter of four years, emancipation, Confederate defeat, and the Reconstruction acts had worked a social revolution in Broadus's white southern world. Almost overnight, planter families and middling gentry like the Broaduses found themselves to be "masters without slaves." The daily domestic sphere was permanently altered, as Lottie Broadus, visiting Locust Grove Plantation in Charlottesville, commented in 1866. Lottie's mother now "has to pay $70 a month for servants' hire. The yankee raiders stripped the farm of hay, straw, corn, ham so that all last summer she had to buy those things on credit, to be paid for by next crop," she wrote. Greenville society had also been turned upside down. "Is it tolerable?" Crawford Toy, considering a move to Greenville in 1868, asked Broadus. "Are negroes and scalawags not worse than elsewhere?" Broadus encouraged Toy to come, though he marveled at the number of former slaves milling about the city, as well as at their transformed behavior. He found some loud and boisterous, some impudent and sassy, while others affected gentility. Broadus recalled one "Greenville Negro" greeting him "with a stiff air": "Good morning, Mr. Broadus." Quickly feeling sheepish, this particular freedmen "caught himself and doffed his hat with a hearty 'Howdy, Marse Jeems,'" as before.[7] If white southern honor before the war had derived largely from mastery, how was Broadus to understand who he was in this strange new world?

Real and rumored Republican corruption further diminished his opinion of Reconstruction. "We have had a most ridiculous, or rather hateful, election canvass for two offices," he told Boyce in 1874. "W. C. Cleveland united 1) family, 2) the Radical leaders, 3) Gower, and 4) whiskey to beat Stradley," he wrote. "They got up the greatest excitement. Free whiskey for a week before the election. He protested in advance against our students voting, and kicked up quite a fuss about it. The ladies at the Cleveland House sat in the porch all day, inviting gentlemen in to drink wine, and sending messengers to negro men that they wanted to see them, etc. I heard Miss Cleveland do so as I was passing myself. Carriages were sent to bring negroes to the polls (rainy day)."[8] White Democrats like Broadus and Boyce fumed helplessly. Such stories fueled the tragic narrative of Reconstruction that lived on in Lost Cause memory for generations.

Many upcountry whites in South Carolina reacted with violence. Vigilante terrorists patrolled the countryside, intimidated Black families, and burned Black churches and schoolhouses. "I had laid out in the woods for months," recalled one South Carolina freedmen, "like I was a dromedary or a hog or a cow afraid to go in to the house; that was hard, I think, for poor negroes." The killing of a Black man in a fight with a white man on July 15, 1866, touched off a riot in Greenville that resulted in the burning of two buildings. Manly complained at the unrest that boiled over "whenever any low fellow of either color chooses to provoke or practice violence." In 1871, Boyce told Broadus of a "fracas" in Newberry that involved "about seven or eight hundred men arranged on both sides," though it "was quieted by the Negroes promising to make no more disturbances." Boyce blamed the trouble on South Carolina's carpetbag governor, Robert Scott of Ohio, and his armed militia of former Union officers and freed Blacks. "Our men are lending every effort to keep our side quiet, and advising to submit to all, rather than bring such calamity," he added.[9]

Broadus's friend E. T. Winkler, now pastoring in Georgia, defended vigilante tactics. "In a state of society where there is no law, and where men must form temporary organizations for the redress of intolerable grievances and the maintenance of social order, justice itself is perverted by attacks on these organizations," Winkler said. But Boyce, Broadus, and other genteel southerners ("our men") tended to condemn racial violence as the activity of the lower classes, who had never learned the aristocratic white man's duty to care for his Black neighbor. Broadus once administered a "scathing rebuke" to young church members when he learned they were mixed up with the Ku Klux Klan. "He grew eloquent over the woes already inflicted by the organization, and spoke with withering power of the criminality of lawlessness and of the just retribution that was sure to come," recalled H. P. Griffith.[10] Racial violence was the "white trash" way; Broadus believed in a more gentlemanly path for restoring white southern rule.

—»»❖❖«« —

The seminary reopened on November 1, 1865, with an enrollment of seven students. (The Presbyterian Columbia Theological Seminary had been reduced from over sixty students to five.) Broadus had only two in his homiletics course, with one dropping out mid-term. "Made my last lecture in homiletics to-day," he wrote to Lottie on April 17. "Quite possible that it will be the *last* indeed." With the seminary barely meeting operating expenses, Boyce wrote letters, published newspaper articles, dispatched agents, and traveled widely to raise funds in person. His sister wept in her pew at Charleston's fine Citadel Square Baptist Church to hear her once-proud brother making another pitiful appeal for money. "I have begged for this Seminary as I would not beg for myself if I were starving," he would write. Boyce often borrowed at his own risk to make payroll. Professors made do on a reduced salary of $1,000 a year immediately after the war, though this was often behind. At the end of 1871, Boyce could not even scrape this together, and Broadus went unpaid for twelve months.[11] Faculty would again draw no salary during a national depression from July 1873 to January 1874.

The Broaduses purchased groceries and necessities in Greenville on twelve months' credit. "I conclude not to order any more books," Broadus sighed in early 1866, "nor to buy anything I can do without, until I get more money, or see a brighter prospect for the country." He found himself doing "the work of two or three men on half the salary of one man, with that salary in arrears and no certainty of ever receiving it." Constant sickness added to his mounting despondency. "I am quite sick, and utterly broken in spirits—intermittent fever—very weak," he told a friend in 1866: "Doctor Earle says it will take several weeks before I can do anything. I am specially dispirited at being utterly unable to obtain any money in my present condition. It is impossible for an honest man to live in town without money all the time. How much more when he is prostrate on his bed. If any of those who owe me and who, I know, find it exceedingly hard to pay anything, could understand my present state of need and mortification, they would feel like making most earnest effort to pay me something." Having sipped so long from the goblet of popularity and prosperity, the cup of poverty and shame now made for bitter drinking.[12]

Opportunities abounded for Broadus to escape the disgrace of Reconstruction Greenville. Richmond College offered him its presidency in 1866, which would bring him home to Virginia and apparently raise his salary by as much as $5,000. His siblings wondered at Broadus's rejection of such an offer, but it was only one of many he would turn down over the next decade. Both the First and Second Baptist Churches in Richmond also offered him a more comfortable living in a prestigious city pastorate, as did Baltimore's wealthy Eutaw Place Baptist Church. Brown University, Washington College, Vassar, Newton, Crozer Seminary, and Wake Forest all sought Broadus in these years. "Brilliant proposals are made in different directions," he admitted in 1868, "but I have no thought of anything else than adhering to the Seminary, though the salary is not increased, and I shall have hard work to live."[13]

By 1868, the seminary's most obvious source of relief was also the most hateful: soliciting funds from wealthy northern Baptists. As Charles Regan Wilson has noted, accepting northern benefaction was a sore subject in the war-ravaged South. Southern loyalists warned their brethren of becoming like their Yankee conquerors: materialistic, unprincipled, valuing efficiency and profit over relationships and virtue. Broadus and his friends not only felt a personal "repugnance" at going hat-in-hand to the Yankees, they knew that it risked alienating their Southern Baptist constituents. As William Williams observed, "We might gain some little perhaps by going north for aid, but would probably lose more by the feeling which would be excited among the strong southern men that the seminary was too much inclined northwards."[14]

In the end, they chose survival. "I shall not gain half so much by any other help you can give as I shall if you go to New York and increase your acquaintance there," Boyce wrote to Broadus. "Get acquainted with all you can. Keep lists, find out desirable men, and we shall be greatly helped in our New York campaign." Broadus obeyed. Among his marks was one "Col. Morgan L. Smith" of Newark, New Jersey, a "fine looking gentleman, slightly lame." Broadus met Smith in Brooklyn and spent hours talking with him about the seminary over a meal. Though "a native of Poughkeepsie," Smith had spent thirty years in Texas and was "a red-hot Democrat and Southern sympathizer." Smith "still has $250,000 he says, besides 18,000 acres in Texas," Broadus told Boyce. Smith indicated to Broadus that he might divide a gift of $100,000 between the seminary and Madison University. "Much of his talk evidently gas, but if he comes to Greenville, *look after him*," Broadus instructed. "Tell the other Professors, particularly. Let there be no failure to show him attention." Broadus became an expert in finding the money.[15]

He began spending extended time in the north. In the summer of 1870, he accepted a summer pulpit assignment in affluent North Orange, New Jersey. "I was very cordially received at Orange, and handsomely paid," he wrote. "They invited me to supply their pulpit for 2 or 3 months, at $150 a month, and to stay in the families of three of the members, but to have no duties but preaching on Sunday." The pleasant arrangement allowed Broadus to earn desperately needed income for his family while making fundraising connections for the seminary. He resisted the North Orange Baptists' pleas to settle permanently, but he would spend the next twenty summers there. By 1876, the church was sending the seminary $1,200 a year, and Broadus was bending over backward to "keep them friendly." "I think it is in the interest of the Seminary that I should do anything they request," he told Boyce.[16]

Playing both sides of the Mason-Dixon was tricky business. If some white southerners recoiled at accepting northern money, some northern donors were "afraid of being considered southern sympathizers." Speeches made up north required a deft touch: no "truckling to or fawning upon the North" could be tolerated. And some invitations must not even be considered. Boyce bristled when the American Bible Union requested a speech from Broadus; its leader had commented after the war "that he believed that every rebel who did not repent specifically of his sin of rebellion (that particular sin) would go to hell." Boyce was also sensitive to alienating northern Baptist institutions (and their wealthy supporters) by invading their territory. He advised Broadus to decline an invitation to speak in Bloomington, Illinois, for example. "We have to be careful of Illinois as well as the South," Boyce wrote. "I have had several intimations from Ohio and Indiana of help and cooperation with us. And we will expect opposition in Chicago and Rochester if we are not prudent." Broadus and Boyce mastered the delicate footwork of postwar fundraising. "It will pay," Broadus said simply of going to New York. With southern charm and Yankee shrewdness, they walked the thin line of soliciting northern funds without surrendering the seminary's honor.[17]

Though he was happy to collect northern Baptist money, Broadus opposed their overtures for denominational reunion. In 1868, the Home Mission Society invited him to speak in New York on "The Religious Conditions and Wants of the South." The HMS had offended Broadus and other white Southern Baptists by sending missionaries into the South in 1864, and by devoting extensive resources to ministry with former slaves. Broadus urged the Society to respect Southern Baptist institutions, and he personally reissued the Convention's request for the HMS to conduct its work in the region through the boards of the SBC. Broadus preached peace between the sections, yet complained of being "prayed at" and "cursed" in northern Baptist gatherings as a former Confederate. "Unless we acknowledge ourselves to have been criminals, and ask forgiveness and absolution from these men, and admit their superiority, wisdom, and integrity, they refuse to recognize us as equals and fellow laborers in the Kingdom of Christ," he wrote in the *Religious Herald*. Formal reunification would be a sham, for hearts would still "throb with suspicion and dislike and indignation." Worst of all, a national denomination must require subjugation to northern beliefs and ways. "Under Yankee rule, we might not expect to worship God but according to Yankee faith," he warned. Political reconstruction might be unavoidable, but religious reconstruction must be resisted at all costs.[18]

For Broadus, the most loathsome article of "Yankee faith" was, of course, racial egalitarianism. He "distinctly and strongly" asserted "the folly and wrong of trying to bring about social equality between white and black." Many white southerners immediately abandoned their prewar paternalism toward Blacks: if they could not control Black behavior, they wanted total separation. Manly considered the presence of so many freedmen to be an "incubus and plague" on Greenville, and judged that the town would be a better place to live if it "could be cleared of negroes," but Broadus maintained his paternal outlook. In Joel Williamson's framework, he was a "conservative" who never questioned Black inferiority yet also saw their potential for uplift.[19]

Broadus promoted the establishment of "Colored Sunday Schools," considering it "more than ever important that the colored people should be brought under the influence of morality and religion, and that they should become able to read for themselves the blessed Word of salvation." He insisted that white Southerners bore the responsibility to equip former slaves for life in southern society, and criticized northern Baptists for presuming to understand and care for them more. "No other persons can possibly reach them on so large a scale as the whites among whom they live, and no other are likely to have so much influence with them, especially in the wide country districts where they are mainly found," he argued in 1866. "We are solemnly bound to use this influence for their highest good; and we may increase it by kindly and judicious efforts to promote their educational and religious welfare." Broadus's motives involved a complicated mixture of Christian love and unquestionable racism, of genuine compassion and proud defiance of northern influence, of a desire to fulfill Christ's Great Commission and the deposed white aristocrat's drive to prove he still belonged to the master class. This complexity is instructive of how many nineteenth-century southerners blended southern honor culture with evangelicalism, rather than abandoning one for the other.[20]

--»»✢✤«««-

Broadus kept up his four rural pastorates after the war. Most of the congregations were small, unglamorous, and required lengthy trips into the country, one as far as seventy miles from Greenville. Conditions were primitive. One frigid Sunday morning in February, church members dragged benches outside and built a fire. A dozen worshipers huddled near the flame while Broadus, open Bible in lap, preached from his own bench. Broadus advised his students to "take your best sermons to the country," but not all listeners appreciated his polished discourses. One woman declared she "had rather hear dear old Uncle Toll give out one verse of a hime than to hear that 'ar Greenville preacher go through a whole sarmon."[21]

Rural pastoral ministry did as little for Broadus's bankbook as for his vanity. He received $200 for a year's labor at Bethel. Often, the churches had no money at all. Eliza Broadus remembered her father's buggy rolling home with "bacon, milk, eggs and butter, and mighty good sweet potatoes. Wagon-loads of provisions and feed for the horse and cow came to us from time to time." To help with his travels, the Bethel church provided Broadus a buggy and umbrella, and the Cedar Grove church furnished a horse. The women of one congregation wove him "a full suit of jeans," which he wore often.[22]

Broadus gave his heart to these remote Baptist churches. Eliza, who often accompanied her father into the country, recalled how seriously he took their spiritual capacities. He made special sermonic appeals to the children, held Saturday night home prayer meetings, and led the Bethel Baptists to read through the entire Bible in a year. He urged his people, especially men, to pray in public and at home. He admonished H. P. Griffith to "Kneel down with your wife every night, and teach your little girl to be still while you lift up your heart to God," and outlined a simple prayer for him to use. "He did all this with such charming tact, and yet he was so simple and earnest and affectionate, that I was impressed for a lifetime," Griffith wrote. Absentee church members received a home visit and a firm reminder of their Christian duty. A young woman in his Bible class opened a letter to find Broadus pleading with her to repent and be saved without delay. "Is it any harm for me to express the earnest desire that you should become a Christian, and *now*?" he wrote.[23]

In May 1868, seminary trustees formally requested that Broadus "dissolve his pastoral relations, in view of the state of his health." He knew they were right. "What can I say?" he wrote to A. B. Woodruff. "I can hardly bear the thought, but it must be so. I can no longer do both a professor's and a pastor's work, and everything must bend to the Seminary. For it I left my position [in Charlottesville], which was to me the most attractive pastorate in the country." Woodruff called the day Broadus resigned "one of the saddest days our church ever experienced. He was beloved by all, and in fact we could hardly exist without him." As his national fame grew, Broadus would miss the simplicity of the rural pastorate. "No man is fit to be a theological professor who would not really prefer to be a pastor," he asserted. Looking back in 1889, he admitted to "always feeling for these thirty years, that in abandoning the pastorate to guide the studies of others I was giving up the minister's better part. I envy those who are most directly concerned with saving souls."[24]

→>>❖❖<<←

But even after jettisoning his pastorates, Broadus's health still declined. By 1869, he wondered if he could continue teaching under any conditions. He commented frequently on his fragile digestive system, sensitivity to certain foods, and recurring bouts of diarrhea. In May 1870, he celebrated that he was up to 130 pounds. With friends murmuring that he could not live much longer, Boyce intervened. First, he hired Broadus's protege Crawford Toy to relieve the faculty workload in 1869. Then, in the spring of 1870, Boyce convinced the seminary's Board of Trustees to send Broadus on a year-long, all-expenses-paid world tour. The seminary would still pay Broadus's salary, and Boyce volunteered to teach his English New Testament class. The Board accepted Boyce's proposal "unanimously" and "with great cordiality."[25]

It was an extravagant gift under any circumstance, but Broadus felt he could hardly accept it during Reconstruction. "Our struggling Seminary needs all that can be obtained," he protested. Besides, how would it look to the average Southern Baptist, who knew the "Grand Tour" to be a tradition for the South's gentlemanly elites? Surely "the masses could not understand the propriety of indulging me in an expensive luxury." Furthermore, how could he leave Lottie, now "hopelessly an invalid"? But when Lottie urged Broadus to go (she was happy to flee Greenville and spend the year at Locust Grove), he relented. Broadus's wealthy friend James Thomas of Richmond arranged for his two daughters, Laura and Bettie, with a European tour of their own already scheduled, to accompany him. Along the way, Broadus would pen his "Recollections of Travel" for the *Religious Herald*. It was an opportunity few Southern Baptists could imagine. Robert E. Lee himself sent his prayers that the Grand Tour would "entirely restore your health, and that you will return renovated in strength and vigor, to gladden the hearts of your many friends."[26]

The party landed at Queenstown, Ireland (known as Cobh since 1920) on August 5, 1870. Weakened by a seasick voyage (including a violent "sacrifice to Neptune" over the side of the ship), Broadus was initially unfit to leave his room, much less to traverse Europe. A rough carriage ride to Dublin left him "just utterly broken down." He remained laid up in a hotel for ten days "with one of my bilious attacks." Disappointed by his confinement, he nonetheless enjoyed the attentions of Laura and Bettie Thomas—"full of kindness and affection," and "quite skillful in nursing."[27] Once he recovered, Broadus squired the young ladies around Ireland, including stops at Blarney Castle and the Lakes of Killarney. By the end of August, they were in Liverpool.

He felt stronger in England, where he mixed with a number of eminent Christian ministers and academics. He stayed with the distinguished Church of England bishop and theologian Charles John Ellicott. Broadus charmed Ellicott's family with his southern manners and introduced them to the pleasures of eating raw tomatoes. One of Ellicott's houseguests "had never before seen a slaveholder," Broadus noted. The guest "talked quite innocently about having thought they were all fierce-looking," he wrote home, "and I had much fun joking with her." He cheerfully debated the bishop over Greek translations, the doctrine of election, and infant baptism. Ellicott seemed to enjoy the give-and-take, and later introduced Broadus to other leading Anglican scholars. These included the New Testament commentator J. B. Lightfoot and the linguists Brooke Foss Westcott and Fenton John Anthony Hort, then working on their famous critical edition of the Greek New Testament. Broadus also received a cordial reception from the London Baptist Association, which invited him to preach. He particularly relished meeting thirty-six-year-old Charles Haddon Spurgeon, then the most celebrated preacher in the English-speaking world. Spurgeon apparently considered Broadus "the greatest of living preachers."[28]

After two months in England and Scotland, Broadus and his female companions traveled through the Netherlands and into Germany, and then passed a month in Italy. Western Europe allowed Broadus to give full vent to his artistic soul. He filled his letters with praise for architecture, paintings, music, and literary works. "Its grandeur, beauty, sublimity, thrilled and awed me," he wrote of the York Minster Cathedral. He gazed upon the quiet grace of the *Venus de Medici* in Florence, and drank in the great paintings in Antwerp, especially moved by Peter Paul Rubens's portrayals of Christ's Passion. In Munich, Broadus took in a performance of Mozart's *Magic Flute,* claiming that it "contains a larger amount of exquisite music than I ever before heard in one evening." Few experiences left Broadus as giddy as England's great literary sites and libraries. "I feel quite powerless to describe the Shakespeare localities, or to tell aught of the feelings awakened by seeing them," he wrote to Lottie.[29] His Grand Tour had set an aesthetic feast before Broadus; through his vivid descriptions in the *Religious Herald,* he educated the sensibilities of thousands of Southern Baptists.

In February, Broadus left the young ladies with friends in Florence and headed east for a three-month tour of Egypt, Palestine, Greece, and Asia Minor. Here, the pages of his Bible came alive with fresh color and power. He "clapped my hands and laughed and sang" at the sight of Egypt's pyramids. He watched a storm gather on the Sea of Galilee and witnessed a full-scale Middle-Eastern wedding. He wandered Jerusalem, pausing frequently to read pertinent selections of the New Testament; though he found the Holy City a squalid place, he discovered that "by an effort of imagination" he could "sweep away these disagreeable actualities and reproduce what was once there." After leaving Palestine, Broadus retraced the missionary journeys of Paul through Asia Minor. In Athens, he analyzed the oratorical dynamics of Paul's sermon at the Areopagus. Sailing the Isthmus past the Ionian islands, he caught a sight of Corinth before passing two pleasant days in Corfu. When he received the opportunity to add Germany and Switzerland to the itinerary of his return voyage, Boyce urged him to take it. "You must not hurry home," Boyce insisted, promising to make the necessary financial arrangements. Broadus happily accepted. By June he was in Paris, and by late July home in Virginia. "I feel that it really has been a pleasant and profitable trip," he declared.[30]

Broadus's Grand Tour allowed him to experience more of the world than virtually any of his Southern Baptist contemporaries. He picked blue bells for Lottie in the fields of Bannockburn, rode gondolas through Venice, and watched the setting sun from a stone bridge in Florence. Moonlit Athens cast a spell over him, having wandered through ancient Greece in his imagination a thousand times before. He wondered at the grandeur of the Parthenon—"the most perfectly beautiful, the most thoroughly satisfying, of all the artistic creations of man." The sites inspired new exertions. He walked up the cone of Mount Vesuvius in six inches of snow and clambered to the top of an Egyptian pyramid, though the latter climb so exhausted him that he had to be carried once he reached the bottom.[31]

The trip also afforded Broadus a range of worship experiences unimagined by most Southern Baptists. He attended a Coptic church gathering in Cairo, and a high Roman Catholic Mass for the birth of a German prince in Dresden. He worshipped at the Greek Orthodox convent Mar Saba—"Now we are in the Middle Ages," he whispered as the door bolted shut behind him. He witnessed a baptism and shared the Lord's Supper with the believers of a newly constituted "Apostolical Church" in Rome. But he felt most at home in Spurgeon's Baptist Metropolitan Tabernacle, where he reported that "The whole thing—house, congregation, order, worship, preaching, was as nearly up to my ideal as I ever expect to see in this life." Broadus's global travels in 1870 and 1871 had broadened his view of the world and, through his published correspondence, enhanced his reputation as Southern Baptists' leading sophisticate.[32]

Broadus expressed his appreciation to Boyce at the 1872 meeting of the Southern Baptist Convention. After messengers elected Boyce president, Broadus presented his friend with a mallet of balsam and olive wood, purchased in Jerusalem. Subsequent convention presidents would conduct business with the same gavel, a symbol of Boyce and Broadus's friendship and of the Convention's founding era, for generations. In 2021, Convention president J. D. Greear retired the gavel because of Broadus's association with slaveholding. Back in Greenville, Broadus pledged "neither to wear out nor to rust out, but to make the lame horse pay for his grazing by as many years as possible of quiet work."[33]

By 1868, Broadus knew the seminary must leave Greenville to survive. Yet a web of factors complicated the move. The location must appeal to the diverse tastes, demands, and prejudices of all Southern Baptists. He suggested Lynchburg, Virginia, to Boyce. It would be "nearer to every part of our field, except South Carolina and lower Georgia, and would *feel much* nearer to Alabama and Mississippi because on the through line to New York," he reasoned. Besides, Lynchburg would "Seem much nearer to Gulf States than Baltimore, and more distinctively Southern. We should keep our hold on the Atlantic States, and get some nearer to the West. We should not seem (to other States) identified with distinctively *Virginia* operations, as would be the case at Richmond. Town large enough for work, and some literary advantages. In the world and in a white man's country." In August 1872, trustees settled on the burgeoning New South city of Louisville, Kentucky. The northerly migration rankled some; E. T. Winkler complained that "the removal of our seminary from Greenville to Louisville rendered it a general rather than a Southern institution." Yet Louisville was a thriving railroad town, easily accessible to the rest of the South, and home to a large, prosperous Baptist population. Once Southern Baptists and Kentucky Baptists endorsed the plan in the spring of 1873, Boyce moved to Louisville to raise the required $500,000 endowment before relocating.[34]

Almost immediately, the financial crisis of railroad financier Jay Cooke set off a national economic depression. Boyce begged for money all over Kentucky. He made personal calls to prominent Baptists, issued appeals in the *Western Recorder* newspaper, and wrote as many as 180 letters a day. "My arm at times I can hardly move," he told Broadus. He accepted an interim pastorate at wealthy Walnut Street Baptist Church "in order to get in that congregation an influence for my work, and also a position before the community in Louisville." Broadus thought the move "very judicious," and advised Boyce to obtain "a great hold" upon the people through his earnest preaching and pastoral work. Under intense strain, the once robust Boyce now developed numerous physical ailments. These included rheumatic gout that required crutches, and "gravel," or kidney stones, that confined him to bed for days. "By living for the Seminary you will, I am right confident, save it; by dying for it you inevitably kill it—buried in your grave," Broadus cautioned. "So take care."[35]

Back in Greenville, Broadus oversaw seminary operations during the term. He devoted his summers to frantic fundraising. Broadus found the constant arm-twisting to be both "laborious" and "embarrassing." "It makes my head ache to think of it," he complained. Yet he dutifully went wherever Boyce sent him. When classes dismissed in May 1874, Broadus traveled to Jefferson, Texas, for the Southern Baptist Convention, where he and the faculty secured pledges totaling $30,000. Then it was off to Washington, to address the Jubilee meeting of the American Baptist Publication Society. His impromptu, six-minute speech for the seminary set off "overwhelming applause" and a spontaneous hat collection, with pledges amounting to $10,000. Broadus then whisked up the coast to his patrons in Orange, New Jersey, to dedicate their new seven hundred-seat church building before plunging back down to Oxford, Mississippi, for the state Baptist meetings. Finally, he accompanied Boyce on a grueling, forty-day campaign in Kentucky. He preached six days a week, twice on Sundays, and made home visits to prospective donors, which often kept him up until midnight. Two years later,

Broadus could still "feel in every nerve" the strain of that summer campaign, yet it yielded enough support to convince him that the endowment was possible.[36]

During Reconstruction, Boyce spoke repeatedly of resigning, or of closing the seminary, but Broadus would never hear of it. "Somehow, somehow, you are bound to succeed," he wrote in a typical letter. "The Seminary is a necessity. Our best brethren want it. God has blessed it thus far. It is your own offspring. You have kept it alive since the war,—fed it with almost your own heart's blood. It must succeed, somehow, and you are the man that must make it succeed." Their correspondence in the early 1870s shows Boyce and Broadus exchanging fund-raising strategies, preaching advice, spiritual admonition, denominational gossip, Bible commentaries, and even good whiskey (for medicinal purposes). Both grew discouraged, but never at the same time.[37]

-->>>❖❖<<<--

Lottie Broadus believed her husband's commitment to the seminary was killing him. "I feel distressed that you cannot stop and allow yourself more rest. It makes me tired just to think how much you are going all the time," she wrote in 1871. "Well! I suppose it is fated that you are to wear yourself out anyhow and I'd as well learn to submit to the idea." She felt slighted by his long absences. From May to July 1876, for instance, he traveled to Boston, Brooklyn, Buffalo, Philadelphia, Culpeper, Virginia, and Orange, New Jersey. On some occasions, Lottie wished he would exchange the seminary for "a city pastorate, a fine residence, hosts of servants and unbroken repose." On an 1866 trip back to Charlottesville, she declared that "the atmosphere is so beautifully clear, & bright—so pure & sweet—as I breathe it. There *is* a great difference between this & Greenville." Lottie daydreamed of recovering her antebellum station, but she knew Broadus would not leave his post. "You pledged yourself to the seminary and to Dr. Boyce," she sighed.[38]

Grief and sickness compounded her trouble. Lottie had lost two children since the war, eighteen-month-old Ellie in 1866, and sixteen-day-old Julia Duvall in 1869. As early as 1870, Broadus described Lottie as an "invalid," and he routinely referred to her as "feeble" and "nervous" after that. In August 1880, she weighed only ninety-six pounds. "In despair about my own health," she complained in 1871. "In despair about my children, they will do wrong, and I can never do my duty toward them. In despair about my work, and about what people expect of me. I want to rest, and I can't. And can not have the comfort of seeing that you get any rest either." She occasionally took her own retreats without her husband. An 1873 letter from Eliza to Broadus, written from Locust Grove, indicated something of the relief that Lottie found away from Greenville. She mentioned her stepmother laughing with a male caller in the parlor, "having a gay time," while Sam reported that "some unmarried gentleman walked with her at the springs." From Rawley Springs in 1873, Lottie confessed her desire to stay several weeks longer, and that she did "tremble and almost faint when I think of all the work that is to be done" back in Greenville. Broadus soothed her by letter. "I love you, dear wife, always, everywhere I love you," he wrote from Mobile. "Try to bear patiently the ills we cannot cure, and God be gracious to us both."[39]

Torn between his family and the seminary, Broadus tried to curb his travel schedule, but he felt indebted to Boyce. "I cannot forget that Boyce got me my house, Boyce sent me to Europe, and this that I am doing now is not merely work for the Seminary, but a personal help and kindness to him," he explained to an exasperated Lottie. Supplementing family income required weekend travel to supply city pulpits; he cobbled together the rest of their living through visiting lecture series and newspaper articles. He realized that his family had to make "great and bitter sacrifices ... for this Seminary enterprise," and that easier roads were available. He sometimes expressed his own desire to rest and write, "instead of wearing out what is left of me in fatiguing journeys and exciting Conventions and collecting campaigns in June," he confessed from a train car. "But it seems to be my duty, and Providence is wiser than I am."[40]

When he could be home, Broadus determined to make it a happy place. By 1875, Eliza was now twenty-five and Annie Harrison twenty-two. Of his children with Lottie, Samuel was now fifteen, Carrie, twelve, Alice, eight, Ella Thomas, age three, and Boyce had arrived just the year before (the name was not in fact settled until "baby Broadus" was four; Lottie had wanted to call him John Albert). Broadus's stepmother, Eliza Somerville Broadus, also lived with them until her death in 1877. At Broadus's request, the children began each day by tapping on his door, one after another, and announcing, "7 o'clock, papa." At the breakfast table, he apprised them of world affairs from the newspaper and engaged each in the family conversation. He then read from the Bible and led them in morning prayers, and heard them recite the hymns he had assigned. It gratified Broadus in 1873 when Annie and Sam made public professions of faith in Christ. "They seem to be thoroughly in earnest, and I trust they are truly renewed," he wrote to his sister Martha.[41]

Broadus cultivated both learning and industry in his children. They read aloud to one another constantly, including poetry, Shakespearean plays, biographies, and novels. In the evenings, they sat by his study table to learn their lessons while he wrote, though he frequently paused to instruct or to recommend a book. Broadus paid for a variety of private lessons for them when he could, and attempted to pass on his love of flowers. "We children would have pinks in our beds and vie with each other in having one to put in his buttonhole when he went to class, and he was never too absorbed in his work to admire the beauty of a rose and inhale its fragrance," Eliza remembered. Broadus took them on his walks for exercise, had them carry in the firewood he sawed, and sought their help in his vegetable garden. He also played with them, especially relishing family croquet games. He often took a child or two on his trips; when he could not, he wrote affectionate and interested letters to each of them.[42]

The Christmas holiday became sacred to the Broadus children. "Christmas Day was the one morning of the year when we were sure to have our busy father to ourselves," recalled Alice. "It was a leisurely day at home, reciting poems and distributing gifts—always some book, chosen with especial care." Watching him thoughtfully brush his hair in the mirror one morning, Alice recalled thinking, "'I must be better than I have been, with him for a father. . . .' We always felt for him a reverence and even a sort of awe that we compared instinctively to living 'in the fear of God.'"[43]

→»✢✢«←

The national experiment of Reconstruction officially ended with the election of Confederate war hero Wade Hampton as governor of South Carolina. Hampton "embodied both the ideology of the Lost Cause and the memory of the Lost Eden, the Old South." White Democrats framed his fall 1876 campaign as a battle between good and evil, leading revival-style services for his election across the state under the banner of "Hampton or Hell!" On election day, Greenville County went for Hampton and the Democratic ticket by a majority of 2,446 votes. Seminary student Jacob Dill recalled the excitement, and the corruption, of the event, as seminary students received ample opportunity to cast illegal votes. Along with voter fraud, the Democratic Party secured victory by organizing paramilitary "Red Shirts" and rifle clubs to suppress the Black vote—perhaps as many as thirty thousand white men served under arms. Red Shirts assassinated at least 150 Black leaders in the campaign. Normally averse to such tactics, Broadus was by now so eager to reverse Reconstruction that he overlooked the violence and praised the self-control of "our people."[44]

White Greenville went wild at the news of Hampton's victory. "We Seminary boys did join most lustily in the jollification," Dill recalled. For Broadus and his fellow white South Carolinians, it meant nothing less than the South's "Redemption," an event vested with deep religious meaning. Accordingly, Greenville's city dignitaries ushered Broadus to the platform to consecrate the evening's events amid cannon fire. Broadus's opening words hushed the crowds: "Thank God! Thank God! Thank God!" he cried. For Black southerners, Hampton's election held a different meaning. "The whole South—every state in the South—had got into the hands of the very men that held us as slaves," remarked one Louisiana freedman. In a later generation, W. E. B. Du Bois summed up the situation: "the slave went free, stood a brief moment in the sun, then moved back again toward slavery." Despite his own immense gratification at Hampton's election, Broadus would not remain in South Carolina to enjoy the return to white home rule. In May of 1877, the trustees voted to move the seminary to Louisville at once.[45]

Seven

THE LOSS OF A JEWEL

I N THE FALL OF 1876, Alvah Hovey solicited John Broadus's scholarly advice from Newton Centre, Massachusetts. The American Baptist Publication Society had recently named Hovey general editor of the American Commentary Series on the New Testament, and he had already asked Broadus, a longtime friend, to contribute the volume on Matthew. Now Hovey needed to identify competent Baptist academics for the other books in the series. For Broadus, one name instantly stood out: Crawford Howell Toy. As an Old Testament specialist, Toy seemed an odd fit for a New Testament commentary, but Broadus knew he could persuade him to write outside of his field; Toy's work would be superior to anything that any other Baptist could do. "He would do it well, be sure—not so juicy as some, but clear, rigorous, sound," he wrote. Toy was that rarest of gems in Baptist life: a first-rate, German-trained *scholar.* Even better, he hailed from Norfolk, Virginia, and had marched with the 53rd Georgia Infantry Regiment to Gettysburg. Broadus wanted the series to get "a wide circulation at the South, where Baptists are so numerous, and Baptist ministers so generally need instruction," and Toy's name would help. "If you include only Manly and myself, two men out of 12, it will not do so much as I could wish in exciting local interest. But our people believe in Toy, as a great scholar, and he deserves it."[1]

Clearly, Broadus believed in Toy, too. He epitomized the professionalism, scholarly rigor, and southern gentility that Broadus wished to promote among Southern Baptists. He often boasted that his fellow Virginian, as much a younger brother as colleague, was "the jewel of our learning" and "the pride of the seminary." Yet, less than three years after lauding Toy to Hovey, he tearfully consented to Toy's dismissal from the seminary faculty. By the fall of 1879, he was discouraging Hovey from contracting Toy to write any Bible commentaries.[2]

Toy's departure from the seminary was one of the most painful and consequential episodes of Broadus's life. It sparked a major denominational controversy, briefly cast a shadow over his own reputation, and strained the limits of his vision of a learned Southern Baptist ministry. As much as any single event, the Toy affair captured Broadus's suspension between tradition and modernity.

→»»✣✥«←

The lives of John Albert Broadus and Crawford Howell Toy had been closely intertwined for fifteen years when Boyce hired the thirty-three-year-old Toy as professor of Old Testament and Hebrew in 1869. Broadus had become Toy's mentor in the younger man's student days at the University of Virginia. After Toy professed faith during a revival at Broadus's Charlottesville Baptist Church, Broadus baptized Toy and then acted as his intimate spiritual counselor. Toy taught at Broadus's Albemarle Female Institute until a Broadus sermon in February 1859 inspired him to become a missionary, and Broadus delivered the charge at Toy's ordination service. Toy then followed Broadus to Greenville, where he enrolled in the seminary's inaugural class to prepare for mission work in Japan. During his single year at the seminary, Toy lived with Broadus. "Toy is among the foremost scholars I have ever known of his years, and an uncommonly conscientious and devoted man," Broadus wrote in 1860.[3]

At the outbreak of the Civil War, Toy enlisted in the Confederate Army as an infantryman and chaplain to the 53rd Georgia Infantry Regiment. He was captured at Gettysburg and spent a year imprisoned at Fort McHenry, where he reportedly occupied himself by studying Arabic and teaching Italian to fellow inmates. After the war, Toy settled on an academic career. He followed Broadus's encouragement and traveled to Germany to complete his studies. At his departure, Broadus praised Toy in the *Religious Herald* as "one of the foremost young scholars of America, and if he lives twenty years longer, will have few equals in the land in point of real, solid learning." Toy studied Semitic languages at the University of Berlin from 1866–1868. Broadus exchanged regular letters with Toy until he successfully drew him back to teach at the seminary. He saw in Toy the perfect partner in raising up a learned Southern Baptist ministry.[4]

The two scholars undertook their task in a day of rising skepticism regarding the Bible's authority and truthfulness. The emergence of a modern scientific worldview had rendered the Bible's accounts of miraculous and supernatural events increasingly implausible to many rational Americans. Charles Lyell's *Principles of Geology* (1837) declared the earth to be much older than previously believed, and Charles Darwin's *Origin of Species* (1859) cast further doubt on the Bible's doctrine of creation. A new "historical consciousness" was also corroding American confidence in the Bible. Historian Grant Wacker explains "historicism" as the belief that a culture's "ideas, values and institutions of every sort are *wholly* conditioned by the historical setting in which they exist." In other words, "the meaning of events is given not from outside history, not anterior to and independent of the process, but forged wholly within the process." Historicism thus probed the historic and cultural contexts that produced the texts of Scripture, rather than simply reverencing the Bible as God's direct revelation to humanity. Readers informed by modern historicism found in the Bible many ideas that they believed to have been conditioned by the times and circumstances of their composition, ideas that they thought were no longer relevant in the modern world. Historians Mark Noll and Molly Oshatz have shown that antebellum slavery debates, in which antislavery proponents argued that Christian ethics had advanced since the first-century world of the New Testament, accelerated historicist thinking in America.[5]

Within this milieu, German higher criticism offered a compelling solution. Building on the work of eighteenth-century theologian Friedrich Schleiermacher, German biblical scholars of the Tubingen School, including David Friedrich Strauss and Ludwig Feuerbach, endeavored to analyze the Bible historically, eschewing the *a priori* theological assumptions that had traditionally controlled biblical studies. These higher critics assumed all biblical texts to be historically bound—written by human beings at a particular moment in time, in a specific place, and out of a certain set of human motivations. They also employed modern scientific and literary techniques to uncover these historical realties. Some of their conclusions alarmed traditional Protestants: that the Pentateuch was written not by Moses but by a later composite of editors, that the Creation account was a myth, and that the Bible contained numerous historical and factual errors, to name a few. At the same time, many higher critics argued that the Bible, while a flawed, time-bound document, nevertheless contained timeless spiritual insights for the modern world. Rational men and women could thus distill from the Bible's fantastical accounts and outmoded ideas an enduring religious message for daily life. Rather than destroying confidence in the Bible, advocates of this "new theology," eventually termed "liberal theology," viewed the historical-critical approach as the key to preserving the Bible's relevance and respectability in the nineteenth century.[6]

By the 1860s, northern Baptist educators had begun interacting extensively with German higher criticism. Newton Theological Institute professors Irah Chase, Barnas Sears, and Horatio B. Hackett had all studied in Germany, and each advocated for a "scientific study of the Scriptures" in their classrooms. Ezekiel G. Robinson, future president of Brown University, wielded tremendous influence over a generation of Baptist ministers in the mid-nineteenth century as a professor at Rochester Seminary, where he promoted a more progressive approach to biblical interpretation. Under the influence of these educators, dozens of northern Baptist ministers were questioning traditional theological methods during the 1870s.[7]

As the ground shifted in the north, post–Civil War Southern Baptists clung to an older view of inspiration. For instance, when Thomas E. Curtis, author of *The Human Element in the Inspiration of the Sacred Scriptures* (1867), rejected the divine inspiration of the Bible, he resigned his professorship at Howard College in Alabama. Germany, the epicenter for historical-critical ideas, became a specter of infidelity for many Southern Baptists. "It may be well for our young men to visit Germany in search of learning," R. H. Bagby wrote in the *Religious Herald* in 1861, "but it is to be hoped that they will look elsewhere for their theology, and that we of the South shall be spared any communication of the least taint of the heretical doctrines with which that country abounds."[8]

Broadus shared many of Bagby's concerns about "the most destructive criticism" of the age. In an 1876 lecture at Newton Theological Institute, Broadus acknowledged the "painfully rapid growth of religious skepticism," which he saw arising from the apparent "antagonism" between the Bible and science. He urged young preachers to "work quietly on in the assurance that we have truth." At the same time, Germany represented for Broadus the highest ideal of academic rigor. In designing the seminary's curriculum, he had modeled it "upon that of the German institutions." He admired German scholars, commenting appreciatively on their works, and dreamed with James P. Boyce of building a Southern Baptist seminary "like Germany with professors whose reputation shall be like theirs." Broadus knew that "*German* and *infidel* are almost synonymous terms" to many southern minds, but questioned the characterization's fairness. One could benefit from a German education without becoming heterodox. After all, Boyce's mentor, Charles Hodge of Princeton, had studied in Germany, yet returned to become America's most stalwart defender of the Bible's verbal plenary inspiration. Broadus thus encouraged bright young Southern Baptists like Toy and William H. Whitsitt to complete their education in the deep scholarship of continental Europe, and then come back "in the fullness of the blessing of the gospel of Christ."[9]

By 1869, Crawford Toy seemed to embody Broadus's dreams. When Toy returned from Germany, he allayed Southern Baptist fears by critiquing Ferdinand Baur's Hegelian method and the "Tubingen School" in the *Baptist Quarterly*. Toy further bolstered Baptist confidence in his inaugural faculty lecture at the seminary, "The Claims of Biblical Interpretation on Baptists." Toy assured Baptists that "a fundamental principle of our hermeneutics must be that the Bible, its real assertions being known, is in every iota of its substance absolutely and infallibly true."

Southern Baptists concerned for status and respectability thrilled to boast a world-class scholar who yet stood firm for the old orthodoxy. "At last we are on a par with our brethren of other denominations, and our peculiar tenets will no longer be attributed to ignorance and narrow-mindedness," gushed one *Religious Herald* reader. Boyce, also reflecting the old Baptist inferiority complex, proudly declared to trustees that "our Southern Baptist Seminary" was now in a position "to rival, in magnitude and in all respects, the great Pedobaptist institutions," and would soon be the largest theological school in America. Toy, as William Whitsitt remembered, was "the highest toast of Southern Baptists, through the agency of Broadus."[10]

Broadus would later insist on his confidence in Toy's orthodoxy in these early years, a claim that Toy himself corroborated. Yet certain statements in Toy's inaugural lecture indicated that his thought was shifting. "The gems of truth are indeed divine, but the casket in which they are given us is of human workmanship, and its key made and applied by human skill," Toy said of the Bible. "To this human side of interpretation, we may hold fast without weakening our grasp on the spirituality, which is its divine side."[11] Toy would spend the following decade exploring the furthest limits of that metaphor.

→»✤✤«←

Toy quickly arose as the star of the seminary faculty. Students lauded him as "a delightful teacher, a brimful scholar, a sympathetic brother." His pious prayers and scintillating lectures captivated his classes. "In the class room he seemed to know everything about the subject which he taught," recalled David G. Lyon. "He criticized the textbook with freedom, and sought not to fill the mind of the student with facts, though he never minimized the value of fact, but to stir up the mind to the exercise of its own powers." Toy's cultural sophistication also attracted students. He taught classes in the fine arts, led the seminary choir, and paid for students to attend concerts. The bachelor Toy took an interest in his students' personal lives, and devoted many evenings to long walks with seminarians. "His thought and interest, his sympathy and care, touched all of the life of a student from center to circumference," student C. C. Brown remembered.[12]

Privately, Toy had embarked on a relentless quest for truth. Long interested in science, Toy undertook an intensive inquiry that convinced him of the tenets of Charles Darwin and Herbert Spencer. As he sought to reconcile their hypotheses with the biblical record, Toy found support from the Dutch biblical scholar Abraham Kuenen, who had reconstructed the Old Testament according to the principles of evolution. Kuenen taught that the Israelite faith had undergone a "natural development" over time, from a primitive religion in the Pentateuch to a more spiritual ethic of love and justice, as reflected in the psalms and prophets. Following this principle, interpreters could see that the earliest Old Testament books had clearly been redacted by post-exilic authors to reflect the more progressive ethic of their own times. Adopting Kuenen's historical-critical hermeneutic opened an exciting new world to Toy, liberating him to affirm the Bible's spiritual message while discarding the text's outdated and unbelievable elements.[13]

Toy began to share his discoveries with students. The word "day" in the first chapter of Genesis could not mean a twenty-four-hour period, Toy explained, because science had proved the earth to be the result of ages of evolution. The author of Daniel was not a contemporary of Nebuchadnezzar as previously believed, but lived in the second century B.C. The New Testament authors frequently misquoted or misinterpreted Old Testament prophecies. "These commonplaces in the teaching of today were startling to many minds in the South four decades ago," David Lyon observed in 1920. Toy disturbed student A. J. Holt of Texas, for one, by equating the inspiration of the biblical authors to that of Shakespeare. When Holt pressed Toy as to whether or not the Bible was "God's word, without a mistake in it?" Toy replied that "there is always a human element in it." Holt afterward quarreled with his classmates. "You boys remind me of a nest of blackbirds. When Dr. Toy speaks to you, open go your mouths and down goes whatever he brings, whether it be a gravel or a grub worm," Holt grumbled. "I tell you right now, I did not come here to learn that the Bible was not the word of God. I believed that it was before I came and if it is not, I have no business here and I have no business preaching." The students departed in disagreement.[14]

As Toy grew more confident in his conclusions, he carried them beyond the classroom. He advocated for Darwin's theory of human origins in a lecture at the Greenville Court House. At a talk on Genesis and race to the Greenville Literary Club, Toy discredited the Genesis 11 account of the Tower of Babel. Toy lectured on the Assyrian legend of the great flood at the Greenville Baptist Church, calling into question Noah's flood. "Whether in public or private Toy was at no pains to conceal his views," William Whitsitt remarked—including from Broadus.[15]

In his *Memoir*, Broadus pleads ignorance to any changes in Toy's view of the Bible until 1877, the seminary's first year at Louisville. Broadus likely failed to grasp the extent of Toy's evolution until then, but he and Toy were simply too close for Broadus to have been completely unaware. They exchanged letters and confidences throughout the period, and collaborated on scholarly projects. Their annotated translation of Johann Lange's commentary on 1 and 2 Samuel is mostly conservative, though Toy asserted that Samuel, not Moses, had written Deuteronomy 17:14–17. Broadus was present for Toy's Darwinism speech in Greenville, and afterward fielded complaints from an offended audience member. Toy's racy address to the Greenville Literary Club was delivered in Broadus's own home; Broadus apparently defused the tension afterward by remarking, "It was an inestimable privilege to hear from the foremost scholar in America touching an issue to which he had devoted so much attention." Moreover, Broadus directly oversaw the faculty in the years 1875–1877, Boyce having already moved to Louisville. Rather than confront Toy over perceived errors, Broadus appears to have consistently run interference for him during the Greenville years. "The manner in which Broadus was subject to Toy in Greenville is one of the wonders of our Seminary history," Whitsitt asserted. "It would be useless to claim that Broadus was not aware of facts that were well known to his colleagues."[16]

Broadus may have harbored some concerns about Toy's theological trajectory at this time. He may have endeavored to influence Toy back toward a more conservative position. But based on his 1876 letter to Hovey, Broadus primarily seemed excited to have a gentleman theologian doing first-class academic work for the Southern Baptist Theological Seminary. In later years, Whitsitt privately maintained that Broadus had begun to adopt Toy's historicism himself in these years, though there is little evidence to support this claim.[17] In any case, Broadus gave Toy the widest possible latitude in the early 1870s. But in the summer of 1876, the situation came to the attention of James P. Boyce.

→·»»·❖·❖·««·←

William H. Whitsitt once compared Boyce and Broadus to "the twins of the ancient classic world." Close friends as well as cofounders of the seminary, the two men pulled in tandem for the seminary for so long that, in retrospect, they can appear indistinguishable. But the Toy affair exposed significant differences between them. Both Boyce and Broadus would ultimately settle on conservative conclusions regarding the verbal plenary inspiration of the Bible. Yet Broadus consistently showed greater openness to critical scholarship, and a broader tolerance of more liberal viewpoints. Broadus's nonsectarian education at the University of Virginia, his far-flung scholarly correspondence (as with the German expatriate Philip Schaff, who rejected verbal plenary inspiration), and his constant, wide-ranging travels all engendered in him a cosmopolitan intellectual outlook. Boyce, reared in the confessionally oriented Charleston Baptist Association, and trained under Charles Hodge at Princeton Theological Seminary, instinctively drew back from doctrinal innovation, believing that it would destroy the seminary and erode the denomination's confidence in the school. Broadus acknowledged as much in his memoir of Boyce. "Duty to the founders of the institution and to all who had given money for its support and endowment, duty to the Baptist churches from whom its students must come, required him to see to it that such teaching should not continue," Broadus wrote. "From the first he saw all this clearly, and felt it deeply."[18]

Boyce had already demonstrated a more guarded theological outlook than Broadus in the case of Abraham Jaeger. A former Jewish rabbi, Jaeger captured the hearts of Southern Baptist messengers by his 1873 Convention address on "The Conversion of the Jews to Christianity." After an emotional corporate prayer, the Convention appointed Jaeger as a special missionary to the Jews.

Within a year, Jaeger had relocated to Greenville, where a council that included Broadus and Toy ordained him to gospel ministry on April 21, 1874. Broadus was particularly taken with Jaeger. He praised him in the *Christian Index* as a "remarkably attractive and impressive preacher," who "preaches the *real* Gospel, in a singularly interesting way."[19] With Boyce in Louisville, Broadus soon had Jaeger teaching church history in the 1875–1876 term, and expressed interest in hiring him permanently.

But Boyce "earnestly protest[ed]." He saw Jaeger as arrogant and divisive, and believed that his "loose views" on inspiration made him unfit to serve as seminary librarian, much less as a professor. "Do you not feel that his sentiments are not accordant with our abstract of principles upon inspiration if on nothing else?" Boyce asked Broadus. "We must be very circumspect as to the position of influence which we give to a man not thoroughly sound," Boyce cautioned. "I had rather put an ignorant orthodox man in the chair of a professor than the most gifted of men if unsound. Dr. [E. G.] Robinson could not have done Rochester more harm than he did had he been the veriest ignoramus. And in Jaeger's case his unsoundness comes in the most serious direction for scholarship to dread, that of inspiration."[20] Boyce declared by letter that he was prepared to stand against a unanimous faculty vote for Jaeger; Broadus yielded to his judgment.

When similar concerns arose about Toy's position on biblical inspiration, Boyce again took the firmer hand. By June 1876, Boyce had offered Toy "a gentle remonstrance and earnest entreaty on inspiration" by letter. His concern deepened in the next session, when a student informed him that Toy taught that the Apostle Peter wrongly identified Psalm 16 as a prophecy of Christ. "Well," Boyce replied, "as between Doctor Toy and Peter, you and I had better stick to Peter." When seminary graduate William C. Lindsay, writing under the pseudonym of "Senex," urged the historical-critical method on Southern Baptists in the *Working Christian,* Boyce immediately identified this as "some fruits of Toy's teaching." He informed Broadus of other graduates he now regarded as "unsound on inspiration," among them seminary trustee J. C. Hiden. Boyce muttered that he "never had no use for Hiden," and directed Broadus to rescind Hiden's invitation to represent the seminary at a meeting in Virginia.[21]

The Senex newspaper controversy prompted Boyce to ask Toy for a full account of his position on the Bible. After reading Toy's response, Boyce declared his theory of inspiration to be "in itself well enough," and not "beyond the statements of others." At this point, Boyce seemed hopeful that Toy still had a future at the seminary. "I do hope we can keep all right for I prize Toy more than all," Boyce told Broadus. "I love him very much. He is a noble fellow and adds greatly to the glory of our institution."[22] A superior scholar like Toy was vital to the kind of seminary Boyce and Broadus wanted for Southern Baptists. Yet Toy was also in danger of progressing beyond what the conservative denomination could tolerate.

The 1877 move to Louisville revealed that Toy already had. His views had continued to develop, as Boyce and Broadus now observed at closer range. (Broadus attended some of Toy's Old Testament lectures in the 1878–1879 session.) Students all recognized that Toy handled the Bible differently than did the rest of the faculty. His behavior outside the classroom caused further alarm. Toy maintained a warm friendship with Abraham Jaeger, now an Episcopal minister and instructor at the University of the South, in Sewanee, Tennessee. It infuriated Boyce to hear Jaeger, while visiting Toy in Louisville, openly mocking Baptists. An incident at the home of Dr. J. Lawrence Smith disturbed Boyce more. The Smiths, among the seminary's most generous donors, hosted a dinner party at their Louisville home to introduce the faculty to the city's church leaders. Toy apparently made a scene by advocating for "the Darwinian philosophy" and "the philosophy of Mr. Herbert Spencer." Toy even called Joseph Cook of Boston—a popular conservative Christian apologist on scientific matters—a "woodenhead," not realizing that Smith, his host, had praised Cook earlier in the evening. Seated at the other end of the table, Boyce squirmed with embarrassment.[23]

At the end of the first term in Louisville, Boyce asked Broadus to meet with Toy. Broadus found his old friend to be unrepentant of his historicism, fully persuaded that his approach would help Southern Baptists keep their Bibles in the modern age. Toy was "convinced that the views he had adopted were correct, and would, by removing many intellectual difficulties, greatly promote faith in the Scriptures." Still, Toy understood Broadus's position; he agreed to refrain from advancing his controversial discoveries, and to teach within the Abstract of Principles.[24]

However well-intentioned Toy's commitment, students continued to ask him questions, and he felt obliged to answer. Toy drew wider attention in a series of "Critical Notes" he wrote for the *Sunday School Times* in January 1878, questioning Mosaic authorship of the Pentateuch. The broader Southern Baptist world now began to take notice. By the summer of 1878, Boyce and Broadus were receiving letters like those they each opened from W. B. Carson. The South Carolina pastor had met a minister who thought "the doctrinal parts of the Bible are inspired," but the rest "liable to error like any other book," and linked the idea to Toy. In August, Carson published his concerns in the *Religious Herald*. More damaging still was a series of articles printed in December by the pseudonymous "E. T. R." alerting readers of two seminary professors unsound in doctrine. "One does not believe in the inspiration of Moses, nor indeed of various other parts of Scripture," and presumed to "decide what part to receive and what to reject," wrote E. T. R. The article demanded that these professors be replaced "by men who will teach what the denomination wishes taught and pays to have taught."[25]

The E. T. R. article awakened Broadus to the threat Toy now posed to the seminary's reputation. He immediately wrote to Boyce. Broadus had learned that E. T. R. was Josephine Eaton Peck, a Virginia woman emerging as a conservative, doctrinal watchdog in the Convention. Broadus believed Peck to be "not only unfair, but impudent and foolish." Yet he also knew that her piece would unleash "an outburst of inquiries" into the seminary's orthodoxy. After twenty years of holding together the delicate Southern Baptist consensus for the seminary, Broadus realized that the time for privately managing Toy had passed. He saw only one path forward: Toy must plainly state his views on inspiration to seminary trustees, and let them decide whether or not he could remain at the seminary. Broadus still did not see the theological issue as clear-cut. "The point is not covered by our Articles of Belief," he admitted to Boyce. Yet Toy had, at the very least, transgressed the bounds of Southern Baptist opinion. "But his views differ widely from what is common among us, and it may be best, probably will be, that he should tell the Board so, and tender his resignation," Broadus wrote.[26]

Broadus was not necessarily pushing Toy out; submitting one's resignation was a common practice for embattled public figures seeking to preserve honor. If Toy resigned, the Board could either accept his letter with quiet dignity or exonerate him from all suspicion. Broadus at this stage expressed openness to either decision. "If he cannot satisfy them he ought not to retain the position. If they are satisfied, we need not care for E. T. R. and Co.," he reasoned. Even now, Broadus hoped the seminary might retain "the jewel of our learning." "The question is a very difficult one, what exactly ought to be done, and we need perfect unreserve among ourselves," Broadus noted, "and that is easy where men have such perfect confidence as we all have in each other's character and spirit."[27] The integrity of these southern gentlemen would ensure an honorable conclusion to a delicate situation.

—·>>·❖·❖·<<·—

Toy indeed responded to Broadus's request like a gentleman: he agreed to submit his resignation at the annual trustee meeting in May, where he fully expected to be vindicated. Yet Toy also appears to have been hurt by Boyce's and Broadus's lack of support. In a set of *Sunday School Times* articles about the book of Job in March, Toy seems to clearly identify with Job—the noble, innocent sufferer, misunderstood by his peers. He also appears to cast his seminary colleagues in the role of Job's counselors: insensitive friends, falsely accusing him of wrong. However Toy perceived the situation, Broadus hoped to shield both Toy and the seminary from controversy. He began inquiring about other teaching positions for his friend around this time. At Broadus's request, Virginia Baptist F. H. Kerfoot approached Basil Gildersleeve about Toy teaching Semitic languages at the University of Virginia. As Broadus saw it, securing a prestigious southern professorship for Toy could prove a satisfactory solution for all. But Gildersleeve demurred that "they perhaps had better not have a theological man in the institution."[28]

Meanwhile, Toy further compromised his position among Southern Baptists. In a pair of April articles in the *Sunday School Times,* Toy offered a historically informed interpretation of Isaiah 42:1–10 and 53:1–12. Evangelicals had traditionally identified the "Servant of the Lord" in these passages as a prophetic reference to Jesus Christ. Toy argued instead that Isaiah's immediate reference was to Israel, though the Servant would find a "final complete fulfillment in the Messiah." This was far from Toy's most radical conclusion. Yet Isaiah 53 was such an iconic Messianic passage for most evangelicals that any perceived tampering with it seemed sacrilegious. Toy's interpretation "provoked a violent denunciation" inside and outside the Convention. North Carolina's *Biblical Recorder,* for example, demanded Toy's immediate resignation. "Whatever may be Dr. Toy's learning and capacity, it seems that he is teaching error, and error too, strikes at the very foundation of Christian religion," thundered the author. "We built the Seminary for other purposes. We sustain it only as it teaches and defends the truths of the revealed word of God." At a popular level, Toy's treatment of the Isaianic Servant of the Lord may have damaged his reputation with Southern Baptists more than anything else he said or wrote. Many believed that the controversy over these April articles (more than Toy's stated views on biblical inspiration) influenced the Board to accept his resignation in May.[29]

Broadus makes no mention of the Isaiah controversy in his memoir's detailed account of the Toy affair. He likely avoided the incident because he had come under fire for a similar interpretation in *The Baptist Teacher* in May of 1879. Broadus agreed with Toy that Isaiah 53 referred immediately to Israel, yet because there existed "a typical relationship between Israel and Messiah," the prophecies found their ultimate fulfillment in Jesus. This interpretation involved nuance, so he urged Sunday school teachers to exercise caution in presenting it. "For more intelligent classes, all this should be carefully explained, having first been carefully studied," he wrote. "For most classes, better to say at once that it means the Savior."[30]

Broadus had always been a gifted "interpreter" in Baptist life, moving deftly between academic and popular audiences, tailoring his message to each with consummate skill. But in these published remarks, the magician pulled the curtain back too far. In differentiating between "more intelligent classes" and "most classes," Broadus came across as elitist and manipulative—a rare *faux pas*. In an equally unusual occurrence, the Baptist public heaped criticism upon him. Virginia Baptist W. E. Hatcher called Broadus's interpretation "fanciful and unreliable." Letters to denominational newspapers lumped Broadus in with Toy as modern manipulators of the Bible, and criticized what seemed a condescending and disingenuous approach toward ordinary Baptists. This unexpected dose of public criticism stung Broadus; Whitsitt remembered it as "the sorest point in the world for Broadus for months."[31] Broadus was still under fire at the May trustee meeting. This weakened his position to defend Toy, had he been inclined to do so.

-→»›❖❖‹«←-

Seminary trustees gathered at the First Baptist Church of Atlanta on May 7, 1879, days before the Southern Baptist Convention. Boyce read to them Toy's nine-page resignation letter, in which Toy acknowledged that his "views of inspiration differ considerably from those of the body of my brethren." Toy nevertheless insisted that he had not violated the Abstract of Principles, which states simply that "The Scriptures of the Old and New Testaments were given by inspiration of God, and are the only sufficient, certain and authoritative rule of all saving knowledge, faith and obedience." "I believe that the Bible is wholly divine and wholly human," Toy declared. A divine message still sparkled in the Bible, even if packaged in "the framework of a primitive and incorrect geology" or "when discrepancies or inaccuracies occur in historical narrative." For Toy, it was "not only lawful for me to teach as Professor in the Seminary," but his view was "one that will bring aid and firm standing ground to many a perplexed mind and establish the truth of God on a firm foundation."[32] Toy believed that he offered Southern Baptists a deeply pious approach to Scripture, updated for the modern world.

The Board appointed a committee of five to meet with Toy for further questioning. Afterward, the committee affirmed Toy's "beautiful Christian spirit" but acknowledged the "divergence in his views of inspiration from those held by our brethren in general." They unanimously recommended accepting Toy's resignation. The Board did so, by a vote of 16–2. By all accounts, the decision "astonished" Toy. According to Whitsitt, he was especially dismayed that Broadus had not interceded for him. "He expected that Broadus at least would stand by him and represent to the Board that his sentiments were harmless and correct enough," Whitsitt recalled. "He was almost frantic with solicitude. He wanted to find Broadus . . . but I was fully aware that the scheme of Boyce and Broadus was now coming to successful issue."[33]

Broadus's role in Toy's dismissal, as Whitsitt's comment suggests, is debated. In public and in private, Broadus characterized Toy's departure as a heartbreaking duty. "Poor bereaved three," he wrote to Lottie on May 10, "we have lost our jewel of learning, our beloved and noble brother, the pride of the Seminary. God bless the seminary, God bless Toy, and God help us, sadly but steadfastly to do our providential duty." In his *Memoir,* Broadus recalled a poignant scene after the resignation, in which he and Boyce accompanied Toy to the railway station. In a waiting room, Boyce threw his left arm around Toy's neck, lifted his right arm into the air and "in a passion of grief," cried, "Oh Toy, I would freely give that arm to be cut off if you could be where you were five years ago, and stay there." Broadus told a story of the seminary's fidelity to the Scriptures, to denominational trust, and to institutional integrity, even at the highest cost. "Never," observed one historian, "was a heretic so beloved by his accusers."[34]

Whitsitt offers a darker account in his diary. According to him, Boyce and Toy loathed one another. Boyce had plotted Toy's removal from the moment that Toy embarrassed him at the Smith residence. At the same time, Toy's hatred for Boyce "unconsciously" influenced him to adopt increasingly radical opinions. Whitsitt paints Broadus, his own one-time mentor, as a turncoat, a deceiver, and a hatchet-man for the Machiavellian Boyce. In Greenville, Toy had "led [Broadus] around by the nose," and Broadus often "stood between Boyce and Toy, shielding Toy from criticism." Then, after moving to Louisville, Broadus deserted Toy to act as Boyce's "toady." Broadus leveraged his friendship with Toy to manipulate him into submitting his resignation, assuring Toy that he would defend him before the Board. All the while, Broadus secretly gathered evidence to present against Toy to the trustees. Toy, the poor "simpleton," fell into Broadus's trap. "Boyce and Broadus could well afford to look through their fingers, and smile at the ease with which they captured the poor silly bird," Whitsitt wrote. "It was pitiful to a man who could see Broadus on the other side to perceive how truly Toy depended on his good offices and support." Broadus's apparently feigned sorrow over Toy's departure disgusted Whitsitt, whose testimony has prompted some historians to accuse Broadus of deception and "character assassination" in the Toy affair.[35]

Whose version of the story is to be believed? There can be little doubt that Broadus's account, which came to symbolize the seminary's heroic doctrinal fidelity, is heavily sanitized. The situation was certainly more complex than indicated in his presentation, written as Southern's president in 1893. Theological, pragmatic, and personal motivations likely all played into the Board's decision to accept Toy's resignation. Boyce's relationship with Toy was also probably more strained than Broadus indicates in his account. (Broadus allows for virtually no relational tension within the faculty.) But whatever his personal animus toward Toy, Boyce's deep concerns regarding the doctrine of biblical inspiration at the seminary had been well established long before the Toy controversy; this was not simply a smokescreen for a private vendetta. Yet it is also indisputable that concern for alienating the seminary's conservative donors factored into Toy's dismissal, as Mikael Parsons and others have brought out. Broadus himself made no secret of this in his *Memoir*. "[Boyce] well knew that nothing of that kind could be taught in the Seminary without doing violence to its aims and objects, and giving the gravest offense to its supporters in general," Broadus wrote.[36] Then and now, attempts to assign a single cause for Toy's removal—whether the seminary's noble defense of the Bible or Boyce's personal grudge against Toy—are ultimately simplistic and unpersuasive.

Yet overall, there are good reasons to accept the basic arc of Broadus's story over Whitsitt's. Toy's own loyal friends David Lyon and George Moore did. Lyon, Toy's protege and longtime colleague at Harvard, praised "the high character of all concerned in this painful affair." Whitsitt, writing in a private diary a decade after the event (a diary that he ordered sealed for one hundred years upon his death), admits that his own sordid account includes much speculation regarding Broadus's and Boyce's motives. His conspiracy theory also does not square with Broadus's December 1878 letter to Boyce, in which Broadus proposes an early, forthright conversation with Toy about his resignation and possible dismissal. While it surely grieved Toy that Broadus did not defend him before the Board, Toy's Job articles in March 1879 indicate that he grasped where Broadus stood before the meeting.[37]

Assessing Whitsitt's narrative is further complicated by his own undisguised loathing of Boyce. At the time of Toy's resignation, Boyce's daughter Lizzie had rejected Whitsitt's marriage proposal. By the time Whitsitt recounts the Toy affair, Boyce—who Whitsitt consistently curses as a "dunderhead"—had generally subjected Whitsitt to second-class treatment on the faculty for more than a decade. Broadus's account of the Toy affair is far from objective, but it seems just as unlikely that Whitsitt's overt hatred of Boyce did not color his own interpretation. Whitsitt's diary provides valuable texture to the Toy controversy, but his private writings contain so many professional jealousies, faculty intrigues, and personal vendettas as to weaken his credibility.[38]

Broadus's continued friendship with Toy raises further questions about his supposed betrayal. The two men were exchanging warm letters within a month of the resignation. Broadus continued to try and secure other teaching positions for Toy, including at Baltimore's Johns Hopkins University. In the fall of 1879, Toy was encouraging Broadus to complete his volume on Matthew in the American Commentary series, and interceding with editor Alvah Hovey to allow Broadus a higher word count. While Broadus supported Hovey in passing over Toy's authorship of commentaries on 1 and 2 Timothy and Titus for the Baptist series, he also wrote a "most cordial" recommendation letter for Toy to Harvard, where his progressive ideas posed no obstacle. In subsequent years, Broadus consulted Toy about faculty hires at the seminary, and Toy invited Broadus to preach at Harvard Divinity School.[39]

Toy himself affirmed Broadus's interpretation of the events in Broadus's 1893 *Memoir*. "You are quite right in describing my withdrawal as a necessary result of important differences of opinion. Such separations are sometimes inevitable, but they need not interfere with general friendly cooperation," he wrote. In his *Memoir*, Broadus explicitly rejects Toy's theology, yet praises Toy as "not only a remarkable scholar, but a most honorable and lovable gentleman, but also a very able and inspiring teacher, and a colleague with whom, as to all personal relations, it was delightful to be associated."[40] To all appearances, Broadus and Toy held one another in mutual respect and affection for the remainder of their lives.

Whitsitt may have dramatized his account of the Toy affair, but the incident drove a real wedge in the seminary faculty. Whitsitt had previously considered Broadus "my advisor in all things," but he never trusted him again. When Broadus requested a statement of Whitsitt's own views on inspiration in 1880, Whitsitt spoke "pleasant words about the complete unreserved of our friendship," but believed that Broadus was laying a trap for him as he had for Toy. After sending Broadus a guarded reply, he congratulated himself that there had in truth "never been the slightest trace of unreserved" between them since Toy's resignation. "I keep to my side of the house and allow Boyce and Broadus to keep to their side of the house," Whitsitt confided to his diary in 1886. "Our official relations, the Lord be thanked, are peaceful enough; I desire to cultivate no other relationship with them. Toy cultivated exceptionally kind relations with Broadus and I have shown above what came of it. Is there any good reason why I should imitate his example?" When Broadus repeatedly praises the close-knit faculty relationships in his *Memoir*, he is either unaware of or is glossing over Whitsitt's disgust for his senior colleagues, and their own dismissive posture toward him. The Toy affair concluded the faculty's era of good feelings.[41]

--->>>�֍✦✧✧<<<--

Trustee Chairman J. B. Jeter's explanation of Toy's resignation in the *Religious Herald* stirred confusion and outrage among Southern Baptists. Jeter's report suggested that the trustees dismissed Toy not for doctrine or any other principled reason, but strictly to curry public favor with a conservative donor base in a critical fundraising season. Noting the "conceded divergence in [Toy's] views from those generally held by supporters of the seminary," Jeter wrote, "the Trustees deemed it inexpedient to subject it to the disadvantages which would inevitably arise from a protracted controversy on an important theological subject, especially while efforts are being made to obtain an endowment."[42] Many Southern Baptists, especially seminary graduates, expressed outrage at Jeter's crass pragmatism. George B. Eager believed that Toy had been "badly treated" and that the trustee action "not only involved injustice to him, but was fraught with peril to our case and to the interest of higher learning among us." The public outcry prompted Jeter to clarify that, in addition to compromising the seminary's financial position, trustees judged that Toy's views on inspiration violated the seminary's Abstract of Principles and contained "the seeds of dangerous errors."[43] In November 1879, Jeter's *Religious Herald* published Toy's own candid explanation of his position in his resignation letter, allowing Southern Baptists to judge the matter for themselves.

The publication of Toy's views launched a debate over the doctrine of inspiration that roiled the Southern Baptist Convention for years to come. Some, like seminary trustee E. T. Winkler and Landmark news editor J. R. Graves, commended the Board's action against Toy—Graves warned Southern Baptists of seeking a "finishing touch" in German schools in the future. Others, including many of Toy's former students, argued that Toy had not violated the Abstract of Principles and that Southern Baptists needed his progressive approach to the Scriptures. Toy himself entered the debate in January 1880, explaining his theological journey and defending his views in numerous *Religious Herald* articles. Toy remained so popular among South Carolina Baptists, where he enjoyed the defense of the *Baptist Courier,* that Furman University elected him president and professor of languages in 1880. Toy instead chose to move to New York City. Soon after, he was named Hancock Professor of Hebrew at Harvard Divinity School, the first non-Unitarian elected to the faculty. Toy would enjoy a long and celebrated career at Harvard.[44]

Broadus attempted to keep a low profile during the controversy. When the *Religious Herald* asked him to participate in a symposium about inspiration, Broadus declined, believing that a public discussion would generate more heat than light around the various personalities. "Toy's having been connected with us has tied our hands in various ways, & I believe we do more good by silence than we would do by the wholesomest things it might be in our power to say," he wrote, "I come out strongly in my lectures whenever there is occasion."[45]

Yet many Southern Baptists questioned Broadus's orthodoxy regarding inspiration in the wake of the Toy controversy. Broadus rebuked a former student for telling the *Western Recorder* office that he shared Toy's view of the Old Testament. In May 1880, J. R. Graves divulged to *Tennessee Baptist* readers that "It was affirmed by those who spoke from their personal knowledge that Profs. Whitsitt and Broadus fully sympathize with the views of Prof. Toy touching inspiration." Boyce, who refuted Graves's claim in the *Western Recorder,* believed that Toy supporter S. F. Thompson had spread this story about Broadus to legitimize Toy's position. Charles Manly reported to his brother Basil in 1881 that a "Bro. J. Q. Adams" had said that Broadus was "in the finest state of uncertainty as to the canonicity and inspiration of the 1st chapter of Genesis" and that "he would not feel warranted in preaching from any part of it as a text of God's word." A month later, Charles told Basil that Adams had changed his story. But rumors about Broadus still swirled; he would spend the next decade publicly reaffirming his commitment to a conservative, evangelical doctrine of biblical inspiration.[46]

·→»⧉⚜⧉«←·

The Toy controversy accentuated Broadus's suspension between two worlds in the late nineteenth-century South. It also marked a turning point in his career. Having spent his adult life promoting a more learned and sophisticated Southern Baptist ministry, he celebrated the emergence of Crawford Toy as the realization of his fondest hopes. But after giving latitude to Toy's avant-garde views during their Greenville years, Broadus by 1879 realized that Toy's historical-critical approach to the Scriptures represented a bridge too far. Moving into the 1880s, Broadus would still promote a Southern Baptist scholarship conversant with the latest German higher critics, but explicitly committed to the verbal plenary inspiration of the Bible.

Whitsitt afterward claimed that Broadus had adopted Toy's historical-critical approach in the early 1870s, then sided with Boyce in Louisville out of self-preservation.[47] This is certainly possible, as Broadus endeavored to remain on the cutting edge of biblical and linguistic learning throughout his career. But it appears that he personally maintained a conservative evangelical view of biblical inspiration, as his evaluation at the time of New Testament scholar and personal friend Bishop Charles John Ellicott indicates. Ellicott affirmed that the Bible was "pervaded by God's Spirit" yet contained "trifling, historical inaccuracies." Broadus judged Ellicott to be "profound, suggestive, and devout, but very objectionable as to inspiration." It seems that when the Toy the controversy broke in Louisville, Broadus found himself walking a tightrope of academy, piety, constituency, and personal friendship. As Grant Wacker has shown, virtually all of Broadus's peers in the evangelical academy were formulating their convictions regarding the Bible in this day of dynamic theological innovation. If some of Broadus's actions can be confusing in retrospect, perhaps he was attempting to follow the advice he issued to a Newton seminary audience in 1876, to "unite breadth of view, and charity in feeling, with fidelity to truth . . . the age is in love with *liberality,* and allows that word to cover many a falsehood and many a folly. But the age will feel more and more its need of *truth,* and 'speaking truth in love' will meet its double want."[48]

William Owen Carver, a seminary student under Broadus in the late 1880s, would go on to agitate for more modern views of the Bible and theology as a missions professor at Southern Seminary for over fifty years. Just before his death in 1952, Carver grew wistful as he reflected on the Toy controversy, and what might have been. Had Toy remained at the seminary, Carver asserted, he could have "led into a deeper and more comprehensive understanding of the principles of progress." Carver conjectured that Toy "might have become the leader of a new era of insight and interpretation of the Old Testament and of a better understanding of the Hebrew religion and of the principles of religion in general. He might have given to this Seminary an outstanding position in Old Testament scholarship such as is achieved in the New Testament field, and such as it has waited for until just now."[49]

Toy had indeed led Broadus, and Southern Baptists, into a valley of decision regarding modernity and tradition. As Carver recognized, their choice of the latter still bore consequences seventy years later. In 1879, Broadus felt the tension more acutely than ever between what southern historian Dewey Grantham termed "the reconciliation of progress and tradition" at his seminary and in his denomination. Broadus would continue to struggle to hold both of these dynamics together as he moved into the New South era.

Eight
SOUTHERN INTERPRETER

I N FEBRUARY 1888, John Broadus opened a letter from an old Virginia neighbor, Presbyterian theologian Robert Lewis Dabney. Born seven years apart, the two men shared much in common. Both had been reared in the Old Dominion and educated at the University of Virginia. Both had trained a rising generation of professional ministers within their respective denominations. Both had also passionately served the Army of Northern Virginia during the war, Broadus as a camp evangelist for Robert E. Lee and Dabney as Stonewall Jackson's chief of staff. Broadus and Dabney had corresponded occasionally through the years; Dabney, a man not easily impressed, revered Broadus as a leader in "enlightened Biblical piety" and listed him among the Southern Baptists he most admired.[1]

This particular epistle was vintage Dabney, who by now had established a reputation for his curmudgeonly protests of the South's modernization. He spent several pages alerting Broadus to certain "monster-evils in our American Protestantism," focusing especially on the "spurious religious excitement" of contemporary revivalism and the American Sunday school movement. Dabney judged the latter to be "a pitiful system of wheedling and coaxing, with marks, merit-tickets, premiums and pennies, mostly resulting in futility," and ultimately serving Satan's designs. He repeatedly voiced his "deep anxiety" at the "strong contrast" he detected "between the depth and earnestness of the religious profession" from earlier in the nineteenth century "and its superficiality now." Complaints about the deterioration of southern religion and culture were nothing unusual for Dabney; from Lee's surrender until his own death in 1898, he spent his best energies urging white southerners back from the siren calls of the "New South" to a glorious past.[2]

Broadus's reply does not survive. He likely would have sympathized with Dabney's concerns regarding reckless revivalism, though, after forty years of Sunday school work, one can imagine Dabney's diatribe against that movement drawing a smile. More important, the letter points to a fundamental difference in how the two aristocratic Virginians responded to Confederate defeat. Twenty years after Appomattox, Dabney remained oriented backward, resisting modernity in favor of a mythical South. As a result, he lived out the nineteenth century in defiant isolation, marginalized by North and South alike. Broadus, on the other hand, enjoyed a surge of prosperity and national popularity from 1880 to 1895, thanks to his adaptability to the new social, political, and economic realities of postbellum American life.

Since Charles Regan Wilson's groundbreaking study, *Baptized in Blood*, Southern historians have taken for granted the prevalence of a "Lost Cause" civil religion among white southern Protestants after the Civil War. Lost Cause advocates praised the Edenic character of the antebellum South, the virtues of the Confederate government, and the bravery of the rebel army. Even through the fiery trial of Reconstruction, white southerners maintained that God yet had a plan for his chosen people; meantime, the duty of the hour was to maintain fidelity to the Old South's defining principles and resist assimilation to the Yankee conquerors. In the latter decades of the nineteenth century, Lost Cause acolytes nurtured the memory of the Old South through literature, speeches, and a host of cultic rituals that included Memorial Day celebrations, parades, and monuments to Confederate heroes. This civil religion of the Lost Cause continues to hold tremendous explanatory power for why the South has so long remained a region set apart. Yet the contrast between Broadus and Dabney also suggests a greater variety within Lost Causism than has always been acknowledged.

From one viewpoint, Broadus believed as deeply as Dabney in southern exceptionalism. After the war, he wished to preserve what he considered the best southern ideals, including its pervasive evangelical theology and morality, its genteel decorum, and, especially, its stratified social order based on white supremacy. Publicly, Broadus celebrated white southern redemption, defended a separate Southern Baptist denomination, and praised the nobility of the conquered southern people. Privately, he instructed his children in the Confederacy's true principles, cautioning young Boyce Broadus to screen his history books for unfair treatments of secession. He had a sweet tooth for moonlight-and-magnolias nostalgia, attending Southern Society poetry readings, corresponding with Lost Cause novelists such as Thomas Nelson Page, and entertaining company by reading Joel Chandler Harris's "Uncle Remus Tales." He found Susan Dabney Smedes's idyllic *Memorials of a Southern Planter* (1887) to be "delightful," and hoped the southern slaveholder might "be better understood" as a result of its publication. In summary, Broadus "was always loyal to his section," as William Whitsitt asserted, and "kept his feet always firmly planted on Southern soil."[3]

But if Broadus gazed "to the past for . . . inspiration and guidance," he also "marched forward to modernity," to borrow David Goldfield's phrase. As suggested by his 1877 flight from embattled Greenville to emerging Louisville, Broadus was a practical man. He could sympathize with an intransigent like Dabney, or L. M. Jones of Trenton, Tennessee, who grumbled, "I have not yet learned to speak flippantly of the New South. I am a man of the South, of the Old South. Her people are my people. Her afflictions are my afflictions; her sorrows are my sorrows." But Broadus resonated more with the forward-looking vision of southerners like Louisville's Henry Watterson, to whose *Courier-Journal* newspaper Broadus often contributed. He shared Watterson's enthusiasm for southern revitalization through reconciliation with the north, the growth of industry and business, the development of southern cities, and participation in a national system.[4]

But as historians like Paul M. Gaston and James C. Cobb have demonstrated, this "New South Creed" was never intended to disconnect the South from its past, but to preserve its old cultural values. Broadus seems to have shared the perspective that embracing the New South Creed was "the best means by which, short of restoring slavery, the social ideals of the Lost Cause might actually be secured. Far from repudiating the Lost Cause, the New South would make southern society essentially impervious to Yankee interference in the conduct of its affairs while forcing northern whites to acknowledge the just and honorable nature of the white South's position in 1861."[5] After Reconstruction, John Broadus promoted southern progress in the service of preserving southern tradition.

→»❖❖«←

Money topped Broadus's list of concerns in the late 1870s. Before the Civil War, he "had dwelt long in affluence and culture, in the gratification of refined tastes."

By December 1878, he and the seminary had been living hand to mouth for over fifteen years. Desperate to raise an endowment, he met with potential donors in the border city of Baltimore; Lottie Broadus dubbed his trip "the Gettysburg of the seminary's fate." Broadus attested to "pulling every string"—preaching in churches, delivering evening lectures, and holding private meetings—yet he could not open Baltimore's deepest purses. "The rich men all failed us," he lamented. Though Broadus "laid vigorous siege to them in private," many "refused point blank." The common folk, on the other hand, "did *nobly.*" Humble pledges of $50, $125, and $250 yielded $10,760 for the seminary endowment. "This is not success, my friend," Broadus reported to Boyce, "but it is far from being failure."[6] The Baltimore campaign attested to Southern Baptists' essentially popular character. But if the seminary were to survive, it would need friends in higher places.

A year later, Boyce had still collected only 10 percent of the needed endowment, and the seminary was clearly "going to ruin." In a pitiable newspaper appeal in December 1879, Boyce revealed his prayer for a single $50,000 donor. It seemed as unlikely as it was desperate. Yet in February 1880, Boyce triumphantly displayed a letter to Broadus and announced "here is the answer to our prayer." In this case, heaven's provision carried the decidedly earthy address of Atlanta, Georgia, home of controversial New South industrialist Joseph Emerson Brown.[7]

Few southerners had adapted to postwar conditions as comfortably as Brown. After serving as Georgia's Democratic wartime governor, Brown had acquiesced to the Reconstruction Radicals and become a Scalawag Republican. His pliancy yielded both power and profits, as Brown reaped appointments as state supreme court chief justice and U.S. senator. He also amassed a fortune in the coal and railroad industries. The Radical Georgia governor Rufus B. Bullock praised Brown as "a representative of this New South" who "fully understands her practical needs and will foster her commercial advantage." Brown certainly understood the economic advantages of Georgia's convict lease system, which amounted to little more than post-emancipation slavery. Critics protested the corrupt legal system, which drafted the mostly Black convicts, often jailed on tenuous grounds, to work in brutal conditions for wealthy industrialists like Brown. "If there is a hell on earth," declared a Georgia legislator in 1892, "it is the Dade coal mines." Progressive Georgia politicians would abolish the convict lease system in 1908, but in the postwar years state convicts provided a cheap and apparently disposable labor force for Brown's mining, manufacturing, and railroad empires.[8]

Brown's opponents sneered that his Southern Baptist piety and philanthropy was a smokescreen for his dubious political and commercial practices. Yet Boyce hurried to meet Brown in Atlanta, where he collected $50,000 in cash and first-class securities. Seminary trustees promptly appointed Brown as Board chairman and named the seminary's first endowed chair of theology in his honor. For generations, the seminary celebrated Brown as its financial savior.[9]

Brown's gift inspired Boyce to launch a $200,000 endowment campaign. He immediately turned to another New South capitalist, George Washington Norton. The son of a successful cut nail factory owner in Russellville, Kentucky, Norton had moved to Louisville after the war. There, with brothers William F. and Eckstein Norton, George formed the G. W. Norton and Company private banking firm. Like Brown, the Nortons were ardent Southern Baptists as well as savvy businessmen: the Convention would elect George its first treasurer (a position subsequently filled by both his son and his grandson), and the Nortons' support influenced Boyce to bring the seminary to Louisville. Besides giving generously to the 1880 endowment, the Norton brothers advised Boyce to alter the seminary charter to protect the endowment's principal from use on current expenses. They formed a board of local businessmen to invest the principal, hold the securities, and pay over the income to the seminary treasurer. The new charter inspired donor confidence and set the seminary on a firm footing.[10]

When New South money could not supply all the seminary's needs, Broadus turned to New York City. He traveled there in February 1881 for what he called "one of the great crises of my life-work." Addressing himself to Gotham's wealthiest financiers, Broadus pitched the endowment campaign as an investment in uplifting the benighted South. "There is still much ignorance among the membership and ministers of vast numbers of our Southern churches," he explained. "We are trying to lift up the rising ministry, through graduating the best teachers of the people at large, and this must improve the social, political, and business prospects of the South, as well as its strictly religious condition." Broadus proposed "an agreeable co-partnership" between the seminary's southern professors and "talented and successful business men" of the North. "We put our lives into the enterprise, they put in money to endow it, and thus together we shall achieve good usefulness of a kind neither could accomplish without the cooperating of the other." Broadus's New York solicitations yielded nearly $40,000. Major gifts from other donors would produce the remaining $150,000 for the endowment. "The Seminary is now safe, humanly speaking" Boyce exclaimed.[11]

After two decades of precarious survival, the seminary gained solvency through Boyce's and Broadus's nimble adjustments to post-Reconstruction economic realities. As C. Vann Woodward has shown, the necessity of propping up sectional denominational causes ultimately overcame the resistance of many conservative southern clergy to embracing northern laissez-fare capitalism. While Dabney and other Confederate die-hards railed against "money-mania," the betrayal of Jeffersonian agrarianism, and decaying southern virtue, Broadus had a seminary to save. He yoked himself with titans of industry, North and South, to do it.[12]

Broadus formed lucrative partnerships with the wealthiest men of the Gilded Age. He corresponded regularly with Joseph E. Brown, and also kept the Nortons close—the family would pour over $1 million into the seminary over the next three generations. The affluent Baltimore twins Joshua and Eugene Levering also entered Broadus's orbit as critical benefactors. Among the most generous Baptist philanthropists of the era, the Leverings had grown their father's coffee business into one of the largest in the nation before ascending to fabulously successful banking careers. The Leverings loved Broadus, sharing his passion for Baptist life as well as temperance reform (Joshua Levering ran as the Prohibition Party's U.S. presidential candidate in 1894). After failing to lure Broadus to their Eutaw Place Baptist Church as pastor, the brothers bankrolled the seminary for decades; Joshua served for fifty-four years on the trustee board, forty as its chairman. When Eugene endowed a lectureship at Johns Hopkins University in 1890, he invited Broadus to deliver the inaugural series, which Broadus later published as *Jesus of Nazareth* (1890).[13]

Yet nothing underscores Broadus's comfort with Gilded Age capitalism like his association with John Davison Rockefeller. Inheriting the strict northern Baptist faith of his mother (who wished him to become a Baptist minister), Rockefeller believed God had gifted him to make money. After breaking into the oil business in the 1860s, he quickly became the wealthiest man in America. Rockefeller founded the Standard Oil Company in 1870, and spent the decade crushing his competitors en route to gaining total mastery of the industry; in the so-called "Cleveland Massacre" of 1872, Standard obtained twenty-two of the city's twenty-six refineries. All the while, Rockefeller remained a committed Baptist church member, Sunday school teacher, teetotaling family man, and philanthropist. Broadus connected with Rockefeller in the late 1870s, and thereafter tapped him, his brother, William, and J. A. Bostwick for regular seminary donations. In 1886, Broadus secured from the oil magnates $25,000 to build dormitories, which he aptly named "New York Hall." Broadus praised Rockefeller as "a very noble man, of wonderful insight into character, and a marvel of mild perseverance in carrying through what he undertakes." In a telling aside in his *Jesus of Nazareth* lectures, Broadus argued that Jesus' commendation of Mary's lavish sacrifice of costly perfume gave precedence for the wealthy making large philanthropic donations, even in the presence of poor and needy individuals.[14]

Broadus developed an intimate friendship with Rockefeller. By 1880, the oil mogul was attaching personal notes to his donations, such as, "Mrs. R. and the children join me with kind remembrances." Rockefeller sought Broadus's advice on the education of his children and on pastoral candidates for his Fifth Avenue Baptist Church. Whenever Broadus was in New York, he lunched daily with Rockefeller, and worked from a desk at the Standard Oil offices. Concerned for Broadus's health, Rockefeller sent him and Lottie on "a little vacation" in 1882, paying for three weeks in New Orleans. The Broaduses stayed with the Rockefellers at their New York and Cleveland homes, explored Mammoth Cave and sailed the Hudson together on holidays, and exchanged family photographs with them. In 1888, Broadus distributed for Rockefeller one hundred copies of a pamphlet defending "Trusts." "Shall be very pleased to send more, if you can place them where they will do good," Rockefeller wrote. Broadus's support for the robber baron was only natural; Standard Oil had enriched both Southern Seminary and the Broadus family throughout the 1880s. Rockefeller purchased a $1,000 share of Standard Oil stock in the mid-1880s for Broadus, who thereafter increased his holdings and received regular invitations to shareholder meetings.[15]

Broadus strengthened these ties in 1883 when he solicited Rockefeller's advice regarding a job for his son. Like his father, Samuel Sinclair Broadus had completed a master's degree at the University of Virginia in Greek and Latin. But while grateful for his classical, Old South education, Sam had set his heart on the New South Creed, and a career in business. Broadus was delighted. "Sam is a decided Christian man, active in religious work, and has never tasted alcoholic liquor nor used tobacco," he wrote to Rockefeller. As he praised Sam's virtues, Broadus sounded more like a sharp-eyed Yankee merchant than a genteel Virginia planter:

> He shows some talent for business. He can buy things cheaper than most folks, always informing himself, and able to wait patiently till he can get them at a fair price. He has been very economical, both with my money, and with his own. Yet he makes a good appearance, and is welcome in the best society. He likes to square up an account, and get it straight. He has always been fond of tools, liking to make little conveniences, and to repair furniture, etc. He knows perfectly well that he has to make his way in the world, by work and character and sense and patience, and while I do not imagine him to be anything remarkable, I think he has a good deal of grip and stick. He must of course begin at the beginning of some business pursuit, and see if he can work his way up.[16]

The former slaveowner had embraced the New South's middle-class business values. Broadus's query resulted in a six-year stint with Standard Oil for Sam. One of the "new men" of the South's "ascendant business class," Sam would go on to a highly successful career in banking and in the cotton mill industry.[17]

-->>❖-❖-<<<-

In another Lost Cause anomaly, Broadus spent nearly as much time north of Dixie as within it during the 1880s. He devoted virtually every summer to supplying prominent northern churches, including North Orange, New Jersey; Brooklyn's Washington Avenue and Emmanuel Baptist churches; Chicago's First Baptist Church; the First Baptist Churches of Indianapolis and Boston; and Woodward Avenue Baptist Church in Detroit. These northern preaching gigs invariably prompted invitations to permanent pastorates; one wealthy congregation offered Broadus an annual salary of $10,000. But Broadus always returned to the seminary. "I am satisfied that in the probable remainder of my life I can do most good by remaining in my present position," he informed one suitor.[18] No one could dislodge Broadus from the South, but he happily plundered the northern larders so that he could remain there.

Baptists nationwide sought Broadus to add a touch of Old South charm to their ceremonies. It seems that no major Baptist building constructed in the late nineteenth century was fit for use until dedicated with a Broadus sermon; he performed the honors in Louisville, New York City, St. Louis, Brooklyn, Detroit, Kansas City, Indianapolis, and more. He received dozens of requests from rural southern churches, too, such as from the Baptists in little Paris, Tennessee. Northern Baptist organizations clamored to secure Broadus as keynote speaker for their annual gatherings, and their publishers sought his byline for their periodicals. One Brooklyn editor claimed that his readers inquired with every issue, "Do you give us something from Dr. Broadus this time?"[19] For white northerners eager for reconciliation in the 1880s, Broadus was an authentic southern gentleman they could trust.

Nor was Broadus's appeal limited to Baptists. Methodist layman John R. Mott invited Broadus to speak at the annual meeting of the North American YMCA. "We believe that you stand for the most helpful, most spiritual, and most enduring Bible work of our time," Mott wrote. Broadus also accepted invitations from popular northern evangelist Dwight L. Moody to teach at his Northfield Bible Conference in Massachusetts and the Moody Bible Institute in Chicago. When Chicago Baptist B. F. Jacobs founded the International Sunday School Committee in 1872, he called on Broadus, declaring that he wanted a "Baptist from the South—a man that we would all thoroughly appreciate and admire." Broadus spent the next two decades preparing Sunday school lessons for students all over North America.[20]

Few of Broadus's engagements highlight his cultural versatility like his long-standing relationship with the annual Chautauqua Assembly. Founded by Methodist Sunday school leaders as a kind of high-class camp meeting for education and cultural improvement, Chautauqua declared in its progressive motto that "every man has a right to be all that he can be, to know all that he can know, to do all that he pleases to do." Each summer, up to two thousand attendees flocked to an open-air auditorium at picturesque Chautauqua Lake in Fair Point, New York, to receive college-level instruction from the nation's best speakers. Students took careful notes from shaded benches, enjoying innovative teaching aids like the 120-foot by 75-foot "Palestine Park," a plaster scale relief model of the holy land. By night, the Chautauquans savored lakeside concerts and plays before retiring to their tents or cottages. The camp culminated in an extensive examination (some students took five hours to complete their tests) and the awarding of diplomas. Chautauqua's success inspired the opening of other camp sites, a lecture circuit, publications, and a popular home study course.[21]

Chautauqua's self-improvement program symbolized many of the ideals of middle-class white Americans in the Progressive Era, and few of its speakers enjoyed greater popularity than Broadus. He delivered sixty-six lectures at the Fair Point campground in the 1880s. Chautauqua drew Broadus into a swirl of ideas largely foreign to the Old South. Featuring speakers like Jane Addams, Washington Gladden, and Richard T. Ely, one historian has dubbed Chautauqua "the cradle of progressive culture." But Broadus relished Chautauqua's natural beauty, stimulating lectures, and lucrative pay (Chautauqua paid Broadus as much as $750 per visit). He also enjoyed the elevated conversation it afforded him with university professors, authors, scientists, and even former U.S. presidents. Broadus's heavy investment in Chautauqua points to an overlooked strain of social progressivism among certain Southern Baptist elites that would develop further in the generation after his death.[22]

By 1880, John A. Broadus, unrepentant Confederate, may have been the most beloved Baptist in America. "I have been accustomed to look on you, not as infallible, but as near to the point of infallibility as men get in this world," wrote J. M. Pendleton from Pennsylvania's Crozer Seminary in 1882, and New York Baptist Thomas Armitage selected Broadus's image for the cover of his 1885 publication of the *History of the Baptists*.[23] Broadus's incessant travels and cozy rapport with northern evangelicals and business people indicate the eagerness of many white northerners to see the conflict of Reconstruction melt away (even, as we will see, at the expense of Black rights). It also demonstrates how gracefully Broadus moved between worlds.

→»»❖❧《《←

Broadus's national popularity soared on the wings of his optimistic message of reconciliation over recrimination. "It is useless now to raise the question who was right," he told a Memorial Day audience at Louisville's Cave Hill Cemetery in 1886. Standing among graves of both Yankee and Rebel soldiers, Broadus supposed that "one side was nearest right according to document and argument," while the other was right "according to the slowly changing condition of our national affairs." But Broadus called for a truce, maintaining that "neither side can claim any monopoly of good intentions, of patriotic aims, nor even of wisdom." Rather than point fingers, Broadus praised "the rapid restoration of good feelings in this country." As he saw it, the war had settled antebellum America's two most divisive issues: the power of the federal government and slavery. At a steep cost, the national conflict had "established mutual respect, and opened the way for mutual good will between the long hostile sections of our great country." While other southern ministers nursed Confederate grudges on Memorial Days, Broadus preached a sunny message of healing and hope. "Let the dead past bury its dead," he urged in 1883. "Forgetting the things which are behind, let us reach forth to those things which are before." If, as Steve Longenecker has suggested, the Lost Cause is "a house with many rooms," then Broadus resided in "the reconciliationist wing." David W. Blight has identified this message that "everyone was right, no one was wrong" as playing an important role in reuniting whites north and south, even as it pushed the nation's ongoing racial problems out of sight.[24]

Broadus still carefully guarded his white southern honor, and he refused to grovel over the South's slaveholding past. But unlike many of his Lost Cause peers, he also stopped defending it. After Appomattox, he called the institution of slavery "impossible to justify and useless to censure." He still thought that northerners misunderstood and mischaracterized southern slavery, yet he resigned himself that God had willed its eradication. He now winced at southern misuse of the Bible during antebellum slavery debates; he even admitted that he was "coming around" to the anti-slavery arguments of antebellum northern Baptist Francis Wayland. "Providence changes our stand-point, and we see Scripture in a different light," he confessed. Robert Lewis Dabney certainly never said anything like that; in these same years, Dabney's *Defence of Virginia* (1867) provided the classic Lost Cause argument that slavery constituted "the best possible relationship between white and black Americans." Broadus fits historian Gaines Foster's model of a white southerner who employed the Lost Cause in the service of reunification.[25]

Broadus made his Confederate loyalties transparent, but he wore them with a good humor that endeared him to northern crowds. "I was a rebel and George Washington was a rebel; but he succeeded and I failed. That is about the difference between us," he told a Boston gathering. He ribbed Yankee listeners about their extreme economic advantages over the superior southern soldier during the war. "We have not forgotten what we have suffered," he admitted. "If we had beaten you half as hard as you beat us, *you* would have found it difficult to forgive *us*. And if we had half as much money as you had, I am not sure but we *should* have beaten you." Yet Broadus insisted that time had obliterated all "unkind feeling" between the sections, forging a stronger and more unified America than ever before. "How we did hate you twenty-five years ago! And after Bull Run, and after Fredericksburg, your love for us was not perfect!" he told the Bostonians. "But you whipped us, and I am not sorry that we did not whip you. We have one country—North, South, East, West—we are one. God bless the *United States!* Let us love one another."[26]

Northern audiences ate it up. The *Examiner* lauded Broadus's "inimitable manner and spirit," and especially "the underlying and but half-suggested proud Southern tone, perfectly reconciled with gentleman-like comity and with Christian love." Indeed, praises for Broadus's sectional peacemaking are ubiquitous. In 1877, W. E. Gellalty credited Broadus's "visits and preaching and social interviews" for promoting "real union and fraternal feeling" between northern and southern Baptists. In 1895, New York's A. H. Strong opined that Broadus "has done more than any other man to bind North and South together, for the whole country loved him." As Grant Wacker has observed about Billy Graham in the twentieth century, Broadus discovered in his southernness "an attractive, exportable cultural commodity."[27] His fears that the Civil War had extinguished his hopes for imminence and influence had proved a happy miscalculation.

-→»❖❖«←-

But if Broadus embraced certain modern changes in the New South, he also wished dearly to preserve many ideals of the Old. Neither emancipation nor Reconstruction had altered his belief that society functioned best when under the rule of an educated, genteel class of white men. "The fact is, the masses need, and always have, leaders, to tell them what to do," he explained, "and the only question is whether they shall be led by low demagogues, or persons not much wiser than themselves, or on the other hand by men worthy to lead, qualified to lead wisely." With the restoration of white home rule after 1877, Broadus reassumed the gentry's burden of providing guidance and uplift to both Blacks and poor whites. "We Southern white people are trying to deal with the most formidable problem that civilized mankind ever had to face," he explained to the *Louisville Courier-Journal* in 1893. "Besides a great many ignorant and often degraded white people, we have this mighty mass of colored people." It was "a vast and difficult task" to "lift up the lower races into Christian enlightenment."[28]

In this arduous social task, Broadus fit the profile of a white southern conservative as outlined by C. Vann Woodward. Broadus argued for the benefits of universal southern education, or "the enlightenment of the masses." He had advocated for slave education before the Civil War ("It never was a necessary part of the institution of slavery to keep the slaves in ignorance," he argued), and he continued to insist on Black southerners' teachability in the New South. He held that African Americans constituted the race "farthest removed, perhaps, in their physical, mental and moral characteristics from us," yet also argued that "intellectual and moral endowments are not radically different; and there are individual negroes, as everybody knows, who are greatly superior, in intelligence and character, to some white men." Though deeply flawed and painfully condescending, his perspective was relatively advanced for a southern white man in 1876. Broadus persistently urged white southerners toward the duty of educating their Black neighbors, as on the night of Wade Hampton's election to the South Carolina governorship: "There will be a noble opportunity for them to win the full confidence of the colored citizens. Let it appear that all the rights of these citizens are scrupulously respected, that they are treated with fairness and kindness. Let their common schools and higher institutions be well supported and well conducted. Let our Christian white people encourage and assist their Sunday schools, and our intelligent ministers show fraternal feeling toward their ministers and churches. And all this not only in some cases, but as a general thing."[29]

Far better for southern whites to oversee Black uplift than to leave the task to the Yankees, he argued. "The teachers who came from [the North] must be mainly such as are not greatly in demand at home," he reasoned. "These, with all the prejudice and fanaticism of ignorance, would exert an evil influence by alienating the colored people from the Southern whites to whom, under God, they must mainly look, not only for employment and protection, but for education and religion." Broadus regularly preached to independent Black congregations, which multiplied at a stunning rate after the Civil War. He praised the participatory sermon-listening of Black worshipers, and scolded stuffy white critics of demonstrative Black praise. "Perchance the angels have a rather low opinion of your worship," he quipped. Black church leaders like Memphis's R. N. Counter of First Baptist Church of Beale Street looked to Broadus as a "generous friend" in times of financial need, though other Black southerners discouraged reliance on southern whites. "It would be better to fail in an honest, manly effort to lead, govern, and elevate ourselves," Rufus Perry announced, "than to suffer the shame of committing this important trust either to our late masters that made merchandise of us, or to those who proscribe us and deny us the social and ecclesiastical rights and privileges ... necessary to constitute a recognition of our manhood."[30]

Upon the establishment of the John F. Slater Fund for Black education in 1882, its directors asked Broadus to recommend as trustee "a gentleman of strong and commanding character; a representative Southerner, with no sign of the carpet bag about him; a man who regards 'our brother in black' in a true, humane, generous and Christian spirit, as a 'brother for whom Christ died'; and a man who ... may be counted on to stand up chivalrously and without flinching on the side of the weak and ignorant."[31] Though the description fit Broadus well, he nominated James P. Boyce, who served as a Slater Fund trustee until his death in 1888. Broadus then took over Boyce's position, advancing Black education reform alongside such luminaries as Johns Hopkins University President Daniel Coit Gilman, former U.S. President Rutherford B. Hayes, and Broadus's own longtime friend Jabez Lamar Monroe Curry.

A southern renaissance man, Curry served variously as a Southern Baptist pastor and college president, Confederate congressman, university professor, and diplomat to Spain under President Grover Cleveland. But he became nationally known as the "Horace Mann of the South" in the 1880s for his tireless promotion of public, tax-funded education for white and Black southerners. Curry's arguments for the fundamental right of Black children to develop their faculties elicited praise from both Booker T. Washington and W. E. B. Du Bois. The latter judged Curry's "singularly wise administration" of the Slater Fund to be "perhaps the greatest single impulse toward the economic emancipation of the Negro." Curry also served as general agent for the Peabody Education Fund, the most important program for state-funded white education in the late nineteenth century. Broadus identified closely with Curry's vision for public southern education, and would dedicate his only volume of published sermons to Curry.[32]

For Broadus, universal education fit with his deep-rooted Whiggish instincts to provide moral formation for society's lower classes. But not all the old southern gentry shared his views. Robert Lewis Dabney, for one, condemned universal education as a fool's errand. "If our civilization is to continue, there must be, at the bottom of the social fabric, a class who must work and not read," Dabney argued. Of course, Curry and Broadus operated no less than Dabney from white supremacist assumptions. "The white people are to be the leaders, to take the initiative, to have the directive control in all matters pertaining to the civilization, and the highest interests in our beloved land," Curry declared in 1899. Broadus's and Curry's efforts to educate "our brother in black" reflected both a desire to love their Black neighbor and to serve the interests of white southerners. "If you do not lift them up they will drag you down to industrial bankruptcy, social degradation, and political corruption," Curry advised. Broadus's advocacy for Black education included no visions of social equality. He remained staunchly committed to segregated classrooms at the seminary, for instance. As Wayne Flynt has noted, southern education reform often comprised "a means of checking social anarchy and promoting middle class values."[33]

Broadus still condemned racial violence, which he considered the product of low-class "negrophobes," in Woodward's phrase. This included the "epidemic of lynching" that swept the South in the 1880s and 1890s. If Broadus and the former planter class tended to look on southern Blacks as children needing guidance and protection, a new generation of white southerners born after slavery regarded free Black men as dangerous criminals, and they lashed out against them in terrible acts of racial violence during the New South era. In Louisville's *Courier-Journal*, Broadus condemned lynching as both "wrong" and "ruinous" to southern society, acknowledging that Black men were the victims in nine out of ten cases. He sympathized with the "wrath almost intolerable" felt by southern white men when "a negro murders a white man, or outrages a white woman or child," though he also pointed out that "the mere accusation or innuendo of such crimes often served as a pretext for southern lynchings." He knew that white southerners had no confidence in the court system, and felt compelled to rectify Black crimes as a point of honor. Yet lynching simply provoked society's criminal elements to further rage. Pragmatically, lynching hurt the southern economy; the brutal newspaper reports alienated the region from "the better class of Northern fellow-citizens," just when their sympathy and financial assistance were most needed. Lynchings also provoked the enmity of the South's "better negroes," and convinced them that "we are enemies of all their race." In cases of "horrid crimes" such as arson, murder, and rape, Broadus urged communities to appoint investigative committees of thoughtful citizens, from all social classes, who could administer "prompt, stern, but real and civilized justice." The suggestion that local committees would obtain justice for Blacks accused of crimes demonstrates some naiveté on Broadus's part, but his repudiation of lynching was forthright. "This is in no sense a question of party politics," he concluded. "It is a question of justice, of fundamental right, of essential civilization, of human welfare."[34]

Broadus did not deny the New South's racial problems, but he bristled at northern criticism. Rebuilding southern society was a far more difficult task than Yankee meddlers could understand. "We must not forget that the negroes differ widely among themselves, having come from different races in Africa, and having had very different relations to the white people while held in slavery," he explained in 1893. "Many of them are greatly superior to others in character, but the great mass of them belong to a very low grade of humanity. We have to deal with them as best we can, while a large number of white people stand off at a distance and scold us. Not a few of our fellow citizens at the North feel and act very nobly about the matter; but the number is sadly great who do nothing and seem to care nothing but to find fault," he complained.[35]

Broadus tried to educate northerners with a pseudoscientific racial analysis reminiscent of Thomas Jefferson's *Notes on the State of Virginia*. Those he classified as "brown negroes" had come from "half civilized" towns in Central Africa, and were "almost uniformly intelligent." Similarly, Broadus considered the "black Negroes," with their "good features—sharp nose, thin lips, good foreheads," to be "relatively intelligent." But he judged the "typical Negro," identified by "thick lips, flat nose, protruding jaws, narrow and retreating forehead," to be "vastly inferior in point of intelligence." Besides genetics and geographical origins, civilizing contact with southern whites also contributed to relative Black social competence. Slaves from smaller plantations in the grain country had worked alongside white owners and played with white children, which "materially improved the intelligence of the slaves." On the other hand, slaves from large plantations had been left "destitute of such educating contact," and thus retained "the horrid superstitions and low moral sentiments which they had brought from Africa." Southern Blacks drew these same distinctions among themselves, Broadus insisted. Those Black southerners more assimilated to white culture regarded the rest with "aversion and contempt," as "thorough savages." Broadus based his now cringe-inducing conclusions on personal anecdotes and unexamined racist assumptions. Yet peers north and south regarded him as an authority on southern racial conditions, and frequently consulted him on the subject.[36]

—·>>·❖·❀·<<·—

Broadus eyed other aspects of the South's march to modernity as mixed blessings. Temperance, his pet cause since the 1840s, made strides among Southern Baptists in the late nineteenth century. Long resistant to organized alcohol reform, Southern Baptists by the 1880s began to identify the liquor industry as a major contributor to the region's poverty, violence, family dissolution, and racial conflict. Accordingly, messengers to the 1886 Southern Baptist Convention pledged to work for "the speedy overthrow" of the manufacture and sale of intoxicating liquors, and Southern Baptist leaders emerged as prominent prohibition advocates. Scholars have noted that temperance served as the gateway through which Southern Baptists entered the Progressive Era.[37]

Broadus celebrated these developments and voted in favor of local prohibition in Louisville in 1887. But he also acknowledged certain excesses in the temperance movement. These included some Southern Baptists' clumsy efforts to explain away the Bible's references to alcohol. A. C. Dixon argued in 1891, for example, that "there was not a drop of alcohol" in the wine that Christ served at the Last Supper. Broadus groaned at these specious exegetical arguments. "No man who is a thorough Hebrew or Greek scholar, as far as I know, at all takes any such position," he insisted. "It seems to me a great pity that advocates of the great cause of total abstinence should take up so utterly untenable a position." He did, however, argue that Jesus and other biblical figures partook of a "mixed" wine ("a man who 'drinks unmixed,' among the Greeks, meant a hard drinker," he explained), which, used in moderation, "was about as stimulating as our tea and coffee." Were Jesus to live in the present day, Broadus conjectured that the Lord would opt for one of these milder beverages.[38]

More serious to Broadus was the temperance crusade's alteration of women's roles, a rising point of concern in the New South. By the 1880s, temperance had thrust many American women out of the domestic sphere and onto the public stage, where they formed independent organizations, agitated for social change, and assumed speaking platforms. Though a longtime advocate for female higher education, Broadus was far more apt to praise a woman's "beautiful delicacy" than her assertive agency. In keeping with the Old South ideal of "true womanhood," Broadus maintained that a woman's greatest contribution to society lay in her ennobling influence on men. "Here lies the great power of Christian women," he preached, "there is much they can do personally, with their own voice and their own action, but there is more they can do by that wondrous influence which men vainly strive to depict, that influence over son and brother and husband and friend whereby all the strength and power of the man is softened and guided and sobered and made wiser through the blessed influence of the woman."[39]

As more Christian women adopted public speaking roles in the wake of the temperance crusade, concerned church leaders reached out to Broadus. One man, disturbed by the rise of female Sunday school teachers, asked Broadus to write "a series of articles clearly defining woman's work as a church member." An Indiana pastor sought Broadus's advice when his congregation pressed for a "sister" to lead the mixed prayer meeting. H. C. Woods of Lincoln, Nebraska, related that "one excellent sister has already been ordained to the Ministry in this state," and wanted Broadus to back up his resistance. "Let the Methodists have the 'novelties,'" sneered one correspondent, "but, let the great Baptist communion stand firm in the old paths, say I."[40]

Broadus responded with the 1890 pamphlet "Should Women Speak in Public Assemblies?" Working carefully through pertinent Pauline passages like 1 Corinthians 14:34 and 1 Timothy 2:11–15, Broadus found the New Testament witness unequivocal in forbidding women to publicly teach men. "There is no prohibition of feminine discourse in female prayer-meetings or missionary societies," he wrote, "only keep the men out." He even warned against the "entering-wedge" of allowing male reporters or newspaper editors to attend a female speech. Contemporary efforts to pit Paul's clear instructions against other parts of Scripture particularly troubled Broadus for their implications regarding biblical authority, for this issue would "cut at the roots of Christianity." He traced the current trend of female preachers to Methodist practices, to temperance societies, and to denominations which now hold "loose views of inspiration." He believed that Baptist women had been "gradually drawn" into the movement by "unreflecting sympathy, or by mere considerations of supposed expediency." Broadus urged female readers rather to stand against the cultural tide in favor of biblical fidelity. "If Baptists are going to abandon New Testament teachings for the sake of falling in with what they regard as a popular movement, the very reason for their existence has ceased."[41]

At the same time, his daughter Eliza was stretching his categories. Intelligent, independent, and unmarried, Eliza had been her father's right hand since the Civil War. She mended all his clothes, trusting no one else to meet his particular standards for "neatness and order." With her sisters, she took dictation for his letters and publications, and she alone could locate particular books and papers in his cluttered study. The whole family marveled at her "executive abilities" in running the large, active Broadus household. Broadus personally instructed her in history, mathematics, literature, philosophy, French, German, "a little Greek and a great deal of Latin," and even in public speaking. He intended to send her to Vassar College in the mid-1870s, but cash flow and her early partial deafness kept her at home. She instead found an outlet for her talents in the women's missionary movement.[42]

Southern Baptist women had organized for missions support since the 1830s. By 1876, the Convention was encouraging "a female missionary society in every church." When the Foreign and Home Mission Boards began forming "Central Committees" of women to lead the work in each state in 1877, Kentucky's organizers chose Eliza, along with five other unmarried women in Louisville. By 1884, Kentucky's Central Committee included seventy local societies, and the total number of women's missionary societies across the South totaled more than 650. In 1888, Southern Baptists formally united this South-wide work as "the Executive Committee of the Women's Missionary Societies, Auxiliary to the Southern Baptist Convention." It was soon known as the Women's Missionary Union, or WMU. Eliza's peers asked her to represent Kentucky as a vice-president on the new Executive Committee. She consulted her father. Having examined the constitution, Eliza found "nothing that can be objected to . . . and none of the very progressive ones are connected with it." She inclined toward accepting the position, but deferred to Broadus's judgment. "If you think it of doubtful propriety for me to try it, say so, by all means, and I will promptly decline," she wrote.[43]

The missions movement had indeed vaulted Southern Baptist women into unprecedented public leadership. Among these pioneering leaders was another Broadus protege, Charlotte Digges Moon. As a student at Broadus's Albemarle Female Institute in the 1850s, Moon had established a reputation for intelligence and impiety; she claimed that her middle initial "D." stood for "devil." But she attended an inquirer's meeting during a revival at Broadus's Charlottesville Baptist Church "to see what that old fool had to say," and his words hit home. "I went to the service to scoff, and returned to my room to pray all night," she recalled. Broadus soon baptized her into the Charlottesville Baptist Church. Denominational legend holds that she also came close to marrying Crawford Toy, before breaking the engagement over his heterodoxy. Moon moved to China with the Foreign Mission Board in 1873, and by the 1880s she was galvanizing Southern Baptist mission support through her passionate newspaper editorials. Moon declared that she did not "want Northern ideals of womanhood introduced into our Southern Baptist missions." But she pushed back against male authoritarianism in other ways, such as when she threatened to resign from the mission if not given voting rights in the field along with men. Her example contributed to refashioning a more activistic piety among Southern Baptist women.[44]

Moon, Eliza Broadus, and WMU Secretary Annie Walker Armstrong, all single, "well-educated, upper-middle class women" drawn from "the Southern Baptist elite," rose to denominational prominence through missions. They formed organizational networks, traveled to distant meetings, addressed large gatherings of women, discussed social reform issues, stewarded significant sums of money, published articles, and corresponded with male leaders as peers. By 1911, over ten thousand chapters of the WMU contributed almost $240,000 for Southern Baptist missions. WMU leaders reflected many of the modern sensibilities of the broader women's progressive movement in America, while maintaining certain conservative social boundaries, such as refusing to publicly address men. Still, the WMU's activity stirred no little consternation among male Southern Baptist leaders. In 1885, the Convention changed its constitution to prevent women from being seated as messengers.[45]

Broadus blessed Eliza's acceptance of the WMU vice-presidency in Kentucky, a position she would hold for forty years. She remembered her father providing "constant encouragement and help." He had read to her from the *Foreign Missionary Journal* since she was a child, and now supplied her with missionary biographies and other literature. He took her to Baptist meetings for networking, and "taught her himself to speak in a large room." Eliza and her coworkers encountered frequent criticism from conservative voices. "Many pastors and churches still looked on our efforts as interfering and upsetting, and many years of slow, patient, quiet work were needed to overcome opposition and indifference, before great progress was made," Eliza remembered. But she could always turn to her father. "Whenever I was faint-hearted over WMU, he would say, 'Just keep on, daughter, the stars in their courses will fight for you.'"[46]

Certain aspects of the WMU still made him nervous. Annie Armstrong revered Broadus but observed regretfully in 1895 that he "seems to be a little fearful of the outcome of this movement." She confessed frustration with his guarded support. "I never heard him make an address on Woman's Work to refer to it that I did not feel very sorry he had touched on it at all, for while he spoke as approving of it, he always ended with a warning that we should not forget Paul's teaching—'let the women keep silence in the churches,' etc. etc.," she wrote. Armstrong believed that the WMU had earned the trust of conservative Convention leaders, and "always hoped that Dr. Broadus would give our work his unqualified endorsement, but as far as I know, he never did, and certainly in the Seminary our work was not spoken of." He had long advocated female education, but it would take his proteges, including Eliza and son-in-law A. T. Robertson, to expand public roles of Southern Baptist women in the next generation.[47]

→»»✣•✣«←

By the time Robert Lewis Dabney visited Louisville in November 1894, Broadus was too ill to accept an invitation to visit his old friend. Despite Dabney's prolific output in the closing decades of the nineteenth century, he had steadily lost influence among the southerners who had once revered him as a great intellectual leader. "I have no audience," Dabney admitted in 1879. Among the antebellum South's most brilliant theologians, the Virginian died in lonely isolation in Victoria, Texas, 1898. "I am the Cassandra of Yankeedom," he sighed in 1894, "predestined to prophesy truth and never be believed by her country until too late." Yet in these same years, the star of John Albert Broadus ascended as high as any southern minister's in America. When he finished his earthly course in 1895, the *Louisville Courier-Journal* declared, "There is no man in the United States whose death would cause more widespread sorrow." Indeed, Broadus "was as much loved in New York as Virginia," marveled William Whitsitt. "Whatever he spoke from any platform on either side of the line was applauded to the echo on both sides of the line."[48]

The diverging paths of the two Virginia clergy demonstrate that not all Lost Cause devotees traveled the same road in the late nineteenth century. In his book *Masters Without Slaves,* James L. Roark suggests that white southerners responded to the rapid social changes of war, emancipation, and Reconstruction in one of three ways. At the two extremes, "transformationists" jettisoned the past to make something fundamentally new, while "restorationists" remained past-oriented, fleeing to tradition to escape a terrifying future. In between, the "accommodationists" demonstrated "a willingness to compromise, an acceptance of a blend of the past, present, and future. Its focus is on immediate circumstances, the goal being to carve out a place in the new environment, while at the same time to maintain integrity." If Dabney represents the classic restorationist, then Broadus was a remarkably successful accommodationist. His peers praised him as an "interpreter" in the New South era. "He could interpret Southern people to Northern audiences, and Northern people to Southern audiences," John R. Sampey remembered.[49] As a preacher, Broadus had long displayed a masterful ability at adapting his message for any audience; emerging from the Civil War and Reconstruction, he now exercised this skill on the larger stage of American life.

Nine

SCHOLARLY CONSERVATIVE

I N THE SPRING OF 1883, seminary graduate George B. Eager poured out his heart to John Broadus in a candid letter detailing his "intellectual difficulties" with his Bible. Eager had arrived at the Southern Baptist Theological Seminary in Greenville in the mid-1870s with his mind already "aroused and perplexed" about the Bible's reliability. He had spent the previous eighteen months of his Louisiana pastorate obsessively reading, debating, and fretting over the doctrine of inspiration. Staggering into the classroom of Crawford Toy, Eager immediately found relief from his mental anguish. Toy's distinction between "the truthfulness and scientific accuracy of the inspired writers" intrigued Eager. So too did Toy's dismissal of "the folly of attempting to harmonize science and the Bible." Aided by frequent evening walks with Toy, at which time "we conversed more or less freely about these matters to my intense interest and satisfaction," Eager's old anxieties about the Bible abated. "I felt that I was attaining to more rational and spiritual views of the subject," he explained to Broadus, "and never once suspected that I was drifting away from orthodoxy."

But after graduation, when Eager accepted a pastoral call to Lexington, Virginia, his doubts resurfaced. Cut off from Toy's guidance, Eager now "puzzled over the great questions of Immortality, Atonement, Future Punishment." By the winter of 1877–1878, he was "almost overwhelmed with a sense of the mystery of life—its darkness, painfulness, and perplexity." Eager's angst threw him into a "spell of sickness," requiring him to take six weeks' vacation that spring. In an attempt to divert his mind, Eager attended a meeting of the local Franklin Society, only to find that the night's discussion topic was "Do the Scriptures teach that the Future Punishment of the wicked is endless?" When Eager declined to voice his affirmation, he was "called out and charged with heresy." As he left the hall, several friends, including a few educated pastors, followed Eager back to his hotel. They "talked freely" until 12:30 a.m. When Eager was finally alone, he said, "[I] threw myself across my bed & sobbed like a child." He wept and prayed for two hours before calming down, but he never slept. The experience marked a turning point in his spiritual and intellectual development:

> I have felt from that day to this, that I carried in my heart a secret sense of the solution of life's mystery. Like "a child crying in the night"—"a child crying for the light, and with no language but a cry," I yielded myself into the arms of my Father God, and found rest. From that day to this, tho' often disturbed *in mind* over these great questions, I have never been so *troubled in heart* as before. I have concerned myself much less about the *philosophy* of life and the *theories* of Atonement, Inspiration, & c., and have given myself up more to *living* and *doing.*[1]

Eager's experience provides a small window into what he called "these tempestuous times" for a rising generation of southern evangelicals seeking to reconcile their traditional faith with modern learning. For intellectually inclined Southern Baptists like Eager, determining the nature and authority of the Bible amid the onslaught of modern ideas formed "the most momentous, blazing question of our day." Many conservative southerners stuck to the old paths, unafraid to "call out and charge with heresy." The more daring sought solutions in Crawford Toy's "more rational and spiritual views" of the Bible. Others opted to table their intellectual quandaries for a focus on piety and ethics, or "living and doing," as Eager put it. As Molly Worthen has written, these evangelicals "had an authority problem," and they had begun the long and violent struggle to reconcile tradition and modernity, faith and reason, the church and the academy.[2] In their search for certainly, many of these younger evangelicals, like Eager, would seek direction from John Broadus, their gold standard of pious scholarship. As usual, he offered a mediating position.

→»·✦·✦·«←

By 1880, Broadus had long been Southern Baptists' leading voice for a scholarly ministry. But Crawford Toy's apostasy from denominational orthodoxy had forced him to reevaluate his mission. Toy had been Broadus's protege, intimate friend, and beau-ideal of Southern Baptist scholarship; in the spring of 1879, seminary trustees also made Toy the first professor in America dismissed over German higher criticism. It had immediately sparked an intense public debate over biblical inspiration in Southern Baptist life. "[Toy] was for several years a sore thorn in the flesh of Boyce and Broadus," recalled William H. Whitsitt, "nearly half the Baptists were on his side."[3]

At the most conservative end of the Southern Baptist spectrum were those Eager called "the self constituted 'heresy hunters' and noisy guardians of orthodoxy in our own ranks, who make it their business to give to the breeze every whispered rumor of unsoundness in their brethren, & consider it their right to demand of each one an account of his creed." Chief among these "heresy hunters" was Mrs. Josephine Peck, who had initially blown the whistle on Toy in the *Religious Herald,* under the pseudonym "E. T. R." Eager expressed to Broadus the "indignation and contempt" that he and other young, educated clergy felt toward Peck and her ilk:

> Mrs. Peck among others has shown herself as entirely too much of a busy-body in such matters to suit my taste. Though an entire stranger to me, she has not only been industrious in circulating reports of my unsoundness, of the truthfulness of which she could not have evidence, but she has even undertaken to dictate to me what course I must pursue in order to set myself right with the public! "Write to the Herald," she directs, "advocating and asserting Plenary Inspiration, & giving the reasons of Baptists for considering that a fundamental doctrine, as much as the existence of God, &c. Show that you believe with all your heart that down to the least jot or tittle of the original writings of the Bible is God's word, and the Holy Ghost is responsible for every word in it as if He had written them with His own hand and handed them to us from the opened heavens"—and much more of the same sort.[4]

In some ways, Peck was a forerunner of the fundamentalist position that emerged in the biblical debates of the 1920s.[5]

At the most progressive end of Southern Baptist life were Toy's disciples. Mostly seminary graduates, they believed Toy's views to be sound, and that he had been martyred to denominational opinion. Eager confessed to Broadus his own distaste for the "policy of repression" that he detected behind Toy's removal. Eager believed that the Board's action "was fraught with peril to our cause and to the interests of higher learning among us." For seminary-trained pastors like Eager, losing a scholar of Toy's caliber represented a massive step backward in the professionalization of Southern Baptist ministry. "I did not think it right, to sacrifice such a man as Dr. Toy to popular clamor . . . not even for the sake of the denominational peace or the future prosperity of the Seminary," he wrote. Broadus, careful to speak no ill of his friend Toy, quietly informed Eager that "a good many did not understand how far he had really gone."[6]

In this charged environment, Broadus and James P. Boyce led a swift conservative retrenchment at the seminary. Immediately upon Toy's resignation, Boyce asked Basil Manly Jr., who had taken the presidency of Georgetown College in 1871, to resume his old teaching position. Manly consented, though he understood the delicacy of replacing Toy. "If I agree with him, I shall be censured for unsoundness, if I differ, I shall be thought to be actuated by prejudice or narrow views, clinging to orthodoxy rather than Truth," Manly wrote. "There is nothing for it but just to go ahead and try to do right, for folks will talk."[7]

In his introductory faculty address, "Why and How to Study the Bible," Manly distanced the seminary from Toy with a ringing affirmation of biblical inspiration. "From the doubt or denial of God's book, the road is short to doubt and denial of God," he thundered, "and after that comes the abyss, where all knowledge is not only lost but scoffed at except that which the brute might enjoy as well." In the classroom, Manly forged an even more cautious path on Old Testament issues than in his previous tenure, though he did study abroad in Germany in 1881, partly to gain a modicum of "prestige." Manly's publication of *The Bible Doctrine of Inspiration Explained and Vindicated* (1888), a defense of the Bible's full verbal plenary inspiration in the tradition of Princeton Theological Seminary, became Southern Baptist orthodoxy on the subject.[8]

With Manly, Broadus walked back his earlier enthusiasm for German critical scholarship as he witnessed the spread of Toy's ideas among Southern Baptists. In 1880, Broadus urged Manly's brother, Charles, to accept the presidency of the University of South Carolina, a state where Toy's influence was especially strong. Charles's placement "will *keep out* undesirable men, and postpone possible tendencies, and will give you additional influence towards maintaining and restoring conservatism in the state at large." Broadus began rigorously screening potential seminary instructors by asking if their "belief in inspiration has become in any respect relaxed" since graduation. Often, he discovered that it had. When Toy provided him with a list of his brightest students as potential instructors, Broadus and Boyce determined that all but two were unsound in their views.[9]

When Boyce learned that seminary alumni John Stout and T. P. Bell allowed for mistakes in the Bible, he intervened with the Foreign Mission Board to rescind their appointments to China. Seminary graduate and vocal Toy devotee William C. Lindsay howled in the papers over this latest instance of the "policy of repression" descending on Southern Baptist life. But Broadus affirmed the Foreign Mission Board decision, and helped find two conservative replacements. He now refused to recommend graduates who rejected traditional views of inspiration for jobs in the pastorate or in the academy, even to teach English in a university.[10]

For years, Broadus had extolled the benefits of German graduate studies. Now, he warned younger men of the damage that a European sojourn could inflict on their faith and reputations. "In Germany, and in some parts of Great Britain and America, it requires great independence of mind and carefully maintained devoutness, in order to stand firm against—not the arguments, but—the cool assumptions, that all 'traditional' views of the Bible are antiquated, and that the orthodox are weak and ignorant," Broadus cautioned F. W. Boatwright of Richmond. "There is much to be learned, much good impulse to be gained, also prestige, and familiarity with languages in which you must be reading through life," he wrote, "but I am persuaded you will find it desirable to maintain, quietly and distinctly, just such habits about Sunday, about beer and wine, about theaters, etc., about private prayer, as you would do at home in Richmond."[11] He now saw that the southern piety of good Virginia boys like Boatwright, future president of Richmond College, would receive a fierce test on the Continent.

Broadus made an even stronger case to David G. Lyon, a bright 1880 graduate and prospective seminary faculty member. But Lyon listened to Toy over Broadus, and took his Ph.D. in Semitic languages at the University of Leipzig. Hoping to hire Lyon a year later, Broadus asked in 1881 if he could "teach, as to inspiration, in accordance with and not contrary to the opinions which prevail among intelligent American Baptists." Lyon could not. "The tears fill my eyes and sincere grief my heart as I reflect that the demand is an impossibility," he wrote to Broadus, "for you wish a man who can assert the absolute infallibility of the biblical writers, and that I cannot do."[12] Lyon would join Toy at Harvard

Divinity School in 1882, launching a distinguished academic career as the Hollis Professor of Divinity.

Broadus also failed to preserve Toy protege George Manly, son of Basil, from Germany's wiles. Nor could he dissuade seminary graduate Lewis J. Huff, who left his pastorate when he could no longer "preach to them and at the same time be free and honest." Huff knew that his decision disappointed Broadus. "It pains me deeply to think that I have come short of what you had hoped for me, and it is not in my power to express the sorrow which this whole matter has given me," Huff wrote in an apologetic letter, "there are few in the world to whom I am under such obligations as to you."[13] The Broadus correspondence repeatedly testifies to the emotional turmoil that young Southern Baptists experienced in the conflict of faith and learning. Having opened the door of Germany to a generation of Southern Baptist seminary students, Broadus now watched in distress as many streamed through it.

To Broadus's relief, some seminary graduates retreated from Toy as his published views grew more radical. Toy had inspired J. O. Lowry to pursue German studies, but by the fall of 1881 Lowry could follow his mentor no further. "Dr. Toy's views and mine part company now, not because of a decayed intellectual sympathy," he wrote to Broadus, "but because of the practical destructiveness, the gulf, to which they tend." George Eager had initially been incensed at the trustees' "policy of repression" in dismissing Toy. But by 1883 he admitted that "at last, by degrees, I came to see how far he was going and drew back amazed and startled." Eager revised his opinion of the trustees' actions in 1879, understanding that "Dr. Toy's views were even then believed by some of the wisest men to be radically wrong." South Carolina Baptist J. Hartwell Edwards also backed away from Toy's increasing skepticism. "I still believe as firmly as ever in the value of biblical criticism, but I feel that its researches must be conducted in a very conservative spirit," Edwards explained. "For Dr. Toy personally I still entertain feelings of affection and esteem, and sincerely regret his present extreme position."[14]

For Broadus, too, the shifting theological winds of the late nineteenth century created painful relational tensions. In the aftermath of the Toy controversy, he would endeavor to forge a model of evangelical scholarship that was both learned and pious.

·->>>✧✦✧<<<·

Broadus's reputation as a preacher and seminary founder has today overshadowed his academic *bona fides,* but his peers praised him as a "consummate scholar." After graduating valedictorian at the University of Virginia under one of antebellum America's most advanced philologists, Broadus ever after maintained the most rigorous of study habits. He read widely and deeply, and committed many important works to memory, until he had gotten them "into his blood." He read fluently in Latin, Greek, French, Anglo-Saxon, Hebrew, and Coptic. Broadus read in German virtually every day, keeping up with the latest periodicals and academic works. He also had a working knowledge of Italian, Spanish, Gothic, modern Greek, and Sanskrit, which he took up at age sixty. "The class-room presents great advantages," Broadus said, "but through life a man must be his own teacher, his own pupil, and his own fellow-student, and bring all the energies of his being to bear upon the persistent effort to fill each of these positions worthily."[15]

He kept a scholar's company. He corresponded with a range of academics regarding Greek grammar, translation, and textual criticism: James Hope Moulton of Manchester, Ezra Abbott of Harvard, A. E. Dunning of Yale, J. B. Lightfoot and B. F. Westcott of Cambridge; Joseph Henry Thayer of Andover and Harvard, and B. B. Warfield of Princeton Theological Seminary. The nation's most prestigious learning centers invited him to speak on their campuses, including the University of Virginia, Johns Hopkins, Cornell, Yale, the University of Chicago, and Vanderbilt. In 1886, Harvard University honored Broadus with a Doctor of Divinity degree at its 250th anniversary celebration.[16]

In short, Broadus's contemporaries viewed him as a credible scholar who advocated careful, technical, and even critical study of the Bible. He would always appreciate many aspects of German scholarship, and remained open to the new light its methods cast on traditional biblical interpretations. Albert Henry Newman, who studied with Broadus in the 1870s, recalled that he "combined in a remarkable degree deep devoutness and spirituality with interest in the critical work of German scholars." Broadus "encouraged his ablest students to master the German language so as to have full access to the treasures of German learning and when practicable to pursue graduate courses in German universities," Newman wrote. While Broadus "warned his students against accepting the more radical results of the so-called higher criticism, he did not, so far as the writer is informed, denounce Biblical criticism as a wicked impertinence." This openness compelled Newman in 1915 to retrospectively ascribe to Broadus an "intermediate position" between the fundamentalist and modernist views of the Bible.[17]

Yet throughout the 1880s, Broadus also acknowledged his pre-commitment to the truthfulness of the Bible and to historic Christian orthodoxy. He did so in his 1883 Southern Baptist Convention message, later published as "Three Views as to the Bible." He did so again in an 1887 address to the annual gathering of Northern Baptist Societies, in a sermon titled "The Paramount and Permanent Authority of the Bible." Amid the "noisy and clamorous" voices of modern scientists and "German infidelity," Broadus identified with those "who believe that the Bible is the Word of God; not merely that it contains the Word of God, which wise persons may disentangle from other things in the book, but that it is the Word of God." Modern scholarship may prove certain traditional interpretations of the Bible to be erroneous, but the Bible itself remained "completely inspired," infallible, and authoritative. "The great principle in all such inquiries," Broadus maintained, "is that while it is lawful to re-investigate the meaning of Scripture in the light of current opinion and feeling, it is not lawful to put anything as authority above God's word."[18]

In the 1880s, Broadus began to defend the Bible's reliability against the claims of modern science, even as prominent evangelicals embraced Darwinian evolution. He explained that the Bible was not a science textbook, but employed poetic and phenomenological language to describe natural events. Still, it spoke accurately to the issues it addressed. "Even today," he asserted, "I know of no discrepancies in the Bible which impair its credibility." He pushed back against modern science's anti-supernatural presuppositions, and noted how the constantly changing nature of scientific hypotheses should temper evangelicals' rush to adjust the biblical witness. "I am waiting for evolution to evolve itself," he preached, "Let us not be over hasty to reconcile the Bible with the present theories of evolution." He compared evangelicals who conceded error in the Bible to make "peace" with science to a man who treats his toothache by shooting himself in the head—they chose a deadly cure. Though he valued scientific research, he insisted that "there are facts of existence which its processes cannot explain or even detect," including "our sense of right and wrong, our quenchless longings after immortality, our invincible belief in the Almighty, All-wise and All-loving."[19]

Broadus also grappled with the era's emerging historical consciousness. Modern critics stressed that the Christian Scriptures had arisen *within* history, rather than *apart from* it. In their emphasis on the cultural contexts that produced the biblical texts, they claimed that the Bible's theology reflected its time-bound human authors, not divine revelation. Broadus appreciated how modern criticism had pushed interpreters to take seriously the cultures, personalities, and styles of the human authors—God had not delivered his Word through a heavenly dictaphone, as skeptics charged. Yet Broadus stressed that the Bible was both a divine and human document, "a supernatural phenomenon," as well as "a product of historical forces." "God here speaks *through men,*" he told the Southern Baptist Convention. "The sacred writings are truly and thoroughly human. Here is human observation, recollection, and reflection. Here are three different human languages.... here are the peculiarities of individual writers, as strongly marked in thought and style as anywhere else in literature, and requiring consideration in all careful interpretation. I repeat, the Scripture writings are thoroughly human."[20]

And yet, "this is not saying that they are only human," he maintained. The inspired authors had been so "moved by the Holy Ghost" that they "not only say what He wishes, but say it as He wishes. In this sense we naturally hold to the verbal inspiration of the Scriptures." While reading the Bible as a legitimate historical document, Broadus urged modern interpreters to remember that it is ultimately "a history of redemption, of God's mightiness and mercies," which culminated in Jesus the Savior. "We cannot understand the Old Testament, except we read it in its bearing upon Christ, as fulfilled in him."[21]

By the 1880s, Broadus recognized progress, not conservatism, to be the *zeitgeist* of late nineteenth-century America. "The passion for something new is all-absorbing," he observed. Broadus acknowledged his own "delight" in pursuing and discovering new truth, and his repulsion at "blind Bourbonic conservatism." "There is a really exalted feeling, of sympathy with progress, and love of inquiry, which powerfully affects us all, and ought to affect us," he allowed. Yet an unexamined love of novelty spelled peril for American Christianity. He cautioned against an overly "progressive orthodoxy" that "forsakes or adds to the teaching of Christ," and thereby "becomes heterodoxy." "If a man is going to be a Christian at all, I think the New Testament will surely make him an orthodox Christian," he wrote to his son Samuel Broadus in 1886. "If it does not teach the divinity of Christ, I wonder how that could be taught." Broadus pleaded with daring young

Baptist scholars to "go slow, and be cautious about announcing anything essentially novel in doctrine."[22] It was a perspective Broadus endeavored to model in his own academic work.

·—→»◈⚬◈«←·—

Despite his scholarly inclinations, Broadus by the mid-1880s boasted no major publications in his chosen academic field. He had published a constant stream of popular articles, academic book reviews, and two highly regarded preaching books, notably his best-selling *A Treatise on the Preparation and Delivery of Sermons* (to be treated in the next chapter). But seminary demands and financial pressures had hindered his production of serious Greek and New Testament scholarship. Broadus complained in 1880 that his teaching load had "become almost intolerably burdensome," as he now covered homiletics, English New Testament, and junior and senior Greek, along with special graduate studies, with an ever-increasing enrollment. "How with all this I can write much for the *Religious Herald* as I must do, and work on my poor commentary, is more than I can see," he sighed, "but I intend to do my best."[23] In his final decade he found success.

Broadus's most important academic contribution involved the American Commentary on the New Testament (ACNT) series, produced by the American Baptist Publication Society, and edited by Newton Theological Institute President Alvah H. Hovey. Friends since the early 1850s, Hovey and Broadus occupied similar positions within the evangelical academy. Both had committed their lives to a single institution: Broadus would give thirty-six years to Southern Seminary and Hovey fifty-four to Newton, where he taught virtually every subject and served as president from 1868–1898. They were both decidedly conservative theologians, though also as "hospitable" to the "newer learning" as possible. Both could also raise eyebrows by the fast company they kept. Hovey befriended notorious liberal Baptist William Newton Clarke, and also hired the controversial Ezra Palmer Gould to teach at Newton, before regretfully dismissing him over biblical inspiration in 1882, in a replay of the Toy affair. Hovey's son George called his father "a harmonizing influence between a progressive thinker and the conservatives," which makes a serviceable description for Broadus, too. As editor of the ACNT, Hovey relied on Broadus to help him select the right mix of contributors: northern and southern, old and young, conservative and progressive. Broadus also agreed to write the volume on the Gospel according to Matthew.[24]

Producing a first-rate commentary on Matthew had preoccupied Broadus since at least 1863. After more than twenty years of painstaking, stop-and-start work, he completed it in the fall of 1885. "I have labored to make a clear, sound, and useful commentary," he wrote, "and I shall be very glad and thankful if it proves acceptable and helpful to earnest readers of the Bible." He dedicated the finished volume to Gessner Harrison, his beloved mentor and father-in-law. "At your feet I learned to love Greek, and my love of the Bible was fostered by your earnest devoutness," Broadus wrote, now two decades after Harrison's death.[25]

In the hefty, 610-page book, Broadus commented on virtually every line in Matthew's twenty-eight chapters. With pastors and "the better class of Sunday School teachers" as his primary audience, he wrote with characteristic warmth and simplicity, interlacing technical comments with "Homiletical and Practical" suggestions. He challenged popular misunderstandings gently. Broadus showed off his learning in the footnotes, where he engaged in extensive discussions of Greek grammar and syntax, as well as questions of textual criticism. He interacted with more than 350 ancient and modern sources, including the latest and most speculative German scholars. Yet Broadus himself was "safely conservative" in his own conclusions. "The solicitude, and even alarm, which some persons feel in regard to the encroachments of text-criticism, must be regarded as without cause," he asserted. "Instead of shaking faith in Scripture, these researches will ultimately strengthen faith." Broadus confronted apparent errors in the text with a calm directness that assured his readers "that the inspiration of Scripture is complete, that the inspired writers have everywhere told us just what God would have us know."[26]

Critics hailed *Matthew* as a career achievement. "No doubt it will prove to be *the* Commentary of the whole series," wrote Hovey, "you will certainly be remembered with honor, if all the rest of us are forgotten." Henry C. Vedder, soon to import modernism into northern Baptist life, declared, "Every Baptist ought to hold up his head a little higher when our own scholars are proved capable of writing books such as this." H. H. Harris of Virginia also lauded the book's "scholarly honesty, its safe conservatism, its picturesque vividness, its homiletical helpfulness, and its devotional spirit." Outside of Baptist life, Andover's J. H. Thayer judged it "probably the best commentary in English on that Gospel." Broadus's learned but reverent treatment of Matthew announced to the Gilded Age that the New Testament still bore the closest scrutiny. "One not only breathes freer, but feels more restful in his own mind after he has seen that a candid and scholarly investigator and critic can wade through all 'the theories' and yet come out substantially holding to the old views," observed one reviewer. *Matthew* would eventually be published in Spanish, Portuguese, and Chinese.[27]

Hovey pressed Broadus to write the ACNT volumes on Ephesians and Colossians as well. Though Broadus declined these projects, he agreed to help Hovey with his own work on the Gospel of John. His insights so impressed Hovey that he begged to include them in the final printed edition, in brackets bearing Broadus's initials. "I will give you all the honor, gladly sit at your feet, and I will try to let you have something else for your time," Hovey wrote. "Even help on a few passages will do much for the commentary. It will also show my respect and love for you as well as your goodwill to me." Upon publication, Hovey sent Broadus a check for $35, to express "my sense of obligation and of friendship, wishing that I could do more."[28]

Completing the Matthew commentary freed Broadus for further scholarly pursuits. His wealthy benefactor Eugene Levering invited him in 1890 to inaugurate a new lecture series that Levering had endowed at Johns Hopkins University, Baltimore's groundbreaking, German-style research university, established in 1876. Selecting "Jesus of Nazareth" as his topic, Broadus prepared a conservative response to the naturalistic "lives of Jesus" that dominated New Testament studies in the era. Beginning with D. F. Strauss's *Life of Jesus* (1835), numerous German New Testament critics had endeavored to sift the Jesus of history from the "Christ" created by the early church. While Broadus appreciated the interest these studies had generated in the life of Christ, he regretted their denials of biblical inspiration and their anti-supernaturalism. Preparing these lectures, Broadus confessed that he "had never in his life, undertaken such a difficult piece of work and that he felt weighed down by the task."[29]

The seven-hundred-seat auditorium at Johns Hopkins filled for Broadus's lectures, with "many turned away" for lack of room. He delivered three addresses, focusing on Jesus' personal character, his ethical teaching, and the historicity of his miracles. Broadus confronted the skeptical dismissals of German scholars F. C. Baur and Theodore Keim, of scientists Thomas Henry Huxley and Charles Darwin, and the iconoclastic American theologian Theodore Parker.

He warned against separating the moral beauty of the Sermon on the Mount from Christ's call for repentance and divine forgiveness. "You deceive yourselves!" Broadus preached, "For Jesus Christ stands before men not only as an ethical and religious teacher, but also as Lord and Savior!" The lectures culminated in an unflinching defense of Christ's bodily resurrection. "If I do not know that Jesus of Nazareth rose from the dead, then I know nothing in the history of mankind," he declared. "If the evidence, when fully examined with a calm willingness to be convinced, does not in this case warrant a practical certainty, then there is no adequate evidence of any historical event."[30]

Evangelical critics praised the lectures upon their publication as the 105-page *Jesus of Nazareth* (1890). "They are scholarly in composition, beautiful in diction, and masterly in thought," announced the *Philadelphia Presbyterian*. "In these days, when naturalism is engaged in a continually closer contest with the spiritual, it is pleasant to hear ring a true message from above, addressed in so attractive a manner, to young men engaged in scientific and philosophic study." The *Presbyterian and Reformed Review* likewise lauded the volume as "the fruit of life-time studies . . . remarkable for their lucidity, comprehensiveness and conclusiveness in thought." *Jesus of Nazareth* would see five English editions and a Spanish translation.[31]

Broadus's classroom teaching also yielded a handful of publications in his latter years. Most notable was his *Harmony of the Gospels* (1893), immediately hailed as the new standard among conservative New Testament scholars. Quickly adopted as a course text by seminaries and Bible colleges, Broadus's *Harmony* went through six editions in its first ten years, and a dozen more after updates by A. T. Robertson, his protege and son-in-law. Robertson further disseminated Broadus's teaching by publishing his *Syllabus for New Testament Study* (1900), which included Broadus's teaching outlines and annotated bibliographies for each New Testament book. The *Syllabus,* also designed for classroom use, saw multiple print runs in the early twentieth century.[32]

Other projects showcased Broadus's translation ability. In 1887, the distinguished church historian Philip Schaff invited Broadus to revise the Oxford translation of John Chrysostom's (347–407) homilies on Philippians, Colossians, and Thessalonians. Broadus considered "John of the Golden Mouth" to be history's greatest preacher. He called Chrysostom a man "fully in earnest, and all alive," whose "straight-forward, careful, and usually sober interpretations" contrasted with the wild allegorizing typical of the fourth century. While Chrysostom's homilies lacked the system of modern sermonic tastes, Broadus challenged contemporary preachers to learn from their "freedom, versatility, and skill in practical application." Indeed, Broadus mused as to whether "the modern careful preparation and orderly arrangement, combined (*mutatis mutants*) with the ancient freedom and directness . . . might constitute the best type of expository preaching."[33] English readers of Chrysostom have followed Broadus's translation for more than a century.

Broadus had also developed a keen interest in textual criticism, the comparison of ancient manuscripts to determine the most accurate modern translation. He viewed this discipline as an outflow of his belief in divine, word-for-word biblical inspiration, arguing that "the highest views of Inspiration should lead to the greatest zeal for Text-criticism." Broadus instructed his students in the science of text criticism, he regularly waded into public debates regarding the best Greek texts and the newest Bible translations, and he delivered three lectures on the subject at Newton Theological Institute in 1884. His peers considered Broadus to be "one of the half-dozen American scholars who may properly be called experts in this department."[34]

In 1887, the American Baptist Publication Society offered him $1,000 to join Alvah Hovey and Henry G. Weston in revising the old American Bible Union New Testament. The original project, conceived as a kind of "Baptist Bible," stirred controversy for translating the Geek "*baptizo*" as "immerse," rather than keeping the standard transliteration of "baptize." Broadus had previously opined against this decision as impractical and unnecessary in the *Religious Herald*. He now shrank from the revision, believing his involvement in a sectarian translation project would damage his scholarly reputation. But C. C. Bitting of the ABPS prevailed on him, and Broadus spent the final years of the 1880s revising Matthew, Mark, and Luke. The "American Bible Union Version Improved Edition" was published in 1892. Its exposure was limited, as Broadus predicted, but critics praised his translations.[35]

Broadus's sudden flurry of publications between 1886 and 1893 burnished his reputation as a Greek and New Testament scholar. He was, in Mark Wilson's summary, a "comprehensive, conventional scholar" who "conserved the Christian and Baptist tradition with supreme ability and accepted, or rejected, new knowledge as it could be used to enrich and correct that tradition in incidental phases." In the twilight of his career, Broadus enjoyed respect and influence within the highest circles of the American academy. This was becoming an increasingly rare experience for a conservative evangelical scholar, and especially for a southerner, as the professionalization of biblical studies and the secularization of the American academy would drive a deep wedge between faith and scholarship by the early twentieth century.[36] Broadus's growing stature also enhanced the academic credentials of the seminary, where his colleagues published comparatively little. Moving forward from Toy and the inspiration controversy, Broadus hoped to stamp the seminary as a center for scholarly religious conservatism in a rapidly changing environment.

-->>✣✣<<-

Broadus took a fatherly interest in the rising generation of biblical scholars, especially those in the Baptist world. "Allow me to say, as one who is growing old, and has all his life been brought in close connection with successive generations of fine young men, that every year I hold young men in deeper respect," he noted cheerfully in 1883. Perhaps he saw in them a faint reflection of his own, ambitious younger self. "I delight in observing their ardor and magnificent hopefulness, their undeveloped potencies and rapid unfolding. I see at times in their very faults and errors a promise of power for good, when years shall have tempered impulse and deepened reflection."[37] Among the energetic young scholars who attracted Broadus's attention in the 1880s, none simultaneously delighted and dismayed him like William Rainey Harper.

Born in Concord, Ohio, in 1856, Harper matriculated at Yale at age seventeen. In two years, he had earned a Ph.D. in ancient languages. Harper had grown up in a Presbyterian home (he would identify with the Baptists while teaching at Denison College in Ohio), but he already doubted traditional Christian faith when he discovered the historical-critical study of the Bible at Yale. Harper concluded that pre-modern readings of the Scriptures were Christianity's single greatest threat. "The cry of our times is for the application of scientific methods in the study of the Bible," he declared in 1889. "If the methods of the last century continue to hold exclusive sway, the time will come when intelligent men of all classes will say, 'If this is your Bible we will have none of it.'"[38]

By age twenty-four, Harper, a zealous, entrepreneurial educator, had launched a crusade to popularize modern biblical studies. He opened a Hebrew summer school and correspondence course in 1880. A monthly journal, the *Hebrew Student,* followed in 1882. In 1883, Harper debuted at Chautauqua, establishing himself as the most popular and demanding professor at the camp. "You are neither to eat, drink, or sleep," he drilled. "You will recite three times a day, six days a week. Study nothing but Hebrew. Go to no side interest. Begin with the rising of the sun Monday and stop with the chimes Saturday night." In 1885, Chautauqua named Harper as principal of its rapidly expanding College of Liberal Arts. In 1886, the thirty-year-old accepted appointment as the Woolsey Professor of Hebrew at Yale.

In the midst of his meteoric rise, Harper formed an unlikely friendship with Broadus. Then in his late fifties and always ailing, Broadus was a slow-moving southerner trained in the antebellum world. The boyish, bespectacled Harper was a "young man in a hurry," a northerner thirty years Broadus's junior who embodied the modern obsession with progress and speed. But Broadus formed a paternal bond with the young scholar. He regarded Harper as "a man of extraordinary powers and possibilities," and Harper admired Broadus's careful scholarship, dynamic lecturing, and irenic demeanor. Harper insisted that Broadus teach at Chautauqua each year. "There are so few men who are able to make such work attractive and valuable," he told him. Refusing to accept Broadus's excuses, Harper sometimes personally intervened to extricate him from various scheduling conflicts. In 1886, he asked Broadus to help him start a Hebrew school at the University of Virginia, as he felt "the necessity of gaining the support of Southern men." He sought Broadus's endorsement for other initiatives as well, noting how "just a word from you would mean a lot." They exchanged frequent letters and telegrams, and Harper planned to visit Broadus and "spend at least a day attending your classes."[39]

The two men knew that they read their Bibles differently. "You know the nature of my views . . . in reference to inspiration," Harper wrote after receiving a certain preaching invitation. "In a careful and cautious putting forward of my views would I do anything that would be out of place under such circumstances?"

But they were eager to keep in sympathy. Harper often minimized the distance between their views, and Broadus always interpreted Harper as charitably as possible. Harper offered to publish Broadus's lecture on "Our Lord's Teaching as to the Old Testament" in the *Hebrew Student*. "While I cannot agree with you in all details, I feel confident that essentially we are agreed," Harper wrote. Discussing German theologian August Dilmann in 1889, Harper insisted, "I agree with you that one may hold to the existence of different documents without believing that they are mutually contradictory or that they have been blunderingly combined." He added that he "appreciated the force" of Basil Manly Jr.'s "little book on Inspiration," and assured Broadus of their shared reverence for the Scriptures. "After all, as you say, the great thing is to keep in devout sympathy with the supernatural and the spiritual in the Bible," he purred, "and this is the thing I am trying to do, and it is a great source of satisfaction to me that I appreciate this element more and more every year."[40]

Broadus did his best to influence Harper in a safer direction. In 1888, for instance, Harper proposed to argue in support of what Broadus termed the "destructive views" of the Pentateuch, against Princeton Seminary's conservative Hebrew scholar William Henry Green. Harper claimed the exercise to be merely academic, but Broadus warned that it would damage his reputation among "conservative scholars and conservative circles." Worse, it could confirm Harper's own mind in the "destructive views." "I am scared at the very idea of your undertaking such an advocacy," Broadus confessed, "I dread it for the sake of what I believe to be vital truth." If Harper needed a spokesman for naturalistic views of the Bible, he should ask former Southern Baptists Crawford Toy or David Lyon, two able scholars ("Lyon would make [Green] see stars in the daytime," Broadus assured) who were already committed to the destructive position. "I am not intruding into another man's affairs," Broadus explained, "for I am profoundly interested in the movements of American Biblical learning, and in the wholesome progress of your own influence and usefulness." But Broadus would "have nothing to express but regret" were Harper to openly defect from orthodoxy.[41]

He offered fatherly guidance to Harper until his death. Broadus commended to the rising generation of Baptist thinkers a scholarly conservatism that he had found to be both intellectually satisfying and faithful to Christian orthodoxy. But with the emergence of the University of Chicago, Harper, like Toy, proved to be a wayward son.

-→>>-❖-❖-<<←-

In the late 1880s, Augustus Hopkins Strong, the president of Rochester Theological Seminary and a leading northern Baptist theologian, yearned to establish a large, prestigious, modern, Baptist seminary in New York City. To realize his dream, Strong would need the money of John D. Rockefeller. Conveniently for Strong, his own son Charles would marry Rockefeller's daughter, Elizabeth, in 1889. Strong exploited this family connection relentlessly in the late 1880s, pressing Rockefeller to underwrite his grand plan. But Strong thought that he would also need the mind and the influence of John Broadus.

Strong considered Broadus to be "a wise and true man," whose "name would go far to give reputation to the institution"; he also knew Broadus to be the evangelical leader most likely to secure Rockefeller's financial support. Accordingly, Strong pitched Rockefeller the idea of Broadus, rather than himself, as the school's first president, with Strong and William Rainey Harper filling out the star-studded faculty. "There is no man in the country who has at once the confidence of Mr. Rockefeller and of the denomination like yourself," Strong wrote to Broadus in 1887. "There is no man whose wisdom and experience are more needed or would be more influential than your own, in the molding and shaping of such an institution as I have in mind, even as there is no man who could exert a stronger influence in favor of its establishment. I ask you favorably to consider the proposition to give yourself for the remainder of your life to this work rather than to the more limited work of the Southern Baptist Theological Seminary."[42]

At Strong's urging, Rockefeller summoned Broadus to his home in October 1887 to discuss the presidency of the new school. Now sixty years old, Broadus had received many flattering professional invitations, but this one must have carried special force. Between Strong and Rockefeller, perhaps Broadus would finally behold a vision grand enough to dislodge him from parochial Southern Seminary and his home region. But Broadus instead respectfully declined the presidency. Rockefeller afterward told Strong that Broadus "has not many more years," and "seems rather infirm." Broadus was open to a faculty appointment at the new school, provided that he could retain his position at Southern Seminary. Strong chose to take what he could get. He expressed his pleasure in obtaining "the use of his name," convinced that "Dr. Broadus, Prof. Harper and myself *together,* will command the confidence of the country, and absolutely ensure the success of the project."[43]

But it was not to be. A separate movement among northern Baptists materialized at this time to revitalize the old Morgan Park Theological Seminary in Chicago and, to Strong's shock, swallowed his dream whole. Ultimately, this rival movement captured all of Rockefeller's money for a modern research university and divinity school in the burgeoning Midwest metropolis of Chicago. Its founders would look to the Baptist *wunderkind* Harper as its founding president, tasked to build the University of Chicago into America's most cutting-edge academic institution. There was no place in the new plan for Strong, left seething in Rochester. Broadus soon found himself drawn into the bitter theological and relational conflict.[44]

Hoping to discredit Harper with Rockefeller, Strong found his opportunity in Harper's unguarded 1888 remarks at Vassar University, where Strong served as a trustee. In a lecture attended by Strong's daughter, Harper declared the Pentateuch to be a composite document, he rejected Jesus' assertions of Mosaic authorship, and he called the Old Testament historical records "idealized history" that "contain errors." It was all the ammunition Strong needed. He immediately fired off letters to Broadus and other prominent Baptist leaders, hoping to relay their outrage on to Rockefeller. "Are such views as these taught in the Southern Baptist Theological Seminary?" Strong demanded. "Would you wish to return in the service of your Seminary a teacher who held such views? Can we as Baptists safely permit such teaching to go unquestioned in any of our institutions?" Yet Broadus, while assuring Strong that Southern rejected Harper's views, also declared that Harper "tends towards orthodoxy and that if left alone he will come around right." Receiving the same message from his other correspondents, Strong retreated.[45]

By 1890, however, Broadus's influence with Harper was clearly diminishing. He urged Harper to recruit for the University of Chicago "men who incline to conservative views about biblical inquiries and about the relations between Christianity and critical science." He added his hopes that Chicago Divinity School would "always be distinctly and decidedly Baptist." Harper responded with his usual charming reassurances, and then proceeded to assemble the most liberal university faculty in the nation. Under Harper, the University of Chicago would become the headquarters of American theological modernism in the twentieth century.[46]

Their widening gap became evident in 1891, when Harper invited Broadus to the university to deliver four lectures for his Bible Institute. One conservative reporter called the gathering "an infidel institute," led by "destructive critics" making "a deliberate effort to introduce these loose views of the Bible among the ministers and churches of this country." After speeches by Harper and Charles A. Briggs, T. T. Martin judged that "the Bible did not have half a dozen friends left in the audience." But when someone noticed Broadus in the crowd, a spontaneous ovation swept him to the platform. Like a true southern gentleman, Broadus first complimented the new university and his fellow speakers. But then, something changed. "All at once, he seemed electrified!" Martin remembered. "Trembling all over, he raised his clenched right fist in the air and, shaking it, let fly a thunderbolt, 'But beware, my brethren!' And again raising the clenched fist over his head and shaking it, his eyes flashing, his face livid, he again shouted, 'Beware, my brethren! Jesus said, 'Moses wrote of me.' Jesus said, Moses wrote of me." Broadus's words had an "electrical" effect on the crowd. As he left the stage, Martin said, "It looked as if every one wanted to go and get a rope and hang Briggs and Harper."[47] Martin, an anti-evolutionary warhorse in the 1920s, may have exaggerated the account. Still, the story highlights Broadus's efforts to maintain a voice of scholarly conservatism within his increasingly liberal circles.

Some of his brethren urged Broadus to practice a stricter separatism. Boyce frowned on his 1886 invitation from Toy to preach at the Harvard Divinity School chapel, for instance. At Harvard, Toy assured Broadus, he would find "Much kicking, of course, against the commonly received orthodoxy, or rather a great indifference to it, yet at the same time a deep interest in fundamental religious truth in its bearing on life." But Boyce strongly discouraged Broadus's acceptance. "There is great danger in any encouragement we give to Dr. Toy and Lyon," he wrote. "We do not know what harm we may do by making people think that their differences from us are not of importance. Besides, I do not like to see the Unitarians helped by favors from others, and especially by sermons from which the 'gospel' must be left out so as not to say what would be unacceptable to Unitarians." Broadus tolerated greater diversity in his associations than did the implacable Boyce, but he meekly sent Toy his regrets.[48]

Broadus faced similar pushback when he invited Harper to speak at Southern Seminary in 1891. A. H. Strong immediately confronted him by letter. "And now I do not see how you can give your help and support to Dr. Harper's endeavors to disseminate his views, and prepare our own denomination to accept them," Strong wrote; "I am filled with alarm for the future of our Seminaries and Churches." C. I. Scofield also expressed dismay at Broadus's liberality toward Harper. "Thousands of Southern Baptists will never dream that there can be fatal error in teaching to which Dr. Broadus gives the sanction of his fellowship," Scofield wrote.[49] As former friends drew doctrinal lines, Broadus again found himself between worlds. Few seriously suspected his own theological commitments, but some questioned his choice of companions.

→>>✤✦✤<<←

Though Broadus always maintained that a preacher called of God needed no education to proclaim the gospel, he never abandoned his efforts to "elevate our ministry" by training Southern Baptist scholars. "I think that scholarly tastes, so far from being useless in the ministry, are now very especially needed among Southern Baptist ministers," he wrote from Chautauqua in 1889. "Most people think scholarship is impracticable, if not undesirable, in the working pastorate, and we greatly need examples to the contrary." Broadus offered up his own example in the 1880s and 1890s of a conservative scholarship, open and updated, yet unapologetically orthodox. "Let our conservatism be progressive and our progress conservative," he urged in one of his final public statements.[50] Moving toward the twentieth century, his balance of piety and scholarship would become even more difficult to maintain.

Ten

TEACHING THE "BROADUS STYLE"

A DONIRAM JUDSON HOLT typified many of the aspiring ministers who came under John Broadus's influence in the latter nineteenth century. He had been converted in 1868 at "an old-fashioned country Baptist church meeting" in Jackson Parish, Louisiana, in which he stepped out of his seat after the sermon and collapsed in a heap of tears. Holt soon felt the call to preach, but he found his first attempt so overwhelming that he had to break off his sermon in the middle to sit and weep. "In those days," he recalled, churches "taught a young preacher to preach by making him preach. It was like breaking a colt; they just put the harness on and made him pull." Holt later admitted that his early sermons "did not amount to anything," and consisted largely of pointing and hollering "Repent! Repent! Repent!" Yet over the next seven years, Holt experienced no mean success in the revival meetings he held in Louisiana and Texas; on one occasion in 1871, he baptized eighty-six new disciples in the Colorado River. Most considered him to be the best preacher in his association.[1]

In 1874, Holt attended the annual meeting of the Southern Baptist Convention in Texas. The young revivalist was "all eyes" at the assemblage of famous town preachers, for "every minute I saw men whom I had been hearing about all my life." He wanted most of all to hear Dr. John A. Broadus, slated to speak on behalf of the seminary. At the appointed hour, every chair was filled, so Holt sat at the pulpit steps. He was disappointed by the appearance of a "small, insignificant looking man," dressed in a "common suit" of "jeans clothes." The stranger began softly and looked "frightened and abashed." Based on the preacher's rustic dress, Holt assumed him to be an "ignorant boob." Yet Holt soon noted his "surprisingly good English," "faultless inflection," and "admirable rhetoric," and leaned in with attention. That's when the speaker carried him away. "He just caught me and flew off with me," Holt remembered. "He soared and took me with him. I forgot where I was, forgot that I had come to hear Dr. Broadus. How long he kept on this flight I can not say." After they "lighted," the stunned Holt asked his neighbor the speaker's identity. To his shock, it was Broadus. Holt dug out a $100 note for Broadus's collection and "resolved to try to go to that Seminary." His decision aroused dismay in his Texas church. "You preach jest to suit us now," exclaimed one deacon. "If you go and git better educated, you will leave us; I don't want you to go." Holt expressed his appreciation, but he now knew that he could not "preach up to what I heard at the Convention." "That Convention has spiled you," the deacon muttered.[2]

For many young Southern Baptists like A. J. Holt, Broadus embodied a new ministry ideal for the New South. The "Broadus Style" that dazzled Holt from the Convention platform involved all the marks of the growing professionalism that scholars have identified among nineteenth-century southern evangelicals: learning, eloquent speech, genteel manners, and the notoriety and influence that landed one a preaching slot at a big denominational meeting. At the same time, Broadus never lost sight of his audience. Even as he promoted education and cultural sophistication, he remembered that he belonged to an essentially popular religious movement, full of skeptical, tobacco-chewing deacons, and fueled by the shouts and tears of frontier revival meetings. However respectable he himself might be, Broadus knew to remain "in sympathy with the common mind" if he hoped to retain influence among Southern Baptists. (Was the "suit of jeans" an unselfconscious wardrobe choice, or a savvy rhetorical move that communicated his solidarity with ordinary southerners on hard times?) As Holt and other young preachers sat at Broadus's feet, they learned a style of ministry that combined eloquence with accessibility, erudition with old-fashioned evangelical piety, and professionalism with a popular touch. By again bridging disparate worlds, Broadus made a higher ministry culture accessible to Southern Baptists. As with Holt, it all began by showing them how to preach.[3]

→»»✣✤《《←

In the fall of 1865, the seminary's first semester back after suspension for the Civil War, Broadus found his resolve tested with each meeting of his homiletics class. Just two students had enrolled, and one dropped out halfway through the course. The remaining student, William Lunn, was blind. Unable to assign the usual course readings, Broadus developed his lectures more extensively. "Really it is right dull to deliver my most elaborate lectures in homiletics to one man, and that man blind," he complained to Lottie. Four years later, when Broadus's failing health required him to turn the homiletics class over to Basil Manly Jr., Broadus expanded those lecture notes for his colleague's use, and his thoughts turned to publication. He assumed that few presses would be interested in "an unknown Southern author," but, with the aid of a Richmond donor group, he submitted the five hundred-page manuscript to Smith & English of Philadelphia in June 1870, just as he was leaving the country for his year-long Grand Tour.[4] By the time of his death in 1895, *A Treatise on the Preparation and Delivery of Sermons* had already seen some forty printings, well on its way to becoming the most widely used preaching manual in history.

Broadus could not have timed the market better. American evangelicalism had exploded during the First and Second Great Awakenings on the strength of preaching much like that of the young A. J. Holt: a revivalistic style that privileged passion, directness, and personal charisma over eloquence and learning. Some of the most successful preachers, not least among the Baptists, were unlettered itinerants, who preached to crowds under the open sky and with Christ's injunction in their hearts: "take no thought how or what ye shall speak: for it shall be given you in that same hour what ye shall speak" (Matthew 10:19). Trusting in the Holy Spirit's immediate inspiration rather than human artifice, these preachers clutched their Bibles and opened their mouths. The flood of unrehearsed words that ensued, along with the conversions and other spiritual manifestations in the crowd, confirmed for many the essentially supernatural character of preaching. According to this tradition, preachers required no education, training, or even much sermon preparation—just "a good set of lungs . . . a flair for the dramatic, and a willingness to let the Spirit take over," as Brian Jackson put it. While this style of ministry remained effective and popular among southern evangelicals throughout the nineteenth century, many, like A. J. Holt, underwent a change in their tastes and expectations for preaching. One witness to this alteration was the proliferation of preaching manuals.[5]

By the end of the Civil War, dozens of publications offered instruction in the art of sermonizing. These included books by New England Baptist Henry Jones Ripley and the Reformed Frenchman Alexander Vinet, both of which Broadus assigned to his early classes. Preaching books continued to flood the market in the decades after the war, with popular titles by Robert Lewis Dabney, Phillips Brooks, Henry Ward Beecher, Austin Phelps, and more. While each manual offered its own slant on the subject, all assigned a greater agency to the human speaker than did the "spontaneous inspiration" model of the old revivalists. Evangelical homileticians drew heavily from the "New Rhetoric," popularized by Scotsmen John Witherspoon, George Campbell, and Hugh Blair, who retrieved classic rhetorical theory while updating it with Enlightenment insights about epistemology and human nature. Neither Broadus nor his colleagues would dare deny the necessity of supernatural influences in preaching; at the same time, they demonstrably shifted the attention of evangelical preachers from the unseen realm to the observable principles of persuasive human speech.[6]

Indeed, Broadus's *Treatise* plainly declared preaching to be "a branch of rhetoric." Effective sermon delivery required more than showing up and being overwhelmed by the Spirit; it was "an art" to be studied and a "skill" to be refined, as a carpenter or blacksmith gained mastery over his own craft. Personal godliness and divine empowerment remained essential for successful preaching, but a little "eloquence" also went a long way, which Broadus defined as "speaking as not merely to convince the judgment, kindle the imagination, and move the feelings, but to give a powerful impulse to the will." Broadus frequently, and with apparent sincerity, registered his respect for those "uneducated preachers" who wielded power with "the masses." Yet he also looked elsewhere for his own pulpit exemplars. He praised "those noble Baptist preachers" who, "beginning with hardly any education have worked their way up to the highest excellence in their calling." Broadus's ideal preachers were industrious craftsmen who attained "their power of clear and precise expression, and of attractive delivery," through "sharp, critical attention, of earnest and long-continued labor." If the "immediate inspiration" model of the old-time exhorters diminished human agency in preaching, Broadus sought to magnify it. The preaching task called for "heedful, thoughtful practice," as well as the study of rhetoric, "those fundamental principles which have their basis in human nature."[7]

Broadus devoured all the newest homiletical works, but the ancients held the key to true eloquence. He listed Aristotle, Quintilian, and Cicero as his greatest influences, and referenced Demosthenes, Tacitus, and other Greco-Roman orators throughout the volume. Virtually all of the era's preaching manuals shared this neoclassical bent, but Broadus, the genteel southerner and classics scholar, especially idealized the original rhetoricians. "The Greeks have left monuments of mental power which the world can never cease to admire," he declared elsewhere. "One need not be a mere praiser of the past to assert that the productions of the Athenian mind have hardly ever been passed, and not very often been equaled, by the noblest kindred works of modern times." Even Saint Augustine had recognized the wisdom of the classical orators when he wrote "*Veritas patent, veritas placate, veritas moved:* make the truth plain, make it pleasing, make it moving," Broadus noted. He structured his preaching book around Aristotle's five "canons of rhetoric": *inventio, dispositio, elocutio, actio,* and *memoria.*[8]

Eloquent preaching began with "invention," the gathering of the speech's materials. Rather than "take no thought how or what ye shall speak," Broadus called for assiduous preparation. Along with enthusiastic expostulation, preaching involved an informed "exposition" of a biblical passage. "The primary idea is that the discourse is a development of the text," he wrote, "an explanation, illustration, application of its teachings. Our business is to teach God's Word." Subsequent homileticians have dubbed Broadus "the father of the modern expository sermon" for his commitment to teaching while preaching. He devoted many pages to the basics of biblical hermeneutics while also commending the reading of systematic theology, church history, and other pertinent books. The alert preacher who carried a "commonplace book" could also capture pulpit fodder from everyday incidents. Whatever the sources, Broadus left no doubt that excellent preaching demanded diligent, thoughtful planning.[9]

Next came *dispositio,* the artful arrangement of one's material. "Two things are obviously necessary to an effective discourse," Broadus instructed, "that there shall be a plan, as we have all seen, and that there shall be movement, progress." Rough-hewn preachers gloried in a discursive, Spirit-led stream of consciousness; the eloquent preacher meticulously planned the sermon around a finely honed "proposition," or thesis statement. This proposition should be "complete (i.e., including all that it is proposed to treat), simple and clear, brief and attractive." A well-crafted proposition brought unity and focus to the sermon, setting it apart from the meandering messages of untutored preachers. "A discourse that has not unity, both offends taste and lacks power—in fact, is not a discourse at all. Let there be unity at whatever cost. And not only this, but structure," Broadus maintained. With the proposition settled, the preacher could develop an appropriate introduction, divisions in the main body, transition statements, and a conclusion. Broadus noted that this progression conformed to "the natural laws of human thinking." Sermon structure benefitted both the preacher and the audience, who found a well-arranged message more intelligible, pleasing, persuasive, and memorable.[10]

Style, or *elocutio,* considered the most effective expression of one's ideas. Broadus focused on three major elements: clarity, energy, and elegance. Clarity required attention to word choice, sentence structure, and the construction of logical paragraphs. (Broadus commended extensive reading in the best literature to develop these skills.) Energy involved the "animation, force, and passion" of delivery, not to be neglected by educated pulpiteers. Indeed, Broadus suggested in another place that "A truly great orator will sometimes go almost wild with excitement, almost beside himself with impassioned concern." But fervor in the pulpit must also be regulated by attention to elegance, the ability to "touch the feelings, and thereby bring truth powerfully to bear upon the will." An instinct for elegant speech required the extensive development of the imagination, through an immersion in nature, art, and literature.[11]

If much of Broadus's counsel thus far would strike the average evangelical preacher as a bit highbrow, he administered heavy doses of common sense in his treatment of *actio,* or delivery. After twenty years' experience, Broadus remained committed to extemporary preaching over reading or reciting written manuscripts. Among its other advantages was simple pragmatism. "With the masses of people, it is the *popular* method," Broadus stated flatly. Amid his Latin quotations and literary allusions, Broadus cautioned preachers to keep their eyes on "the masses," referring to them as such over twenty times in *A Treatise.* He warned against "sneer[ing] at the folly of the masses, in so often preferring ignorant preachers who thoroughly sympathize with them, and speak in the way they like." Aristotle had long ago observed that "uneducated men have more power of persuasion among the rabble"—Broadus utilized the pejorative term unselfconsciously—because they can "say the things that lie close to their hearers." Accordingly, Broadus urged preachers to "make almost everything bend to retain their hold upon the people," from sermon delivery to method of argumentation to word choice. "Study the common mind," he exhorted, and learn how to "fall in with the modes of thought which are familiar and agreeable to the masses," like a stump speaker or a jury lawyer. Broadus maintained that a skilled preacher could connect with ordinary folks "without the sacrifice of truly profound thought or the violation of refined taste." After all, history's best preachers had always done so, not least of all "that Great Teacher of whom it was said—O exalted eulogium!—'the common people heard him gladly.'"[12]

Broadus received the initial reviews of *A Treatise* while still abroad on his Grand Tour. Baptists of all stripes celebrated the publication. "Your book is going like hotcakes," wrote W. D. Thomas from Charlottesville. Friends published warm reviews in Virginia's *Religious Herald,* Georgia's *Christian Index,* and other Southern Baptist periodicals. Landmark Baptist J. M. Pendleton purchased thirty-seven copies, one for each student at Pennsylvania's Crozer Theological Seminary. Baptists overseas also praised the book. Broadus gave a copy to Charles Spurgeon, who called it "invaluable," and to Joseph Angus, president of Regent's Park College, who had it reprinted in London with his own introduction.[13]

But Broadus also pitched *A Treatise* beyond his own denomination. The wife of one Missouri Presbyterian minister requested Broadus to send her a copy as a Christmas gift for her husband, and J. L. M. Curry passed on favorable notices from Methodist, Presbyterian, and Congregational journals. "We unhesitatingly recommend this book to *Methodist* preachers," wrote one reviewer, who deemed it "the very best book" on the subject. The same Methodist author praised Broadus as "so large and liberal in his views as to place him beyond the contracted and petty sphere in which bigots and sectaries move and revolve." Another Methodist reviewer also remarked that, while the *Treatise* contained "a grain or two of Calvinism with a slight admixture of anti-pedobaptism," it was only a "homeopathic dose," producing "little effect."[14]

The *Treatise* became the most popular preaching textbook in America. It soon made its way into mission schools around the world, and was translated into multiple languages. It remained in print and wide usage throughout the twentieth century. Broadus's grandson John Broadus Mitchell noted that the thirty-two grandchildren still received regular royalties in 1977. Twenty-first-century American homileticians continue to cite Broadus with authority, and typically regard *A Treatise* as the most influential preaching manual in history.[15]

More than one observer has noted how Broadus's *Treatise* contributed to the modernization of American preaching. John P. Hoshor has identified Broadus's *Treatise* as completing the transition of American preaching from a theological discipline to a rhetorical one. David J. Randolph called it a "fateful day" when "the venerable John A. Broadus" declared preaching to be "a branch of rhetoric. American homiletics has not yet been completely reconstituted after this stroke which severed the head of preaching from theology and dropped it in the basket of rhetoric held by Aristotle." James F. Kay of Princeton Theological Seminary also lamented the rationalism and minimization of divine influences in Broadus's homiletic theory. Kay registers surprise that Broadus makes no reference to the preacher's dependence on God's activity until page 504.[16]

These evaluations may be overstated. For instance, Broadus declares in the introduction:

> Now the things which ought *most* to be thought of by the preacher, are piety and knowledge, and the blessing of God. Skill, however valuable, is far less important than these; and there is danger that rhetorical studies will cause men to forget that such is the case. It is lamentable to see how often the remarks made by preachers themselves, in conversation and in newspaper critiques, are confined to a discussion of the performance and the performer. Unsympathizing listeners or readers have, in such cases, too much ground for concluding that preachers are anxious only to display skill, and gain oratorical reputation.[17]

While similar statements can be found throughout *A Treatise* and the Broadus corpus, his enthusiasm for human eloquence and classic rhetorical theory is undeniable. For frontier preachers like A. J. Holt, the perspective represented a dramatic change from the style they had always known. The first thing Holt learned under Broadus, he claimed, was "that I did not know one single thing about preaching." By the end of his first seminary term, Holt had committed nearly all of Broadus's textbook to memory.[18]

The truth is, Christian ministers had wrestled over the relationship between human eloquence and supernatural influence in preaching since before Augustine's *On Christian Doctrine,* as Brian Jackson has pointed out. However one evaluates Broadus's balancing of the equation, his *Treatise* does represent an important transition in popular American preaching. Broadus and his disciples maintained that the Holy Spirit was the true persuader in the pulpit, but they also settled "into an Augustinian middle road," in which the "rhetoric of the invisible" played a "complementary" rather than a "totalizing" role in the preaching moment. As Southern Baptists joined the evangelical "pilgrimage toward respectability" in the nineteenth century, it fell to more radical out-groups, such as the Mormons, and later the Pentecostals, to carry on the spontaneous inspiration preaching model.[19]

-→>>❖-❖-<<←-

The Broadus Style attracted hundreds of aspiring pastors like A. J. Holt to the Southern Baptist Theological Seminary in the late nineteenth century. In 1877, the first term in Louisville, eighty-nine students enrolled, besting the previous high mark in Greenville of sixty-seven. Enrollment would climb to 120 in 1882, and to 164 in 1888. Atlantic states continued to supply many students, but the Louisville location also made the school more accessible to the southwest and to the north, attracting pupils even from Canada. Classes grew so large—forty-one students crowded into Broadus's homiletics course in 1888—that some criticized the seminary for having "too many students." "I think the Seminary stands on trial, as to whether we can really handle so many students," Broadus told Boyce in 1888.[20]

The student body remained remarkably eclectic. "A Texas cowboy, who had never before seen the inside of a school, sat side by side with a learned Presbyterian doctor of divinity who had been professor in a seminary," recalled J. H. Farmer. Bernard Spillman of North Carolina marveled at how "Doctrinal candidates and scholars from German universities sat next to men 'caught wild on the plains of Texas without knowing what kind of thing a high school was,' men from the south and from the north, a great mixture." Country preachers like A. J. Holt did not always find easy acceptance among their urbane classmates. Holt thought he had stepped into "another world" when he reached the seminary. "I was from the frontier of Texas, with little or no culture, and was wholly a child of nature," he remembered. "I used such provincialisms as were in vogue among the people where I lived. . . . My dress and habits were different from that of these young college boys from the East. There was not a day that I was not humiliated."[21]

Holt's early classroom encounters with Broadus, now "in his prime and glory" in the lecture hall, further awed him. Students claimed that it was "worth a day's journey to hear Broadus in New Testament and Preaching"—while they groaned over William H. Whitsitt's droning monologues, and the rote recitation of textbook outlines Boyce required. Students described Broadus with two primary metaphors: the throne and the spell. "Broadus was on his throne in the English New Testament," declared A. T. Robertson. "Students were often so completely under the spell of the teacher as to find it difficult to write down the thoughts as he presented them," added John Sampey. Certain lectures in his English New Testament course became anticipated annual events, with former students showing up "to hear Broadus curl."[22]

One starstruck pupil, T. H. Pritchard, considered Broadus "the most instructive, stimulating and inspiring teacher that I have ever known." Pritchard's description, while worshipful, nevertheless captures Broadus's effect on many of his wide-eyed trainees:

> There you saw the keen, clear, discriminating Damascus knife of his intellect, separating truth from error; there his mind, like the sun, would make luminous the darkest subject, while his enthusiasm would seize hold of you and shake you and lift you out of yourself, and make you long to be something and do something for God and humanity. It was something grand and beautiful to see this little giant, with a soul as big as a mountain, hew his intense personality into the hearts of a hundred fine young fellows and stir up from the depths of their nature all that was good and true in them. No man that ever sat under such teaching can ever forget Dr. Broadus.[23]

As Pritchard indicates, Broadus did more than dispense Greek verb tenses and homiletical strategies in his classroom. He was "hewing his intense personality into the hearts of a hundred fine young fellows," imparting an impressive ministerial ethos to a generation of church leaders.

--->>>�֍֍<<<-

In addition to preaching, Broadus transparently wished to reform Baptist worship patterns. He believed that "Highchurchmen" typically gave too little attention to the sermon, but that Baptists "too generally think little of the service." Because most Baptists treated the elements of worship as preliminaries to preaching, many of their services could be characterized by "coldness, lack of animation, want of connection, and general slovenliness." Yet Broadus did not recommend a more elaborate liturgy. "Externals, however they may appeal to aesthetic sentiment, can never create devotion," he cautioned. For all his sophistication, Broadus remained a Baptist, and insisted that "the freedom, spontaneity, simplicity, spirituality, of the New Testament worship must be maintained at all costs."

Baptist preachers need not don a clerical gown or adopt the Book of Common Prayer to infuse Sunday mornings with a sense of the holy. But they *should* plan their services. Broadus guided ministers through the fine details of Scripture reading, public prayer, hymn singing, time management, and pulpit decorum. On the latter point, Broadus warned against fussing with one's hair or necktie, sloppy or showy dress, taking a drink of water or a chew of tobacco during prayer, talking during the singing, and more. He cautioned equally against affecting "an elaborate solemnity of air," for "there should be nothing self-important, or formal, in the preacher's manner." He commended an evangelical worship pattern that steered between both foolishness and formalism, "thoroughly simple in form, so as not to encourage the people to rest in externals, but full of interest, animation, devoutness, solemn sweetness, and with a specific but inelaborate adaptation to the occasion."[24]

He gave particular attention to the church's singing. While many New South Baptists adopted the folksy gospel songs of D. L. Moody and Ira Sankey, Broadus raised a standard for classic hymnody. He was a legitimate expert in the field. From the seminary's opening semester, Broadus incorporated lectures on the history of hymns and their writers into his homiletics class, and eventually developed a twenty-three-page "Syllabus as to Hymnology" for his students. In 1885, Broadus led advanced students through a course in "Foreign Hymnology," reading hymns in Latin, Greek, German, and French, with Broadus lecturing on the history of each. The upper-level course was the first of its kind at an American Protestant seminary. He taught students to identify a "good" hymn as: (a) correct in sentiment, (b) devotional in its spirit, (c) poetical in imagery and diction, (d) rhythmical, and (e) symmetrical.[25]

He knew that he was fighting uphill. Rank-and-file Baptists preferred simple, catchy gospel tunes over the complex rhythms, archaic language, and transcendent themes of the old hymns. His colleague Basil Manly Jr. complained in 1891 that "the rage for novelties in singing, especially in our Sunday Schools, has been driving out of use the old, precious standard hymns." Manly assured readers that his *Manly's Choice* hymnal "contains no trash, and no unreal sentiment or unsound doctrine." Both Manly and Broadus believed that the aesthetically attuned ought to instruct the singing tastes of the masses. While appreciating many of the "livelier religious songs and sprightlier tunes," Broadus deemed some "unendurable." These "wretched ditties ought to be carefully avoided, and . . . judiciously discouraged where they have become popular," he advised. He allowed that music selection "will vary somewhat according to the art culture of the worshipers," but did not conceal his conviction that "the more spiritual and at the same time more intelligent of the church" should guide the church's singing, yet also exhibit "careful consideration of what is best for all classes." The latter extended to "giving out" the words of the hymn, with brief explanations, so that illiterate white and Black churchgoers could "share in this delightful part of the worship."[26] Under his leadership, the seminary became a center for a higher-toned Baptist worship, suitable for the South's stateliest town churches. When the seminary opened its School of Music in 1953, leaders credited its origins to Broadus.

Broadus also shaped the theology of Southern Baptist ministry students by holding the line for traditional Calvinism. In 1856, Boyce had voiced alarm over a "crisis of Baptist doctrine" in the South. Boyce saw the theology of the Charleston Confession, which once "had almost universal prevalence," especially in his native South Carolina, rapidly giving way to the "leaven" of Alexander Campbell's Restoration movement. The "distinctive principles of Arminianism," via Campbell and camp meeting Methodism, were being "engrafted upon many of our churches," Boyce warned. By the 1880s, both frontier revivalism and the softer evangelicalism of D. L. Moody had eroded much of Calvinism's popular influence among Baptists. Broadus found that most students arrived at the seminary "rank Arminians," but he and Boyce quickly went to work on them. Boyce, known for his "old, straight, up-right, outright" Calvinism, drilled his systematic theology students in the doctrines of Old Princeton. Broadus, who approached the issue by way of New Testament exegesis, equally praised Calvinism as "that exalted system of Pauline truth."[27]

Among Calvinism's many advantages, Broadus extolled the system for its enrichment of the mind. The classic doctrines of grace "compel an earnest student to profound thinking, and, when pursued with a combination of systematic thought and fervent experience, makes him at home among the most inspiring and ennobling views of God and of the universe he has made." Besides providing intellectual stimulation, Broadus believed Calvinism to be the most faithful synthesis of biblical truth. "The people who sneer at what is called Calvinism might as well sneer at Mount Blanc," he wrote in 1891. ". . . I do not see how any one who really understands the Greek of the Apostle Paul or the Latin of Calvin and Turretin can fail to see that the latter did but interpret and formulate substantially what the former teaches." Broadus himself found immense practical value in Calvinistic piety. He makes constant references in his personal writings to God's providential control over human affairs, especially in times of uncertainty or sorrow. "Try to believe that there is a reality in what we call Providence, & to trust therein with sincere & simple trust," he encouraged his daughter, Annie, during a child's illness. "That great thought sometimes becomes dearer to us when we are in danger—may it be so with you now."[28]

Broadus traced most popular objections to Calvinism to "misapprehension, or misapplication through iron inferences." Anti-Calvinists typically feared that affirming God's absolute control would lead inevitably to fatalism. But Broadus often pointed out how God's initiating activity harmonized with human freedom in Christian experience. In his lectures on the "Pauline System of Christian Doctrine," for instance, Broadus reasoned that "Every Christian acknowledges the divine influence, of which he is conscious, to be a *gift of grace,* & feels entirely dependent, for spiritual life, upon God. This is acknowledged & established, *an election of grace,* while, at the same time, the Christian is conscious of freedom. And this consciousness of freedom establishes human responsibility, and demolishes that fatalism which regards man as a mere machine & seeks to excuse his sinfulness." In daily life, all believers reconciled the complimentary realities of divine agency and human responsibility. "The blindest 'Hardshell,' [ultra-Calvinistic Baptist] who has 'no message to the unconverted,' does not neglect to plough his corn," Broadus observed, while "the most ultra and heated Arminian believed in the doctrines of grace whenever he goes to prayer." Under Broadus and Boyce, seminary students became known for their "vigorous adherence to the old doctrines."[29]

On the other hand, Broadus resisted end-times debates. One Baptist observed in the 1870s that details regarding Christ's personal return and millennial reign were "presented, elaborated, and defended, sometimes with conspicuous power." The post-millennial position, which affirmed that the gospel would steadily advance in the culture until Christ returned to reign on earth for one thousand years, had dominated American evangelicalism since the late eighteenth century. But the 1880s also witnessed the rise of a pre-millennial viewpoint. The details could vary, but this model generally viewed the culture as declining rather than ascending. Christ would disrupt humanity's slide into chaos by his personal return, at which time he would inaugurate a thousand-year earthly reign. Post-millennialists stressed the present progress of God's Kingdom, culminating in Christ's return, while pre-millennialists looked to a future, any-moment crisis in history, for which all were obligated to prepare through evangelism and pious living.[30]

Broadus saw little value in popular eschatological disputes, though he understood why the details of end-time prophecies captured evangelical imaginations. He considered himself neither pre- nor post-millenarian in the standard sense. His lectures on Revelation presented all the major views, while focusing on "the moral and spiritual instructions of the letter," and showed that one could derive edification from each perspective. He had sympathized with revivalistic post-millennialism in his youth, he explained to seminary student E. Y. Mullins. But reading his New Testament had convinced Broadus of the Lord's imminent return—though whether Christ would appear in the next week or ten thousand years in the future, we could not know. Broadus pleaded ignorance as to the precise meaning of the "thousand years" in Revelation, and was unsympathetic to the popular charts and conferences of pre-millennial Bible teachers. He found their authoritative timelines "unwarranted" and resting on "very doubtful interpretations of very obscure expressions." Besides, Jesus himself had "forbidden" precise calculation of his parousia. "I confine myself to what is clearly taught by the Savior and his apostles, and we ought to be looking for his second coming and trying to be ready for it."[31] Resistance to wild-eyed speculation and unnecessary doctrinal disputes were all part of the genteel Broadus Style.

→»❖❖«←

Like A. J. Holt, many seminarians arrived in Broadus's classroom with minimal preparation. W. O. Carver judged that in the 1890s "little more than half the students were college graduates and not a few lacked even high school graduation." William H. Whitsitt privately complained that "nearly half our men are the merest tyros." Broadus acknowledged the challenges of teaching large classes with "first rate College men . . . all the way down to men who cannot write a sentence without blunders." He remained committed to receiving every

Baptist God had called to preach, but he would hold them to exacting standards. "What you know, learn to know straight," he often said. Broadus demanded total consecration to studies, including two hours of daily devotional Bible study. He cautioned students against neglecting schoolwork for preaching, as well as for romance. "A pair of blue eyes can get between a man and the seminary course," he warned Carver.[32]

Broadus's rigor alarmed A. J. Holt, who, besides being a successful revivalist, had been a country schoolmaster. Broadus returned Holt's first paper "written in red ink all over every page." Holt's classmates "guyed me about my 'bloody paper.'" Broadus's withering classroom remarks further intimidated Holt. He once became so enthralled in a Broadus lecture on the star of Bethlehem that he leaned forward and asked, "Dr. Broadus, did that star really move?" Annoyed by the interruption, Broadus curtly replied, "I do not know. I was not there," inspiring jeers from across the class. Fifty years later, Holt judged Broadus to have been "unnecessarily severe on some of his untrained students. We were doubt-less a trial to him. We were silly and unwise, but we needed what he sometimes failed to extend—sympathy." In these first encounters, Holt doubted if Broadus had any kindness in his nature. Many interruptors and idlers also testified that Broadus could be "impatient and severe," "sarcastic," and even "cruel." The arro-gant and indifferent, along with time-wasting question-askers, found themselves "slaughtered by some rapier thrust of wit or sarcasm," recalled A. T. Robertson. "He would cut the man's head off so smoothly that he would not know it till he sneezed." R. J. Williams believed that his students "feared him hardly less than they loved him."[33]

But at the end of his first semester, Holt learned another side of Broadus. He answered a knock at his door to greet the professor, come to break the news that Holt had failed his exams. "I had hoped to put you through, Brother Holt, in homiletics," Broadus began, "but while you were almost perfect in your recita-tions, you had formed such habits of speech, that we felt we could not afford to let you go out as a graduate in our most characteristic department." Holt wept with disappointment. But Broadus reassured him that his natural speaking gifts surpassed those of his more polished classmates, and urged him to retake the course. Holt did so, and passed. "Dr. Broadus was tenderness itself," Holt remem-bered. Broadus often regretted snapping at students, and more than once pursued his victim to personally apologize. One emerged from such a private meeting, brushing away tears. "You know that great man begged my pardon," he told his classmate. Most students came to love Broadus. They spoke of him reverently, imitated his preaching posture, and repeated his aphorisms. On Broadus's sixtieth birthday, students pooled their money to buy him a saddle and bridle; the citizens of Louisville supplied the horse.[34]

Graduates continued to rely on Broadus, especially when their vision of professional ministry collided with the unglamorous realities of rural church life. From Columbus, Georgia, S. M. Provence lamented the prejudice he encountered against his written sermons. Provence carried a manuscript into the pulpit, but he assured Broadus that he did not read it, and "not one in twenty of the best listeners would observe it." He believed that his method, learned from Boyce, secured "the precision of a written style with the directness and vigor of extempore speech." Even if some listeners complained, Provence was sure that his preaching had "impressed intelligent people." Seminarians also found their financial expectations disappointed. A cash-strapped George B. Eager sought Broadus's help in securing a summer pulpit supply, stipulating that he could accept no less than $75 a month. Many graduates grew wistful for the seminary's intellectual stimulation. E. Y. Mullins was likely the only resident of Harrodsburg, Kentucky, interested in the oratorical style of Demosthenes; searching for the best translation of the ancient Greek orator prompted a letter to Broadus. "To those who were once students at the Seminary you remain the highest authority on such subjects," Mullins wrote. "We learned to lean on you while we were there, and hope that when we trespass a little on your time, you will forgive us on the ground of our dependence."[35]

If rural congregations failed to satisfy seminarians' professional longings, prestigious town churches posed their own challenges. Broadus received many letters from churches expressing lofty expectations for their next pastor. One representative of a 275-member church in Austin, Texas, sought "an efficient man for this field . . . we need one who is both a *good preacher* and a *good pastor* and a man of social refinements." The Central Baptist Church in Memphis, Tennessee, likewise required a "a *strong man,* one whose voice and influence will reach throughout the city, and draw the people to him, one to lead and build up the Baptist cause in Memphis and place it where of right it belongs—in the front rank." Broadus tried to prepare his students for the practical demands of high-profile charges. "But in every *town* church there are from 2 to 7 'ladies' who are most excessively fastidious & conceited & at the same time nervous," he warned his son-in-law W. Y. Abraham, "& who 'can't *bear*' some little peculiarity of the Teacher, & sometimes they make such a fuss with their nervous intolerance as really to influence a good many people." Broadus heard from dissatisfied churches, too. One Baptist from Milledgeville, Georgia, complained of seminary alumni's lofty, unintelligible pulpit offerings. J. M. Morris of Grand Junction, Tennessee, "lectured" Broadus about the newfangled theology, academic sermons, and salary-greed among seminarians. "Oh!" Morris exclaimed, "For more Pauls and Judsons who love the Gospel more than filthy lucre!"[36]

Broadus understood well that the refined ministry model he offered required careful calibration for the typical southern congregation. He shook his head at educated preachers who got "away from all sympathy with the common man." Lacking the imagination to "comprehend the way that people in general look at things," they "don't know how to talk to the people" or "present things as the people have to see them," and so failed to "get hold of the people." Even Whtsitt, who yearned for middle-class respectability as much as any nineteenth-century Baptist, grasped this principle, at least in the abstract. "Brethren, the Lord is always going to look after the plain people," Whitsitt told his classes. "The Episcopalians were eminently respectable; and the Lord raised up the Methodists and the Baptists to look after the common people. And now, Brethren, the Methodists and the Baptists are getting to be eminently respectable: look out for the Salvation Army."[37] Broadus's own rare combination of refinement and relatability, learned from his politician father, may have been the great secret of his success.

→»✢✢«←

In January 1889, Broadus traveled to New Haven, Connecticut, for the crowning achievement of his preaching life. He was going to deliver the Lyman Beecher Lectures on Preaching at Yale University, the nation's premier homiletics lectureship. To this day, Broadus remains one of only three Southern Baptists to receive this prestigious invitation. Gathering up the major themes of his ministry and teaching career, he presented the Broadus Style at one of America's most venerable institutions.[38]

His first of seven lectures, "The Young Minister's Outfit," represents his most mature and comprehensive manifesto for ministry students. Though he would say much about the preacher's intellectual life, culture, and eloquence, Broadus made old-fashioned evangelical piety his top priority. Seeking the "indwelling and perpetual aid of the Spirit of God" remained the "indispensable" element of successful ministry, he told his Yale audience. "We need this in our every-day thought and activity, that we may be enabled to form a strong and symmetrical Christian character. We need it in all our studies. We need it in every stage of preparation and in preaching the sermon, beginning with the selection of the text and the topic, which should be made with special prayer," he preached. "And whenever we come to preach—ah! Young brethren dwelling at this formal seat of education, I do not wish you to think less of genius and culture and energy, but let us all remember that the source of real power in preaching must be 'an unction from the Holy One.'" If any had found his *Treatise* too humanistic, he made up for it now. Broadus reminded his scholarly audience how often God chose to "stain the pride of intellect and knowledge by making some poorly instructed but deeply devout man a greater power for good, whose word the people rightly receive as in some just sense 'the word of God.'"[39] Perhaps he was lecturing himself as much as the Yalies.

Broadus made no attempts to hide his southernness throughout the series. He urged the New Haven students to learn from the passion of southern speakers, noting that northerners were known for thought, energy, and culture, but "are often comparatively deficient in passion." Southern deficiencies ran in the opposite direction, he quickly added, which is why the North tended to produce writers, while the South produced speakers. But while he was on the subject, New England preachers could take a few notes on southern manners. "Above all men among us, a minister ought to be a gentleman," he counseled, "considerate of people's feelings, heedful as to all the delicate proprieties of life," and exhibiting "genuine courtesy and refinement." Without these qualities, the minister lacked a complete Christian character. Moreover, his private influence over "cultivated and refined people" will be "far less strong and wholesome," and even "plain people" would instinctively withdraw from their "want in real courtesy." Along these lines, learning to smile and make friendly conversation would not kill the Yankee ministers. "To Southerners the people of New England usually seem reserved in manner," Broadus shared. "Many men who are not wanting in real kindness of heart, fail to take a strong hold upon others, especially upon strangers, because they lack cordiality of manner." He knew they could hardly help their flinty personalities, tracing the trouble to the chilly climate and the old Puritan aversion to elaborate manners. Nevertheless, a minister who manifested "a certain undue reserve in greeting strangers, and in ordinary intercourse with society," curtailed his usefulness. With due allowance for cultural differences, "a more effusive cordiality would generally be better."[40]

Broadus completed his sketch with a paean to ministerial ambition. In a transparently autobiographical passage, he called preachers to develop "elevated aspirations" and "a quenchless longing to do better," spurning "the evils of contentment." "God forbid if you should be content with any sermon you have preached," he thundered. "*Nil credens actum*": believe nothing done so long as anything remains to be done. "Ah!" he soared, "Try to make the best of your native powers, and of your providential opportunities. Shame on the young man, yea, and on an old man, who does not burn with desire to improve, in character, knowledge, and usefulness. What is the use of being alive?" Broadus closed with a story, perhaps a personal experience, of an American traveler in Germany who asked directions from Eisenach to Wartburg. "*Immer hinaus und hinauf,*" the German stranger had said, pointing along the road: keep on outward and upward. "It might not be a bad motto for a young minister's career," Broadus concluded, "a motto still encouraging him to the very bound of life, and then only taking on a new meaning. *Immer hinaus und hinauf*: always onward and upward."[41] The motto had served Broadus for nearly half a century.

His second lecture, "Freshness in Preaching," urged the communication of old truths in new, interesting, and inspiring ways. Ministers could avoid riding their old ruts through continuous study of the Bible and systematic theology, as well as from careful listening to the individuals in one's pastoral charge. The preacher's own "penetrating and preserving reflection" about life also leant a depth of insight sorely lacking from most sermons. He urged his students to "never fall into stereotypical methods." They should "cherish and cultivate a restless longing to preach better, and try frequent experiments in preaching differently." Broadus balanced his emphasis on innovation with his third lecture, "Sensation Preaching," warning that "not everything . . . that draws a crowd, is to be commended." He touched on titillating sermon advertisements, gimmicky preaching topics, incautious political pronouncements, fostering applause in church, and unseemly pulpit humor.[42]

His fourth lecture, "Freedom in Preaching," commended the virtues of ex-

temporaneous speaking to divinity students he suspected were inclined to a literary style. While most Episcopalians and Congregationalists tended to read
their sermons, Broadus reminded his listeners that the best preachers in those
traditions, like Phillips Brooks and Henry Ward Beecher, did not. He addressed
all the most common fears associated with "free preaching": sloppy language
and grammar, misstatements of facts, repetition of ideas, long and meandering
sermons, and, perhaps undergirding all of these, the loss of control and the fear of
failure. Above all, Broadus stressed that oratory operated by a different set of rules
than did written communication, and the seminarian who failed to recognize this
did so to the detriment of himself and his hearers. "No matter how he prepares,
no matter if he reads closely, he ought to make us feel the speaker, rather than
the speech," he asserted. "Yes, and a man born to speak well always impresses us
as hearing more in him than he has said, more than words can express. We feel
the man."[43]

The Yale community packed Marquand Chapel for each of Broadus's seven
sessions (his remaining speeches covered the well-traveled Broadus topics of
"The Minister's General Reading," "The Minister and his Hymn Book," and "The
Minister and his Bible"). Many stood to listen to the famous southern preacher.
Afterward, the organizers declared that Broadus's lectures had stirred more enthusiasm than any since Henry Ward Beecher had inaugurated the series in 1871.
Broadus's audience thrilled to his deep learning, practical mastery, and Virginia
charm. "For the most part our hope of usefulness in the world is through you,"
he told the students in conclusion. "Preach your best before God, for your own
sakes, and then think of us and preach a little better still." He sat down to loud
and prolonged applause.[44]

Broadus's New England sojourn culminated on January 24, 1889, in a special dinner party in honor of his sixty-second birthday. The aging southerner
sat down to dinner at Radcliffe's with fifty prominent guests, all invited by Yale
professor William Rainey Harper. Amid the clinking glasses on that wintry New
Haven night, Broadus enjoyed a program that included speeches by Judge Francis Wayland III, dean of the Yale Law School; Connecticut's former lieutenant
governor, James L. Howard; the well-known financier Julius Twiss; and Harper.
All feted Broadus with toasts, speeches, and poems. Preaching had carried him a
long way from the farm. He had wanted to "rise and be something in the world";
now he was the man of the hour, at the summit of his career.

·→›› ❖·❖·‹‹←·

A. J. Holt failed three of his six classes in his first term at the seminary, including homiletics and New Testament with Broadus. Yet Holt had received "an everlasting benefit" from the experience. He "learned more in those eight months than I had in the previous eight years of my ministry." But the real test came when he returned to Webberville, Texas, and to the folk-Baptists he had left behind. After preaching his first post-seminary sermon, that skeptical deacon who had discouraged Holt's studies invited him home for a meal. "Brother Holt, your eddication hain't hurt you a bit," the deacon admitted. "When you get ready to go back, I'll send you." From Charlottesville to Louisville and from New Haven to the Red River, the Broadus Style seemed to play well just about everywhere in the late nineteenth century. Holt went on to raise money for the seminary in Texas, engage in Indian missions, and rise to prominence in Texas Baptist denominational life. Broadus corresponded with Holt until his death, securing him preaching positions, commenting on his book manuscripts, and providing Holt with a letter of introduction to Charles H. Spurgeon when the Texan visited London. Holt always considered Broadus the greatest man he had ever known.[45]

Eleven

OUR LIFE WORK

AN ESTIMATED ten thousand Louisvillians had to be turned away from D. L. Moody's tabernacle on the final night of his 1888 evangelistic campaign. "Not since the days of old when men spoke as they were inspired of God, has any man attracted the attention, enlisted the interest and so impressed his theme upon people as Dwight Lyman Moody," reported the *Courier-Journal*. Those who did secure seats included an array of "Baptist deacons, Episcopal vestrymen, Presbyterian elders and officials from all the Protestant churches." As they waited for the evangelist, the crowd belted out gospel songs like "Beulah Land," "Let the Saviour In," and "Oh, Jesus Is a Rock in the Weary Land." In the midst of the lusty, urban camp meeting, one reporter noted that "Dr. John A. Broadus sat by the side of Mr. Moody, the latter giving a book to join in the singing."

Anyone familiar with Broadus's preference for traditional hymns knew that he was stretching himself. Indeed, Broadus had privately rolled his eyes at Moody's lowbrow evangelicalism before. "Moody did as well as expected for I did not expect much," he told Boyce after hearing him in 1886. Yet he took a leading role in the 1888 meetings, issuing welcome speeches, invocations, and exhortations to build on Moody's work. "Mr. Moody does not preach a gospel that is afar off, but brings the naked truth in living contact with men's minds and consciences, and humbly seeks God's blessing upon his work," he told the *Courier-Journal*. "He combines the power of preaching with administrative power in a higher degree than any other man except Mr. Spurgeon." From the platform, Broadus expressed appreciation to Moody and song leader Ira Sankey on behalf of Louisville, remarking that "the angels must help us to thank these."[1]

His partnership with Moody in the late 1880s signaled important developments in Broadus's southern life. His prominence in the festivities indicated that he had fully recovered his pre–Civil War status as a leader in American evangelicalism. And the shared songbook evoked conciliation beyond worship aesthetics, for he and the Boston-born Moody had served opposite sides in the Civil War. In fact, Broadus and Moody both represented the role that religion played in uniting white southerners and northerners during the Gilded Age. Edward J. Blum has identified Moody as a key figure in "reforging the white republic." "Moody acted as a bridge between the white north and the white south," Blum argued, by de-politicizing the Civil War, reaching out to southern whites, and following regional customs when in Dixie—including the segregation of the races that was becoming common in the New South.[2]

Indeed, while the *Courier-Journal* reported that "colored people" joined the singing that night "with a will," they did so from their own, separate section. The policy disappointed many of Louisville's African American Christians. "I see no reason why there should be a color line in matters of this sort," explained William M. Hargrave, Black minister of the Knox Presbyterian Church. "We don't want to perpetuate the sins of our fathers." The white committee who organized the Moody meetings "probably thought they were dealing with the old time negroes, such as their fathers used to own; but there is a new generation on hand now," Hargrave said. "The whites and the blacks ought to cooperate in the work of God. Why, white and black men co-operate in the election of men to office, and I don't see why they can't do the same in religious matters." Questioned about Black Louisville's lukewarm response to Moody, Hargrave observed, "Any union meeting where the people are classified according to race or color will be a failure as far as the colored people are concerned." Hargrave saw no point in Moody's offer to come back to preach to Louisville's Black community. "No, he could do us no good. He could not reach the colored people."[3] If religion was drawing northern and southern whites together, it seemed that southern whites and Blacks were drifting steadily apart. These elements and more formed an important backdrop to Broadus's final decade.

·—>>>◦❖◦<<<—·

After relocating to Louisville, Broadus shared with Boyce his prayer that God would "grant that we may live to rest a little while under the shadow of our com-

pleted work—if it please him." Broadus indeed experienced his greatest produc-
tivity and popularity in the 1880s, and enjoyed more material comforts than he
had known since the war. George Norton arranged for the seminary to purchase
a fine house for the Broadus family at 821 Fourth Avenue, in Norton's own neigh-
borhood. The Nortons often shared their box seats at the Louisville auditorium,
where the Broaduses took in symphony performances of *Messiah, Elijah,* and
The Creation. Broadus acquired the scores beforehand so he could follow along.
"He always wished to have the notes before him for the fullest enjoyment in
listening," daughter Eliza remembered. The family also enjoyed trolleying over
to Jacob's Park (now Iroquois Park) to walk the scenic trails. After a long fall
from prosperity, the aging gentleman recovered nicely in New South Louisville.[4]

Boyce also enjoyed a season of satisfaction in the 1880s. Finally able to relax his travel schedule, he stayed home to teach his beloved systematic theology
class—Broadus thought his neglect of teaching for fundraising to have been
Boyce's greatest sacrifice for the seminary. Boyce even published his lecture notes
in 1887; his *Abstracts of Systematic Theology* offered a final tribute to Charles
Hodge and Old Princeton. But gout tormented Boyce by then, and decades of
anxious toil from 5 a.m. to 11 p.m. had worn him out. He wept when students
surprised him with a gold-headed cane in 1886. "God bless the boys," he told
Broadus. "We do not know sometimes how kindly they think of us, in our consciousness of our short comings in many ways."[5]

Feelings ran cooler between Boyce and William H. Whitsitt, who had joined
the faculty in 1872. Whitsitt was raised a strident Landmark Baptist in Middle
Tennessee, but broadened his outlook with studies at the University of Virginia
and, at Broadus's encouragement, two years in Leipzig and Berlin. He returned
disillusioned with his narrow Baptist upbringing. "I am greatly oppressed by
the fact that the spirit of my people is foreign from my spirit; that they are far
more narrow & pharisaical than accounts with my conception of Christianity,"
Whitsitt confided to his diary. In other candid entries, he questioned the valid-
ity of Baptist church government, restrictive communion, and even immersion.
He considered becoming a respectable Presbyterian or Episcopalian, if not for
Broadus. "The prospect of losing his friendship," Whitsitt wrote, "is one of the
worst things in the world." As for Broadus, he struggled to find the best fit for
Whitsitt, who he considered a poor lecturer; he finally settled him in church

history. Boyce was even less impressed, and made it clear that he would not mind losing Whitsitt in the move to Louisville.[6]

Whitsitt felt slighted by Boyce throughout the 1880s. Boyce's daughter Lizzie rejected his marriage proposal in 1879. When Whitsitt married Florence Wallace in 1881, Boyce agreed to officiate, but then failed to show up for the ceremony. (Broadus stood in at the last minute.) Boyce also repeatedly ignored Whitsitt's requests for a raise. After many failed solicitations, Whitsitt finally confronted Broadus over the discrepancy between his own humble living conditions and the "palaces" that Boyce and Broadus occupied at seminary expense. (Boyce had purchased a large house from the widow of Henry Clay.) Broadus admitted that Boyce opposed his raise, and that he would always side with Boyce. Whitsitt also felt intellectually disrespected, as when Broadus asked to review his upcoming seminary lecture in Baptist history. "Broadus is sure I have no common sense in the world and I am sure that his own common sense is his chief blemish," Whitsitt sulked. "I cannot endure it; [he] is always offering advice; and in the most unseemly places." Whitsitt had come to reject the Landmark view of Baptist origins, and Broadus may have been concerned that his remarks could alienate this powerful constituency. He believed Broadus shared his views but was "unwilling for a Professor in the Seminary to speak the truth about it. I am greatly hampered by these restraints upon research." Whitsitt quietly awaited the day when he could say just what he thought.[7]

Broadus hid it better than Boyce, but both likely viewed the Tennessean as something of a parvenu, and an interloper on their aristocratic society. Whitsitt labored to project sophistication—he put on "full dress" to make formal calls on New Year's Day, he gave addresses to the Greenville Literary Club, and he sniffed at the general backwardness of the Baptist masses—but he comes across as trying too hard. Whether because of his background, his personality, or both, Whitsitt never seemed to gain the same acceptance from the seminary founders as did Virginia faculty Crawford Toy or Franklin Kerfoot. The latter was a personal favorite of Boyce, and Whitsitt's most hated rival. Publicly, Whitsitt was friendly enough to earn the nickname "Uncle Billy," but he privately savaged his colleagues, especially the "ignoramous" Kerfoot, and Boyce the domineering "dunder-head."[8]

Boyce attempted to recover his health with a long family vacation to Alaska and California in the summer of 1887. He improved some, but Kerfoot had to teach all his classes in the 1887–1888 session. In May of 1888, Boyce sailed for England. Broadus provided letters of introduction to Charles Spurgeon and others, but Boyce was too sickly to enjoy the visit. He suffered a heart attack in London and spent two weeks in bed. By October, he knew he would never teach again. On his doctor's recommendation, the Boyces removed to southern France, where Boyce exchanged letters with Broadus. Dispersed among reports of seminary business and health advice are many wistful reflections on what they called "our closely coupled life." "I think we have both of us more to learn of the duty of faith and confidence in the working of the Lord for our seminary," Boyce mused. "With all our anxiety and hopes and fears how true it is that in our agony of trouble as to what will occur we find that God has found us ways of which we have never dreamed."[9]

Humanly speaking, no one had done more than Boyce to bequeath a seminary to Southern Baptists, his dream since his student days at Princeton. The patrician Boyce—even Whitsitt acknowledged that he embodied "elevation of character" and "Southern nobility"—had epitomized the desire of early denominational leaders to elevate Baptist ministry. Yet he was prescient enough to envision an innovative Baptist school that respected God's democratized call to ministry, while also equipping a "band of scholars." His dogged commitment to an educated ministry provided an important counterweight in the story of nineteenth-century southern evangelicalism. It had cost him his fortune, his health, and finally his life. In the end, even his most implacable foes gave him his due. "I feel a thrill of regret in view of the early departure of my old enemy," Whitsitt wrote in his diary. "He has been for nearly ten years sternly opposed to me and has done me a deal of damage, but he has many good qualities, and I cannot avoid respecting him."[10]

Boyce knew that he would have failed without Broadus. Thirty years after talking him into the uncertain seminary enterprise, Broadus had become his closest confidante, loyal lieutenant, and constant encourager. Broadus's national popularity had attracted students and donors, his scholarship bestowed academic credibility, and his winsomeness kept the school amenable to the spectrum of Southern Baptists. "No one knows how much I owe you for your help and your influence in that matter of the establishment of what you call my life work, but which ought to be called 'our life work,'" Boyce wrote from Paris.[11]

Students discerned their differences. Boyce was always more doctrinaire, the seminary's immovable confessionalist. Broadus was the seminary's scholar, skillfully navigating Southern Baptists through a sea of modern ideas. "Broadus impressed his students with the danger of trusting too much to human scholarship and logic. Boyce impressed them with reliance absolutely on things revealed," Z. T. Cody recalled. "Broadus carried his students through the intellectual problems that beset them. Boyce made them feel that all their problems were already solved. Broadus was a careful pilot, on a great ship loaded down with theological students in dangerous waters. He steered safely between great dangers. Boyce was a granite rock in a stormy sea, against which and beneath which ships could anchor in confidence."[12]

Isla May Mullins, wife of later seminary president E. Y. Mullins, insisted that there had been "jealousy and rivalry" between Boyce and Broadus. There must have been isolated incidents over three decades of close and stressful work.[13] But the overwhelming impression of the record conforms to the judgment of John R. Sampey, who compared them to the Bible's Jonathan and David. "They loved and admired each other, and each would grow eloquent in talking of his comrade and friend," Sampey remembered. Whitsitt called them "the twins of our Southern Baptist world. The twins of the ancient classic world were set as stars in the skies, to serve as a guide to mariners who might sail over wide and dangerous seas." The Lutherans had Luther and Melanchthon, the Reformed had Calvin and Beza, but "Southern Baptists may find their twins in Boyce and Broadus, who will stand side by side in our history till the end of time."[14]

Boyce died in Pau, France, on December 28, 1888. His family transported his body to Louisville's Cave Hill Cemetery, where they buried him on January 20, 1889. Among the attendees was Fanny, once Elizabeth Boyce's enslaved maid, who had telegraphed from Memphis to obtain information about the services. Fanny had been a wedding gift to the Boyces, but was herself married to a skilled carpenter named George, enslaved by another Greenville family. Boyce had endeared himself to Fanny by purchasing George, for the "very high price of $3,500," though, according to Boyce's daughter Lizzie, "his services he did not need at all." Boyce would hire George out for contract work. After the couple gained their freedom, they moved to Memphis, where George became a successful builder using the toolkit Boyce had given them as a parting gift. When Boyce and Basil Manly Jr. visited Memphis for a meeting, Fanny invited them to dine in her home. "They accepted, and she received them with pride and joy, seated them at a well-laden table, and waited on them herself," recalled Lizzie Boyce. Fanny's presence at Boyce's funeral bore witness to a more troubling aspect of Boyce's legacy, though also to the complex relationships of evangelical masters and slaves. Lizzie Boyce intended the story to testify to Boyce's generous spirit; it also speaks eloquently to the grace of Fanny.[15]

Broadus spent the next four years composing his memoir of Boyce's life, and of their shared life work in the seminary. "O Brother beloved, true yokefellow through years of toil, best and dearest friend, sweet shall be thy memory till we meet again!" Broadus would write in conclusion. "And may the men be always ready, as the years come and go, to carry on, with widening reach and heightened power, the work we sought to do, and did begin!" The seminary may die, he had said after the war, but we will die first. Half of those covenanters were now gone, their end hastened by their fidelity to that agreement. To seminary trustees, it was a "foregone conclusion" that Broadus would succeed Boyce as president. He urged the enfeebled Manly to gather his last energies for their final season of service. "I shall be constantly needing your advice, about measures and men, about great things and small. Now that Boyce is gone, I value your advice in Seminary matters beyond that of all other men," Broadus told him. "We must husband our strength, and stand together, like two old oxen, nearest to the wagon."[16]

·→»✣·✤·«←·

The seminary presidency accelerated the pace of Broadus's strenuous life. He traveled constantly now: in the winter of 1888–1889 alone, he preached in Indianapolis, Knoxville, New York City, and New Haven, Connecticut. Each summer, he delivered commencement speeches, kept up his northern pulpit supplies and Chautauqua lectures, and attended denominational meetings. He gave leadership to the International Sunday School Committee, the YMCA, the Slater Fund, and the Kentucky School of Medicine, of which he was made regent. He traveled to receive honors from Harvard University, Princeton's Cliosophic Literary Society, and more. Locally, Broadus preached in Louisville churches of all denominations, penned articles for the *Courier-Journal,* and was a favorite after-dinner speaker for social groups. His correspondence also piled higher than ever; his daughters, to whom he dictated his responses, called his study "The Letter Factory." Most correspondents were searching for something: a pastor, a keynote speaker, an article for their journal, vocational direction, answers to theological questions—one single man was even looking for a good Baptist wife. Each believed Broadus could help them find what they were looking for, and somehow felt close enough to ask.[17]

The seminary expanded under his administration. When the endowment reached $400,000, the Norton family donated $60,000 to build a chapel, recitation rooms, and offices; Broadus cut the ribbon on "Norton Hall" in 1892. Academic sophistication grew with the campus, as Broadus led trustees in 1892 to overhaul all the old degree programs. This included the creation of a new Doctor of Theology (Th.D.) degree, thirty years after Yale University had awarded the first American Ph.D. With enrollment climbing to nearly 280 in the fall of 1894, Broadus declared it "considerably more than any other theological seminary in the United States of any denomination." Many factors contributed to this, including the increased wealth of the New South, the triumph of professional ministry expectations among Baptists, and improved transportation to Louisville from all over North America. But John R. Sampey preferred a simpler explanation: "the name and fame of John A. Broadus."[18]

He also enlarged the faculty, though his scholarly conservatism required utmost care in appointments. By the 1890s, few Baptist academics remained unsullied by the new theology. He hoped to hire graduate George B. Eager, for instance, until Eager disclosed his altered views on the Bible. "I have struggled with these problems and held what view I have arrived at in almost absolute silence," he wrote. "You are the first one to whom I ever attempted to give anything like a history of my mental struggles and changes, or a full statement of my views or doubts." Broadus counseled Eager, but did not hire him. Yale graduate Edward B. Pollard, an Old Testament scholar, evaded Broadus's questions regarding biblical inspiration and secured his recommendation. But while Broadus coveted Pollard's academic pedigree for his faculty, trustees rejected him as a theological liberal; Pollard went on to promote the new theology at Crozer Seminary.[19]

Guarding the seminary's conservative identity now strained many old relationships. In 1891, the Presbyterian Church charged Union Theological Seminary's Charles Augustus Briggs with heresy for openly denying biblical authority and inspiration. Months earlier, Broadus had shared a platform with Briggs, a fellow University of Virginia alumnus, at William Rainey Harper's Chicago Bible Conference. Harper publicly supported Briggs, but Broadus remonstrated with him.

Harper's "spirit and method stand in the most gratifying contrast to those of my friend, Dr. Briggs," Broadus wrote. He considered Briggs to be "a regular sensationalist," and took offense at his "sneering attacks upon theologians and apologists, his delight in assuming the boldest and most startling positions, his arrogant claim that every opinion of the group of critics to which he belongs is science." But Harper by contrast had shown "a discrimination, sobriety, earnest effort to find the real truth, readiness to recognize that this or that question cannot now be settled, that on one point or another Christian scholars are much divided—in a word your general tone and spirit please me greatly in the comparison." But when Harper continued to defend Briggs, Broadus told Whitsitt that "he and Harper must now part company." Still, he refused to publicly criticize the younger man. When A. T. Robertson published a sharp critique of Harper's naturalistic interpretation of Genesis 11, Broadus admitted that he found the review "severe."[20]

His relationship with John D. Rockefeller also cooled now, as the University of Chicago brought Broadus and Harper into direct competition for Rockefeller's philanthropy. Harper remarked to Thomas Goodspeed in 1889, for example, that, "Dr. Broadus is pushing him unmercifully for $50,000 for Louisville, as a thank-offering for Mrs. R's recovery (he will not get it)." Indeed, Rockefeller would sink nearly $35 million into the University of Chicago, dwarfing his total gifts to Southern Seminary. The university's modernistic theological trajectory suited Rockefeller, who declared the school to be the greatest investment of his life. After Rockefeller failed to lure Broadus to Fifth Avenue Baptist Church, he spent a decade under the ministry of W. H. P. Faunce, the future president of Brown University and an ardent modernist. Rockefeller now carefully avoided identifying with conservative views of inspiration. His son, John D. Rockefeller Jr., would be a major financier of Protestant liberalism in the twentieth century.[21]

Most Baptist seminaries in America underwent significant theological transition in the 1890s. New presidents sympathetic to the new theology hired new professors trained at Harper's University of Chicago. A. H. Newman observed in 1915, "At present all the older theological seminaries of the North have on their faculties scholars of the modern type who are outspoken in their acceptance of modernistic views of the Bible, of the evolutionary philosophy, and no one of them, so far as the writer is aware, has among its professors a stalwart and aggressive advocate of the older conservatism." Newman located Southern Seminary somewhere between the University of Chicago and the "fundamentalist" elements in northern Baptist life, a position he credited to Broadus. Virtually the whole Southern Seminary faculty in 1915 had been "trained by Broadus," and were now "conducting the institution in his spirit." By implementing Broadus's spirit, Newman predicted, "it is easy to see that the Southeast is becoming gradually assimilated in thought and attitude to the Northeast, though still distinctly more conservative." Southern Seminary's faculty had in fact pushed beyond Broadus's theological boundaries by then. Yet the institution's avoidance of the fundamentalist-modernist conflicts of the 1920s can be attributed partly to his gentlemanly spirit of moderation.[22]

-→>>✤-❖-<<←-

Broadus's seminary leadership also required the political management of denominational factions. He believed it to be "eminently our duty at the Seminary to be as nearly as possible impartial and fair on points that divide the denomination," but this proved a constant challenge. For instance, his own "liberality" toward non-Southern Baptists set the teeth of the sectarian Landmarkers on edge; some even rumored that Broadus sprinkled his infant children like a Presbyterian. Seminary student E. E. King of Mississippi told Boyce that Broadus ridiculed Landmark tenets in class and socially excluded them. "The students sometimes, I believe, get up hot debates among themselves, and I suppose that leads to unintentional exaggeration and distortion as to what we have said," Broadus explained to Boyce. "I have been, and am, heartily desirous of respecting not only the opinions, but the most sensitive feelings, of all brethren throughout the South. As to Landmarkism, many of my cherished friends hold those views, and I, while not accepting them, feel no call whatever in my position to antagonize them."[23]

In 1876, J. R. Graves publicly accused Broadus of condemning Landmarkism in Virginia's *Religious Herald* under the pseudonym "Pike." Broadus denied the charges in Graves's *Tennessee Baptist*. But Graves still threatened to oppose the seminary in his newspaper if Broadus did not terminate his association with the *Herald*, or write equally for him. "How can I submit to such dictations?" Broadus fumed to Boyce, "I do not wish to be foolish, but a man must have some self-respect." Abandoning the *Herald* would alienate old friends and send more Virginia Baptists to Crozer Seminary in Pennsylvania. "You try to put the Seminary in a neutral position," he told Boyce. "But neutrality will not satisfy him. . . .

Don't you see it plainly? Have we not long known that every man whom Graves cannot make his *subject* he regards as his enemy? Why delude yourself with the notion that he is your friend, or that you can manage him. When my father died, he thought he was leaving his son a scholar and a gentleman." Through the years, Boyce and Broadus alternately appeased and challenged influential dissidents like Graves.[24]

At the end of his life, Broadus managed another mercurial Southern Baptist leader named T. T. Eaton. The Broadus family in 1880 joined Louisville's Walnut Street Baptist Church, a merger of Louisville's First and Second Baptist churches, and home to many of the city's most prominent Baptists. In 1881, the church called Eaton as pastor. The thirty-six-year-old Eaton was a gifted preacher, a staunch conservative sympathetic to Landmarkism, and a frequent newspaper controversialist—his sister, Josephine Peck, was the chief agitator of the Southern Baptist inspiration debate of the 1870s and 1880s. Under Eaton's energetic leadership, the Walnut Street church exploded from around seven hundred members in 1881 to over two thousand in 1887, while also sending out over seven hundred members to start mission congregations in Louisville. Many considered it the South's leading Baptist church. Eaton expanded his influence when he acquired the *Western Recorder* newspaper in 1887 (sister Josephine, under the pseudonym "Senex," helped advance their aggressive conservative agenda), and the Baptist Book Concern in 1891.[25]

Eaton freely criticized many Baptist leaders, but he revered Broadus and supported the seminary. He took particular comfort in the Abstract of Principles, that "very definite creed drawn up by Dr. Boyce," as it ensured that "the denomination can know just what doctrines are taught to the students." Broadus, in turn, encouraged Eaton's pastoral leadership. When Walnut Street planted McFerran Memorial Baptist Church in 1890, Broadus urged seminary faculty to join the startup congregation. Professors Sampey and Kerfoot obliged, though Whitsitt thought the move beneath him. "I shall stay where I am," he wrote in his diary. "I have something more dignified to do than to be going about to fill up holes for my colleagues which they had no business to leave open." Despite their friendly rapport, Whitsitt claimed that Broadus grew "dreadfully impatient of the extremes of Dr. Eaton and the *Western Recorder*. His whole heart loathes the stuff that is often dished up there, but he does not dare speak a word. I have often heard him say he sometimes felt like bursting things to pieces but he holds his peace." Broadus believed the ambitious Eaton wished to succeed him as seminary president, and told friends emphatically that this "would be a mistake." Yet somehow, Broadus deftly maintained what Bill J. Leonard termed "The Southern Baptist Consensus," keeping ultra-conservatives like Eaton on his side, even as he maintained friendships with northern liberals like William Rainey Harper.[26]

-->)>·❖·❧·«<-

President Broadus also carefully curated the seminary's Old South ethos, as prospective students of color quickly discovered. The first record of a Black student requesting admission is in 1877, when the faculty informed him that "no provision has been made here for colored men." Broadus told one Native American applicant that he would be received "if he had no negro blood in him." He questioned the racial origins of one Jesse Murrow in 1883, but Murrow's adopted father assured Broadus that he was "a *pure* Indian—Not a *drop* of negro blood in his veins." Though Murrow lacked "brain power," his father insisted that he had "good clean blood and is a pure minded Christian gentleman." The faculty accepted Murrow, but Broadus politely rebuffed A. D. Chandler, a young Black man from Detroit. Chandler had attended Ohio's Denison College alongside white students, and appealed Broadus's rejection. "All I desire is to be admitted to the class rooms," he pleaded. Broadus replied stiffly that "as sufficiently intimated in my former letter," the faculty did "not think it desirable." Should Chanler show up for class, "the faculty would decline to admit you." Broadus saw "no real hardship" in this for Chandler, who could attend many other "excellent seminaries" closer to Detroit, "in which you would have many fellow students with whom you would most likely be specially associated through life in ministerial labor." Chandler, a future leader in the National Baptist Convention, was one of numerous Black applicants to receive a Broadus rejection letter in the 1880s and 1890s.[27]

Broadus saw no conflict in restricting his seminary to whites while at the same time advocating for Black theological education. He actively supported all-Black institutions like Louisville's Simmons University and Richmond Theological Seminary. He also personally tutored several Black students, including Charles A. Parrish, pastor of Louisville's Calvary Baptist Church, who would teach Greek at Simmons. But these scenarios posed no threat to his white southern honor; indeed, they served the same paternalistic impulse that had once motivated his ministry to slaves. Broadus's insistence on segregated classrooms based on "pure blood" represents the darker side of the "Southern nobility" that his admirers praised in him, but it comprises a significant feature of his legacy at the seminary. In 1922, his successor and former student E. Y. Mullins was still declaring that "the institution here has, from the beginning, been for white students."[28]

--→>>◆◆◆<<←--

Broadus's seminary leadership belonged to a larger effort to preserve distinctly southern, white religious institutions after the Civil War. Eighteen years old when the Southern Baptist Convention formed during the slavery controversies of 1845, Broadus served the denomination's sectional aims for the rest of his life. For instance, he famously opposed a proposal for a formal plan of cooperation with northern Baptists in 1879 because he believed that it would lead to "a full merging of the work of this Convention into that of the Northern societies." While Broadus himself "loved to go North and loved to speak for their objects," Southern Baptists must maintain independence. "As matters now stand, we are not responsible for what at the North we object to, and they are not responsible for what at the South they object to," he reasoned, "but put us together and a good many of us might object, and the old feeling might again be revived." He proposed to communicate to northern brethren that, "while firmly holding to the wisdom of policy of preserving our separate organizations, we are ready, as in the past, to co-operate cordially with them in promoting the cause of Christ in our own and foreign lands." Southern Baptists adopted his motion; subsequent generations celebrated Broadus for saving the Convention at one of its lowest points.[29]

In addition to their own denomination, Broadus believed that white Southern Baptists needed their own religious literature, as seen in his leadership of the Sunday School Board in the mid-1860s. This venture folded after the war due to financial troubles, but an 1890 controversy with the American Baptist Publication Society (ABPS) presented an opportunity for its revival. Southern Baptists had relied on the literature of the Philadelphia-based ABPS for decades, but its northern perspective rankled many former Confederates. Broadus often wrote for the ABPS, but he pleaded with its leader, Benjamin Griffith, to give his publications "such a truly religious character, and succeed in keeping it so free from all that ought to give offense, that we of the South may find no difficulty in yielding it a hearty support." At the same time, Black Baptists were beginning to lobby Griffith to platform their own writers. "The time has come when the freedmen want a voice in things that they are called upon to support," S. A. Neal, a Black minister from Augusta, Georgia, declared in 1889. Griffith responded by inviting Black Baptists William J. Simmons, Emmanuel K. Love, and William H. Brooks to contribute to the *Baptist Teacher*.[30]

The decision enraged white Southern Baptists. "Southern people refuse to have negroes set up as their instructors," reported one periodical. Southern editorialists painted the three Black writers as "notorious negroes" and "incendiaries." They accused the ABPS of encouraging "the wickedly ambitious, unprincipled elements among them, to a contempt for law and order and to deeds of violence and death." "When will we unitedly rise up and rebuke such an insult to our Christian manhood!" demanded one white North Carolina Baptist. Under pressure, Griffith rescinded his invitation to the Black authors, asking them to instead write a series of tracts for an exclusively Black audience. In turn, Black Baptist ministers in Washington, D.C., condemned the ABPS for "ignoring the rights of the colored race in matters or religious co-operation."[31]

With many white Southern Baptists now calling for "Southern literature for Southern churches," Virginia Baptist J. M. Frost proposed the creation of a new publication board at the 1890 Convention meeting. But Frost's pitch sparked a major floor debate, for many viewed the plan as another effort by denominational elites to centralize power and homogenize Southern Baptist thought. When the uproar drowned out discussion, Broadus took the floor to calm "all this hullabaloo." The Convention appointed a committee to prepare a report on the proposed board for its 1891 annual meeting. Over the next year, Southern Baptist newspapers debated the issue, while the ABPS did its best to discourage the project. Each party attempted to co-opt Broadus as supporting its own position, but he refrained from public comment.[32]

Tensions ran high at the 1891 Southern Baptist Convention. After J. M. Frost's committee delivered its report, messengers expected an impassioned speech from Frost, followed by a hostile floor discussion. Instead, Broadus rose, unrecognized, and pled for peace. Southern Baptists would never reach unanimity regarding Sunday school literature, he reasoned. Thus, if a majority favored establishing a Sunday School Board, it should be done, though "let us not say that anyone is disloyal . . . when he buys his literature where he pleases." Acknowledging the reporters present, Broadus urged his brethren to refrain from hot words, and then he sat down in a hushed room. Without further discussion, the Convention adopted the Board almost unanimously. "The great throng bowed to his will," marveled one observer. Broadus's speech became "one the classic stories in Southern Baptist life." "Plain and uneducated men could understand him, and they came to trust him as a safe leader," John Sampey observed. "He was aware of the weaknesses in our ultra-democratic denominational life, but he believed in our Baptist doctrines and polity. He held the confidence and loyalty of the Baptist brotherhood to the close of his life."[33]

Soon the new Board was churning out Sunday school literature, tracts, hymnals, and books—all from a conservative, white southern viewpoint. Broadus boosted the new enterprise with his own writings. When the ABPS asked him to compose a Baptist catechism, he agreed on the condition that it be published jointly with the Southern Board, and his widely used *Catechism of Bible Teaching* was printed in 1892. Under the aggressive leadership of J. M. Frost, the Sunday School Board by 1910 had driven the once-dominant ABPS from the South. Embracing a New South business ethos, Frost and his successors grew the Board into an impressive corporate organization, with assets increasing from $53,000 in 1900 to almost $760,000 by 1920, at which time the Board employed 115 workers in its growing downtown Nashville headquarters. In a tribute to the early contributions of Broadus and Basil Manly Jr., the Board named its publishing house "Broadman Press" in 1933. Into the twentieth century, this common religious literature would forge Southern Baptists' religious and cultural identity.[34]

The ABPS controversy also spurred Black Baptists to form their own publication house. "It is plainly evident that as a [Black] denomination we shall never attain to the broad influence and elevated dignity worthy of so vast a body of Baptists, so long as our literary productions remain unpublished, our work unsystematized, and its success remains dependent upon the option of our friends for prosecution," reported one committee. Savannah minister Emmanuel K. Love, one of the three spurned authors in the controversy, now accepted that "he is both blind and foolish who does not recognize the fact that the color line is already drawn. I do not believe that a white man is color blind." Love concluded that "there is not so bright and glorious a future before a Negro in a white institution as there is for him in his own." Black Baptists accordingly established the National Baptist Publishing Board in 1896.[35]

-→))-❖-❧-(((←-

Broadus continued to promote his genteel brand of Black uplift through another sectional institution, the Southern Baptist Home Mission Board (HMB). Like virtually all Southern Baptist entities, the HMB floundered after the Civil War, prompting many southern states to partner with the wealthy northern Baptist Home Mission Society. But in 1882, the HMB tapped Isaac Taylor Tichenor, a former Confederate marksman and president of Alabama Polytechnic Institute (Auburn University), as its new executive. Over the next decade, Tichenor revitalized the HMB, thanks in no small part to his stoking of white southern race fears. He warned of ceding Black mission work to white northerners, with their "ideas of negro suffrage, of social equality, of miscegenation, of agrarianism, and every mischievous outgrowth of the fanaticism of that clime," which would "infuse these things into the minds of the negroes." Tichenor's strategy proved so effective that by 1892 he proudly reported that "there was not a missionary to the white people of the South who did not bear a commission from the Home Mission Board of the Southern Baptist Convention, or one of our state boards in alliance with it." Under Tichenor, the HMB had "won the confidence of the denomination and justified its own right to live."[36]

Tichenor's HMB promoted ministry to Blacks in the familiar antebellum tones of white paternalism. "Nothing is plainer to any one who knows this race than its perfect willingness to accept a subordinate place, provided there be confidence that in that position of subordination it will receive justice and kindness," Tichenor reported in 1891. "That is the condition it prefers above all others, and this is the condition in which it attains the highest development of every attribute of manhood. Whenever it shall understandingly and cheerfully accept this condition, the race problem is settled forever." Black Baptist Walter Brooks scoffed at the statement as "simply absurd." Tichenor and other white Southern Baptists may be "perfectly sincere" in such comments, Brooks said, but they were "blinded by their own prejudices and false education." As such, "they deserve our pity," along with Black prayers that God may "grant enlightenment of mind, and forgive them for so grossly misrepresenting the facts of the Afro-American's history and the sentiment of his heart." But Tichenor doubled down in his next report, calling Blacks an "inferior race" that must be "subordinated to our control" if they hoped to survive the modern world. Broadus was himself more than satisfied with Tichenor's leadership; he urged young ministers to "read the reports of I. T. Tichenor, for their information, their interpretation of the South industrially, for his statesmanship, and for his religious insight—and if for no other reason, for his English, simply pure."[37]

Black and white Baptists parted climactically in September 1894. After decades of territorial feuding, white northern and southern Baptist leaders met at Fortress Monroe, Virginia, for what Keith Harper has called the "Baptist Appomattox." In essence, northern Baptists agreed to withdraw their missionaries and concede the South to white Southern Baptists, allowing them to conduct ministry to Blacks in their own way. Black separatist Baptists seized the opportunity of Fortress Monroe to unify previously divided Black Baptists leaders around a single African American denomination. Black leaders met in Atlanta in 1895 to create the National Baptist Convention, which would direct various boards parallel to those of the Southern Baptist Convention. After Fortress Monroe, white northern Baptists, white Southern Baptists, and Black Baptists would travel separate paths into the twentieth century.[38]

Occurring less than a year before his death, the events of Fortress Monroe provided a fitting end to Broadus's career. Disappointed with Confederate defeat, Broadus, Boyce, Frost, Tichenor, and others reestablished cultural control in the Southland by maintaining a regionally distinctive, white southern denomination. While he acknowledged that social problems remained, Broadus pronounced his benediction on the New South's racial progress in 1893. "It was not [the Convention's] duty to deal with social questions," he stated, for "society is a thing that would settle its own variances in time. The colored people have done much better since their emancipation than any one who know them had any reason to expect. On the other hand, the white people of the South have done better by them than anybody else who know their pride had any reason to expect. . . . Let us work together cheerfully, and hopefully, thankfully." Into the twentieth century, Broadus's Southern Baptist Convention provided a powerful cultural bond in a South increasingly detached from broader American culture. Yale's Liston Pope observed in 1942 that "the churches have been the strongest forces in maintaining a spirit of isolation and in idealizing antebellum civilization in the region; the Southern churches, it is said, have never been reconstructed."[39] This, too, belonged to John Broadus's life work.

Twelve
CAVE HILL

A N EXPECTANT CROWD stood at Louisville's Tenth and Broadway Depot on October 4, 1893. They awaited a "magnificent special train," full of Confederate veterans and their families from Tennessee, scheduled to stop at 12:30. The *Courier-Journal* had advertised the visit, and invited all "ex-Confederates and friends" to come meet them. Accordingly, forty former Kentucky rebels, accompanied by their wives and daughters, showed up to extend their Tennessee comrades a bluegrass welcome. The train ran two hours late that day, but Professor Erhard Eichorn's popular brass band entertained the greeters by playing "My Old Kentucky Home," "The Bonnie Blue Flag," and "Dixie." Tapping his foot at a nearby table sat perhaps the city's most distinguished Confederate, Dr. John A. Broadus. At sixty-six, he was considerably grayer and feebler than when he had preached to Lee's army in 1863. But he would not miss this opportunity to represent the Confederate Association of Kentucky.[1]

When the Tennesseans arrived, Broadus laid on the southern charm. He welcomed his "fellow Confederates," complimented "these fair women and brave men," and offered to show the guests around "our lovely city" and into "our homes." He grew poignant at the sight of the old soldiers' lined faces, and remarked that "the tender buds and blossoms of spring are not as beautiful as the golden leaves of autumn." But then he turned to their shared identity as southern Americans. They had come today to "clasp hands again with those endeared to us by reason of a high and almost holy cause." "We have nothing to be ashamed of," he declared, for "when we laid down our arms and took the oath of allegiance, no people were more true to their obligation." The vanquished Confederates had "made the best of it," and proved themselves loyal Americans. Now, as they crossed the Ohio River, "will not every one of you be glad that it is not the border line into a foreign land, and when you see the glorious Stars and Stripes floating over the Magic City on the Lake, will you not rejoice that it is our flag?" Certainly they would. What they also knew, and what few outside that circle could understand, is that their hearts still throbbed for the Stars and Bars, too. "Some say that we ought never to mention with love the flag which we lost, that we thereby dishonor the flag now ours," Broadus said. "They do not know what love is. Does the husband not love his wife, though he mentions a buried loved one of the long ago?" As if to recall that shared lost love, he held up a gray CSA coat, to loud cheers.[2]

The old Confederacy had long since been interred on that October afternoon. In the nearly thirty years since Lee's surrender, Broadus had himself "made the best of it," pledging allegiance to the Union, preaching national reconciliation, and emerging as a beloved American patriot. But in the late autumn of his own life, the old man could no more forget his love of the South that was—"the flag which we lost"—that "high and almost holy cause"—than he could forget falling in love with Maria Harrison on the campus of the University of Virginia. Some memories never faded.

--->>>◆※◆<<<--

Broadus's fragile body had long frustrated his outsized ambitions. By age thirty-three, he had known that he would "never again have vigorous health." Throughout his life he was described as "small" and "frail," and was given to bouts of sickness and exhaustion that interrupted his prodigious plans. His personal writings are littered with references to being "laid up" or "prostrate," usually from some "derangement of the bowels," "dyspepsia," "diarrhea," or other gastric malady. Friends and family worried constantly over his health and pleaded with him not to drive so hard. "His brain seemed too much for his body," remarked one colleague.

Broadus learned to alternate his exhausting labors with extended retreats. He annually visited Virginia's springs, and wealthy friends gifted him a number of vacations, including his extravagant Grand Tour in 1870–1871. He consulted frequently with his physician brother-in-law, George Harrison. He weighed himself scrupulously, celebrating every pound gained, and he carefully monitored his diet. He became an exercise fanatic. He rode horses, chopped wood, took long walks, lifted weights, and used other fitness "apparatuses." He frequently sermonized on ministerial health, including lengthy excursuses in his *Memoir of James Petigru Boyce,* and in his funeral sermon for colleague George Riggan. He instructed listeners in the science of digestion, and warned against exchanging fresh country air and wholesome manual labor for the city's "incessant strain, without adequate bodily exercise or mental rest." He pleaded with students to join a gymnasium, as he had, for "exercising the muscles in some proportion to the exhausting and incessant strain he puts upon brain and nerves." In 1897, the Levering family would fulfill Broadus's long desire by building a gymnasium on the seminary campus. "A man of ardent nature, impulsive, enthusiastic and resolute enough to become a notable force in the world, will always find it hard to control himself and keep within the conditions of physical health," Broadus cautioned at Riggan's funeral. He knew from long experience.[3]

Since childhood, he had yearned "to be something and do something in the world," though after his Christian conversion he had endeavored to yield his aspirations to God's will. "Deliver me, O Lord, from wrong ambition, from every improper desire to be first among my brethren," he prayed in 1851. "May I be enabled to subordinate all my desires and plans and hopes to Thy will, and when I labor and strive for success and eminence and fame, may I 'do all for the glory of God.'" His earnest evangelical faith supplied a ballast to his will to ascend, but never destroyed it. After shuttling restlessly between careers as a denominational pastor and southern academic, by 1859 he found in the Southern Baptist Theological Seminary a means of combining his two loves, and a cause large enough to devote his life. As a seminary founder, Broadus helped lift up the denomination's humblest preachers into professional ministers. Through the hardships of Civil War and Reconstruction, he submitted every personal consideration to the institution's survival. His commitment exacted a steep cost on his family, finances, and personal health. But the seminary lived on, just as he had pledged.[4]

The years of sickness and strain now showed. City congregants had once called him "the handsomest man" they "had ever seen." But when William H. Whitsitt observed Broadus shambling down a Louisville sidewalk, he declared that he had seen healthier looking scarecrows. "One shoulder hung down forward, as if it might be broken; the other stood at the contradictory opposite, backwards and very erect; his long crooked neck bent over in front; he walked with a rapid hitch and altogether was a spectacle to witness," Whitsitt wrote, marveling that this "ungainly figure" was considered "the foremost man & preacher of the city." "Perhaps his physical defects go far to recommend his graces," he wondered. In the summer of 1884, Broadus passed out with a high fever in the pulpit at North Orange, New Jersey. The episode received embarrassingly wide newspaper coverage and inspired a flood of concerned letters. "My real difficulty as to work and rest is one I see no way to cure," he complained to Boyce. "I cannot live on my salary, I know it cannot possibly be enlarged, and in one way or another I am compelled to do extra work for which I lack strength. I make mistakes. But am trying very hard to act right and wisely."[5]

He had always held in taut tension the competing claims of professional aspirations and godly humility, the stewardship of his gifts, physical health, financial need, family obligations, and denominational expectations. The demands only increased in his final years. "'Busy' seems no adequate word for what his life always was," his daughter Alice recalled. "We often waited for weeks, to get a chance for ten minutes' talk with him about something important, and then if such a time seemed to have come, had no heart to interfere with his first moment of rest." To Alice, the weight under which he labored seemed "cruelly heavy." In unguarded moments, she heard him murmur that he was "working within an inch of his life." He had long ago accepted this as the price of "being something" in the world, but he confessed to daydreaming about reading himself to sleep under a Virginia shade tree, and "having nothing to do."[6]

Perhaps these conditions sweetened his trip to Europe in the summer of 1891. Twenty years after his first Grand Tour, the seminary rewarded him with another vacation abroad—though this time with an important difference. Lottie Broadus, who had stayed home so many times from her husband's travels, accompanied him overseas. "We have run around, and had much enjoyment, and only now and then extreme fatigue," Broadus reported. "Lottie holds up finely, especially when examining an old castle or cathedral, or surveying some inspiring scenery." They left behind a bustling Louisville household. Their home now included two unmarried daughters, forty-year-old Eliza and twenty-year-old Ella, and high school-aged Boyce, plus two married daughters and their spouses. Annie had married Virginia pastor W. Y. Abraham in 1878, and this union gave Broadus his first two grandchildren: John Broadus and Annie Louise. Alice and her new husband, Samuel Chiles Mitchell, also lived with the Broaduses in 1891. Samuel Broadus, now working for the Florence Railroad and Improvement Company, visited frequently. Eliza "kept house for this assorted crowd and kept everything going," Ella remembered. Broadus delighted in his grandchildren, giving them rides across the floor like a horse, writing them letters from his travels, and presenting them with books, such as James Fennimore Cooper's *Leatherstocking Tales*.[7]

The death of Basil Manly Jr. on January 31, 1892, returned Broadus's thoughts to his mortality. At the funeral, he praised his old friend as "the most versatile man I have ever met." He conjectured that, had Manly devoted himself to only two or three things, "he would have stood out as the most famous man of his age." Manly had died, in part, from lingering effects of a violent head injury suffered at the hands of a Louisville mugger in 1887. Broadus, in a rare loss of public control, vented his anger at the "assassin," whom he charged with "the murder of an aged minister of Christ." "O wretched man that slew my friend," he shouted, "where are you—in all the round world, where are you?" Regaining his composure, Broadus expressed hope that the robber would find salvation in Christ. The funeral party, led by two hundred seminary students, transported Manly's body to his plot in Cave Hill Cemetery, next to Boyce. Ella Broadus remembered her father talking more of death, heaven, and his own funeral after this.[8]

He remained a romantic to the end. However demanding his schedule, he never failed to make time for enjoying music, novels, and poetry—especially Wordsworth. "He is in some respects the great poet of the age, yet one that the crowd will never appreciate," he commented. With Wordsworth, nature still held matchless wonder for him. He stole away frequently for walks in the countryside or at Jacob Park—his "constitutionals," he called them. His young colleague John Sampey, who often accompanied Broadus, noted his unaffected "love for the beautiful in nature." "He would stop suddenly in view of a brilliant sunset and point to the glories of the clouds, or break off the thread of conversation to admire a tiny flower in his path." He still relished the baths, the mountains, and the genteel companionship of Virginia's springs. "How delightful it is to drink from the copious flowing stream that has so often done you good through and through," he wrote from Rawley Springs in 1893. "To climb high mountain sides with fresh and unwearied vigor, and revel in the beautiful scenery; then to sleep, drinking in at every breath the cool, pure mountain air." One of his companions that summer remarked that he seemed to have reached "the type of a perfect Christian character, 'a glorified childhood.'"[9]

In the spring of 1892, he took Lottie and his two youngest daughters to his boyhood home in Culpeper. They toured Old Jack's stables, the garden where Uncle Griffin told him Br'er Rabbit stories, and the ice house where he and his slave playmates, Henry and George, invented their own languages. They drank from his favorite spring and sat at the old family hearth as he described where each family member had sat when he read aloud to them on winter nights. He was now the only one left. "I know papa must have sad thoughts here, but he was merry and tender, and all of cheery anecdotes all the while," wrote Alice. A visit to the University of Virginia also stirred deep sentiment. "Every locality and object here has memories for me," he told his grandson, "and they grow more pathetic as I grow older, so that it is hard to control my feelings, in public and in private." He preached in Richmond at the dedication of Grace Street Baptist Church's new building, to an adoring crowd that included the governor and the city's most prominent people. "It was really pathetic," wrote A. T. Robertson. "It was Virginia's farewell to her great son."[10]

Unwell at the end of the spring 1894 semester, Broadus skipped the Southern Baptist Convention in Dallas to recuperate at Kentucky's Dawson Springs. In June, he delivered a couple of commencement sermons, finishing at Vanderbilt University in Nashville, Tennessee. "There is one thing about Doctor Broadus's preaching and speaking," reported Tennessee Baptist E. E. Folk. "Whenever you hear him you feel like you want to be a better man, and that by God's help you are going to be a better man." No one knew that it would be Broadus's final sermon. Back in Louisville, his doctor informed him that his heart was failing. He immediately canceled all preaching appointments and went to Rawley Springs. By September, he had gained six pounds and felt stronger. "I cannot wholly escape the weak feelings, and doubtless never shall, but I hope to do steady work—not too burdensome—with hearty relish," he told Alice. During his convalescence, he drew comfort from a photograph of his daughters, borrowed from a local relative. "Pray don't forget," he wrote to Alice, "amid whatever engrossments, that the old gentleman you call papa loves you, more in fact than he can state or you can imagine." In the fall, he resumed teaching and an ambitious writing project, completing five chapters of an inter-biblical history. By November, he could not lecture.[11]

The winter brought pleasant diversions. The Broadus family had scattered by 1894: Boyce Broadus was a student at Georgetown College in Kentucky, where Alice's husband, Samuel Mitchell, was a professor. Annie and W. Y. Abraham now served a church in Columbia, South Carolina, and Sam Broadus had launched a banking career in Florence, Alabama. At home in Louisville, Ella had become engaged to Broadus's greatest protege. The brilliant Greek student Archibald Thomas Robertson had arrived at the seminary in 1885 and immediately caught Broadus's attention. His "discovery of Robertson was like one discovering a diamond mine," recalled a classmate. The two formed a deep bond. "No man has left such a deep impress upon my life and cast of thought as he," Robertson wrote in 1888. "I shall bear his mark upon me as long as I live. His personality is intense." After joining the faculty, Robertson fell in love with Ella Broadus, though he told John Sampey that "I can't afford to marry her; I'd be known all my life as Dr. Broadus' son-in-law!" But Robertson overcame his hesitations and proposed marriage. He told Broadus that he anticipated the day "when I can call you my Father, as well as my truest earthy friend."[12] The Robertsons would move in with the Broaduses after the wedding.

Broadus grew reflective as his family flocked home for the ceremony in November 1894. "My home is lively with the daughters and their children, come beforehand to the wedding, and they help me a great deal on what would otherwise have been days hard to bear, in all the monotony of sickness," he wrote to a friend. In the rush of his working life, he had often wondered if he had sacrificed his family on the altar of personal ambition and public duty. As the work neared completion, he took satisfaction in the affectionate relationships he enjoyed with each of his children. "I take great pride in my daughters," he wrote. "They are quite unlike in appearance and character, and I admire each one. The fond pleasure I take in each one makes me all the more delight in the others. I love to talk with them, and quietly observe their quiet ways."[13] Nearly all of his children would name a grandchild "John Broadus" in his honor.

After the wedding, Broadus escaped to Florida to avoid Louisville's punishing winter. But when he returned for the spring semester, temperatures in Louisville hovered near zero for weeks and he realized that he had come home too soon. As he climbed the stairs to bed one night, he remarked to Robertson that "the next three weeks would decide everything for him." As his body weakened, Broadus found himself leaning consciously on "the guidance and sustaining power" of the Holy Spirit. Citing Jesus's words from John 16:7, he reminded W. D. Powell that "we are actually better off, if we only knew it and would fully avail ourselves of the privilege, in that we can constantly seek the blessings of the Holy Spirit in his blessed mission with his people, than we would be if the Savior himself were still moving among us." Preaching to himself, he wrote, "we should be always seeking the Holy Spirt's help in determining the meaning of the inspired teachings, in applying them to our guidance, and using them for our support in every question of truth and duty with which we are called to deal."[14]

The following week, his English New Testament class, sensing the end was near, carefully recorded his closing lecture:

> "Young gentlemen, if this were the last time I should ever be permitted to address you, I would feel amply repaid for consuming the whole hour in endeavoring to impress upon you these two things, *true piety* and like Apollos, to be men 'Mighty in the Scriptures.'" Then pausing, he stood for a moment with his piercing eye fixed upon us, and repeated over and over again in that slow but wonderfully impressive style peculiar to himself, "*Mighty in the Scriptures,*" "*Mighty in the Scriptures,*" until the whole class seemed to be lifted through him into a sacred nearness to the Master. That picture of him as he stood there at that moment can never be obliterated from my mind.[15]

The next day, Broadus took pleurisy. The following week, Robertson announced to the student body that the president was dying. When he slipped in and out of consciousness, he would call for a class book or pencil, as if lecturing. At times, he dictated long, intricate instructions regarding textual criticism. He died at 3:45 a.m. on March 16. That night, he was heard singing "Jesus, Lover of My Soul" and "Loving Kindness," repeating the line "And sing my Great Redeemer's praise."[16]

→»✢⊹✢«←

They committed the earthly remains of John A. Broadus next to those of Boyce and Manly in Cave Hill Cemetery. The city of Louisville had purchased the three hundred-acre Cave Hill farm in 1830 and transformed it into an enormous, undulating, Victorian garden, complete with basin ponds, thick plots of trees, flower gardens, and winding walking paths. The Norton family would erect a towering, marble monument above Broadus's grave, as "a feeble token of esteem and veneration for his memory." He doubtless would have appreciated this final act of generosity from his benefactors. But he may also have wondered at the humanistic inscription they affixed beneath his bronzed image: "On earth there is nothing great but man. In man there is nothing great but mind." Nearby, an unassuming footstone offers a contrasting epigram, from the apostle Paul: "J. A. B. 'I count all things but loss for the excellency of the knowledge of Christ Jesus my Lord.'" The conflicting tributes witness to something of Broadus's complexity.[17]

So too did his eulogists. Standing sentinel at his funeral was a mass contingent of the Confederate veterans who "idolized" him. Acknowledging the old soldiers, William Whitsitt reminded the mourners that Broadus throughout his life "kept his feet always firmly planted on Southern soil." And yet, "he was as much loved in New York as Virginia. Whatever he spoke from any platform on either side of the line was applauded to the echo on both sides of the line." Broadus stands as a striking example of how loyal Confederates could zealously promote national peace and reconciliation while also clinging to the Lost Cause. It is fitting that Broadus is buried among both Union and Confederate soldiers in Cave Hill.[18]

His mediating role can also be observed in the subsequent history of Southern Baptists, who quickly felt the loss of his leadership. Whitsitt realized his long-held dream of leading the seminary when trustees named him president in 1895. But the denominational factions Broadus had united since 1859 splintered under Whitsitt. He had resented Broadus's interference in publicizing his anti-Landmark views of Baptist origins in the 1880s, and had anonymously published his conclusions in a Presbyterian magazine. When Southern Baptists discovered this shortly into his presidency, T. T. Eaton, Whitsitt's rival for the presidency and his pastor at Walnut Street Baptist Church, led a campaign for his removal. To Eaton and seminary trustee B. H. Carroll, Landmark sympathizers who also considered themselves Broadus disciples, Whitsitt had betrayed the Convention's trust. They also insisted that Broadus would see it their way.[19] Meanwhile, Broadus's most intimate circle vigorously supported Whitsitt, including A. T. Robertson, John Sampey, Boyce Broadus, and Alice Broadus's husband, Samuel Mitchell, who pleaded with trustees to side with "the forces of progress" and uphold Whitsitt's freedom of research.[20] But Eaton and his cohorts had hounded Whitsitt from office by 1899. He finished his career among progressive Virginia Baptists, bitterly grieving his martyrdom to intellectual freedom. But the caustic

Whitsitt had also failed to follow Broadus's adroit maintenance of the fragile Southern Baptist consensus. "When Dr. Broadus died, so very short a time ago, the seminary was in the hearts of all our people," Carroll opined in 1897. "In two years' time under the present executive, and by his own course, what a sad change! The wisdom of thirty years reared an imposing structure, a veritable lighthouse, and two years of unwisdom threatens its overthrow!"[21]

Trustees elected Edgar Young Mullins to succeed Whitsitt. Mullins had adored Broadus as a seminary student in the 1880s, and corresponded with him until Broadus's death. Scholarly, refined, cosmopolitan—the Mississippi native spent fifteen years pastoring in Baltimore and Boston—he closely approximated Broadus's own sophisticated southern profile. Until his death in 1928, Mullins would lead the seminary as a New South business executive, expanding the seminary's enrollment and academic prestige while also moving the institution in a more theologically progressive direction. Mullins also shrewdly managed the Southern Baptist consensus, witnessed in his authorship of the denomination's first confession of faith, the Baptist Faith and Message (1925), a document both conservative and broad enough to satisfy most Southern Baptists during the divisive evolution debates of the early 1920s. In this mediating role, Mullins saw himself as stewarding the Broadus legacy.

So too did Texas Baptist preacher and educator B. H. Carroll. A massive, bearded, cigar-smoking former Confederate scout, Carroll declared in 1895 that Broadus had "exercised a greater influence over my own life than all other men put together." In 1896, Sampey told Carroll, "You are now—since Broadus is gone—our natural leader in the Southern Baptist Convention." Carroll obtained a charter for what would become Southwestern Baptist Theological Seminary in 1905, motivated in part by liberalizing trends at Southern Seminary. Carroll's seminary would develop a reputation as a more conservative, practical, evangelistically focused alternative. He believed his Southwesterners to be the true heirs of the Broadus legacy, and he honored his hero by naming a major campus road "Broadus Street." The two seminaries would follow different paths in the twentieth century, but both looked to Broadus as their guide.[22]

Broadus's family provides another vantage point for observing the complexity of his legacy. After learning the ropes under John D. Rockefeller at Standard Oil, Samuel Broadus made his fortune in North Alabama by founding a successful chain of eighteen Merchants' Banks (later Tennessee Valley Banks) and the Broadus Cotton Mill in Stevenson. He lured his younger brother, Boyce, to Decatur, where he joined Sam in business and in faithful Baptist churchmanship. But the Broadus boys inherited their father's poor health along with his faith and ambition. Boyce died in 1902, at age twenty-seven, and Sam died in 1916 at age fifty-six. The *Decatur Daily* called Sam Broadus's funeral "one of the most impressive ever held in North Alabama."[23]

Eliza Broadus, almost totally deaf by her mid-fifties, moved in with Ella and A. T. Robertson after her father's death. But she continued to lead the WMU, ear trumpet and all, until 1928. She also helped open a women's Training School at Southern Seminary in 1907, over the objections of many disapproving Southern Baptists. "I know change has come in the opinion of Dr. Broadus's daughters," WMU secretary Annie Armstrong complained, "but Dr. Broadus is in his grave and can no longer exercise authority in the matter." The Training School eventually developed into the seminary's School of Social Work, one of the most socially progressive wings of Southern Baptist life, until its controversial closure in 1997. After a speeding truck killed Eliza in 1928, seminary professor J. B. Weatherspoon referred her mourners to the biblical story of Enoch. "Eliza S. Broadus went for a walk one evening and was not, for God took her," he said. Ella Robertson chose a different biblical allusion: "The Lord sent a chariot for Elijah and a truck for Eliza." Since 1975, Kentucky Baptists have collected their annual state missions offering in Eliza's name. "Make choices," she often told young Baptist women, "don't wait for chances."[24]

Alice and Samuel Chiles Mitchell carried the Broadus legacy in still other directions. Samuel Mitchell became well known for his progressive views on race and labor relations in the New South. He rose to the presidency of the University of South Carolina, but was forced to resign in 1913 for routing Peabody Fund gifts to the state's Black colleges. Though Alice Broadus Mitchell had been close to her father, she and her husband drifted from his faith. Samuel remained outwardly religious, but his son John Broadus Mitchell judged that "later in life that meant very little to him. I think it was social values that took the place of individual goodness or devotion or anything of that sort." As for Alice, Broadus Mitchell believed that his mother "was less religious than he was, though she was a daughter of a Baptist clergyman." Alice knew her Bible exhaustively, but her son did

not think that "any of the supernatural part won through to her at all." She preferred a "sensible" and "very realistic view of religious legend," Broadus Mitchell
explained, citing her rejection of Christ's virgin conception. "My mother believed
in the sperms rather than in the miracles," he laughed.[25]

Broadus Mitchell, a journalist, economic historian, and activist for labor and
civil rights, extended his parents' progressive legacy. His published dissertation
from Johns Hopkins University celebrated the South's industrial revolution as
a "romantic" tale of progress for the region's white laboring class. "Formerly, a
landed aristocracy shut out the average man from economic participation; but
with the rise of the cotton mills, the poor whites were welcomed back into the
service of the South," he explained. Like his father, Samuel, Broadus Mitchell
believed that the South had lost the Civil War "because it placed itself in opposition to the compelling forces of the age," and that "the task since 1865 has been
to liberalize the South in thought, nationalize it in politics, and industrialize it in
production." His interpretation of the New South remained standard (featured
prominently in such influential works as W. J. Cash's *The Mind of the South*) until challenged by C. Vann Woodward and others in the mid-twentieth century.
Mitchell became an ardent Socialist during the Great Depression, and ran for
governor of Maryland on that party's ticket in 1934. In 1977, he confessed to
being as religiously indifferent as his parents.[26]

After initial concerns about being overshadowed, A. T. Robertson quickly
embraced his proximity to John A. Broadus. In 1901, he published as his first
book, *The Life and Letters of John A. Broadus*, a 450-page work of filial devotion.
Robertson would go on to publish another forty-four books, as the leading evangelical New Testament scholar of his generation. No volume was more significant
than his comprehensive *Grammar of the Greek New Testament* (1914), which was
hailed by scholars around the world. Robertson dedicated the volume "to the
memory of John A. Broadus," and he related in the preface how his mentor had
charged him to complete the work. "I have never lost the intellectual impulse
from the impact of Broadus who with a frail body had a genius for work," he
remarked elsewhere. Robertson stood among the last of the "scholarly conservatives" in the Broadus tradition, a denominational scholar who yet gained notoriety in the broader American academy.[27] He far surpassed Broadus's output, but
Robertson insisted that he simply carried out the work that his mentor would
have done, had Providence allowed him the time and repose.

In 1933, after forty-six years at the seminary, Robertson died from a stroke suffered in the middle of a class lecture. His family buried him in Cave Hill Cemetery. At Robertson's request, they marked his grave with a moderate-sized, ground-level cross, now covered with ivy, situated behind the imposing monument of his famous father-in-law. Robertson was content to await the resurrection, with a generation of southern ministers, in the shadow of John A. Broadus.

NOTES

ABBREVIATIONS

AHP   Alvah Hovey Papers

AHS   Augustus Hopkins Strong

ATR   A. T. Robertson, *Life and Letters of John A. Broadus*. Philadelphia: American Baptist Publication Society, 1901.

BMJ   Basil Manly Jr.

BP   Broadus Papers, James P. Boyce Centennial Library, Archives and Special Collections, Southern Baptist Theological Seminary.

CEB   Charlotte Eleanor (Sinclair) Broadus

CHT   Crawford Howell Toy

JAB   John Albert Broadus

JDR   John D. Rockefeller

JMB   James Madison Broadus

JPB   James Petigru Boyce

MCB   Maria Carter (Harrison) Broadus

Memoir   John A. Broadus, *Memoir of James Petigru Boyce*. New York: A. C. Armstrong and Son, 1893.

MFC   Manly Family Collection, The University of Alabama Libraries Special Collections

MFP   Manly Family Papers, The University of Alabama Libraries Special Collections

RAC   Rockefeller Archive Center

SBTS   Southern Baptist Theological Seminary, Archives and Special Collections

WHW   William Heth Whitsitt

WRH   William Rainey Harper

INTRODUCTION

1. JAB, *Memoir*, 198–99; J. William Jones to JAB, 18 May 1867, in ATR, 224. For Lee's tenure at Washington College, see Guelzo, *Robert E. Lee,* 378–92.

2. JAB to CEB, 6 June 1867, BP.

3. ATR, 224–27.

4. ATR, 214; Wilkinson, "John Albert Broadus," 327, 332–33.

5. "Proceedings of Sons in Louisville," *The Confederate Veteran Magazine* 13, no. 1 (1905), 241; Longenecker, *Pulpits of the Lost Cause,* 4.

6. For the Lost Cause facilitating incorporation into the Union, see Foster, *Ghosts of the Confederacy,* 6–8, 195–98, and Foster, *The Limits of the Lost Cause,* 1–18. David W. Blight also argues that the Lost Cause assisted reconciliation by sweeping the issues of race and slavery under the rug, in *Race and Reunion,* 385–91, though Caroline Janney argues for the Lost Cause as a more divisive than unifying force in *Remembering the Civil War,* 3–11.

7. Williams, *Isaac Taylor Tichenor,* 67; Grantham, *Southern Progressivism,* passim.

8. George in Dockery and Duke, eds., *John A. Broadus,* 5; Holifield, *Gentlemen Theologians,* 24; T. T. Eaton, in ATR, 435.

9. Hatch, *Democratization of American Christianity,* 16; Robertson, "An Educational Revival in the South," 2.

10. *Richmond Dispatch,* 17 May 1869, 3.

11. Sampey, "John A. Broadus," 10.

12. Dockery and Duke, eds., *John A. Broadus: A Living Legacy.* The most comprehensive dissertation is Barron, "The Contributions of John A. Broadus to Southern Baptists."

13. See "Dedication of John A. Broadus Memorial Chapel (video)," 12 October 1999, at https://repository.sbts.edu/handle/10392/5532. In his popular textbook, Bryan Chapell calls Broadus's *Treatise* "the seminal volume for the codification and popularization of the expository method as we now know it." Chapell, *Christ-Centered Preaching,* 79, 129.

14. Wills et al., "Report on Slavery and Racism"; Alison Collin Greene critiqued the report as insufficient in *Southern Baptists Re-Observed,* 242–63; Bailey, "Southern Baptist President."

15. JAB, *Memoir,* 186–87.

1. DETERMINED TO BE SOMETHING

1. ATR, 28.

2. Elder, *The Sacred Mirror,* 141–46. For more on oratory in the Old South, see Wyatt-Brown, *Southern Honor,* 330–31; O'Brien, *Conjectures of Order,* passim; Fox-Genovese and Genovese, *The Mind of the Master Class.*

3. JAB, *A Treatise on the Preparation and Delivery of Sermons,* 17–18.

4. See Ragosta, *Wellspring of Liberty;* Schweiger, *Gospel Working Up,* 14; Little, *Imprisoned Preachers.*

5. For Leland, see Smith, *John Leland.*

6. ATR, 4.

7. For Andrew Broaddus, see Sprague, *Annals of the American Baptist Pulpit,* 6:291–296; Andrew Broaddus, ed., *Sermons and Other Writings of the Rev. Andrew Broaddus;* and Holifield, *Gentlemen Theologians,* 53–55.

8. Sprague, *Annals of the American Baptist Pulpit,* 6:291–296.

9. On the early influence of his family, see Fuller, "The Way to Learn to Preach Is to Preach," in Dockery and Duke, eds., *John A. Broadus,* 47–48. On William F. Broaddus and "Kentucky" Andrew Broaddus, see Nettles, *The Baptists,* 290–93.

10. Taylor, ed., *Virginia Baptist Ministers,* Third Series, 237–47.

11. Schweiger, *Gospel Working Up,* 24.

12. For an introduction to the Whig Party and Henry Clay's American System, see Pearson, *The Whigs' America,* and Holt, *The Rise and Fall of the American Whig Party.*

13. *Richmond Times-Dispatch,* 4 July 1846, 2; ATR, 13–15.

14. *Kind Words* article cited in ATR, 24.

15. JAB to James P. Boyce, 6 December 1876, Boyce Papers.

16. ATR, 18.

17. ATR, 29.

18. JAB, *A Treatise on the Preparation and Delivery of Sermons,* 426–27.

19. ATR, 21–22.

20. "Citizens Petition," 20 February 1839; "Citizens Petition," 25 January 1836.

21. Caroline M. Broadus to JAB, 30 January 1849, BP.

22. ATR, 26–27.

23. ATR, 30–32; for education in the Old South, see Schweiger, *A Literate South*; Wyatt-Brown, *Southern Honor,* 192–95; for a typical Virginia field school, see Hatcher, *Life of J. B. Jeter,* 48–56.

24. ATR, 32.

25. JAB, "The Baptism," in *Kind Words* 52, no. 5 (May 1867), 1.

26. ATR, 33–34. For modern evangelicalism and the individual self, see especially Hindmarsh, *The Evangelical Conversion Narrative,* and Hindmarsh, *The Spirit of Early Evangelicalism.* For southern evangelicalism's blending of honor culture and modern self-identity, see Elder, *The Sacred Mirror.* Older but still valuable studies of antebellum southern revivalism include Loveland, *Southern Evangelicals and the Social Order,* and Boles, *The Great Revival.* All quotations from the Bible are from the King James Version.

27. JAB to Edmund Broadus, 11 April 1845, BP. For evangelicals seeking "an everlasting name," see Elder, *The Sacred Mirror,* 176–99.

28. JAB to a college student, 7 July 1889, BP.

29. Edmund Broadus to JAB, 4 January 1844, BP; JAB to Maria Broadus, 29 April 1856, BP.

30. Letters from Martha and Carrie Broadus cited in ATR, 37; for the treacherous vocation of a schoolmaster, see Wyatt-Brown, *Southern Honor,* 161–63.

31. Edmund Broadus to JAB, 7 May 1844, in ATR, 38–39, emphasis in the original.

32. JAB, diary, 15 October 1845, BP. For Broadus's Sunday school leadership, see Barron, "The Contributions of John A. Broadus to Southern Baptists," 11–12.

33. William Morton to JAB, 30 August 1844, in ATR, 43; JAB, diary, 26 June 1845, in ATR, 47; JAB to T. W. Lewis, 26 February 1846, in ATR, 49; JAB, diary, 13 February 1846, BP.

34. JAB to Edmund Broadus, 11 April 1845, in ATR, 45.

35. JAB to T. W. Lewis, 26 February 1846, in ATR, 48–49.

36. J. M. Broadus to JAB, 21 August 1849, BP.

37. *Richmond Times-Dispatch,* 4 July 1846, 2; JAB, "College Education for Men of Business," in *Sermons and Addresses,* 267.

38. Schweiger, *Gospel Working Up,* 19. For Poindexter, who figures prominently in the founding of Southern Seminary, see Taylor, *Virginia Baptist Ministers,* Third Series, 146–64.

39. JAB, "Memorial of A. M. Poindexter," in *Sermons and Addresses,* 397–99.

40. JAB, "American Baptist Ministry of A. D. 1774," in *Sermons and Addresses,* 237; Elder, *The Sacred Mirror,* 187; JAB, "Memorial of A. M. Poindexter," in *Sermons and Addresses,* 399.

2. ON THE RISE

1. Taylor, *Virginia Baptist Ministers,* Third Series, 232.

2. *Alexandria Gazette,* 23 January 1844, 2; Taylor, *Thomas Jefferson's Education;* Thomas Jefferson to Joseph C. Cabell, 13 January 1823, *Founders Online,* National Archives, https://founders.archives.gov/documents/Jefferson/03-19-02-0217; Bruce, *The History of the University of Virginia,* 3:8–15.

3. Thomas Jefferson to William Roscoe, 27 December 1820, *Founders Online,* National Archives, https://founders.archives.gov/documents/Jefferson/03-16-02-0404; Bruce, *History of the University of Virginia,* 3:133; Taylor, *Thomas Jefferson's Education,* 300–307. For Jefferson's conflicted religious life, see Kidd, *Thomas Jefferson.*

4. Bruce, *History of the University of Virginia,* 3:113–18, 121–26; Taylor, *Thomas Jefferson's Education,* 305; JAB, *A Memorial of Gessner Harrison, M.D.,* 28–29; ATR, 64.

5. ATR, 69.

6. JAB to Martha Broadus Bickers, 4 February 1849, in ATR, 70.

7. ATR, 64–65, 69; *University of Virginia Alumni News,* vols. 1–3, 174.

8. Bruce, *History of the University of Virginia,* 3:90–92; Taylor, *Virginia Baptist Ministers,* Fourth Series, 234–35.

9. JAB, *A Memorial of Gessner Harrison, M.D.,* 22; Bruce, *History of the University of Virginia,* 3:136.

10. Barron, "The Contributions of John A. Broadus to Southern Baptists," 17.

11. ATR, 71.

12. For more detail on the courtship of Maria Harrison and Broadus's illnesses at the end of his college experience, see Reeder, *Broadus Unbound,* 18–31.

13. ATR, 74.

14. ATR, 56; JAB, *A Memorial of Gessner Harrison, M.D.,* 39; Longenecker, *Pulpits of the Lost Cause,* 153.

15. JAB to MCB, 7 October 1850, in ATR, 81; JAB to MCB, 14 October 1850, in ATR, 81–82; JAB to MCB, 5 November 1850, in ATR, 83.

16. JAB to MCB, 9 September 1850, in ATR, 79–80; J. M. Broadus to JAB, September 1849, in ATR, 72; ATR, 79.

17. ATR, 97; Holifield, *Gentlemen Theologians,* 74–77.

18. Andrew Broaddus to JAB, 3 March 1851, in ATR, 89.

19. JAB to MCB, 7 October 1850, in ATR, 80; for Cocke and Bremo Seminary, see Moore, "General John Hartwell Cocke of Bremo 1780–1866," 207–218, and Taylor, *Thomas Jefferson's Education,* 250–53.

20. See Mary Pinkard to JAB, 22 July 1851, BP; JAB to "Turpin," 18 September 1851, BP; JAB to MCB, 7 October 1850 and 15 October 1850, in ATR, 80–82.

21. J. H. Cocke to JAB, 1 August 1850, in ATR, 78; Taylor, *Thomas Jefferson's Education,* 146–47; Coyner, "John Hartwell Cocke of Bremo," 305–308, 311.

22. Genovese, *Roll, Jordan, Roll;* ATR, 81; "John A. Broadus, Chairman of Committee for the Religious Instruction of Colored People," *Religious Herald,* 23 October 1856, 1; Irons, *The Origins of Proslavery Christianity,* 173–76; Barron, "The Contributions of John A. Broadus to Southern Baptists," 36.

23. JAB, *Memoir,* 91–92.

24. Quoted in Sparks, *Religion in Mississippi,* 63; see also Schweiger, *Gospel Working Up,* 22–23, and Holifield, *Gentlemen Theologians,* 31.

25. Gessner Harrison to Mr. Tutweiller, 23 December 1850, in ATR, 84.

26. William F. Broaddus to JAB, 2 February 1851, BP; William F. Broaddus to JAB, 13 April 1851, BP; William McGuffey to JAB, 13 March 1851, BP; William F. Broaddus to JAB, 9 May 1851, BP; ATR, 88.

27. ATR, 92–93.

28. Taylor, *Virginia Baptist Ministers,* Fourth Series, 241; ATR, 93.

29. Bruce, *History of the University of Virginia,* 3:97.

30. JAB to Charlottesville Baptist Church, 5 September 1851, BP.

3. GENTLEMAN PASTOR

1. Maxwell, ed., *Virginia Historical Register,* 1850, 56; James Thomas to JAB, 22 August 1856, BP. For railroads and the growth of southern towns, see Ayers, *The Promise of the New South,* 3–33, 55–80.

2. Holifield, *Gentlemen Theologians,* 10–11, 39; Schweiger, *Gospel Working Up,* 35; JAB, "America's Baptist Ministry in A.D. 1774," in *Sermons and Addresses,* 243.

3. Wyatt-Brown, *Southern Honor,* 43–45, 92–95; O'Brien, *Conjectures of Order,* 1:326–27, 372; Taylor, *Virginia Baptist Ministers,* Fourth Series, 248; Bruce, *History of the University of Virginia,* 3:219; Clarke, *To Count Our Days,* 30–31.

4. Wyatt-Brown, *Southern Honor,* 89–92; McGlothlin, "John Albert Broadus," 159; ATR, 100–102, 138.

5. J. M. Broadus to JAB, 11 November 1851, BP; MCB to JAB, 16 November 1856, BP; MCB to JAB, 6 December 1856, BP; MCB to JAB, 26 July 1857, BP; MCB to JAB, 1 December 1857, BP; JMB to JAB, 17 November 1851, BP; Mr. Hansbrough to JAB, 17 November 1851, BP; William Farish to JAB, 29 April 1853, BP; O'Brien, *Conjectures of Order,* 1:382–84.

6. JAB, "America's Baptist Ministry in A.D. 1774," in *Sermons and Addresses,* 243; J. M. Broadus to JAB, September 1849, in ATR, 72.

7. Frederickson, "Interview with Broadus Mitchell"; "Criticisms on Some of the Ablest Representative Preachers of the Day," 101; Riley, "The Pulpit Oratory of the South," 150.

8. ATR, 107, 110; JAB to CEB, 13 August 1888, in ATR, 367; Hoyt, "Fifty Years of Practical Theology," 155; Carver, "Recollections," 19.

9. JAB to CEB, 7 November 1858, in Reeder, *Broadus Unbound,* 105; JAB to CEB, 15 October 1858, in Reeder, *Broadus Unbound,* 100; ATR, 123–24; Taylor, *Virginia Baptist Ministers,* Fourth Series, 248–49; JAB, "Essay on the Best Mode of Preparing and Delivering Sermons," 14 December 1854, *Religious Herald;* JAB, *A Treatise on the Preparation and Delivery of Sermons,* 18; Longenecker, *Pulpits of the Lost Cause,* 159.

10. Taylor, *Virginia Baptist Ministers,* Fourth Series, 147, 244; Bruce, *History of the University of Virginia,* 3:219; for Romanticism in Broadus's preaching, see Edwards, "The Preaching of Romanticism in America," 297–312; JAB to CEB, 15 February 1877, in ATR, 304.

11. "Criticisms on Some of the Ablest Representative Preachers of the Day," 101; JAB, "Some Laws for Spiritual Work," in *Sermons and Addresses,* 39.

12. *Richmond Dispatch,* 3 June 1854, 1; JAB to MCB, 22 September 1852, in ATR, 106; Schweiger, *Gospel Working Up,* 42; Holifield, *Gentlemen Theologians,* 21–22.

13. Bruce, *History of the University of Virginia*, 3:34–36; Taylor, *Virginia Baptist Ministers*, Fourth Series, 241.

14. Taylor, *Virginia Baptist Ministers*, Fourth Series, 241–42.

15. W. H. Harrison to JAB, 3 January 1852, BP.

16. JAB to MCB, 4 September 1852, BP; Lewis, *Ladies and Gentlemen on Display; Richmond Dispatch*, 6 August 1882, 2.

17. JAB to MCB, 1 September 1852, BP; JAB to MCB, 4 September 1852, BP; ATR, 100–101; for the modernizing influences of evangelical women, see especially Brekus, *Sarah Osborn's World;* Elder, *The Sacred Mirror*, 209.

18. JAB to MCB, 4 September 1852, BP.

19. JAB, "Some Account of the Revival in the Charlottesville Church in October and November, 1852," BP; JAB to MCB, 17 September 1852, BP; Loveland, *Southern Evangelicals and the Social Order*, 65–90.

20. JAB to Cornelia Taliaferro, 5 September 1853, BP.

21. For the 1852 revival, see JAB, "Some Account of the Revival in the Charlottesville Church in October and November, 1852," BP, and Fuller, "The Way to Learn to Preach Is to Preach," in Dockery and Duke, eds., *John A. Broadus*, 58–66; Elder, *The Sacred Mirror*, 176–99.

22. JAB to MCB, 14 May 1853, BP; MCB to Martha Broadus Bickers, 27 April 1853, BP; ATR, 112.

23. A. H. Hovey to JAB, 10 March 1855, BP; A. H. Hovey to JAB, 24 January 1855, BP.

24. ATR, 107–108, 118, 122.

25. See J. B. Jeter to JAB, 31 December 1856, BP; on church discipline practice in the nineteenth-century South, see Wills, *Democratic Religion;* W. E. Eliott to JAB, 30 May 1858 and June 1858, BP.

26. Hatcher, *Life of J. B. Jeter*, 381; JAB, "Essay on the Best Mode of Preparing and Delivering Sermons," 14 December 1854, *Religious Herald;* R. B. C. Howell to JAB, 16 October 1854, BP; Schweiger, *Gospel Working Up*, 69; Holifield, *Gentlemen Theologians*, 43.

27. Barron, "The Contributions of John A. Broadus to Southern Baptists," 35; Baptist General Association of Virginia, *Minutes of the Baptist General Association of Virginia . . . June, 1855*, 46; MCB to Martha Bickers, 11 June 1855, in ATR, 127–28.

28. Schweiger, *Gospel Working Up*, 26–27; Southern Baptist Convention, *Proceedings of the Southern Baptist Convention . . . 1853*, 10; Southern Baptist Convention, *Proceedings of the Fifth Biennial Meeting . . . 1855*, 11, 61–62; Southern Baptist Convention, *Proceedings of the Seventh Biennial Session . . . 1859*, 5, 26, 20, 94–95; for a detailed account of Broadus's denominational work, see Barron, "The Contributions of John A. Broadus to Southern Baptists," 31–41.

29. Schweiger, *Gospel Working Up*, 47; ATR, 104–105; Guthman, *Strangers Below*.

30. For Albemarle Academy, see Sullivan, *Lottie Moon*, 23–26; Schweiger, *Gospel Working Up*, 63–64; JAB, "College Education for Men of Business," in *Sermons and Addresses*, 256.

31. JAB, "Address to Berryville Total Abstinence Society"; Wills, *Southern Baptist Theological Seminary*, 178–79; Minutes, *Grand Division of the Sons of Temperance of the State of Virginia, 1855*, 97, 105–107, 111–13; Schweiger, *Gospel Working Up*, 83; Pflugrad-Jackisch, *Brothers of a Vow*, 63, 83, 96–97. Broadus used his 1856 communication to the Sons of Temperance to urge the restriction of membership to men only. For antebellum Baptists and social reform, see Menikoff, *Politics and Piety*.

32. ATR, 117, 121; JAB to MCB, 7 November 1853, BP.

33. ATR, 147; William F. Broaddus to JAB, 4 June 1853, BP.

34. JAB to MCB, 4 June 1853, BP; JAB to MCB, 22 August 1853, BP.

35. "A Friend" to JAB, 5 November 1855, BP; Enquirer to JAB, 27 February 1857, BP; Enquirer to JAB, 14 April 1857, BP; Oliver Lillibridge to JAB, 3 February 1856, BP.

36. Stuart White to JAB, 15 December 1856, BP. A century later, Billy Graham would provide a similar ministry of letter responses, albeit on an exponentially larger scale; see Wacker, *America's Pastor,* 250–81.

37. *University of Virginia Alumni News,* vols. 1–3, 36; Bruce, *History of the University of Virginia,* 3:120; J. B. Jeter to JAB, 29 January 1855, BP; William F. Broaddus to JAB, 12 March 1855, BP.

38. JAB to W. A. Whitescarver, 26 March 1855, BP; JAB to W. A. Whitescarver, 18 June 1855, BP; ATR, 144.

39. JAB to Cornelia Taliaferro, May 19, 1856, BP; Schweiger, *Gospel Working Up,* 22. For Dickinson, see Brown, "Pastoral Evangelism."

40. JAB to W. A. Whitescarver, 4 February 1856, BP; JAB to MCB, 9 July 1855, in ATR, 130.

41. Barron, "The Contributions of John A. Broadus to Southern Baptists," 25; JAB to Cornelia Taliaferro, 19 May 1856, BP, in ATR, 134–35.

42. W. H. Baynham to JAB, 16 May 1879, BP; Prof. William M. Thornton, "Alumni Bulletin," May 1895, in ATR, 142–43; "Madison Hall: The University Young Men's Christian Association," *University of Virginia Alumni News,* vols. 1–3, 36; Hiden quoted in Brown, "Pastoral Evangelism," 102–103; Moore, *Apostle of the Lost Cause,* 12.

43. Thomas T. Devan to JAB, 4 October 4 and 15 October 1856, BP; JAB to MCB, 11 June 1855, BP; MCB to Martha Broadus Bickers, 11 June 1855, BP.

44. JAB to MCB, 29 April 1856, BP.

45. Andrew Broaddus to JAB, 26 August 1858, BP; William Williams to JAB, 25 September 1856, BP; ATR, 99; J. B. Jeter to JAB, 20 March 1856, BP.

46. BMJ to JAB, 22 August 1856, BP; JMB to JAB, 16 March 1852, BP; Edward J. Willis to JAB, 15 March 1854 and 27 March 1854, BP; E. H. Sanford to JAB, 26 March 1854, BP; William Robinson to JAB, 27 March 1854, BP; Osgood C. Wheeler to JAB, 11 May 1854, BP; ATR, 98; James Edmunds and W. B. Caldwell to JAB, 1 June 1857, BP.

47. JMB to JAB, 16 July 1856, BP.

4. CASTING THE DIE

1. JAB, *Memoir,* 97.

2. Miller, *Piety and Intellect,* 1–83; Fraser, *Schooling the Preachers,* 29–47; Clarke, *To Count Our Days,* 1–8.

3. BMJ, "The Beginnings of the History of the Seminary," 114; Snay, *Gospel of Disunion,* 104–109; Manley, "The Southern Baptist Mind in Transition," 45–62.

4. JAB, *Memoir,* 116–17; Wills, *Southern Baptist Theological Seminary,* 3–14; Baptist General Association of Virginia, *Minutes of the Baptist General Association of Virginia . . . June, 1855,* 30–31.

5. For Boyce's early development, see Nettles, *James Petigru Boyce,* 13–91.

6. South Carolina Baptist Convention, *Minutes,* 1856, South Carolina Baptist Historical Collection, 18–19.

7. JAB, *Memoir,* 142–45; JPB, *Three Changes in Theological Institutions,* 15–19, 24–25, 46–48.

8. JPB, *Three Changes in Theological Institutions*, 29, 30.

9. JPB, *Three Changes in Theological Institutions*, 34, 35, 38; Miller, *The Utility and Importance of Creeds*, 11–13; Mohler, "'To Train the Minister Whom God Has Called'"; Clarke, *To Count Our Days*, 7.

10. JAB, "American Baptist Ministry in A.D. 1774," in *Sermons and Addresses*, 243; JAB, "Ministerial Education," in *Sermons and Addresses*, 202–203; Harvey, *Redeeming the South*, 137–44.

11. JAB, "The Theological Seminary," *Religious Herald* 26 (9 April 1857), 3; Barron, "The Contributions of John A. Broadus to Southern Baptists," 46–47.

12. JAB to MCB, 11 May 1858, BP.

13. JAB to Cornelia Taliaferro, 28 July 1857, in ATR, 145.

14. JAB, *Memoir*, 156–63; Wills, *Southern Baptist Theological Seminary*, 26–30; JAB to Cornelia Taliaferro, 28 July 1857, in ATR, 145.

15. JAB to Cornelia Taliaferro, 28 July 1857, in ATR, 145; MCB to JAB, 1 August 1857, BP; Birdwhistell, *Eliza Broadus Biography*, 3.

16. L. C. to JAB, 24 October 1857, BP; J. B. Jeter to JAB, 22 October 1857, BP; J. M. Broadus to JAB, 31 October 1857, BP.

17. JAB, *Memoir*, 152–53; JAB to JPB, 15 May 1858, Boyce Papers; BMJ to JAB, 14 May 1858, in ATR, 152.

18. ATR, 149; William P. Farish to JAB, 8 May 1858, BP.

19. JAB to JPB, 15 May 1858, Boyce Papers; BMJ to JAB, 18 May 1858, BP; E. T. Winkler to JAB, 26 May 1858, BP; Sarah Rudolph Manly to BMJ, 21 June 1858, MFP.

20. JAB to CES, 16 July 1858, 8 September 1858, 24 August 1859, in Reeder, *Broadus Unbound*, 81, 86, 71.

21. James M. Broadus to JAB, 31 October 1857, BP; Margarett S. Swann to JAB, 9 December 1857, BP; Somerville Ward Broadus to JAB, 7 June 1858, BP.

22. JAB to CES, 18 August 1858, in Reeder, *Broadus Unbound*, 78.

23. Reeder, *Broadus Unbound*, 107; ATR, 155–56.

24. JAB to JPB, 4 April 1859, in ATR, 157; JPB to JAB, 11 April 1859, in ATR, 157–58.

25. JAB to JPB, 21 April 1859, in ATR, 159; JPB to JAB, 26 April 1859, in ATR, 159–60.

26. JAB to JPB, 16 July 1859, in ATR, 165; "Southern Baptist Theological Seminary," *Western Recorder*, 18 July 1859, 1, quoted in Nettles, *James Petigru Boyce*, 159.

27. William F. Broaddus to JAB, 10 June 1859, BP; William F. Broaddus to JAB, 12 December 1859, BP; William F. Broaddus to JPB, 28 December 1860, Boyce Papers.

28. JAB to BMJ, 21 April 1859, quoted in "The Seminary's Troubles from Extreme Landmarkers," A. T. Robertson Papers; for Graves, see Patterson, *James Robinson Graves*.

29. J. R. Graves, "Convention Items—Odds and Ends," *Tennessee Baptist*, 6 June 1857, 2; Wills, *Southern Baptist Theological Seminary*, 50–52; Harvey, *Redeeming the South*, 88–89; JAB to JPB, 23 July 1859, Boyce Papers.

30. JAB to JPB, 20 June 1860, Boyce Papers; JAB, *Memoir*, 166–67; Huff, *Greenville*, 122–23.

31. JAB, *Memoir*, 153; JPB to JAB, 26 April 1859, in ATR, 160.

32. JAB to JPB, 16 July 1859, Boyce Papers; JAB, *Memoir*, 169–72; ATR, 173.

33. Ryland, "Recollections of the First Year," 9.

34. Sampey, *Memoirs*, 23; BMJ to Charles Manly, 11 October 1859, MFP; BMJ to Basil Manly Sr., 11 October 1859, MFC; BMJ to Basil Manly Sr., 29 December 1860, MFP.

35. Eager, "Rev. William Williams," 407, 414.

36. See Manley, "The Southern Baptist Mind in Transition," 165–66; BMJ to Basil and Sarah Manly, 5 April 1860, MFP; BMJ to Basil and Sarah Manly, 16 October 1860, MFP; BMJ to Basil and Sarah Manly, 5 April 1860, MFP.

37. Nettles, *James Petigru Boyce*, 102–106, 173; Wills et al., "Report on Slavery and Racism," 10.

38. See Wills et al., "Report on Slavery and Racism," 9; Clarke, *To Count Our Days*, 7.

39. JAB to Cornelia Taliaferro, 18 February 1860, BP.

40. JAB, *Memoir*, 172–73; JAB to Cornelia Taliaferro, 28 March 1860, in ATR, 172.

41. For the hymn, as well as the "missing" stanzas, see Haykin, "'Soldiers of Christ, in Truth Arrayed,'" 34–39.

42. JPB, *Three Changes in Theological Institutions*, 6; Hatch, *Democratization of American Christianity*, 16; Elder, *The Sacred Mirror*, 152.

43. JAB to James P. Boyce, 23 July 1860, in ATR, 174; JAB to CEB, 25 July 1860, in ATR, 175; JAB to JPB, 31 August 1860, Boyce Papers.

5. THE GREAT DISRUPTION

1. JAB to Cornelia Taliaferro, 25 October 1860, in ATR, 176; JAB to JPB, 31 August 1860, Boyce Papers; J. M. Broadus to JAB, 7 December 1860, BP.

2. JAB to JPB, 31 August 1860, BP; J. M. Broadus to JAB, 27 April 1861, BP; J. M. Broadus to JAB, 26 February 1861, BP; Bertram Wyatt-Brown, "Church, Honor, and Secession," in Miller, Stout, and Wilson, eds., *Religion and the American Civil War*, 89–91; J. B. Jeter to JAB, 11 December 1860, in ATR, 180. Rable further surveys the views of secession among American clergy in *God's Almost Chosen People*, 33–50.

3. JAB to Cornelia Taliaferro, 22 January 1861, BP. For Basil Manly Sr. and secession, see Fuller, *Chaplain to the Confederacy*, 287–308.

4. JAB, *Memoir*, 183–84. For Greenville's secession crisis, see Huff, *Greenville*, 130–34. Stephanie McCurry highlights the role of Baptist ministers in South Carolina secession in *Masters of Small Worlds*, 239–304.

5. JAB, *Memoir*, 185.

6. JAB to Cornelia Taliaferro, 22 January 1861, BP; JAB, *Memoir*, 186–87; J. M. Broadus to JAB, 27 April 1861, BP; JAB, *Memoir*, 186.

7. JAB, *Memoir*, 185.

8. Tichenor's "Fast-Day Sermon," cited in Rable, *God's Almost Chosen Peoples*, 282–83; JAB, in T. T. Eaton, Lecture Notebook, 30 March 1882, T. T. Eaton Papers, SBTS; Douglass quoted in Harvey, *Through the Storm, Through the Night*, 66.

9. Wills et al., "Report on Slavery and Racism," 17–18; Rable, *God's Almost Chosen Peoples*, 12–14.

10. Richard Hackley to JAB, 5 November 1860, in ATR, 177; James Madison Broadus to JAB, 21 October 1857, BP; James Madison Broadus to JAB, 11 November 1857, BP.

11. Noll, *The Civil War as a Theological Crisis*, 91–92.

12. JAB, *Memoir*, 179; Byrd, *A Holy Baptism*, 87–90. Stout traces the use of civil religion to justify unprecedented slaughter in *Upon the Altar of the Nation*.

13. JPB to JAB, 5 February 1862, BP; JPB to JAB, 23 December 1861, BP.

14. JPB to JAB, 16 May 1862, in ATR, 191.

15. JAB to JPB, 14 March 1862, in ATR, 191; JPB to G. W. Randolph (CSA secretary of war), 20 August 1862, in ATR, 194–95; JAB, *Memoir*, 180; William Williams to JAB, 15 August 1860, BP.

16. William Williams to JAB, n.d., BP; Wills et al., "Report on Slavery and Racism," 21–22; ATR, 189.

17. Southern Baptist Convention, *Proceedings of the Ninth Biennial Session . . .* , 18–19, 54. In one of the few times the two men publicly disagreed, Boyce opposed these resolutions on the grounds that churches and denominations should stay removed from political activity. JAB, *Memoir*, 178–79. The southern use of the jeremiad plays a prominent role in Stout's *Upon the Altar of the Nation*.

18. S. S. Kirby to JAB, 18 February 1862, BP; Rable explores the issue of camp vice in *God's Almost Chosen Peoples*, 90–106; JAB, "We Pray for You at Home," 4–5; ATR, 190–91.

19. Daniel W. Stowell, "Stonewall Jackson and the Providence of God," in Miller, Stout, and Wilson, eds., *Religion and the American Civil War*, 187–207; ATR, 197–98; for Jones, see Moore, *Apostle of the Lost Cause*.

20. JAB to CEB, 27 June 1863, BP. Ayers describes the scene in Staunton in *The Thin Light of Freedom*, 82–85.

21. JAB to CEB, 7 July 1863, BP; JAB to CEB, 8 July 1863, BP; JAB to A. E. Dickinson, 21 July 1863, in Jones, *Christ in the Camp*, 314.

22. JAB to CEB, 6 July 1863, BP; JAB to A. E. Dickinson, 21 July 1863, in Jones, *Christ in the Camp*, 315.

23. JAB to CEB, 12 September 1863, BP; Jones, *Christ in the Camp*, 329; Jones, "Dr. John A. Broadus as Evangelist in Lee's Army," 53–58. Moore explores interdenominational networking in the southern camps, as well as the limits of camp ecumenism, in *Apostle of the Lost Cause*, 33–68.

24. Quoted in Jones, *Christ in the Camp*, 248.

25. Jones, *Christ in the Camp*, 248; JAB, *Memoir*, 189.

26. McPherson, *For Cause and Comrades*, 62–76; see also Byrd, *A Holy Baptism*, 230; Rable, *God's Almost Chosen Peoples*, 204–221. Stout emphasizes the manipulative nature of the revivals and revival reports in the prosecution of an unjust war in *Upon the Altar of the Nation*, 286–94.

27. See Moore, *Apostle of the Lost Cause*, 33–37. Harry S. Stout and Christopher Grasso also explore the longterm impact of the revivals on southern memory in "Civil War, Religion, and Communications: The Case of Richmond," in Miller, Stout, and Wilson, eds., *Religion and the American Civil War*, 313–49.

28. CEB to JAB, 4 September 1863, BP; JAB to CEB, 6 July 1863, BP; JAB to CEB, 28 August 1863, BP.

29. JAB to JPB, 6 August 1863, Boyce Papers; JAB to CEB, 5 August 1863, BP.

30. CEB to JAB, 9 September 1863, BP; Eliza Broadus, "Recollections" (unpublished mss, December 1925), 21–22, quoted in Reeder, *Broadus Unbound*, 181; JAB to CEB, 17 August 1863, BP; Faust, *Mothers of Invention*.

31. JAB to CEB, September 1863, BP; JAB to CEB, 2 September 1863, BP; Reeder, *Broadus Unbound*, 179–81. Broadus may have been thinking of this episode in his comments in a later sermon: "Perhaps I may suggest about it, in passing, that when money is scarce and there are so many other things to be done with it, we may compensate for making the gifts less expensive than usual by taking more than ordinary pains in the way of adapting them to the particular persons. The loving care we

thus show may give more pleasure than would be given by greater financial cost." JAB, "Glad Giving," in Bogard, ed., *Pillars of Orthodoxy*, 318–19.

32. CEB to JAB, 4 September 1863, BP; CEB to JAB, 21 August 1863, BP.

33. JPB to JAB, 30 November 1864, BP; Albemarle County: Record of Slaves that have escaped to the enemy during the war [1861–1863].

34. Southern Baptist Convention, *Proceedings of the Ninth Biennial Session . . .*, 45–47; Baker, *The Story of the Sunday School Board*, 14–16; Burroughs, *Fifty Fruitful Years*, 21, 24; Rable, *God's Almost Chosen Peoples*, 245. For the Sunday school movement in its broader American context, see Boylan, *Sunday School*.

35. Southern Baptist Convention, *Proceedings of the Ninth Biennial Session*, 45–47; Baker, *The Story of the Sunday School Board*, 14–16; Burroughs, *Fifty Fruitful Years*, 21, 24.

36. ATR, 210.

37. Southern Baptist Convention, *Proceedings . . . held at Russellville, Kentucky*, 30–32; Boylan, *Sunday School*, 26–29; see especially McMillen, *To Raise Up the South;* Schweiger, *Gospel Working Up*, 72–74. Keith Harper uncovers various aspects of Southern Baptist social Christianity in *The Quality of Mercy.*

38. Southern Baptist Convention, *Proceedings of the Ninth Biennial Session . . .*, 45–47. For the influential role of nineteenth-century evangelical women in Sunday schools, see Boylan, *Sunday School*, 114–32.

39. Southern Baptist Convention, *Proceedings . . . held at Russellville, Kentucky*, 27–28; JAB to CEB, 17 April 1866, in ATR, 217.

40. Thomas E. Skinner to JAB, 11 July 1863, Basil Manly Papers; Manley, "The Southern Baptist Mind in Transition," 193.

41. Southern Baptist Convention, *Proceedings . . . held at Russellville, Kentucky*, 31. Paul Harvey explores the growth of this denominational sectionalism in *Redeeming the South*, 17–44.

42. Huff, *Greenville*, 138; JAB to CEB, 4 September 1863, BP; JAB to BMJ, 11 April 1865, BP.

43. Huff, *Greenville*, 144.

44. JAB, *Memoir*, 197.

6. SURVIVAL

1. Quoted in Sampey, *Southern Baptist Theological Seminary*, 14; JAB, *Memoir*, 198–206.

2. JAB, *Memoir*, 199–200.

3. Elder, *The Sacred Mirror*, 187–94; Whitehead, "Hold the Mirror Up," 19, in Slatton, *W. H. Whitsitt*, 47; Foster, *Ghosts of the Confederacy*, 24.

4. Jones, *Christ in the Camp*, 461–62; Boyce's speech is quoted in Andrews, *The South Since the War*, 72; Edgar, *South Carolina*, 383–84; ATR, 302.

5. Zuczek, *State of Rebellion*, 37; Edgar, *South Carolina*, 385; *Proceedings of the Colored People's Convention*, 23.

6. Edgar, *South Carolina*, 386–87; Zuczek, *State of Rebellion*, 47–51; Foner, *Reconstruction*, 281–82; Herbert Aptheker, "South Carolina Negro Conventions, 1865," *Journal of Negro History* 31, no. 1 (January 1946): 93–94, cited in Holt, *Black Over White*, 21–22; Harvey, *Freedom's Coming*.

7. CEB to JAB, 29 March 1866, BP; for the altered household status of southern women, see Fos-

ter, *Ghosts of the Confederacy,* 31–38, and Roark, *Masters Without Slaves,* 149–50; C. H. Toy to JAB, 2 December 1868, BP; ATR, 215–16.

8. JAB to JPB, 22 September 1874, Boyce Papers; Huff, *Greenville,* 424; Edgar, *South Carolina,* 394–95.

9. Blight, *Race and Reunion,* 108–122; Basil Manly Jr. to unspecified recipient, n.d. [circa 18 July 1866], Manly Family Collection, Southern Baptist Historical Library and Archives; JPB to JAB, 24 September 1870, BP; for Scott's militia, see Zuczek, *State of Rebellion,* 72–89.

10. Winkler, *Christian Watchman and Reflector,* 4 January 1872, quoted in Harvey, *Freedom's Coming,* 39; ATR, 221–22.

11. JAB to CEB, 27 January 1866, BP; JAB to CEB, 17 April 1866, BP; JAB, *Memoir,* 212; Wills, *Southern Baptist Theological Seminary,* 69.

12. JAB to CEB, 27 January 1866, BP; JAB, *Memoir,* 207; JAB to H. P. Griffith, 5 October 1866, in ATR, 220–21.

13. J. M. Broadus to JAB, 1 November 1866, BP; JAB to B. A. Woodruff, 18 May 1868, in ATR, 228.

14. See Wilson, *Baptized in Blood,* 79–99; BMJ to JAB, 17 July 1868, BP; Manly quotes Williams in BMJ to JAB, 30 June 1868, BP.

15. JPB to JAB, 4 April 1877; JAB to JPB, 8 July 1870, Boyce Papers.

16. JAB to JPB, 30 April 1870, Boyce Papers; W. A. Gellatly to JAB, 30 May 1870, in ATR, 235; JAB to JPB, 16 February 1875, Boyce Papers; JAB to JPB, 24 February 1876, Boyce Papers.

17. JAB to JPB, 8 August 1867, Boyce Papers; JAB to JPB, 26 May 1874, Boyce Papers; JPB to JAB, 6 August 1875, Boyce Papers; G. S. Bailey to JAB, 23 November 1872, BP; JPB to JAB, 10 December 1872, BP; JAB to JPB, December 1874, Boyce Papers.

18. Baker, *Relations Between Northern and Southern Baptists,* 105–106, 170–71; Southern Baptist Convention, *Proceedings of the Southern Baptist Convention . . . 1867,* 79; Nathan Bishop to JAB, 28 May 1868, in ATR, 230; JAB, *Religious Herald,* 19 October 1865, in Harvey, *Redeeming the South,* 23; Harvey, "'Yankee Faith' and Southern Redemption," in Miller, Stout, and Wilson, eds., *Religion and the American Civil War,* 176.

19. JAB, "Speech of Dr. Broadus in New York," *South Carolina Baptist,* 26 June 1868, 2; Basil Manly Jr. to Basil and Sarah Manly, 21 July 1865, Manly Collection of Manuscripts, Southern Baptist Theological Seminary; Williamson, *The Crucible of Race,* 4–7.

20. Harvey, *Redeeming the South,* 39; Southern Baptist Convention, *Proceedings . . . held at Russellville, Kentucky,* 30–32; Boylan, *Sunday School,* 26–29; Elder, *The Sacred Mirror,* 1–11.

21. JAB to CEB, 19 February 1866, BP; JAB, "Ministerial Education," *Sermons and Addresses,* 204.

22. Eliza Broadus, "Early Days of the Southern Baptist Theological Seminary," in Reeder, *Broadus Unbound,* 151; JAB to CEB, 24 April 1866, in ATR, 217; ATR, 229.

23. ATR, 223, 215.

24. JAB, *Memoir,* 213, 245; ATR, 228–29; JAB to a College Student, 7 July 1889, in ATR, 382.

25. JAB to JPB, 23 May 1870, 16 May 1870, Boyce Papers.

26. JAB to JPB, 30 April 1870, 23 May 1870, Boyce Papers; Robert E. Lee to JAB, 21 June 1870, in ATR, 238. For antebellum southerners' experiences on the Grand Tour, see O'Brien, *Conjectures of Order,* 1:100–157.

27. ATR, 239.

28. JAB to Eliza Broadus, 8 October 1870, in ATR, 247; ATR, 243–50, 356.

29. ATR, 243, 249–50.

30. ATR, 262, 272–73; JPB to JAB, 10 March 1871, 21 May 1871, in ATR, 263–64, 277.

31. JAB to JPB, 21 May 1871, 28 January 1871, Boyce Papers; JAB to William Williams, 6 June 1871, in ATR, 277.

32. ATR, 243, 256.

33. JAB to CEB, 9 May 1872, in ATR, 284; Bailey, "Southern Baptist President"; JAB to JPB, 21 July 1871, Boyce Papers.

34. JAB to JPB, 23 April 1868, Boyce Papers; JPB to JAB, 18 November 1872; "Alabama State Convention," *Christian Index,* 14 November 1872; JPB to JAB, 23 August 1875, BP; JPB to JAB, 17 April 1873, BP; Wills, *Southern Baptist Theological Seminary,* 79–81. Boyce called Winkler's remarks "ruinous to me."

35. JPB to JAB, 2 October 1873, BP; JAB, *Memoir,* 238–39; JPB to JAB, 18 November 1872, BP; JPB to JAB, 6 March 1873, BP; JAB to JPB, 14 March 1874, Boyce Papers; JPB to JAB, 30 November 1874, BP; JAB to JPB, 3 December 1874, Boyce Papers; JAB, *Memoir,* 221; JPB to JAB, 9 March 1875, BP; JAB to JPB, 19 March 1874, Boyce Papers.

36. JAB to JPB, 30 April 1871, Boyce Papers; JPB to JAB, 14 April 1874, BP; JAB, *Memoir,* 240–41; JAB to CEB, 23 May 1874, in ATR, 296; JAB to CEB, 1 June 1874, in ATR, 296; JAB to Caroline Broadus, 4 August 1874, in ATR, 297; JAB to JPB, 26 June 1876, Boyce Papers.

37. JAB to JPB, 14 March 1873, in ATR, 289; ATR, 297.

38. CEB to JAB, 18 June 1871; BP; JAB to CEB, 15 June 1874, BP; WHW to Florence Wallace, 19 November 1873, in Slatton, *W. H. Whitsitt,* 45; CEB to JAB, 6 February 1866, BP; CEB to JAB, 8 June 1874, BP.

39. CEB to JAB, 13 August 1880, BP; CEB to JAB, 18 June 1871, BP; Eliza Broadus to JAB, 10 September 1873, BP; CEB to JAB, 19 September 1873, BP; JAB to CEB, 12 May 1873, in ATR, 291–92.

40. JAB to JPB, 6 April 1874, Boyce Papers; JAB to JPB, 16 February 1875, Boyce Papers; JAB to CEB, 15 June 1874, BP; JAB to JPB, 19 March 1874, Boyce Papers; JAB to JPB, 26 June 1876, Boyce Papers; JAB to JPB, 30 March 1877, Boyce Papers; ATR, 310; JAB to CEB, 23 May 1874, in ATR, 296; JAB to CEB, 23 May 1872, in ATR, 284.

41. JAB to Martha Bickers, 10 April 1873, in ATR, 290.

42. ATR, 328; Birdwhistell, *Eliza Broadus Biography,* 5.

43. ATR, 327; Eliza Broadus to JAB, 18 September 1873, BP; Birdwhistell, *Eliza Broadus Biography,* 5–6.

44. Poole, *Never Surrender,* 116 35; Dill, *Lest We Forget,* 36.

45. Dill, *Lest We Forget,* 36; ATR, 302; freedman's quote from Tisby, *The Color of Compromise,* 97–98; Du Bois, *Black Reconstruction in America,* 30.

7. THE LOSS OF A JEWEL

1. JAB to Alvah Hovey, 27 October 1876, Alvah Hovey Papers, Andover Newton Theological School Collection at Yale Divinity School.

2. WHW, "John Albert Broadus," 348; JAB to Alvah Hovey, 8 August 1879, Alvah Hovey Papers, Andover Newton Theological School Collection at Yale Divinity School.

3. CHT, "Sketch of My Religious Life," May 24, 1860; JAB to Cornelia Taliaferro, 28 March 1860, in ATR, 173. For a recent treatment of Toy, see Parsons, *Crawford Howell Toy.* Parsons engages with the less sympathetic picture of Toy found in Wills, *Southern Baptist Theological Seminary,* 108–49.

4. Hurt, "Crawford Howell Toy," 34–36; JAB, *Religious Herald,* 27 September 1866, in Parsons, *Crawford Howell Toy,* 47.

5. Wacker, "Demise of Biblical Civilization," in Noll and Hatch, eds., *The Bible in America,* 124–26; Noll, *America's Book,* 529–31; Oshatz, *Slavery and Sin,* 4.

6. A summary of the emergence of higher criticism in America can be found in Holifield, *Theology in America,* 191–96, and Noll discusses how mid-century slavery debates pushed many northern abolitionists toward theological liberalism in *America's God,* 413–21. The definitive study of the emergence of American liberal theology is Dorrien, *The Making of American Liberal Theology.*

7. See especially Maring, "Baptists and Changing Views of the Bible, 1865–1918 (Part I)," 30–61. For more on the shifting ground of northern Baptist theology in this era, see Wacker, *Augustus H. Strong,* and Shrader, *Thoughtful Christianity.*

8. R. H. Bagby in *Religious Herald,* 8 November 1861, 1.

9. JAB, *Lectures on the History of Preaching,* 231–32; JAB to Cornelia Taliaferro, 8 July 1857, in ATR, 145; JAB to CEB, 2 March 1866, in ATR, 217; JAB to CEB, 8 October 1870, in ATR, 246; JPB to JAB, 17 April 1876, BP; Whitehead, "Hold the Mirror Up," xxv–xxvi, quoted in Slatton, *W. H. Whitsitt,* 27; E. S. Joynes to JAB, 6 March 1859, in ATR, 156–57

10. CHT, "The Tubingen School," 210–35; CHT, *The Claims of Biblical Interpretation on Baptists,* 44; "Professor Toy's Inaugural," *Religious Herald,* 13 March 1870, in Hurt, "Crawford Howell Toy," 15; *Proceedings of the Board of Trustees,* book 1, 95–97, cited in Mueller, *A History of Southern Baptist Theological Seminary,* 135; WHW, diary, 30 November 1886, 5:105, quoted in Slatton, *W. H. Whitsitt,* 74.

11. JAB, *Memoir,* 262. Toy would tell the seminary Board that "my divergence from the prevailing view in the Denomination . . . has gradually increased in connection with my studies from year to year till it has become perceptible to myself and to others." CHT, Resignation Letter, SBTS, 1; Moore, "An Appreciation of Professor Toy," 3; CHT, *The Claims of Biblical Interpretation,* 42; Duncan, "Crawford Howell Toy (1836–1919)," in George H. Shriver, ed., *Dictionary of Heresy Trial in American Christianity,* 431; Wills, *Southern Baptist Theological Seminary,* 112–15; Hurt, "Crawford Howell Toy," 125–26.

12. Jeffers, "Reminiscences of My Seminary Life," 196–97; Lyon, "Crawford Howell Toy," 6; Brown, "Letter to the Seminary Magazine," 88.

13. JAB, *Memoir,* 260–61; Moore, "An Appreciation of Professor Toy," 12.

14. Lyon, "Crawford Howell Toy," 7; for student notes on Toy's lectures, see Bush and Nettles, *Baptists and the Bible,* 209–212; Holt, *Pioneering in the Southwest,* 90.

15. WHW, diary, 30 November 1886, 5:111, in Slatton, *W. H. Whitsitt,* 76.

16. Erdmann, *The Books of Samuel,* 136–37; WHW, diary, 30 November 1886, 5:106, 5:110, cited in Parsons, *Crawford Howell Toy,* 59–60; Longenecker, *Pulpits of the Lost Cause,* 168–69.

17. WHW, diary, 30 November 1886, 5:106–107, in Slatton, *W. H. Whitsitt,* 76; Parsons, *Crawford Howell Toy,* 75.

18. WHW, "John Albert Broadus," 345; Nettles, *James Petigru Boyce,* 321; David S. Dockery, "Mighty in the Scriptures: John A. Broadus and His Influence on A. T. Robertson and Southern Baptist Life," in Dockery and Duke, eds., *John A. Broadus,* 37–38; JAB, *Memoir,* 261–62.

19. JAB, "Rev. A. Jaeger," 5.

20. JPB to JAB, 24 January 1876, BP; JPB to JAB, 6 December 1876, BP.

21. JPB to JAB, 20 June 1876, in ATR, 301; Dill, *Lest We Forget,* 45; JPB to JAB, 15 June 1877, BP; Nettles, *James Petigru Boyce,* 331.

22. JPB to JAB, 22 June 1877, BP.

23. Lyon, "Crawford Howell Toy," 7; Slatton, *W. H. Whitsitt,* 77; Parsons, *Crawford Howell Toy,* 69–70; William H. Whitsitt to Florence Wallace, 25 January 1878, in Slatton, *W. H. Whitsitt,* 76–77.

24. JAB, *Memoir,* 262.

25. Nettles, *James Petigru Boyce,* 329; W. B. Carson to JPB, 11 June 1878, Boyce Papers; W. B. Carson to JAB, 2 April 1878, BP; Wills, *Southern Baptist Theological Seminary,* 126; W. B. Carson, "The Inspiration of the Scriptures," *Religious Herald,* 15 August 1878, 1; E. T. R. [pseud.], "E. T. R. Again! False Teaching—&c.," *Religious Herald,* 12 December 1878. For the identity of E. T. R., see Winters, "T. T. Eaton," 53–58.

26. JAB to JPB, 12 December 1878, Boyce Papers.

27. JAB to JPB, 12 December 1878, Boyce Papers.

28. Wills, *Southern Baptist Theological Seminary,* 130–31. These Job articles suggest that Toy understood the position of Boyce and Broadus before the trustee meeting, rather than being blindsided by a duplicitous plot, as Whitsitt would have it. F. H. Kerfoot to JAB, 16 March 1879, BP.

29. CHT, "Critical Notes," *Sunday School Times,* 12 April 1879, 231; CHT, "Critical Notes," *Sunday School Times,* 19 April 1879, 246–48; Hurt, "Crawford Howell Toy," 128–43; "Dr. C.H. Toy's Rationalism," *Biblical Recorder,* 7 May 1879, 2; Lyon, "Crawford Howell Toy," 9n7; Moore, "An Appreciation of Professor Toy," 4; Parsons, *Crawford Howell Toy,* 71–77. Hurt questions the relevance of the Isaiah controversy to Toy's dismissal, noting that the *Biblical Recorder* article came out the day of the trustee meeting, too late to influence the Board.

30. JAB, "How to Teach the Lesson," 70; see Parsons, *Crawford Howell Toy,* 74–78.

31. *Biblical Recorder,* 28 May 1879, 2; *Journal and Messenger,* 17 May 1879, 4; A. S. Worrell, "Dr.s Toy and Broadus on Isaiah 53," *Baptist Battle Flag,* 14 May 1879, 156, cited by Hurt, "Crawford Howell Toy," 191–93; WHW, diary, 30 November 1886, 5:106–107, in Slatton, *W. H. Whitsitt,* 83; Parsons, *Crawford Howell Toy,* 75; Hurt, "Crawford Howell Toy," 193–94.

32. CHT, "Letter of Resignation," 2, 4, 8.

33. Furman, "Report of Dr. Toy's Committee of Resignation"; Mueller, *A History of Southern Baptist Theological Seminary,* 139; the two dissenting votes were John A. Chambliss (Toy's classmate at Southern) and D. W. Gwin (married to Toy's cousin); virtually every trustee had a personal tie to Toy; J. A. Chambliss, "The Trustees of the Seminary and Dr. Toy's Resignation," *Baptist Courier,* 12 June 1879, 2; WHW, diary, 30 November 1886, 5:113–14, in Slatton, *W. H. Whitsitt,* 83.

34. JAB to CEB, 10 May 1879, BP, in ATR, 313; JAB, *Memoir,* 264. Joshua Levering, seminary benefactor and longtime trustee, corroborates that Toy's departure was "a great blow, particularly to Boyce and Broadus," who, "with entreaties, tears, and prayers," endeavored to restore Toy to orthodoxy. Levering, "A Backward Glance," 138; Clayton, "Crawford Howell Toy of Virginia," 50.

35. WHW, diary, 30 November 1886, 5:106, 113–14, in Slatton, *W. H. Whitsitt,* 83; Parsons, *Crawford Howell Toy,* 57.

36. JAB, *Memoir,* 261–62; Parsons, *Crawford Howell Toy,* 86–87.

37. Lyon, "Crawford Howell Toy," 9. George Moore challenges Broadus's account of Toy's theological formation, but never questions his integrity in Toy's dismissal. Hurt also writes, "The evidence seems to support the view that Broadus was not actively engaged in securing Toy's resignation from the seminary. His efforts were certainly not such as to cause a breach in the relationship which existed between the two men." Hurt, "Crawford Howell Toy," 193–94.

38. For example: "I half suspect that Broadus had permitted himself to make some sort of representations to that effect which Toy leaned on too heavily," WHW, diary, 30 November 1886, 5:113, in Slatton, *W. H. Whitsitt,* 82; Slatton, *W. H. Whitsitt,* 85–86.

39. CHT to JAB, 22 May 1879, BP; D. G. Gilman to JAB, 24 June 1879, BP; Hurt, "Crawford Howell Toy," 189; CHT to JAB, 31 October 1879, BP; JAB, *Memoir,* 264; Lyon, "Crawford Howell Toy," 11; Boyce would advise Broadus to decline; see JPB to JAB, 14 August 1886, BP.

40. CHT to JAB, 20 May 1893, BP; JAB, *Memoir,* 263. In his impressive revisionist account of the Toy affair, Parsons weights Whitsitt's caustic private interpretation more heavily than the open statements of Toy and Broadus. See Parsons, *Crawford Howell Toy,* 283–84.

41. WHW to Florence Wallace, 3 September 1873, in Slatton, *W. H. Whitsitt,* 46; Parsons, *Crawford Howell Toy,* 82–83.

42. J. B. Jeter, "The Southern Baptist Convention," *Religious Herald,* May 22, 1879, 2. Clayton judges this "practical consideration" to have been decisive in Toy's dismissal in "Crawford Howell Toy of Virginia," 55, as does Parsons in *Crawford Howell Toy,* 86–87. Both point to Joseph E. Brown's major endowment gift of $50,000 to the seminary in the following year as proof of the·primacy of financial considerations.

43. J. A. Chambliss, "The Trustees of the Seminary and Dr. Toy's Resignation," *Baptist Courier,* 12 June 1879, 2; George B. Eager to JAB, 31 December 1883, BP; J. B. Jeter, "News and Notes," *Religious Herald,* 13 November 1879, 2.

44. Flynt, *Alabama Baptists,* 163–68; J. R. Graves, "The Convention: The Seminary," *The Baptist,* May 1879, 229; E. T. Winkler, "Dr. Toy on Inspiration," *Baptist Courier,* 26 February 1880, 1; Wills, *Southern Baptist Theological Seminary,* 138. Toy defenders included John A. Chambliss, J. C. Hiden, William Lindsay, and John Stout. Recounting his journey with science in the Bible, Toy declared, "The true divinity of the Scripture does not depend on its scientific accuracy." CHT, "Genesis and Geology," *Religious Herald,* 6 May 1880, 1; Parsons, *Crawford Howell Toy,* 108. For the debate as to whether or not Toy remained a Baptist or became a Unitarian upon moving to Cambridge, see the discussion in Parsons, *Crawford Howell Toy,* 182–92.

45. JAB to H. H. Harris, 15 October 1881, cited in Barron, "The Contributions of John A. Broadus to Southern Baptists," 101.

46. J. E. Farnum to JAB, 3 July 1879, BP; S. G. Thompson to JAB, 3 July 1879, BP; Barron, "The Contributions of John A. Broadus to Southern Baptists," 76; J. R. Graves, "The Southern Baptist Convention," *Baptist* (Memphis, Tenn.), May 22, 1880, 773; JPB to JAB, 26 May 1880, BP; S. F. Thompson to JAB, 3 July 1879, BP; Charles to BMJ, 18 February 1881, MFC; Charles Manly to BMJ, 11 May 1881, MFC; in Manley, "The Southern Baptist Mind in Transition," 261–62.

47. "Broadus was almost captured by the influence of Toy," Whitsitt writes, citing his interpretation of Isaiah 53. "I was astonished that he should go so far, and it was a sore point with him to meet the questions of brethren when the cataclysm appeared on the first of May in Atlanta. Now he has forgotten all that and is quite as solicitous about his orthodoxy as Jerome was after the conflict with Rufinus." WHW, diary, 24 January 1893, 15:84, in Parsons, *Crawford Howell Toy,* 75.

48. C. C. Brown, "Dr. Hiden and Senex," *Working Christian,* 26 July 1877, 1; JAB, *Lectures on the History of Preaching,* 233. See Wacker's careful treatment throughout *Augustus H. Strong.*

49. Carver, "Recollections," 26.

8. SOUTHERN INTERPRETER

1. R. L. Dabney to JAB, 4 April 1868, BP.

2. R. L. Dabney to JAB, 19 February 1888, BP; Charles Reagan Wilson explored the sustained critique of the New South offered by many southern clergy in *Baptized in Blood*, 79–99; on Dabney, see "The New South," in *Discussions by R. L. Dabney, D. D.*, 4:1–24; and Lucas, *Robert Lewis Dabney*, 165–245.

3. JAB to Boyce Broadus, 9 August 1889, BP. For the southern concern regarding textbooks, see Wilson, *Baptized in Blood*, 141–42; Moore, *Apostle of the Lost Cause*, 168–71; JAB to Eleanor Broadus, 12 May 1888, in ATR, 364; JAB to CEB, 8 May 1890, in ATR, 388; Whitsitt quote in ATR, 434; for the romanticizing of the Old South by New South boosters like Harris, see Gaston, *The New South Creed*, 175–76; Woodward, *The Origins of the New South*, 158; Ayers, *The Promise of the New South*, 340–43.

4. Goldfield, *Still Fighting the Civil War*, 181; L. M. Jones to JAB, 3 November 1887, BP; Margolies, *Henry Watterson and the New South*, 17–62.

5. Cobb, *Away Down South*, 72; Gaston, *The New South Creed*, 27.

6. JAB, *Memoir*, 413; CEB to JAB, 10 December 1878, BP; JAB to JPB, 12 December 1878, Boyce Papers.

7. JAB, *Memoir*, 271–73; JPB, "The Danger to the Seminary," *The Baptist*, 6 December 1879, 409. Many identify Brown's large gift as further proof of the political pragmatism behind Crawford Toy's dismissal the previous spring: see Clayton, "Crawford Howell Toy," 54; Parsons, *Crawford Howell Toy*, 86–87.

8. "Regenerating the South," *New York Tribune*, 25 October 1880, 2, quoted in Woodward, *The Origins of the New South*, 17; Wright and Wheeler, "New Men in the Old South," 363–87; Lichtenstein, *Twice the Work of Free Labor*, 142.

9. Wills et al., "Report on Slavery and Racism," 33–38. The seminary's association with Brown became a public embarrassment in 2020. Trustees moved to vacate the Brown chair, then held by longtime president R. Albert Mohler Jr., and created a new endowed chair, "The Centennial Professor of Systematic Theology." See Baptist Press Staff, "Trustees: SBTS Retains Names, Vacates Chair, Establishes Endowment," *Baptist Press*, October 13, 2020. As recently as 2005, Mohler's election to the Brown chair had been considered a high honor; see Jeff Robinson, "Southern Trustees Elect Mohler to Storied Chair of Theology," *Baptist Press*, April 27, 2005.

10. JAB, *Memoir*, 273. For the Nortons, see Baptist Sunday School Board, *Encyclopedia of Southern Baptists*, 2:1023–24. Eckstein Norton became president of the Louisville and Nashville Railroad in 1887; for its importance in the New South economy, see Woodward, *The Origins of the New South*, 6–11.

11. JAB to CEB, 14 February 1881, in ATR, 318; JAB to JDR, 22 February 1881, BP; JPB to M. T. Yates, 13 July 1881, Letterpress Copy Book 7, June–November 1881, 434, in Wills, *Southern Baptist Theological Seminary*, 160.

12. Woodward, *The Origins of the New South*, 171–74. Wilson argues in *Baptized in Blood* (81–82) that southern clergy were more conflicted over these issues, but Broadus does not fit this mold. For Dabney's critique of capitalism, see Lucas, *Robert Lewis Dabney*, 187–90.

13. Annie Broadus to Mary Adams, 30 March 1890, in ATR, 386. After George W. Norton's death in 1889, his son, George W. Norton II, succeeded him as both chairman of the seminary's financial board and as second treasurer of the Southern Baptist Convention. George II would endow the Norton lectureship at the seminary, which focused on science and theology, and he and his sisters

would give another $150,000 to the school. George Norton II died in 1924 at the age of fifty-eight, at which time the college-aged George III assumed his father's role on the seminary's financial board and as the SBC's third financial secretary. When Margaret M. Norton died in 1950, she left her house and estate to the seminary, in memory of her husband, George W. Norton II, tallying the Norton family gifts to the seminary at over $1 million. Baptist Sunday School Board, *Encyclopedia of Southern Baptists,* 2:1023–24.

14. JAB to SSB, 16 March 1886, BP; ATR, 348; JAB, *Jesus of Nazareth,* 52–64; Mueller, *A History of Southern Baptist Theological Seminary,* 49; Wills, *Southern Baptist Theological Seminary,* 186. The standard biography of Rockefeller is Chernow, *Titan: The Life of John D. Rockefeller, Sr.* More recently, Daren Dochuk has explored Rockefeller's evangelical faith in *Anointed with Oil.*

15. JDR to JAB, 30 March 1880, BP; JDR to JAB, 11 February 1882, BP; JDR to JAB, 24 October 1888, BP; JAB to SSB, 16 March 1886, BP; ATR, 348; JDR to JAB, 9 November 1882, BP; ATR, 323; JDR to JAB, 3 April 1882, BP; JDR to JAB, 10 October 1887, BP; JDR to JAB, 18 June 1883, BP; JAB to JDR, 10 September 1888, John D. Rockefeller, Sr. Papers, Rockefeller Archive Center; Mrs. John D. Rockefeller to JAB, 4 May 1883, BP; JDR to JAB, 24 April 1888, BP; Samuel S. Broadus to JDR, 11 March 1886, John D. Rockefeller, Sr. Papers, Rockefeller Archive Center. For Rockefeller's relationships with ministers, see Chernow, *Titan,* 121. It was Broadus who, in 1889, introduced Rockefeller to northern Baptist minister Frederick T. Gates, who went on to head up Rockefeller's philanthropic activities for decades. Frederick T. Gates to JAB, 24 January 1889, BP.

16. JAB to JDR, 9 June 1883, John D. Rockefeller, Sr. Papers, Rockefeller Archive Center. Samuel had long acted as Broadus's secretary in receiving gifts for the school. Barron, "The Contributions of John A. Broadus to Southern Baptists," 72–73; Samuel S. Broadus to JAB, 9 December 1879, BP.

17. For this post–Civil War generation of southern businessmen, see Doyle, *New Men, New Cities, New South,* 87–110.

18. ATR, 361–62.

19. Frank DuPont to JAB, 5 April 1889, BP; *Brooklyn Magazine* to JAB, 18 March 1885, BP.

20. John R. Mott to JAB, 5 February 1891, BP; J. R. Mott to JAB, 18 January 1893, in ATR, 405; Reuben A. Torrey to JAB, 5 July 1892, BP; ATR, 365; Wills, *Southern Baptist Theological Seminary,* 180; B. F. Jacob to JAB, 18 April 1884, BP; Sampey, "John A. Broadus," 10.

21. For Chautauqua, see Rieser, *The Chautauqua Moment;* Scott, "The Chautauqua Vision of Liberal Education," 41–59; and McGerr, *A Fierce Discontent,* 5–73.

22. JAB to Eliza Broadus, 22 July 1889, BP; ATR, 382; Ashby, "John Albert Broadus," 191–93; WRH to JAB, 31 March 1888, BP; WRH to JAB, 23 February 1889, BP.

23. J. M. Pendleton to JAB, 31 August 1882, BP; ATR, 347; Armitage, *A History of the Baptists,* 869.

24. JAB, "The Confederate Dead," in *Sermons and Addresses,* 371; JAB, "As to the Colored People," *Standard* (Chicago), 1 February 1883, 1; for the ritual of Confederate Memorial Days, see Wilson, *Baptized in Blood,* 18–33; Longenecker, *Pulpits of the Lost Cause,* 4, 163; Blight, *Race and Reunion,* 4, 344.

25. JAB, "Paramount and Permanent Authority of the Bible"; Lucas, *Robert Lewis Dabney,* 31; Dabney, *A Defence of Virginia;* see Foster, *The Limits of the Lost Cause.*

26. *Religious Herald,* 30 May 30, 1889, cited in ATR, 380–81; ATR, 378.

27. ATR, 381; W. E. Gellatly to JAB, 6 January 1877, in ATR, 303–304; ATR, 304–305; Wacker, *America's Pastor,* 111.

28. JAB, "Some Earnest Words as to Lynching," 1; JAB, "Public Opinion," *Baptist Home Mission Monthly,* April 1883, 82–84, quoted in Harvey, *Redeeming the South,* 40.

29. Woodward, *The Strange Career of Jim Crow,* 48–52, 65; Robertson, *The New Citizenship,* 87–98; ATR, 302; JAB, "Miscellanea," *Religious Herald,* 23 November 1876, 2.

30. *Religious Herald,* May 10, 1866, 1, quoted in Spain, *At Ease in Zion,* 85, 86, 90; JAB, "As to the Colored People," *Baptist Courier,* 15 February 1883, 1; R. N. Counter to JAB, 19 April 1880, BP; Consolidated American Baptist Missionary Convention Report 1877, 28–33.

31. Leonard W. Bacon to JAB, 10 February 1882, BP. Bacon was John F. Slater's Congregationalist minister. For the Slater Fund, see Fischer, *The John F. Slater Fund.*

32. Fischer, *The Slater Fund,* xviii–xix; JAB, *Sermons and Addresses,* iv.

33. Dabney, "The Negro and the Common School," in *Discussions by R. L. Dabney, D. D.,* 4:185; Report of the Commissioner of Education, vol. 1. (Washington, D.C. 1904), 368; Weissman, "The Role of White Supremacy Amongst Opponents and Proponents of Mass Schooling in the South During the Common School Era," 703–23; Curry quoted in Bond, *Negro Education in Alabama,* 203; Flynt, *Alabama Baptists,* 187

34. Woodward, *The Strange Career of Jim Crow;* see JAB in the *Louisville Courier-Journal,* 27 September 1886; JAB, "Some Earnest Words as to Lynching," 8. Ayers treats the rise of lynching in *The Promise of the New South,* 153–59. Bertram Wyatt-Brown discusses lynching as an effort to maintain southern honor in the disgrace of defeat in *The Shaping of Southern Honor,* 283–89.

35. JAB, "Some Earnest Words as to Lynching," 8.

36. JAB, "As to the Colored People," *Standard* (Chicago), 1 February 1883, 1; JAB, "The Negro," *Johnson's Cyclopedia,* cited in ATR, 404; J. B. M. Lauchlin to JAB, 5 April 1889, BP. A University of South Carolina student requested Broadus's thoughts on "the education of the negro" as he prepared for a debate on the topic. For the emergence of "scientific" racial theory in the antebellum South, see O'Brien, *Conjectures of Order,* 1:215–52; Noll discusses southern evangelicals' unexamined racial assumptions in *The Civil War as a Theological Crisis,* 52–74. Henry Louis Gates Jr. discusses how grounding racial differences in biology helped justify white supremacy in *Stony the Road,* 56–91.

37. Southern Baptist Convention, *Proceedings of the Southern Baptist Convention . . . 1886* (Richmond, Va.: Dispatch Steam Presses, 1886), 33. When Boyce presided over the 1888 Southern Baptist Convention, he controversially ruled a temperance resolution out of order, to preserve the spirituality of the church. See Wills, *Southern Baptist Theological Seminary,* 176–79. For Southern Baptists and temperance, see Payne, *Gin, Jesus, and Jim Crow;* Coker, *Liquor in the Land of the Lost Cause;* Harvey, *Redeeming the South,* 211–17; Holcomb, *Home Without Walls,* 1–7; Spain, *At Ease in Zion,* 174–97. Several scholars have demonstrated that white southern temperance advocates gained traction in the 1890s by connecting drunkenness with violent Black crime. White southern drys galvanized the South to pass prohibition laws and to eliminate the Black vote, thus launching the Jim Crow era.

38. Dixon quoted in Coker, *Liquor in the Land of the Lost Cause,* 52; JAB to B. W. N. Simms, 28 November 1894, in ATR, 426–27; JAB, *Religious Herald,* 8 April 1875, 1.

39. JAB, "Memorial of Gessner Harrison," in *Sermons and Addresses,* 343; JAB, "Some Laws of Spiritual Work," in *Sermons and Addresses,* 36–37. For the antebellum concept of the "true woman," see Welter, "The Cult of True Womanhood: 1820–1860," 155–74.

40. K. E. Hewitt to JAB, 23 September 1889, BP; T. D. Ware to JAB, 29 January 1890, BP; H. C. Woods to JAB, 20 September 1888, BP; Henry King to JAB, 16 October 1890, BP. The *Chicago Statesman* also requested Broadus to address the relations of women to the state and to the church. *Chicago Statesman* to JAB, 10 April 1889, BP.

41. JAB, "Should Women Speak in Mixed Public Assemblies?" n.p.

42. Ella B. Robertson, "Seeketh Not Her Own," *Baptist Courier,* 10 December 1936; Scales, *All that Fits a Woman,* 70.

43. Birdwhistell, *Eliza Broadus Biography,* 9.

44. Nettles, *The Baptists,* 2:364–65; Sullivan, *Lottie Moon,* 25–26; Harvey, *Redeeming the South,* 212–14; Robert, *American Women in Mission,* 184.

45. Holcomb, *Home Without Walls,* 7; Harvey, *Redeeming the South,* 125–28; Schweiger, *Gospel Working Up,* 157–63. For the WMU and the rise of Southern Baptist women in this era, see Scales, *All That Fits a Woman,* 58–72; and Flynt, *Southern Religion and Christian Diversity in the Twentieth Century,* 179–96.

46. Birdwhistell, *Eliza Broadus Biography,* 9–11.

47. Annie Armstrong to R. J. Willingham, 25 May 1895, in Harper, ed., *Rescue the Perishing,* 91–92. Robertson, for example, celebrates the rise of the "New Woman" and argues for female suffrage and wider employment in *The New Citizenship,* 66–76.

48. Mary Young Allison to JAB, 13 November 1894, BP; Lucas, *Robert Lewis Dabney,* 193; ATR, 431, 434.

49. Roark, *Masters Without Slaves,* 207, drawing from the work of Robert Jay Lifton; Sampey, "John A. Broadus," 10.

9. SCHOLARLY CONSERVATIVE

1. George B. Eager to JAB, 31 December 1883, BP.

2. Worthen, *Apostles of Reason,* 49.

3. Briggs, *General Introduction to the Study of Holy Scripture,* 286; WHW, diary, 5:107, in Slatton, *W. H. Whitsitt,* 84. For Southern Baptist debates over inspiration and modern science in this era, see Wills, *Southern Baptist Theological Seminary,* 136–38, and Flynt, *Alabama Baptists,* 163–68.

4. George B. Eager to JAB, 31 December 1883, BP.

5. See, for instance, Bailey, *Southern White Protestantism in the Twentieth Century,* 1–24.

6. George B. Eager to JAB, December 31, 1883, BP.

7. JAB, *Memoir,* 264; BMJ to Lulie Manly, 13 May 1879, cited in Mueller, *A History of Southern Baptist Theological Seminary,* 96–97. Whitsitt viewed Manly's return as "revenge against Toy," after having been "crowded out of his position as Prof. Of Hebrew" a decade earlier; see WHW, diary, 5:109, in Slatton, *W. H. Whitsitt,* 85.

8. "Why and How to Study the Bible," *Western Recorder* 45, no. 4 (4 September 1879), 1; Parsons, *Crawford Howell Toy,* 99–101. According to Whitsitt, Boyce confided to him that enrollment declined as a result of Manly replacing Toy; Slatton, *W. H. Whitsitt,* 84–85. Charles Manly noted that his brother's German study trip would afford him "prestige as well as the reality of preparation for giving instruction in Hebrew, Arabic, etc." Charles Manly to BMJ, 19 April 1881, MFP. For the significance of Manly's work in preserving the seminary from liberal influences, see Manley, "The Southern Baptist Mind in Transition," 269. In 1995, Broadman Press reprinted Manly's book, a reflection of the new conservative control of the Southern Baptist Convention.

9. JAB to Charles Manly, 23 August 1881, MFP; Edwin C. Dargan to JAB, 4 March 1879, BP; JPB to JAB, 25 August 1883, BP.

10. Lindsay's articles ran in the October 1881 edition of the *Baptist Union,* quoted in George B. Eager to JAB, 31 December 1883, BP; Wills, *Southern Baptist Theological Seminary,* 144–47.

11. JAB to F. W. Boatwright, 25 July 1889, in ATR, 382–83. Boatwright would serve for fifty-one years as president of Richmond College.

12. See David G. Lyon to JAB, 22 May 1880, BP; Wills, *Southern Baptist Theological Seminary,* 145–46; David G. Lyon to JAB, 28 March 1881, BP.

13. Lewis J. Huff to JAB, 18 June 1885, BP.

14. J. O'Bannon Lowry to JAB, 22 October 1881, BP; George B. Eager to JAB, 31 December 1883, BP; J. Hartwell Edwards to JAB, 20 March 1883, BP.

15. Robertson, "Broadus in the Class Room," 162; Mueller, *A History of Southern Baptist Theological Seminary,* 81–2; David S. Dockery, "Mighty in the Scriptures," in Dockery and Duke, eds., *John A. Broadus,* 35; JAB, *Memoir,* 311.

16. ATR, 352; B. B. Warfield, originally from Lexington, Kentucky, achieved fame as the foremost defender of biblical inerrancy and conservative Protestant orthodoxy of his day. Broadus used Warfield's Greek textbook in the classroom and consulted with Warfield when writing commentary on selections of John's Gospel; see B. B. Warfield to JAB, 25 March 1885, BP; B. B. Warfield to JAB, 4 February 1886, in ATR, 344. Warfield invited Broadus to visit him in Lexington during the summer; B. B. Warfield to JAB, 6 May 1885, BP.

17. Newman, *A History of the Baptist Churches in the United States,* 518. Roger Finke and Rodney Starke also note that Broadus was "extremely impressed with the application of critical methods to biblical studies that was going on in European universities, especially in Germany," in *The Churching of America, 1776–1990,* 179.

18. JAB, *Paramount and Permanent Authority of the Bible,* 1–7, 10–13

19. JAB, *Paramount and Permanent Authority of the Bible,* 3–4; JAB, *Three Questions as to the Bible,* 34, 46–47; JAB, "Science and Christianity," in *Sermons and Addresses,* 348–51. For the evangelical embrace of evolution, see Marsden, *Fundamentalism and American Culture,* 22–26.

20. Wacker, *Augustus H. Strong,* 21–42; JAB, *Three Questions as to the Bible,* 23–25; JAB, "The Old Testament Apocrypha," *The Baptist Review* 3 (January 1881), 109.

21. JAB, "Notes on Various Subjects," 12:25, BP. JAB, *Three Questions as to the Bible,* 6, 7, 9, 27; ATR, "As a Teacher," in "Broadus Memorial," *Seminary Magazine* 8 (April 1895), 360; JAB, "The Holy Scriptures," *Sermons and Addresses,* 161. See also his comments regarding the nature of the Bible in *A Catechism of Bible Teaching.*

22. JAB, *Paramount and Permanent Authority of the Bible,* 7–8; JAB, *Three Questions as to the Bible,* 54–56; JAB to Samuel Sinclair Broadus, 31 December 1886, in ATR, 355; JAB to H. E. Truex, 28 January 1893, in ATR, 406.

23. JAB to H. H. Harris, 8 November 1880, cited in Barron, "The Contributions of John A. Broadus to Southern Baptists," 126. Besides his preaching manual, Broadus published *Lectures on the History of Preaching,* five lectures delivered at Newton Theological Institute in 1876. The work claimed to be the first account of preaching from the ancient church to the present day in the English language; see ATR, 300.

24. Hovey, *Alvah Hovey,* 208, 169. See also Shrader, *Thoughtful Christianity,* 23, 179–80. For Clarke's liberalism, see Dorrien, *The Making of American Liberal Theology,* 1:406.

25. J. William Jones to JAB, 30 March 1863, in ATR, 196; JAB to CEB, 28 August 1863, in ATR, 204; Benjamin Griffith to JAB, 31 December 1868, BP. JAB had failed to secure a contract with Gould & Lincoln in 1868; JAB to BMJ, 24 June 1868, in ATR, 230–31; JAB, *Commentary on Matthew,* li.

26. JAB, *Commentary on Matthew,* xlix, xlv, 58.

27. Alvah Hovey to JAB, 20 April 1888, BP; Vedder, Review of *An American Commentary,* 267–68; Harris, "As a Commentator," 375; ATR, 357; R. M. D., "Dr. John A. Broadus' *Commentary on Matthew,*" 1; David S. Dockery, "Mighty in the Scriptures: John A. Broadus and His Influence on A. T. Robertson and Southern Baptist Life," in Dockery and Duke, eds., *John A. Broadus,* 33–37; Barron, "The Contributions of John A. Broadus to Southern Baptists," 139.

28. Alvah Hovey to JAB, 13 October 1888, BP; Alvah Hovey to JAB, 6 March 1885, 16 March 1885, BP; Alvah Hovey to JAB, 8 February 1886, BP.

29. JAB, *Three Questions as to the Bible,* 13; ATR, 387. Broadus called German scholar F. C. Baur a "great man" but an "infidel scholar," and dismissed as arbitrary Baur's judgments on the authenticity of the New Testament books. A. J. Holt, "Lecture Notes in Old and New Testament, 1874–75," 102.

30. JAB, *Jesus of Nazareth,* 10, 84; Mueller, *A History of Southern Baptist Theological Seminary,* 76–80; Barron, "The Contributions of John A. Broadus to Southern Baptists," 140–45.

31. *Philadelphia Presbyterian,* 11 June 1890, quoted in ATR, 387; "Review of John A. Broadus, *Jesus of Nazareth,*" in *Bibliotheca Sacra* 48 (July 1891): 542; James S. Riggs, *The Presbyterian and Reformed Review,* 685; Starr, *A Baptist Bibliography,* 3:151.

32. JAB, *A Harmony of the Gospels.* Robertson divided the royalties evenly with the unmarried Eliza Broadus; see Barron, "The Contributions of John A. Broadus to Southern Baptists," 146. Roberston, *Syllabus for New Testament Study,* v. "The plan and spirit of the course are due to John A. Broadus," Robertson wrote.

33. Philip Schaff to JAB, 16 July 1889, BP; JAB, "St. Chrysostom as a Homilist," in *A Select Library of the Nicene and Post-Nicene Fathers of the Christian Church,* v–vi; see also JAB, *Lectures on the History of Preaching,* 73–74.

34. JAB, *Three Questions as to the Bible,* 58–59; Henry C. Vedder, Review of John A. Broadus, *An American Commentary on the New Testament,* in *Baptist Quarterly Review* 9 (April 1887): 268. Broadus largely commended the work of Westcott and Hort, as well as Constantin Tischendorf's eighth critical edition of the New Testament, and B. B. Warfield's *Introduction to the Textual Criticism of the New Testament* (1887). See JAB, Review of Benjamin B. Warfield, *An Introduction to the Textual Criticism of the New Testament,* in *Baptist Quarterly Review* 9 (April 1887): 266–67; JAB, *Commentary on Matthew,* xlix.

35. JAB to Alvah Hovey, 13 April 1887, AHP; Barron, "The Contributions of John A. Broadus to Southern Baptists," 117–19; Robertson, *Studies in the Text of the New Testament,* 142–43.

36. Wilson, *William Owen Carver's Controversies in the Baptist South,* 162; Noll, *Between Faith and Criticism,* 11–31; Worthen, *Apostles of Reason,* 21–24.

37. JAB, *Three Questions as to the Bible,* 55–56.

38. For Harper, see Boyer, *The University of Chicago,* 67–148; and Marsden, *The Soul of the American University Revisited,* 175–91.

39. JAB to WRH, 17 February 1888, John D. Rockefeller, Sr. Papers, box 1, folder 3, Rockefeller Archive Center; WRH to JAB, 31 January 1888, BP; WRH to JAB, February 18, 1890, BP; WRH to JAB, 3 February 1886, BP.

40. WRH to JAB, 16 February 1891, BP; Harper would also consult Broadus regarding the publication of controversial articles about the Documentary Hypothesis of the Pentateuch in WRH to JAB, 20 April 1888, BP; WRH to JAB, 11 April 1890, BP; WRH to JAB, 28 February 1889, BP.

41. JAB to WRH, 17 February 1888, John D. Rockefeller, Sr. Papers, box 1, folder 3, Rockefeller

Archive Center. For the debate with Green, see W. Boyer, "Broad and Christian in the Fullest Sense," 27–33.

42. AHS to JDR, 3 November 1887, University of Chicago, Founder's Correspondence; AHS to JAB, 25 October 1887, BP.

43. JDR to JAB, 5 October 1887, BP; JDR to JAB, 10 October 1887, BP; JDR to AHS, 10 October 1887, University of Chicago, Founder's Correspondence; AHS to JDR, 26 November 1887, University of Chicago, Founder's Correspondence.

44. For this story, see Boyer, *The University of Chicago,* 67–148.

45. AHS to JAB, 21 February 1889, BP; AHS to JDR, 25 March 1899, box 1, folder 6, RAC. Strong also consulted Alvah Hovey, George W. Northup, and Henry G. Weston.

46. JAB to WRH, 13 October 1890, John D. Rockefeller, Sr. Papers, box 2, folder 12, Rockefeller Archive Center; Dorrien, *The Making of American Liberal Theology,* 1:371.

47. Quoted in AHS to JAB, 10 February 1891, BP; Martin, *Viewing Life's Sunset from Pike's Peak,* 18–19.

48. CHT to JAB, 22 July 1886, BP; JPB to JAB, 14 August 1886, BP; CHT to JAB, 29 October 1886, BP.

49. Mueller, *A History of Southern Baptist Theological Seminary,* 64, 131–32; AHS to JAB, 10 February 1891, BP; C. I. Scofield, "Complicity w Error" *The Truth* 17 (1891), 280–82.

50. JAB, "Ministerial Education," in *Sermons and Addresses,* 198–203, 208–210; JAB to a College Student, 7 July 1889, in ATR, 382; JAB, "Conservatives and Progressives," *Religious Herald* 68 (March 14, 1895), 1.

10. TEACHING THE "BROADUS STYLE"

1. Holt, *Pioneering in the Southwest,* 44, 58.

2. Holt, *Pioneering in the Southwest,* 82–86.

3. Holifield, *Gentlemen Theologians,* 24–49; Schweiger, *Gospel Working Up,* 129–48; Harvey, *Redeeming the South,* 137–66.

4. JAB to CEB, 27 January 1886, BP; JAB to CEB, 1 February 1866, BP; JAB to J. L. M. Curry, 11 January 1870, in ATR, 233–34, 237.

5. Jackson, "'As a Musician Would His Violin,'" 502.

6. Jackson, "'As a Musician Would His Violin,'" 501; Johnson, *Nineteenth-Century Rhetoric in North America,* 50–52.

7. JAB, *A Treatise on the Preparation and Delivery of Sermons,* 20, 25, 30.

8. JAB, "Education in Athens," in *Sermons and Addresses,* 269–70. "It would hardly be extravagant to assert, that in real training of mind, in mastery of principles and knowledge of men, in capacity for every form of mental effort, from the most refined speculation to the conduct of affairs, they were as highly educated a people as the world has yet seen," Broadus continues, in "Education in Athens," 291; Jackson, "'As a Musician Would His Violin,'" 502. For the Old South's bent toward classical Greek oratory, see Elder, *The Sacred Mirror,* 179, and Wyatt-Brown, *Southern Honor,* 92–96. For the neoclassicism of nineteenth-century homiletics manuals, see Hirst, "The Sermon as Public Discourse," 78–103.

9. Chapell, *Christ-Centered Preaching,* 79, 129; JAB, *A Treatise on the Preparation and Delivery of Sermons,* 39, 125.

10. JAB, *A Treatise on the Preparation and Delivery of Sermons*, 262, 296, 305, 245.

11. JAB, "The Young Preacher's Outfit," 10; JAB, *A Treatise on the Preparation and Delivery of Sermons*, 396, 399.

12. JAB, *A Treatise on the Preparation and Delivery of Sermons*, 238, 211, 451.

13. ATR, 249; Nettles, "Enduring Impact," in Dockery and Duke, eds., *John A. Broadus*, 187.

14. Lucy Garrett to JAB, 13 November 1871, BP; J. L. M. Curry to JAB, 28 December 1870, in ATR, 254; "homeopathic dose" quote cited in Nettles, "Enduring Impact," in Dockery and Duke, eds., *John A. Broadus*, 189–90.

15. Old, *The Reading and Preaching of the Scriptures*, 6:272. For a survey of modern homiletics books' treatment of Broadus, see Nettles, "Enduring Impact," in Dockery and Duke, eds., *John A. Broadus*, 201–209.

16. Hoshor, "American Contributions to Rhetorical Theory and Homiletics," 149; Randolph, *The Renewal of Preaching*, 21; Kay, "Preacher as Messenger of Hope," 15. Johnson also credits Broadus for "popularizing the theoretical principles of the New Rhetoric" among American preachers, in *Nineteenth-Century Rhetoric in North America*, 271.

17. JAB, *A Treatise on the Preparation and Delivery of Sermons*, 27. See also his remarks to close his lectures on the history of preaching at Newton Theological Institute in 1876: "In your time, as in all times, the thing needed will be not oratorical display but genuine eloquence, the eloquence which springs from vigorous thinking, strong convictions, fervid imaginations, and passionate earnestness; and true spiritual success will be attained only in proportion as you gain, in humble prayer, the blessing of the Holy Spirit." JAB, *Lectures on the History of Preaching*, 234.

18. Holt, *Pioneering in the Southwest*, 87, 93.

19. Jackson, "'As a Musician Would His Volin,'" 502.

20. JAB, *Memoir*, 275; JAB to JPB, 17 October 1888, Boyce Papers; JAB to JPB, 19 September 1888, Boyce Papers.

21. Reeder, *Broadus Unbound*, 324; Bernard Spillman, "Journal," quoted in Harvey, *Redeeming the South*, 147; Holt, *Pioneering in the Southwest*, 88.

22. Sampey, "John A. Broadus," 10; Robertson, "Broadus in the Class Room," 157, 163.

23. T. H. Pritchard, "John Albert Broadus," *The Watchman*, 29 March 1895, 1.

24. JAB, *A Treatise on the Preparation and Delivery of Sermons*, 476–77; 503–504.

25. JAB, "Syllabus as to Hymnology"; JAB, *A Treatise on the Preparation and Delivery of Sermons*, 349–55; Barron, "The Contributions of John A. Broadus to Southern Baptists," 152–54; ATR, 337.

26. JAB, "President John A. Broadus on Dr. Manly's Last Work," undated newspaper clipping quoted in Manley, "The Southern Baptist Mind in Transition," 290; Harvey, *Redeeming the South*, 97–102; JAB, "Syllabus as to Hymnology," 1–2, 18–19; JAB, *A Treatise on the Preparation and Delivery of Sermons*, 489–90. For the rise of gospel songs among American Protestants, see Blumhofer, "Fanny Crosby, William Doane, and the Making of Gospel Hymns in the Late Nineteenth Century," 152–74. See also Crookshank, "'The Minister and His Hymn Book,'" 135–39.

27. JAB, *Memoir*, 73; *Our Home Field* (February 1889), 6, quoted in Harvey, *Redeeming the South*, 153; Wills, *Southern Baptist Theological Seminary*, 94–96; Holifield, *Theology in America*, 284–90; ATR, 396–97. Broadus commended the study of systematic theology to ministry students, from "the great teachers of the past" such as Turretin and Calvin, to modern writers like John L. Dagg and A. H. Strong. See JAB, "Freshness in Preaching," 3.

28. JAB, *Memoir,* 265; JAB to Annie Abraham, 19 November 1883, Neal Broadus Abraham Collection, in Reeder, *Broadus Unbound,* 322.

29. JAB, "The Pauline System of Christian Doctrine," BP (with thanks to Casey McCall for sharing his transcription); JAB, *Memoir,* 265-66, 310; JAB, *Sermons and Addresses,* 110-23.

30. Clarke, *Sixty Years with the Bible,* 102. For a discussion of eschatology in this era, see Marsden, *Fundamentalism and American Culture,* 48-62. For the Southern Baptist debates, see Harvey, *Redeeming the South,* 154-55. For an updated study of the rise of American pre-millennialism, see Gribben, *J. N. Darby and the Roots of Dispensationalism.*

31. JAB to E. Y. Mullins, 27 January 1894, in ATR, 417-18; Robertson, *Syllabus for New Testament Study,* 274.

32. Carver, "Recollections," 16; Barron, "The Contributions of John A. Broadus to Southern Baptists," 60-61; Slatton, *W. H. Whitsitt,* 150-51; JAB to H. H. Harris, 8 November 1880, cited in Barron, "The Contributions of John A. Broadus to Southern Baptists," 126; JAB, "Ministerial Education," in *Sermons and Addresses,* 208-210; Robertson, "Broadus in the Class Room," 164, 166; Carver, "Recollections," 14. A. H. Newman believed that he lost his job at Rochester for advocating for English Bible instruction; see A. H. Newman to JAB, 26 May 1881, BP.

33. Holt, *Pioneering in the Southwest,* 87-89; Robertson, "Broadus in the Class Room," 164; R. J. Williams, "A Prince and a Great Man," *Western Recorder* 69, no. 21 (4 April 1895).

34. Holt, *Pioneering in the Southwest,* 93; McGlothlin, "John Albert Broadus," 162; Mueller, *A History of Southern Baptist Theological Seminary,* 83; Ramsay, "Boyce and Broadus," 9; Edward Judson to JAB, 31 March 1892, in ATR, 402; Robertson, "Broadus in the Class Room," 167-69; JAB to Samuel Sinclair Broadus, 5 February 1887, in ATR, 358.

35. S. M. Provence to JAB, 4 April 1885, BP; George B. Eager to JAB, 20 June 1884, BP; E. Y. Mullins to JAB, 12 April 1888, BP.

36. R. S. Harrison to JAB, 29 April 1880, BP; W. Williams to JAB, 2 September 1882, BP; JAB to W. Y. Abraham, 22 February 1883, Neal Broadus Abraham Collection, in Reeder, *Broadus Unbound,* 319-21; Williams Rutherford to JAB, 18 December 1882, BP; J. M. Morris to JAB, 27 February 1890, BP.

37. Carver, "Recollections," 17.

38. See George E. Day to JAB, 31 December 1887, BP; ATR, 375-77. For the lectures, see Mark Overstreet, "The 1889 Lyman Beecher Lectures on Preaching and the Recovery of the Late Homiletic of John Albert Broadus (1827-1895)." The two other Southern Baptist Beecher lecturers are Edwin M. Poteat (1940) and John R. Claypool (1979).

39. JAB, "The Young Minister's Outfit," 3-4.

40. JAB, "The Young Minister's Outfit," 13-15.

41. JAB, "The Young Minister's Outfit," 16-17.

42. JAB, "Freshness in Preaching," 4-6, 11; JAB, "Sensation Preaching."

43. JAB, "Freedom in Preaching," 1, in "'Lost' Yale Lectures on Preaching," Boyce Digital Repository, SBTS.

44. ATR, 375-77.

45. Holt, *Pioneering in the Southwest,* 92, 102-104; A. J. Holt to A. T. Robertson, 13 September 1928, A. T. Robertson Papers, Wake Forest University, quoted in Wills, *Southern Baptist Theological Seminary,* 171.

II. OUR LIFE WORK

1. *Louisville Courier-Journal,* 9 January 1888, 6; *Louisville Courier-Journal,* 13 February 1888, 6; JAB to JPB, 12 August 1886, Boyce Papers.

2. Blum, *Reforging the White Republic,* 145.

3. "Do Not Want Moody," *Louisville Courier-Journal,* 13 February 1888, 7.

4. JAB to JPB, 9 December 1878, Boyce Papers; JAB, *Memoir,* 288; E. S. Broadus, "Recollections," 34–35, quoted in Reeder, *Broadus Unbound,* 362–63.

5. JPB to JAB, 26 March 1886, BP.

6. Slatton, *W. H. Whitsitt,* 27, 113, 46, 54; JAB to JPB, 9 February 1876, Boyce Papers; JPB to JAB, 14 August 1876, BP; JPB to JAB, 9 February 1877, BP.

7. WHW to JAB, 8 February 1882, BP; Slatton, *W. H. Whitsitt,* 85–86, 120–21.

8. Slatton, *W. H. Whitsitt,* 36; Parsons, *Crawford Howell Toy,* 64–66; Carver, "Recollections," 15. In May 1887, trustees appointed Franklin H. Kerfoot as co-professor of systematic theology to relieve Boyce. Kerfoot had attended the seminary in the early 1870s, before completing his studies at Crozer and then at Leipzig. Boyce had been trying to hire Kerfoot since 1877, and would recommend him as his own replacement. See JPB to JAB, 4 November 1888, BP; JAB, *Memoir,* 317–18; Slatton, *W. H. Whitsitt,* 131.

9. JAB, *Memoir,* 322–25; JAB to JPB, 24 October 1888, Boyce Papers; JPB to JAB, 31 October 1888, BP.

10. JAB, *Memoir,* 369; Slatton, *W. H. Whitsitt,* 141.

11. JPB to JAB, 31 October 1888, BP.

12. Z. T. Cody, "James Petigru Boyce," *Review and Expositor* 24 (April 1927): 145–66.

13. Broadus objected to Boyce's changing his title from "Faculty Chairman" to "President" shortly before Boyce's death. The "Faculty Chairman" title had been Broadus's idea, based on Thomas Jefferson's model at the University of Virginia. Trustee minutes indicate two years of heated discussion, and observers recalled observable friction between Boyce and Broadus. Broadus finally yielded in his opposition, perhaps in light of Boyce's declining health. JAB, *Memoir,* 199; Slatton, *W. H. Whitsitt,* 130; Carver, "Recollections," 15–16; Mueller, *A History of Southern Baptist Theological Seminary,* 49.

14. Sampey, "John A. Broadus," *Biblical Recorder,* May 11, 1932, 10; Whitsitt, "John Albert Broadus," 345; ATR, 433–34.

15. JAB, *Memoir,* 363–64.

16. JAB, *Memoir,* 371; Joseph Emerson Brown to JAB, 16 May 1889, BP; JAB to BMJ, 28 January 1889, in ATR, 375–76.

17. Birdwhistell, *Eliza Broadus Biography,* 10–11.

18. ATR, 424; Sampey, *Memoirs,* 54, 56–57, 64; Barron, "The Contributions of John A. Broadus to Southern Baptists," 85–87. W. O. Carver noted the many non-Baptists drawn in by Broadus, including future Methodist theologian and historian Gross Alexander; Charles S. Hemphill, founder of Louisville Presbyterian Seminary; and future Nobel Prize winner John R. Mott, the Methodist leader of the YMCA and father of the modern ecumenical movement. See Carver, "Recollections," 17–21.

19. George B. Eager to JAB, n.d.; for Eager, see Flynt, *Southern Religion and Christian Diversity in the Twentieth Century,* 189–90; Wills, *Southern Baptist Theological Seminary,* 184–85.

20. JAB to WRH, 9 February 1891, William Rainey Harper Papers, Special Collections Research Center, University of Chicago Library; Slatton, *W. H. Whitsitt,* 161; A. T. Robertson, "Dr. Harper's

Lectures on Genesis and Kuenen's Theory of OT History," *The Examiner,* 6 September 1894; JAB to ATR, 15 September 1894, A. T. Robertson Papers; Straub, *The Making of a Battle Royal,* 184–85.

21. WRH to Goodspeed, 27 January 1889, William Rainey Harper Papers, Special Collections Research Center, University of Chicago Library; *New York Tribune,* 27 May 1891; Dochuk, *Anointed with Oil,* 90–92, 169–79; Chernow, *Titan,* 325–26.

22. Straub, *The Making of a Battle Royal,* 280; Newman, *A History of the Baptist Churches in the United States,* 518; See Marsden, *Fundamentalism and American Culture,* 103–104, 179; Kidd and Hankins, *Baptists in America,* 183–95.

23. JAB to JPB, 15 July 1876, Boyce Papers; J. William Jones to JAB, 28 January 1874, BP.

24. Pike, "Reciprocal Baptism," *Religious Herald,* 4 May 1876; JAB, "Reply," *Tennessee Baptist,* 18 November 1876; JAB to JPB, 6 December 1876, Boyce Papers.

25. Sampey, *Memoirs,* 35; ATR, 308; T. T. Eaton to JAB, October 14, 1875, BP; Winters, "T. T. Eaton," 66–68, 107, 147.

26. T. T. Eaton to JAB, 8 August 1884, BP; JAB to Samuel Sinclair Broadus, 5 February 1887, in ATR, 358; T. T. Eaton to JAB, 29 March 1876, BP; Winters, "T. T. Eaton," 142, 144; Slatton, *W. H. Whitsitt,* 167; Sampey, *Memoirs,* 80; Leonard, *God's Last and Only Hope,* 43–64.

27. J. S. Murrow to JAB, 13 May 1883, BP; JAB to A. D. Chandler, 16 July 1889, BP; A. D. Chandler to S.B.T.S. Faculty, 7 July 1889, BP; JAB to A. D. Chandler, 16 July 1889, BP; J. C. Lewis to JAB, 26 July 1890, BP; J. C. Rose to JAB, 10 September 1891, BP.

28. JDR to JAB, 14 March 1885, BP; Wills et al., "Report on Slavery and Racism," 48, 51.

29. *Religious Herald,* 15 May 1879, quoted in ATR, 314; Burroughs, *Fifty Fruitful Years,* 32–34; Baker, *Relations Between Northern and Southern Baptists,* 105–106.

30. JAB to Benjamin Griffith, 21 June 1866, in ATR, 219; Washington, *Frustrated Fellowship,* 163.

31. C. Durham, "Negroes and the Publication Society," *Biblical Recorder,* 8 January 1890, 3; McGuinn, *The Race Problem in the Churches,* 57; *Washington Bee* (D.C.), 15 February 1890.

32. Winters, "T. T. Eaton," 109–120, 123; Baker, *Relations Between Northern and Southern Baptists,* 104–107; Baker, *The Story of the Sunday School Board,* 27–30; Harvey, *Redeeming the South,* 28–31; R. H. P., "More About the Convention at Ft. Worth," *Religious Herald* 63 (22 May 1890), 2; Burroughs, *Fifty Fruitful Years,* 85.

33. Baker, *The Story of the Sunday School Board,* 40–43; Sampey, "John A. Broadus," 10.

34. Harvey, *Redeeming the South,* 29–30; Barron, "The Contributions of John A. Broadus to Southern Baptists," 205–6; Burroughs, *Fifty Fruitful Years,* 129; Ammerman, *Baptist Battles,* 39–40.

35. Washington, *Frustrated Fellowship,* 181; Freeman, *The Epoch of Negro Baptists and the Foreign Mission Board,* 87.

36. Harvey, *Redeeming the South,* 39; Southern Baptist Convention, *Proceedings of the Southern Baptist Convention,* 1892, xi.

37. Southern Baptist Convention, *Proceedings of the Southern Baptist Convention,* 1891, Appendix B, 36; Virginia Baptist State Convention, *Minutes, 1892,* 18, cited in Washington, Frustrated Fellowship, 179; Southern Baptist Convention, *Proceedings of the Southern Baptist Convention,* 1892, Appendix A, 4; JAB to B. D. Gray, cited in Meraz, "The Missiology of I. T. Tichenor," 31.

38. Washington, *Frustrated Fellowship,* 183; Harper, "The Fortress Monroe Conference," 123–24; Winters, "T. T. Eaton," 119–31; Harvey, "'Yankee Faith,'" 174–81. For Southern Baptist efforts at radical uplift in the Progressive Era, see Harper, *The Quality of Mercy,* 89–111.

39. "Mission Work," *Nashville Banner* 18, no. 31 (15 May 1893), 1; see especially Leonard, *God's Last and Only Hope*, 11–15; Pope, *Millhands and Preachers*, 34; Hill, *Religion and the Solid South*, 36.

12. CAVE HILL

1. *Louisville Courier-Journal*, 4 October 1893, 6.

2. *Louisville Courier-Journal*, 5 October 1893, 10.

3. See JAB to JPB, 30 July 1860, Boyce Papers; JAB to JPB, 14 July 1877, Boyce Papers; McGlothlin, "John Albert Broadus," 160; JAB to JPB, 31 August 1860, Boyce Papers; JAB, "Funeral Sermon for George W. Riggan, D. D.," in *Sermons and Addresses*, 364–65, 367; JAB, *Memoir*, 314–16.

4. JAB, diary, 2 February 1851, BP.

5. J. M. Broadus to JAB, 30 June 1865, BP; WHW, diary, 3:20–21, in Slatton, *W. H. Whitsitt*, 121; JAB to JPB, 8 June 1884, Boyce Papers; JAB to JPB, 14 August 1884, Boyce Papers.

6. ATR, 335; Reeder, *Broadus Unbound*, 310–11.

7. ATR, 347, 404; JAB to Mrs. JMB, 6 September 1891, in ATR, 397; Reeder, *Broadus Unbound*, 322, 358, 370–71; Birdwhistell, *Eliza Broadus Biography*, 9. Broadus urged his colleagues to invest in some of Sam's speculative financial ventures. According to Whitsitt, Broadus, Kerfoot, and Manly each lost thousands of dollars in one particular investment through Sam. See Slatton, *W. H. Whitsitt*, 144.

8. Manley, "The Southern Baptist Mind in Transition," 270–83; "A Good Man's Burial," *Louisville Courier-Journal*, 3 February 1892, 6.

9. ATR, 243, 412; Sampey, "John A. Broadus," 10.

10. JAB to John Broadus Abraham, 15 March 1894, in ATR, 419; *Richmond Times-Dispatch*, 27 March 1893, 3; Hatcher, *William E. Hatcher*, 356; ATR, 420.

11. ATR, 420–22; JAB to Alice Broadus Mitchell, 14 September 1894, in ATR, 424; JAB to Eliza Somerville Broadus, 10 September 1894, in ATR, 423.

12. Norman, "The Home-Going of Dr. Robertson," 1934, 7; A. T. Robertson, personal journal, 4 March 1888, in Wills, *Southern Baptist Theological Seminary*, 186; Gill, *A. T. Robertson*, 77.

13. JAB to a friend, 24 November 1894, in ATR, 419.

14. JAB to W. D. Powell, 26 February 1895, in ATR, 429.

15. ATR, 430.

16. ATR, 431; Robertson, "Broadus in the Class Room," 162.

17. Other notable persons interred at Cave Hill today include George Rogers Clarke, Muhammad Ali, "Colonel" Harland Sanders, and NFL Hall of Fame running back Paul Horning. The text on the footstone is from Philippians 3:8.

18. ATR, 434.

19. Eaton even cast Broadus as a quasi-Landmarker. In fourteen years as his pastor, Eaton wrote, he "never got from Dr. Broadus the slightest hint that he believed there was any such thing as the 'universal invisible church.'" See T. T. Eaton, "Ridiculous Claim," *Western Recorder*, 15 January 1903, in Winters, "T. T. Eaton," 207.

20. Mitchell, *After Whitsitt, What?*; Slatton, *W. H. Whitsitt*, 298–331. Boyce Broadus voted against censuring Whitsitt at Kentucky's state Baptist convention in 1897, dissenting from his fellow messengers from Eaton's Walnut Street Baptist Church. Kimbrough, *History of the Walnut Street Baptist Church*, 147–48.

21. B. H. Carroll, "The Real Issue in the Whitsitt Case," *Baptist Standard*, 5 August 1897, 5.

22. See ATR, 444; John R. Sampey to B. H. Carroll, 24 August 1896, quoted in Spivey, "Benajah Harvey Carroll," in George and Dockery, eds., *Theologians of the Baptist Tradition,* 167.

23. ATR, 419; "Samuel S. Broadus, Founder of Many Tennessee Valley Banks, Died Today," *Decatur Daily* (Ala.), 1 April 1916, 1.

24. Harper, ed., *Rescue the Perishing,* 285–86; Flynt, *Southern Religion and Christian Diversity in the Twentieth Century,* 188–91; Scales, *All That Fits a Woman,* 60–72; Birdwhistell, *Eliza Broadus Biography,* 17. After World War I, A. T. Robertson would also promote expanded rights and opportunities for "the new woman." Robertson, *The New Citizenship,* 66–76; Gottwig, "Before the Culture Wars," 39–63.

25. Frederickson, "Interview with Broadus Mitchell."

26. Mitchell, *The Rise of Cotton Mills in the South,* vii–viii; Hall, "Broadus Mitchell, Economic Historian of the South," 25–31. Broadus Mitchell would publish sixteen books, including a multivolume biography of Alexander Hamilton.

27. Robertson, "Broadus in the Class Room," 157; Dockery, "The Broadus-Robertson Tradition," in Dockery and Duke, eds., *John A. Broadus,* 102; Noll, *Between Faith and Criticism,* 31.

BIBLIOGRAPHY

PRIMARY SOURCES

Manuscripts and Archives

Andover Newton Theological School Collection at Yale Divinity School
    Alvah Hovey Papers
Archives and Special Collections, Southern Baptist Theological Seminary
    A. T. Robertson Papers
    James P. Boyce Papers
    John A. Broadus Papers T. T. Eaton Papers
    William O. Carver Papers
Rockefeller Archive Center
    John D. Rockefeller, Sr. Papers
Southern Baptist Historical Library and Archives
    Manly Family Collection
University of Alabama Libraries Special Collections
    Manly Family Collection
University of Chicago Library
    University of Chicago Founders' Correspondence 1886–1892

Newspapers and Periodicals

Alabama Baptist (Marion, Ala.)
Alexandria Gazette (Va.)
Baptist (Nashville, Tenn.)
Biblical Recorder (Raleigh, N.C.)
Christian Index (Atlanta, Ga.)
Decatur Daily (Ala.)
Louisville Courier-Journal (Ky.)

Religious Herald (Richmond, Va.)
Richmond Dispatch (Va.)
Southern Baptist (Charleston, S.C.)
Sunday School Times (Philadelphia, Pa.)
Tennessean (Nashville, Tenn.)
Tennessee Baptist (Memphis, Tenn.)
Western Recorder (Louisville, Ky.)

Organizational Publications

Albemarle County: Record of Slaves that have escaped to the enemy during the war [1861–1863]. *Virginia Untold: The African American Narrative Digital Collection,* Library of Virginia, Richmond, Virginia.

Baptist General Association of Virginia. *Minutes of the Baptist General Association of Virginia Held in the Town of Charlottesville, June, 1855.* Richmond, Va.: H. K. Ellyson's Steam Press, 1855.

———. *Minutes of the Eighty-Fourth Annual Session of the Baptist General Association of Virginia.* Danville, Va., 1907.

Proceedings of the Colored People's Convention in the State of South Carolina Held in Zion Church, Charleston, November, 1865. Charleston: South Carolina Leader Office, 1865.

South Carolina Baptist Convention. Minutes. 1856. South Carolina Baptist Historical Collection.

Southern Baptist Convention. *Proceedings of the Southern Baptist Convention, Convened in the City of Baltimore, May 13th, 14th, 16th, and 17th, 1853.* Richmond, Va., 1853.

———. *Proceedings of the Fifth Biennial Meeting of the Southern Baptist Convention, convened in the city of Montgomery, Alabama, May 11th, 12th, 14th, and 15th, 1855.* Richmond, Va., 1855.

———. *Proceedings of the Seventh Biennial Session of the Southern Baptist Convention . . . 1859.* Richmond, Va.: H. K. Ellyson's Steam Presses, 1859.

———. *Proceedings of the Ninth Biennial Session, of the Southern Baptist Convention.* Macon, Ga., 1863.

———. *Proceedings of the Southern Baptist Convention, held at Russellville, Kentucky, May 22nd, 23rd, 24th, 25th, and 26th, 1866.* Richmond, Va.: Dispatch Steam Presses, 1866.

———. *Proceedings of the Southern Baptist Convention, Held in Meeting House of the First Baptist Church, in Memphis, Tennessee, May 9th, 10th, 11th, and 13th, 1867.* Baltimore, Md.: John F. Weishampel Jr., 1867.

———. *Proceedings of the Thirteenth Meeting of the Southern Baptist Convention, Held in the Seventh Baptist Church, Baltimore, May 7 . . . and 12th.* Baltimore, Md.: John F. Weishampel, Jr., 1868.

———. *Proceedings of the Seventeenth Meeting of the Southern Baptist Convention, Held in the Baptist Church, Raleigh North Carolina, May 9th, 10th, 11th, and 13th, 1872.* Baltimore, Md.: John F. Weishampel, 1872.

———. *Proceedings of the Southern Baptist Convention . . . 1891.* Atlanta: Jas. P. Harrison and Co. Printers, 1891.

———. *Proceedings of the Southern Baptist Convention . . . 1892.* Atlanta: Jas. P. Harrison and Co. Printers, 1892.

———. *Proceedings of the Southern Baptist Convention, held with the churches of Nashville, Tennessee, May 12–16, 1893.* Atlanta, Ga.: Franklin Printing and Publishing, 1893.

University of Virginia Alumni News, vols. 1–3. Charlottesville, Va.: Alumni Association of the University of Virginia, 1913.

Books, Pamphlets, and Articles

Andrews, Sidney. *The South Since the War: As Shown by Fourteen Weeks of Travel and Observation in Georgia and the Carolinas.* Boston: Ticknor and Fields, 1866.

Armitage, Thomas. *A History of the Baptists; Traced by Their Vital Principles and Practices, from the Time of Our Lord and Saviour Jesus Christ to the Present.* New York: Bryan, Taylor, 1890.

Boyce, James P. *Life and Death the Christian's Portion.* New York: Sheldon, 1869.

———. *Three Changes in Theological Institutions. An Inaugural Address Delivered Before The Board of Trustees of The Furman University, The Night Before The Annual Commencement, July 30, 1856.* Greenville, S.C.: C. J. Elford's Book and Job Press, 1856.

Briggs, Charles A. *General Introduction to the Study of Holy Scripture.* New York: Scribner's, 1899.

Broaddus, Andrew, ed. *The Sermons and Other Writings of the Rev. Andrew Broaddus with a Memoir of His Life by J. B. Jeter.* New York: Lewis Colby, 1852.

Broadus, Eliza S. "Some Recollections of My Father." *Western Recorder,* July 25, 1929, 3–4.

Broadus, John A. "Address to Berryville Total Abstinence Society." May 1846. Broadus-Mitchell Family Papers, Archives and Special Collections, James P. Boyce Centennial Library, Southern Baptist Theological Seminary.

———. "As to the Colored People." *Standard* (Chicago), 1 February 1883, 1.

———. "The Baptism." *Kind Words* 52, no. 5 (May 1867). Greenville, S.C.: The Sunday School Board of the Southern Baptist Convention.

———. *A Catechism of Bible Teaching.* Philadelphia: American Baptist Publication Society, 1892.

———. *Commentary on Matthew.* American Commentary Series. Philadelphia: American Baptist Publication Society, 1886.

———. "Essay on the Best Mode of Preparing and Delivering Sermons." *Religious Herald,* December 14, 1854.

———. "Freshness in Preaching." "Lost" Yale Lectures on Preaching. Archives and Special Collections, Southern Baptist Theological Seminary.

———. *A Harmony of the Gospels, in the Revised Version, with Some New Features.* New York: A. C. Armstrong and Sons, 1893.

———. "How to Teach the Lesson." *The Baptist Teacher* 10, no. 5 (May 1, 1879), 70.

———. *Jesus of Nazareth.* New York: A. C. Armstrong, 1890.

———. *Lectures on the History of Preaching.* New York: Sheldon, 1876.

———. "'Lost' Yale Lectures on Preaching." Boyce Digital Repository, Southern Baptist Theological Seminary.

———. *Memoir of James Petigru Boyce.* New York: A. C. Armstrong and Son, 1893.

———. *A Memorial of Gessner Harrison, M. D., Professor of Ancient Languages in the University of Virginia.* Charlottesville, Va., 1874.

———. "Miscellanea." *Religious Herald,* November 23, 1876.

———. *Paramount and Permanent Authority of the Bible*. Philadelphia: American Baptist Publication Society, 1887.

———. "Rev. A. Jaeger." *Christian Index and Southwestern Baptist*, May 7, 1874, 5.

———. "Sensation Preaching." "Lost" Yale Lectures on Preaching. Archives and Special Collections, Southern Baptist Theological Seminary.

———. *Sermons and Addresses*. New York: Hodder and Stoughton, 1886.

———. "Should Women Speak in Mixed Public Assemblies?" Louisville, Ky.: Baptist Book Concern, 1880.

———. "Some Earnest Words as to Lynching." *Louisville Courier-Journal*, September 27, 1886.

———. "St. Chrysostom as a Homilist." In *A Select Library of the Nicene and Post-Nicene Fathers of the Christian Church*, ed. Philip Schaff, vol. 13. New York: The Christian Literature Company, 1889.

———. "The Theological Seminary," *Religious Herald* 26 (9 April 1857), 3.

———. *Three Questions as to the Bible: Annual Sermon before the Southern Baptist Convention, at Waco, Texas, May 9, 1883*. Philadelphia: American Baptist Publication Society, 1883.

———. "Syllabus as to Hymnology," 2nd ed. Louisville: Southern Baptist Theological Seminary, 1892.

———. *A Treatise on the Preparation and Delivery of Sermons*. Philadelphia: Smith, English, 1871.

———. "We Pray for You at Home." Raleigh, N.C., n.d.

———. "The Young Preacher's Outfit." "Lost" Yale Lectures on Preaching. Archives and Special Collections, Southern Baptist Theological Seminary.

Brown, C. C. "Letter to the Seminary Magazine." *The Seminary Magazine* (March 1889), 88.

Carver, W. O. "Recollections and Information from Other Sources Concerning the Southern Baptist Theological Seminary." Unpublished mss, 1954. Archives and Special Collections, Southern Baptist Theological Seminary.

Chambliss, J. A. "The Trustees of the Seminary and Dr. Toy's Resignation." *Baptist Courier*, 12 June 1879, 2.

"Citizens Petition," 20 February 1839. Legislative Petitions of the General Assembly, 1776–1865. Accession Number 36121, Box 60, Folder 25, Library of Virginia.

"Citizens Petition," 25 January 1836. Legislative Petitions of the General Assembly, 1776–1865. Accession Number 36121, Box 60, Folder 15, Library of Virginia.

Clark, William Newton. *Sixty Years with the Bible: A Record of Experience*. New York: Charles Scribner's Sons, 1909.

The Confederate Veteran Magazine 13, no. 1 (1905).

"Criticisms on Some of the Ablest Representative Preachers of the Day, by an Eminent Professor of Homiletics, No. VII—Rev. John A. Broadus, D. D." *Homiletic Review* 16, no. 2 (August 1888): 99–106.

Dabney, R. L. *A Defence of Virginia, [And Through Her, of the South]*. New York: E. J. Hale, 1867.

———. "The Negro and the Common School." In *Discussions by R. L. Dabney, D. D.*, 4:176–90. 1876. Reprint, Harrisonburg, Va: Sprinkle Publications, 1994.

———. "The New South." In *Discussions by R. L. Dabney, D. D.,* 4:1–24. 1883. Reprint, Harrisonburg, Va.: Sprinkle Publications, 1994.

Dill, Jacob Smiser. *Lest We Forget: Baptist Preachers of Yesterday That I Knew.* Nashville: Broadman Press, 1938.

Domestic Slavery Considered as a Scriptural Institution: A Correspondence Between the Rev. Richard Fuller and the Rev. Francis Wayland. New York: Sheldon, 1845.

Eager, George B. "Rev. William Williams, D. D., LL.D." *Review and Expositor* 6, no. 3 (July 1909): 401–23.

Erdmann, C. F. D. *The Books of Samuel.* Translated and edited by C. H. Toy and John A. Broadus. New York: Scribner's, 1877. E. T. R. [pseudonym]. "E. T. R. Again! False Teaching—&c." *Religious Herald* (December 12, 1878).

Frederickson, Mary. "Interview with Broadus Mitchell, August 14 and 15, 1977." Southern Oral History Program Collection, #4007. https://docsouth.unc.edu/sohp/html_use /B-0024.html.

Harper, Keith, ed. *Rescue the Perishing: Selected Correspondence of Annie Armstrong.* Macon, Ga.: Mercer Univ. Press, 2004.

Harris, H. H. "As a Commentator." *Seminary Magazine* 8 (April 1895).

Hatcher, William E. *Life of J. B. Jeter, D. D.* Baltimore, 1887.

Holt, A. J. "Lecture Notes of C. H. Toy's O. T. Class, 28 Sept. 1874." Archives and Special Collections, Southern Baptist Theological Seminary.

———. *Pioneering in the Southwest.* Nashville, Tenn.: Sunday School Board of the Southern Baptist Convention, 1923.

Jefferson, Thomas, to Joseph C. Cabell, January 13, 1823. *Founders Online,* National Archives. https://founders.archives.gov/documents/Jefferson/03-19-02-0217.

Jeffers, M. D. "Reminiscences of My Seminary Life." *Seminary Magazine* 5 (January 1892), 196–97.

Jefferson, Thomas. *Notes on the State of Virginia.* Boston: H. Sprague, 1802.

Jefferson, Thomas, to William Roscoe, December 27, 1820. *Founders Online,* National Archives. https://founders.archives.gov/documents/Jefferson/03-16-02-0404.

"John A. Broadus, Chairman of Committee for the Religious Instruction of Colored People." *Religious Herald* 25 (October 23, 1856), 165.

Jones, J. William. *Christ in the Camp, or Religion in Lee's Army.* Richmond, Va.: B. F. Johnson, 1887.

———. "Dr. John A. Broadus as Evangelist in Lee's Army." *Seminary Magazine* 8, no. 7 (April 1895), 53–58.

Kerfoot, Franklin H. "Hon. Joseph Emerson Brown." *Seminary Magazine* 8 (1894), 130–31.

Levering, Joshua. "A Backward Glance." *Review and Expositor* 24, no. 2 (October 1927): 132–44.

Little, Lewis Payton. *Imprisoned Preachers and Religious Liberty in Virginia: A Narrative Drawn Largely from the Official Records of Virginia Counties, Unpublished Manuscripts, Letters, and Other Original Sources.* Lynchburg, Va.: J. P. Bell Co., 1938.

Lyon, David G. "Crawford Howell Toy." *Harvard Theological Review* 13, no. 1 (January 1920): 1–22.

Manly, Basil, Jr. "Beginnings of the History of the Seminary." *Seminary Magazine* 5 (1891).

———. "Dr. Manly and the Colored Man." *South Carolina Baptist,* June 5, 1868, 2.

Martin, T. T. *Viewing Life's Sunset from Pike's Peak: The Life Story of T. T. Martin.* Louisville: A. D. Muse, 1939.

Maxwell, William, ed. *The Virginia Historical Register and Literary Notebook, Vol III, for the Year 1850.* Richmond: Macfarlane and Fergusson, 1850.

McGuinn, Robert A. *The Race Problem in the Churches.* Baltimore: J. F. Weishampel, 1890.

Mell, Patrick H. *Slavery: A Treatise Showing That Slavery Is Neither a Moral, Political, Nor Social Evil.* Penfield, Ga.: Benjamin Brantly, 1844.

Miller, Samuel. *The Utility and Importance of Creeds and Confessions and Adherence to Our Doctrinal Standards.* Philadelphia: Presbyterian Board of Publication, 1839.

Minutes, Grand Division of the Sons of Temperance of the State of Virginia, 1855. Richmond: MacFarlane and Fergusson, 1855.

Mitchell, John Broadus. *The Rise of Cotton Mills in the South.* Baltimore, Md.: Johns Hopkins Press, 1921.

Mitchell, S. C. *After Whitsitt, What?* (Louisville: Charles T. During, 1899).

Moore, George F. "An Appreciation of Professor Toy." *American Journal of Semitic Languages and Literatures* 36, no. 1 (October 1919): 1–17.

Newman, A. H. *A History of the Baptist Churches in the United States,* 6th ed. New York: Charles Scribner's Sons, 1915.

Norman, Don. "The Home-Going of Dr. Robertson," 1934, 7. https://repository.sbts.edu/handle/10392/4146.

Pritchard, T. H. "John Albert Broadus." *The Watchman,* March 28, 1895, 1.

Riggs, James S. Book Review. *The Presbyterian and Reformed Review* 5 (1894): 326. R. M. D. "Dr. John A. Broadus' *Commentary on Matthew.*" *Western Recorder* 53 (7 April 1887), 1.

Robertson, A. T. "As a Teacher." *Seminary Magazine* 8 (April 1895).

———. "Broadus in the Class Room." *Review and Expositor* 30 (1933): 157–69.

———. "An Educational Revival in the South." *Baptist and Reflector,* January 1919, 2.

———. *Life and Letters of John A. Broadus.* 1901; reprint, Harrisonburg, Va.: Gano Books, 2003.

———. *The New Citizenship: The Christian Facing a New World Order.* New York: Fleming H. Revell, 1919.

———. *Studies in the Text of the New Testament.* London: Hodder and Stoughton, 1926.

———. *Syllabus for New Testament Study: A Guide for Lessons in the Class-Room,* 5th ed. London: Hodder and Stoughton, 1923.

Ryland, Charles H. "Recollections of the First Year: 1859–1860." An address delivered before the Seminary at Louisville, Kentucky, Founders Day, January 11, 1911, Boyce Digital Repository, SBTS.

Sampey, John R. "John A. Broadus." *Biblical Recorder,* May 11, 1932, 10.

———. *Memoirs of John R. Sampey*. Nashville: Broadman Press, 1947.

———. *Southern Baptist Theological Seminary: The First Thirty Years, 1859–1889*. Baltimore: Wharton, Barron, 1890.

Scofield, C. I. "Complicity with Error." *The Truth* 17 (1891): 280–82

Sprague, William B. *Annals of the American Baptist Pulpit*, vol. 6. New York: Robert Carter and Brothers, 1860.

Starr, Edward C. *A Baptist Bibliography: Being a Register of Printed Material by and about Baptists*. Vol. 3. Chester, Pa.: American Baptist Historical Society, 1953.

Taylor, George Braxton. *Virginia Baptist Ministers, Third Series*. Lynchburg, Va.: J. P. Bell, 1912.

———. *Virginia Baptist Ministers, Fourth Series*. Lynchburg, Va.: J. P. Bell, 1913.

Toy, C. H. *The Claims of Biblical Interpretation on Baptists*. New York: Lange and Hillman, 1869.

———. "Sketch of My Religious Life," May 24, 1860. Transcribed by Jason Fowler. T. T. Eaton Papers, Special Collections, James P. Boyce Centennial Library, Southern Baptist Theological Seminary.

———. "Letter of Resignation to the Board of Trustees of the Southern Baptist Theological Seminary." E-Text Collection. Archives and Special Collections, Southern Baptist Theological Seminary.

———. "The Tubingen School." *Baptist Quarterly* 3 (1869): 210–35.

United States, Report of the Commissioner of Education. Vol. 1. Washington, D.C.: Government Printing Office, 1904.

Vedder, Henry C. "Review of John A. Broadus, *An American Commentary on the New Testament*." *Baptist Quarterly Review* 9 (April 1887): 375.

Warfield, Benjamin Breckenridge. *An Introduction to the Textual Criticism of the New Testament*. London: Hodder and Stoughton, 1886.

Whitsitt, William H. Diary, vol. 5. Virginia Baptist Historical Society. University of Richmond, Richmond, Virginia.

———. "John Albert Broadus: Address for Founders' Day at The Southern Baptist Theological Seminary, January 11, 1907." *Review and Expositor* 4, no. 3 (July 1907): 339–51.

———. "A New Year's Greeting." *Baptist Courier*, January 2, 1902, 1.

Wilkinson, William C. "John Albert Broadus: The Scholar, the Preacher, the Teacher, the Man of Affairs, the Man, the Christian." *The Biblical World* (May 1895): 327–35.

SECONDARY SOURCES

Books, Articles, Chapters, and Dissertations

Ammerman, Nancy Tatom. *Baptist Battles: Social Change and Religious Conflict in the Southern Baptist Convention*. New Brunswick, N.J.: Rutgers Univ. Press, 1990.

Andrews, Sydney. *The South Since the War: As Shown by Fourteen Weeks of Travel and Observation in Georgia and the Carolinas.* Boston: Ticknor and Fields, 1866.

Ashby, Jerry Paxton. "John Albert Broadus: The Theory and Practice of His Preaching." Th.D. thesis, New Orleans Baptist Theological Seminary, 1968.

Ayers, Edward. *The Promise of the New South: Life After Reconstruction.* New York: Oxford Univ. Press, 2007.

———. *The Thin Light of Freedom: The Civil War and Emancipation in the Heart of America.* New York: Norton, 2017.

Bailey, Kenneth K. *Southern White Protestantism in the Twentieth Century.* New York: Harper and Row, 1964.

Bailey, Raymond. "John A. Broadus: Man of Letters and Preacher Extraordinaire." *Preaching* (November–December 1993): 58–61.

Bailey, Sarah Pulliam. "Southern Baptist President Wants to Retire Famed Gavel Named for Slave Holder." *Washington Post,* June 10, 2021. https://www.washingtonpost.com /religion/2020/06/10/southern-baptist-gavel-grear/.

Baker, Robert A. *Relations Between Northern and Southern Baptists.* New York: Arno Press, 1948.

———. *The Story of the Sunday School Board.* Nashville: Convention Press, 1966.

Baptist Press Staff. "Trustees: SBTS Retains Names, Vacates Chair, Establishes Endowment." *Baptist Press,* October 13, 2020. https://www.baptistpress.com/resource-library/news /trustees-sbts-retains-names-vacates-chair-establishes-endowment/.

Baptist Sunday School Board. *Encyclopedia of Southern Baptists,* vol. 2. Nashville: Broadman Press, 1958.

Barron, James. "The Contributions of John A. Broadus to Southern Baptists." Ph.D. diss., Southern Baptist Theological Seminary, 1972.

Birdwhistell, Jack. *Eliza Broadus Biography.* 1980. Reprint, Louisville: Kentucky WMU, 2013.

Blight, David W. *Race and Reunion: The Civil War in American Memory.* Cambridge, Mass.: Belknap Press, 2002.

Blum, Edward J. *Reforging the White Republic: Race, Religion, and American Nationalism, 1865–1898.* Baton Rouge: Louisiana State Univ. Press, 2007.

Blumhofer, Edith L. "Fanny Crosby, William Doane, and the Making of Gospel Hymns in the Late Nineteenth Century." In *Sing Them Over Again to Me: Hymns and Hymnbooks in America,* edited by Mark Noll and Edith L. Blumhofer, 152–74. Tuscaloosa: Univ. of Alabama Press, 2006).

Bogard, Ben M., ed. *Pillars of Orthodoxy, or Defenders of the Faith.* Louisville, Ky.: Baptist Book Concern, 1900.

Boles, John. *The Great Revival: Beginnings of the Bible Belt.* Lexington: Univ. Press of Kentucky, 1996.

Bond, Horace Mann. *Negro Education in Alabama: A Study in Cotton and Steel.* New York: Octagon Books, 1969.

Boyer, John W. "Broad and Christian in the Fullest Sense: William Rainey Harper and the

University of Chicago." *Occasional Papers on Higher Education,* vol. 15, 27–33. https://
humanities-web.s3.us-east-2.amazonaws.com/college-prod/s3fs-public/documents
/Boyer_OccasionalPapers_V15.pdf.

———. *The University of Chicago: A History.* Chicago: Univ. of Chicago Press, 2015.

Boylan, Anne M. *Sunday School: The Formation of an American Institution, 1790–1880.* New Haven, Conn.: Yale Univ. Press, 1988.

Brekus, Catherine A. *Sarah Osborn's World: The Rise of Evangelical Christianity in Early America.* New Haven, Conn.: Yale Univ. Press, 2013.

Brown, William Earl. "Pastoral Evangelism: A Model for Effective Evangelism as Demonstrated by the Ministries of John Albert Broadus, Alfred Elijah Dickinson, and John William Jones in the Revival of the Army of Northern Virginia in 1863." Ph.D. diss., Southeastern Baptist Theological Seminary, 1999.

Bruce, Philip Alexander. *The History of the University of Virginia, 1819–1919: The Lengthened Shadow of One Man.* New York: Macmillan, 1920.

Burroughs, P. E. *Fifty Fruitful Years, 1891–1941: The Story of the Sunday School Board of the Southern Baptist Convention.* Nashville: Broadman Press, 1941.

Bush, L. Russ, and Tom J. Nettles. *Baptists and the Bible.* Nashville: B&H Academic, 1999.

Byrd, James P. *A Holy Baptism of Fire and Blood: The Bible and the American Civil War.* New York: Oxford Univ. Press, 2021.

Chapell, Bryan. *Christ-Centered Preaching: Redeeming the Expository Sermon.* Grand Rapids, Mich.: Baker Academic, 2005.

Chernow, Ron. *Titan: The Life of John D. Rockefeller, Sr.* New York: Random House, 1998.

Clarke, Erskine. *To Count Our Days: A History of Columbia Theological Seminary.* Columbia: Univ. of South Carolina Press, 2019.

Clayton, John Powell. "Crawford Howell Toy of Virginia." *Baptist Quarterly* 24 (1971): 49–57.

Cobb, James C. *Away Down South: A History of Southern Identity.* New York: Oxford Univ. Press, 2005.

Coker, Joe. *Liquor in the Land of the Lost Cause: Southern White Evangelicals and the Prohibition Movement.* Lexington: Univ. Press of Kentucky, 2007.

Cole, Arthur Charles. *The Whig Party in the South.* Washington, D.C.: American Historical Society, 1914.

Coyner, M. Boyd, Jr. "John Hartwell Cocke of Bremo: Agriculture and Slavery in the Antebellum South." Ph.D. diss.., University of Virginia, 1961.

Crookshank, Esther Rothenbusch. "'The Minister and His Hymn Book': John A. Broadus as Hymnologist." In *Minds and Hearts in Praise to God: Hymns and Essays in Church Music in Honor of Hugh T. McElrath,* edited by J. Michael Raley and Deborah Carlton Loftis, 135–39. Franklin, Tenn.: Providence House Publishers, 2006.

Dochuk, Darren. *Anointed with Oil: How Christianity and Crude Made Modern America.* New York: Basic Books, 2019.

Dockery, David S., and Roger D. Duke, eds. *John A. Broadus: A Living Legacy.* Nashville, Tenn.: B&H Academic, 2008.

Dorrien, Gary. *The Making of American Liberal Theology: Imagining Progressive Religion, 1805–1900*. Louisville, Ky.: Westminster John Knox Press, 2001.

Doyle, Don H. *New Men, New Cities, New South: Atlanta, Nashville, Charleston, and Mobile, 1860–1910*. Chapel Hill: Univ. of North Carolina Press, 1990.

Dubois, W. E. B. *Black Reconstruction in America: Toward a History of the Part Which Black Folk Played in the Attempt to Reconstruct Democracy in America, 1860–1880*. New York: Harcourt, Brace, 1935.

Duncan, Pope A. "Crawford Howell Toy (1836–1919)." In *Dictionary of Heresy Trial in American Christianity*, edited by George H. Shriver, 430–438. Westport, Conn.: Greenwood, 1997.

Edgar, Walter. *South Carolina: A History*. Columbia: Univ. of South Carolina Press, 1998.

Edwards, O. C., Jr. *A History of Preaching*, vol. 2. Nashville, Tenn.: Abingdon Press, 2004.

———. "The Preaching of Romanticism in America." *American Transcendental Quarterly* 14, no. 4 (December 2000): 297–312.

Elder, Robert. *The Sacred Mirror: Evangelicalism, Honor, and Identity in the Deep South, 1790–1860*. Chapel Hill: Univ. of North Carolina Press, 2016.

Faust, Drew Gilpin. *Mothers of Invention: Women of the Slaveholding South in the American Civil War*. Chapel Hill: Univ. of North Carolina Press, 1996.

Finke, Roger, and Rodney Starke. *The Churching of America, 1776–1990*. New Brunswick, N.J.: Rutgers Univ. Press, 1992.

Fischer, John E. *The John F. Slater Fund: A Nineteenth Century Affirmative Action for Negro Education*. New York: Univ. Press of America, 1986.

Flynt, Wayne. *Alabama Baptists: Southern Baptists in the Heart of Dixie*. Tuscaloosa: Univ. of Alabama Press, 1998.

———. *Southern Religion and Christian Diversity in the Twentieth Century*. Tuscaloosa: Univ. of Alabama Press, 2016.

Foner, Eric. *Reconstruction: America's Unfinished Revolution, 1863–1877*. New York: HarperCollins, 1989.

Foster, Gaines M. *Ghosts of the Confederacy: Defeat, the Lost Cause, and the Emergence of the New South, 1865–1913*. New York: Oxford Univ. Press, 1987.

———. *The Limits of the Lost Cause: Essays on Civil War Memory*. Baton Rouge: Louisiana State Univ. Press, 2024.

Fox-Genovese, Elizabeth, and Eugene D. Genovese. *The Mind of the Master Class: History and Faith in the Southern Slaveholder's Worldview*. New York: Cambridge Univ. Press, 2005.

Fraser, James W. *Schooling the Preachers: The Development of Protestant Theological Education in the United States, 1740–1875*. Lanham, Md.: Univ. Press of America, 1988.

Freeman, Edward. *The Epoch of Negro Baptists and the Foreign Mission Board*. Kansas City, Mo.: Central Seminary Press, 1953.

Fuller, A. James. *Chaplain to the Confederacy: Basil Manly and Baptist Life in the Old South*. Baton Rouge: Louisiana State Univ. Press, 2000.

Gaston, Paul M. *The New South Creed: A Study in Southern Mythmaking*. 1970. Reprint, Montgomery, Ala.: NewSouth Books, 2002.

Gates, Henry Louis, Jr. *Stony the Road: Reconstruction, White Supremacy, and the Rise of Jim Crow.* New York: Penguin Press, 2019.

Genovese, Eugene D. *Roll, Jordan, Roll: The World the Slaves Made.* New York: Vintage Books, 1972.

George, Timothy, and David S. Dockery, eds. *Theologians of the Baptist Tradition.* Nashville, Tenn.: Broadman and Holman, 2001.

Gill, Everett. *A. T. Robertson: A Biography.* New York: Macmillan, 1943.

Goldfield, David R. *Still Fighting the Civil War: The American South and Southern History.* Baton Rouge: Louisiana State Univ. Press, 2002.

Gottwig, Danielle DuBois. "Before the Culture Wars: Conservative Protestants and the Family, 1920–1980, Volume I." Ph.D. diss., University of Notre Dame, 2011.

Grantham, Dewey W. *Southern Progressivism: The Reconciliation of Progress and Tradition.* Knoxville: Univ. of Tennessee Press, 1983.

Gribben, Crawford. *J. N. Darby and the Roots of Dispensationalism.* New York: Oxford Univ. Press, 2024.

Guelzo, Allen C. *Robert E. Lee: A Life.* New York: Knopf, 2021.

Guthman, Joshua. *Strangers Below: Primitive Baptists and American Culture.* Chapel Hill: Univ. of North Carolina Press, 2015.

Hall, Jacquelyn Dowd. "Broadus Mitchell, Economic Historian of the South." In *Reading Southern History: Essays on Interpreters and Interpretations,* edited by Glenn Feldman, 25–31. Tuscaloosa: Univ. of Alabama Press, 2001.

Hankins, Barry. *Uneasy in Babylon: Southern Baptist Conservatives in American Culture.* Tuscaloosa: Univ. of Alabama Press, 2002.

Hardin, John A. "Parrish, Charles Henry, Sr." In *Encyclopedia of Louisville,* edited by John E. Kleber, 694–695. Lexington: Univ. Press of Kentucky, 2001.

Harper, Keith. "The Fortress Monroe Conference and Shaping of Baptist Life in America at the End of the Nineteenth Century." In *Mirrors and Microscopes: Historical Perceptions of Baptists,* edited by C. Douglas Weaver, 110–28. London: Paternoster, 2015.

———. *The Quality of Mercy: Southern Baptists and Social Christianity, 1890–1920.* Tuscaloosa: Univ. of Alabama Press, 1996.

———, ed. *Southern Baptists Re-Observed: Perspectives on Race, Gender, and Politics.* Knoxville: Univ. of Tennessee Press, 2022.

———. "What's Wrong with This Picture? James P. Boyce, John A. Broadus, and Reflections on the Lost Cause." *Journal of Southern Religion* 17 (2015): http://jsreligion.org/issues/vol17/harper.html.

Harvey, Paul. *Freedom's Coming: Religious Culture and the Shaping of the South from the Civil War Through the Civil Rights Era.* Chapel Hill: Univ. of North Carolina Press, 2012.

———. *Redeeming the South: Religious Cultures and Racial Identities Among Southern Baptists, 1865–1925.* Chapel Hill: Univ. of North Carolina Press, 1997.

———. *Through the Storm, Through the Night: A History of African American Christianity.* Lanham, Md.: Rowman and Littlefield, 2011.

———. "'Yankee Faith' and Southern Redemption: White Southern Baptist Ministers, 1850–

1890." In *Religion and the American Civil War,* edited by Randall M. Miller, Harry S. Stout, and Charles Reagan Wilson, 167–86. New York: Oxford Univ. Press, 1998.

Hatch, Nathan O. *The Democratization of American Christianity.* New Haven, Conn.: Yale Univ. Press, 1991.

Hatcher, Eldridge Burwell. *William E. Hatcher, D.D. LL.D., L.H.D.: A Biography.* Richmond, Va.: W. C. Hill, 1915.

Haykin, Michael A. G. "'Soldiers of Christ, in Truth Arrayed': The Ministry and Piety of Basil Manly Jr. (1825–1892)." *Southern Baptist Journal of Theology* 13, no. 1 (2009): 34–39.

Hill, Samuel S., Jr. *Religion and the Solid South.* Nashville, Tenn.: Abingdon Press, 1972.

———. *The Spirit of Early Evangelicalism: True Religion in a Modern World.* New York: Oxford Univ. Press, 2018.

Hindmarsh, D. Bruce. *The Evangelical Conversion Narrative: Spiritual Autobiography in Early Modern England.* New York: Oxford Univ. Press, 2005.

———. *The Spirit of Early Evangelicalism: True Religion in a Modern World.* New York: Oxford Univ. Press, 2018.

Hirst, Russel. "The Sermon as Public Discourse: Austin Phelps and the Conservative Homiletic Tradition in Nineteenth-Century America." In *Oratorical Culture in Nineteenth-Century America: Transformations in the Theory and Practice of Rhetoric,* edited by Gregory Clark and S. Michael Halloran, 78–103. Carbondale: Southern Illinois Univ. Press, 1993.

Holcomb, Carol Crawford. *Home Without Walls: Southern Baptist Women and Social Reform in the Progressive Era.* Tuscaloosa: Univ. of Alabama Press, 2020.

Holifield, E. Brooks. *The Gentlemen Theologians: American Theology in Southern Culture, 1795–1860.* Durham, N.C.: Duke Univ. Press, 1978.

———. *Theology in America: Christian Thought from the Age of the Puritans to the Civil War.* New Haven, Conn.: Yale Univ. Press, 2003.

Holt, Michael. *The Rise and Fall of the American Whig Party: Jacksonian Politics and the Onset of the Civil War.* New York: Oxford Univ. Press, 2003.

Holt, Thomas. *Black over White: Negro Political Leadership in South Carolina During Reconstruction.* Urbana: Univ. of Illinois Press, 1979.

Hoshor, John P. "American Contributions to Rhetorical Theory and Homiletics." In *History of Speech Education in America,* edited by Karl Wallace. New York: Appleton-Century-Crofts, 1954.

House, Paul R. "Crawford Howell Toy and the Weight of Hermeneutics." *Southern Baptist Journal of Theology* 3 (Spring 1999): 28–38.

Hovey, George Rice. *Alvah Hovey: His Life and Letters.* Valley Forge, Pa.: Judson Press, 1928.

Howe, Daniel Walker. *What Hath God Wrought: The Transformation of America, 1815–1848.* New York: Oxford Univ. Press, 2007.

Hoyt, Arthur S. "Fifty Years of Practical Theology." *Review and Expositor* 7 (January 1910): 151–59.

Huber, Paul. "A Study of the Rhetorical Theories of John A. Broadus." Ph.D. diss., University of Michigan, 1956.

Huff, Archie Vernon. *Greenville: The History of the City and County in the South Carolina Piedmont,* 2nd ed. Columbia: Univ. of South Carolina Press, 2020.

Hurt, Billy Grey. "Crawford Howell Toy: Interpreter of the Old Testament." Ph.D. diss., Southern Baptist Theological Seminary, 1965.

Irons, Charles F. *The Origins of Proslavery Christianity: White and Black Evangelicals in Colonial and Antebellum Virginia.* Chapel Hill: Univ. of North Carolina Press, 2009.

Jackson, Brian. "'As a Musician Would His Violin': The Oratory of the Great Basin Prophets." In *A New History of the Sermon: The Nineteenth Century,* edited by Robert H. Ellison, 489–520. Leiden: Brill, 2010.

Janney, Caroline E. *Remembering the Civil War: Reunion and the Limits of Reconciliation.* Chapel Hill: Univ. of North Carolina Press, 2016.

Johnson, Nan. *Nineteenth-Century Rhetoric in North America.* Carbondale: Southern Illinois Univ. Press, 1991.

Kay, James F. "Preacher as Messenger of Hope." In *Slow of Speech and Unclean Lips: Contemporary Images of Preaching Identity,* edited by Robert Stephen Reid, 13–34. Eugene, Oreg.: Wipf and Stock, 2010.

Kidd, Thomas S. *Thomas Jefferson: A Biography of Spirit and Flesh.* New Haven, Conn.: Yale Univ. Press, 2022.

Kidd, Thomas S., and Barry Hankins. *Baptists in America: A History.* New York: Oxford Univ. Press, 2015.

Kimbrough, Bradley Thomas. *The History of the Walnut Street Baptist Church, Louisville, Kentucky.* Louisville, Ky.: Western Recorder Press, 1949.

Leonard, Bill J. *God's Last and Only Hope: The Fragmentation of the Southern Baptist Convention.* Grand Rapids, Mich.: Eerdmans, 1990.

Lewis, Charlene M. Boyer. *Ladies and Gentlemen on Display: Planter Society at the Virginia Springs, 1790–1860.* Charlottesville: Univ. of Virginia Press, 2001.

Lichtenstein, Alex. *Twice the Work of Free Labor: The Political Economy of Convict Labor in the New South.* New York: Verso Books, 1996.

Longenecker, Steve. *Pulpits of the Lost Cause: The Faith and Politics of Former Confederate Chaplains During Reconstruction.* Tuscaloosa: Univ. of Alabama Press, 2023.

Loveland, Anne C. *Southern Evangelicals and the Social Order, 1800–1860.* Baton Rouge: Louisiana State Univ. Press, 1980.

Lucas, Sean Michael. *Robert Lewis Dabney: A Southern Presbyterian Life.* Philipsburg, N.J.: Presbyterian and Reformed, 2005.

Mancini, Matthew J. *One Dies, Get Another: Convict Leasing in the American South, 1866–1928.* Columbia: Univ. of South Carolina Press, 1996.

Manley, James M. "The Southern Baptist Mind in Transition: A Life of Basil Manly Jr., 1825–1892." Ph.D. diss., University of Florida, 1999.

Manly, Charles. "The Rise of the Seminary Sentiment Among Southern Baptists." *Review and Expositor* 12, no. 2 (April 1915): 246–259.

Margolies, Daniel S. *Henry Watterson and the New South: The Politics of Empire, Free Trade, and Globalization.* Lexington: Univ. Press of Kentucky, 2006.

Maring, Norman. "Baptists and Changing Views of the Bible, 1865–1918 (Part I)." *Foundations* (January 1, 1958): 30–61.

Marsden, George M. *Fundamentalism and American Culture.* New York: Oxford Univ. Press, 2006.

———. *The Soul of the American University Revisited: From Protestant to Post-Secular.* New York: Oxford Univ. Press, 2021.

McCurry, Stephanie. *Masters of Small Worlds: Yeoman Households, Gender Relations, and the Political Culture of the Antebellum South Carolina Low Country.* New York: Oxford Univ. Press, 1995.

McGerr, Michael. *A Fierce Discontent: The Rise and Fall of the Progressive Movement in America, 1870–1920.* New York: Free Press, 2003.

McGlothlin, W. J. "John Albert Broadus: An Address Delivered at The Southern Baptist Theological Seminary, January 11, 1930, Founder's Day." *Review and Expositor* 27, no. 2 (April 1930): 141–68.

McKibbens, Thomas R. "John A. Broadus: Shaper of Baptist Preaching." *Baptist History and Heritage* 40, no. 2 (Spring 2005): 18–24.

McMillen, Sally G. *To Raise Up the South: Sunday Schools in Black and White Churches, 1865–1915.* Baton Rouge: Louisiana State Univ. Press, 2001.

McPherson, James M. *For Cause and Comrades: Why Men Fought in the Civil War.* New York: Oxford Univ. Press, 1997.

Menikoff, Aaron. *Politics and Piety: Baptist Social Reform in America, 1770–1860.* Eugene, Oreg.: Pickwick Publications, 2014.

Meraz, Aaron. "The Missiology of I. T. Tichenor with Implications on Contemporary Southern Baptist North American Missions." Ph.D. diss., Southern Baptist Theological Seminary, 2012.

Miller, Glenn T. *Piety and Intellect: The Aims and Purposes of Ante-Bellum Theological Education.* Atlanta, Ga.: Scholars Press, 1990.

Miller, Randall, Harry S. Stout, and Charles Reagan Wilson, eds. *Religion and the American Civil War.* New York: Oxford Univ. Press, 1998.

Mohler, R. Albert, Jr. "'To Train the Minister Whom God Has Called': James Petigru Boyce and Southern Baptist Theological Education." *Founders Journal,* no. 19/20 (Winter/Spring 1995). https://founders.org/1995/03/24/to-train-the-minister-whom-god-has-called/.

Moore, Christopher C. *Apostle of the Lost Cause: J. William Jones, Baptists, and the Development of Confederate Memory.* Knoxville: Univ. of Tennessee Press, 2019.

Moore, William Cabell. "General John Hartwell Cocke of Bremo 1780–1866." *William and Mary Quarterly* 13, no. 4 (October 1933): 207–218.

Mueller, William A. *A History of Southern Baptist Theological Seminary, 1859–1959.* Nashville, Tenn.: Broadman Press, 1959.

Nettles, Tom J. *The Baptists: Key People in Forming a Baptist Identity.* Vol. 2, *Beginnings in America.* Fearn, Scotland: Mentor Press, 2007.

———. *James Petigru Boyce: Southern Baptist Statesman*. Phillipsburg, N.J.: Presbyterian and Reformed, 2009.

Noll, Mark A. *America's Book: The Rise and Decline of a Bible Civilization, 1794–1911*. New York: Oxford Univ. Press, 2022.

———. *America's God: From Jonathan Edwards to Abraham Lincoln*. New York: Oxford Univ. Press, 2002.

———. *Between Faith and Criticism: Evangelicals, Scholarship, and the Bible in America*. San Francisco, Calif.: Harper and Row, 1986.

———. *The Civil War as a Theological Crisis*. Chapel Hill: Univ. of North Carolina Press, 2006.

O'Brien, Michael. *Conjectures of Order: Intellectual Life and the American South, 1810–1860*, 2 vols. Chapel Hill: Univ. of North Carolina Press, 2004.

Old, Hughes Oliphant. *The Reading and Preaching of the Scriptures in the Worship of the Christian Church*. Vol. 6, *The Modern Age*. Grand Rapids, Mich.: Eerdmans, 2007.

Oshatz, Molly. *Slavery and Sin: The Fight Against Slavery and the Rise of Liberal Protestantism*. New York: Oxford Univ. Press, 2012.

Overstreet, Mark. "The 1889 Lyman Beecher Lectures on Preaching and the Recovery of the Late Homiletic of John Albert Broadus (1827–1895)." Ph.D. diss., Southern Baptist Theological Seminary, 2005.

Parks, Joseph H. *Joseph E. Brown of Georgia*. Baton Rouge: Louisiana State Univ. Press, 1977.

Parsons, Mikeal C. *Crawford Howell Toy: The Man, the Scholar, the Teacher*. Macon, Ga.: Mercer Univ. Press, 2019.

Patterson, James A. *James Robinson Graves: Staking the Boundaries of Baptist Identity*. Nashville, Tenn.: B&H Academic, 2012.

Payne, Brendan J. J. *Gin, Jesus, and Jim Crow: Prohibition and the Transformation of Racial and Religious Politics in the South*. Baton Rouge: Louisiana State Univ. Press, 2022.

Pearson, Joseph W. *The Whigs' America: Middle-Class Political Thought in the Age of Jackson and Clay*. Lexington: Univ. Press of Kentucky, 2020.

Percy, Will A. *Lanterns on the Levee: Recollections of a Planter's Son*. New York: Knopf, 1941.

Pflugrad-Jackson, Amy. *Brothers of a Vow: Secret Fraternal Orders and the Transformation of White Male Culture in Antebellum Virginia*. Athens: Univ. of Georgia Press, 2011.

Poole, W. Scott. *Never Surrender: Confederate Memory and Conservatism in the South Carolina Upcountry*. Athens: Univ. of Georgia Press, 2004.

Pope, Liston. *Millhands and Preachers*. New Haven, Conn.: Yale Univ. Press, 1942.

Rable, George C. *God's Almost Chosen Peoples: A Religious History of the American Civil War*. Chapel Hill: Univ. of North Carolina Press, 2010.

Ragosta, John A. *Wellspring of Liberty: How Virginia's Religious Dissenters Helped Win the American Revolution and Secured Religious Liberty*. New York: Oxford Univ. Press, 2010.

Ramsey, David M. "Boyce and Broadus, Founders of the Southern Baptist Theological Seminary: Founder's Day Address, Delivered January 11, 1941." E-Text Collection. Archives and Special Collections, Southern Baptist Theological Seminary.

Randolph, David James. *The Renewal of Preaching.* Minneapolis, Minn.: Fortress Press, 1969.

Reeder, Betsy. *Broadus Unbound: The Oversized Will, Intellect, and Influence of a Small Baptist.* Seattle, Wash.: Kindledirect Publishing, 2021.

Rieser, Andrew C. *The Chautauqua Moment: Protestants, Progressives, and the Culture of Modern Liberalism.* New York: Columbia Univ. Press, 2003.

Riley, Benjamin F. "The Pulpit Oratory of the South." In *The South in the Building of the Nation: History of Southern Oratory,* edited by T. E. Watson, 128–57. Richmond, Va.: Southern Historical Publication Society, 1909.

Roark, James L. *Masters Without Slaves.* New York: Norton, 1977.

Robert, Dana. *American Women in Mission: The Modern Mission Era, 1792–1992.* Macon, Ga.: Mercer Univ. Press, 1997.

Roberts, Derrell C. *Joseph E. Brown and the Politics of Reconstruction.* Tuscaloosa: Univ. of Alabama Press, 1973.

Robinson, Jeff. "Southern Trustees Elect Mohler to Storied Chair of Theology." *Baptist Press,* April 27, 2005. https://www.baptistpress.com/resource-library/news/southern-trustees -elect-mohler-to-storied-chair-of-theology/.

Scales, T. Laine. *All That Fits a Woman: Training Southern Baptist Women for Charity and Mission, 1907–1926.* Macon, Ga.: Mercer Univ. Press, 2000.

Scales, T. Laine, and Melody Maxwell. *Doing the Word: Southern Baptists' Carver School of Church Social Work and Its Predecessors, 1907–1997.* Knoxville: Univ. of Tennessee Press, 2019.

Schweiger, Beth Barton. *The Gospel Working Up: Progress and the Pulpit in Nineteenth-Century Virginia.* New York: Oxford Univ. Press, 2000.

———. *A Literate South: Reading Before Emancipation.* New Haven, Conn.: Yale Univ. Press, 2019.

Scott, John C. "The Chautauqua Vision of Liberal Education." *History of Education* 34, no. 1 (January 2005): 41–45.

Shrader, Matthew C. *Thoughtful Christianity: Alvah Hovey and the Problem of Authority Within the Context of Nineteenth-Century Northern Baptists.* Eugene, Oreg.: Pickwick Publications, 2021.

Sizer, Sandra S. *Gospel Hymns and Social Religion: The Rhetoric of Nineteenth-Century Revivalism.* Philadelphia, Pa.: Temple Univ. Press, 1978.

Slatton, James H. *W. H. Whitsitt: The Man and the Controversy.* Macon, Ga.: Mercer Univ. Press, 2009.

Smith, Eric C. *John Leland: A Jeffersonian Baptist in Early America.* New York: Oxford Univ. Press, 2022.

Snay, Mitchell. *Gospel of Disunion: Religion and Separatism in the Antebellum South.* Chapel Hill: Univ. of North Carolina Press, 1997.

Spain, Rufus B. *At Ease in Zion: A Social History of Southern Baptists, 1865–1900.* 1961. Reprint, Tuscaloosa: Univ. of Alabama Press, 2003.

Sparks, Randy J. *Religion in Mississippi.* Oxford: Univ. Press of Mississippi, 2011.

Stout, Harry S. *Upon the Altar of the Nation: A Moral History of the Civil War*. New York: Penguin, 2007.

Straub, Jeffrey. *The Making of a Battle Royal: The Rise of Liberalism in Northern Baptist Life, 1870–1920*. Eugene, Oreg.: Pickwick Publications, 2018.

Sullivan, Regina D. *Lottie Moon: A Southern Baptist Missionary to China in History and Legend*. Baton Rouge: Louisiana State Univ. Press, 2011.

Taylor, Alan. *Thomas Jefferson's Education*. New York: Norton, 2019.

Tisby, Jemar. *The Color of Compromise: The Truth About the American Church's Complicity in Racism*. Grand Rapids, Mich.: Zondervan, 2020.

Wacker, Grant. *America's Pastor: Billy Graham and the Shaping of a Nation*. Cambridge, Mass.: Harvard Univ. Press, 2014.

———. *Augustus H. Strong and the Dilemma of Historical Consciousness*. 1985. Reprint, Waco, Tex.: Baylor Univ. Press, 2018.

———. "Demise of Biblical Civilization." In *The Bible in America: Essays in Cultural History*, edited by Mark A. Noll and Nathan O. Hatch, 121–38. New York: Oxford Univ. Press, 1982.

Wallace, Karl R., ed. *History of Speech Education in America: Background Studies*. New York: Appleton-Century-Crofts, 1954.

Washington, James Melvin. *Frustrated Fellowship: The Black Baptist Quest for Social Power*. Macon, Ga.: Mercer Univ. Press, 1986.

Watkins, Jordan T. *Slavery and Sacred Texts: The Bible, the Constitution, and Historical Consciousness in Antebellum America*. New York: Cambridge Univ. Press, 2021.

Weissman, Rebecca. "The Role of White Supremacy Amongst Opponents and Proponents of Mass Schooling in the South During the Common School Era." *Pedagogica Historia* 55, no. 5 (October 1, 2019): 703–23.

Welter, Barbara. "The Cult of True Womanhood: 1820–1860." *American Quarterly* 18, no. 2 (Summer 1966): 155–74.

Williams, Michael. *Isaac Taylor Tichenor: The Creation of the Baptist New South*. Tuscaloosa: Univ. of Alabama Press, 2018.

Williamson, Joel. *The Crucible of Race: Black-White Relations in the American South Since Emancipation*. New York: Oxford Univ. Press, 1984.

Wills, Gregory A. *Democratic Religion: Freedom, Authority, and Church Discipline in the Baptist South, 1790–1900*. New York: Oxford Univ. Press, 1997.

———. *Southern Baptist Theological Seminary, 1859–2009*. New York: Oxford Univ. Press, 2009.

Wills, Gregory A., et al. "Report on Slavery and Racism in the History of the Southern Baptist Theological Seminary." 2018. https://cf.sbts.edu/sbts2023/uploads/2023/10/Racism-and-the-Legacy-of-Slavery-Report-v4.pdf.

Wilson, Charles Regan. *Baptized in Blood: The Religion of the Lost Cause, 1865–1920*. Athens: Univ. of Georgia Press, 2009.

Wilson, Mark R. *William Owen Carver's Controversies in the Baptist South*. Macon, Ga.: Mercer Univ. Press, 2010.

Winters, Adam G. "T. T. Eaton and the Politicization of Baptist Ecclesiology." Ph.D. diss., Southern Baptist Theological Seminary, 2016.

Woodward, C. Vann. *The Origins of the New South, 1877–1913.* 1951. Reprint, Baton Rouge: Louisiana State Univ. Press, 1971.

———. *The Strange Career of Jim Crow.* New York: Oxford Univ. Press, 2002.

Worthen, Molly. *Apostles of Reason: The Crisis of Authority in American Evangelicalism.* New York: Oxford Univ. Press, 2013.

Wright, G. Richard, and Kenneth H. Wheeler. "New Men in the Old South: Joseph E. Brown and His Associates in Georgia's Etowah Valley." *Georgia Historical Quarterly* 193, no. 4 (Winter 2009): 363–87.

Wyatt-Brown, Bertram. *The Shaping of Southern Honor: Honor, Grace, and War, 1760s–1890s.* Chapel Hill: Univ. of North Carolina Press, 2001.

———. *Southern Honor: Ethics and Behavior in the Old South.* 1982. Reprint, New York: Oxford Univ. Press, 2007.

Zuczek, Richard. *State of Rebellion: Reconstruction in South Carolina.* Columbia: Univ. of South Carolina Press, 1996.

INDEX

www.ingramcontent.com/pod-product-compliance
Lightning Source LLC
Chambersburg PA
CBHW020038170226
39823CB00002B/21